STABILITY AND CHANGE IN RELATIONSHIPS

Understanding interpersonal relationships requires understanding actors, behaviors, and contexts. This volume presents cutting-edge research from a variety of disciplines that examines personal relationships on all three levels. The first section focuses on the factors that influence individuals to enter, maintain, and dissolve relationships. The second section emphasizes ongoing processes that characterize relationships and focuses on issues such as arguing and sacrificing. The third and final section demonstrates that the processes of stability and change are embedded in social, cultural, and historical contexts. Chapters address cultural universals as well as cross-cultural differences in relationship behaviors and outcomes. The emergence of new relational forms, such as the interaction between people and computers, is also explored. *Stability and Change in Relationships* will be of interest to individuals in a broad range of fields including psychology, sociology, communication, gerontology, and counseling.

Anita L. Vangelisti is a well-known researcher in the field of communication whose work focuses on family interaction and the communication of emotion in personal relationships. She has coauthored and edited several books and has served as associate editor of *Personal Relationships*.

Harry T. Reis is an eminent social psychologist who is known for his research on intimacy as an interpersonal process as well as his work on the development of theories of social interaction. He previously served as editor of the *Journal of Personality and Social Psychology*, published by the American Psychological Association.

Mary Anne Fitzpatrick, a leading figure in the field of communication, has done extensive research on communication in marriage and has established one of the best-known typologies of marital interaction. She has published more than 75 articles and chapters and has authored and edited several books.

ADVANCES IN PERSONAL RELATIONSHIPS

Series Editiors
HARRY T. REIS
University of Rochester

MARY ANNE FITZPATRICK
University of Wisconsin, Madison

ANITA L. VANGELISTI
University of Texas, Austin

Advances in Personal Relationships represents the culmination of years of multidisciplinary and interdisciplinary work on personal relationships. Sponsored by the International Society for the Study of Personal Relationships (ISSPR), the series offers readers cutting-edge research and theory in the field. Contributing authors are internationally known scholars from a variety of disciplines, including social psychology, clinical psychology, communication, history, sociology, gerontology, and family studies. Volumes include integrative reviews, conceptual pieces, summaries of research programs, and major theoretical works.

PREVIOUSLY PUBLISHED

Valerie Manusov and John H. Harvey, eds., *Attribution, Communication Behavior, and Close Relationships*

Stability and Change in Relationships

Edited by

ANITA L. VANGELISTI
University of Texas, Austin

HARRY T. REIS
University of Rochester

MARY ANNE FITZPATRICK
University of Wisconsin, Madison

CAMBRIDGE UNIVERSITY PRESS
Cambridge, New York, Melbourne, Madrid, Cape Town,
Singapore, São Paulo, Delhi, Tokyo, Mexico City

Cambridge University Press
The Edinburgh Building, Cambridge CB2 8RU, UK

Published in the United States of America by
Cambridge University Press, New York

www.cambridge.org
Information on this title: www.cambridge.org/9780521790765

© Cambridge University Press 2002

This publication is in copyright. Subject to statutory exception
and to the provisions of relevant collective licensing agreements,
no reproduction of any part may take place without the written
permission of Cambridge University Press.

First published 2002

A catalogue record for this publication is available from the British Library

Library of Congress Cataloguing in Publication data
Stability and change in relationships / edited by Anita L. Vangelisti, Harry T. Reis, Mary Anne Fitzpatrick.
p. cm. – (Advances in personal relationships)
Includes bibliographical references and index.
ISBN 0-521-79076-x (hardcover)
1. Interpersonal relations. 2. Change (Psychology) I. Vangelisti, Anita L. II. Reis, Harry T. III. Fitzpatrick, Mary Anne, 1949– IV. Advances in personal relationships (Cambridge, England)
HM1106 .S75 2002
302 – dc21   2001035611

ISBN 978-0-521-79076-5 Hardback

Cambridge University Press has no responsibility for the persistence or
accuracy of URLs for external or third-party internet websites referred to in
this publication, and does not guarantee that any content on such websites is,
or will remain, accurate or appropriate. Information regarding prices, travel
timetables, and other factual information given in this work is correct at
the time of first printing but Cambridge University Press does not guarantee
the accuracy of such information thereafter.

Contents

Contributors		*page* ix
Preface		xi

PART ONE: ACTORS: THE SCAFFOLDING OF STABILITY AND CHANGE

1 Change in Relationship Knowledge Representations   5
Paula R. Pietromonaco, Jean-Philippe Laurenceau, and Lisa Feldman Barrett

2 Personality Effects on Personal Relationships over the Life Span   35
Jens B. Asendorpf

3 An Intergenerational Model of Romantic Relationship Development   57
Chalandra M. Bryant and Rand D. Conger

4 How Relationships Begin and End: A Genetic Perspective   83
David T. Lykken

PART TWO: BEHAVIORS: THE PROCESSES OF STABILITY AND CHANGE

5 Serial Arguing over the Relational Life Course: Antecedents and Consequences   107
Michael E. Roloff and Kristen Linnea Johnson

6 Communication, Relationship Concerns, and Satisfaction in Early Marriage   129
Patricia Noller and Judith A. Feeney

7	Sacrifice in Romantic Relationships: An Exploration of Relevant Research and Theory *Sarah Whitton, Scott Stanley, and Howard Markman*	156
8	Stability and Change in Social Relations: Perspectives from Gerontology and Stress Research *David A. Chiriboga*	182
9	What Microanalysis of Behavior in Social Situations Can Reveal about Relationships across the Life Span *Rebecca M. Warner*	207
10	Developing a Multifaceted View of Change in Relationships *Ronald D. Rogge and Thomas N. Bradbury*	228

PART THREE: CONTEXTS: SOCIAL ENVIRONMENTS FOR STABILITY AND CHANGE

11	Social Networks and Change in Personal Relationships *Susan Sprecher, Diane Felmlee, Terri L. Orbuch, and Marion C. Willetts*	257
12	Creating a Context for Change: Integrative Couple Therapy *Jennifer Wheeler and Andrew Christensen*	285
13	Passionate Love and Sexual Desire: Cultural and Historical Perspectives *Elaine Hatfield and Richard L. Rapson*	306
14	Rules for Responsive Robots: Using Human Interactions to Build Virtual Interactions *Joseph N. Cappella and Catherine Pelachaud*	325

Author Index	355
Subject Index	370

Contributors

Jens B. Asendorpf, Humboldt-Universität zu Berlin

Lisa Feldman Barrett, Boston College

Thomas N. Bradbury, University of California, Los Angeles

Chalandra M. Bryant, Iowa State University, Ames

Joseph N. Cappella, University of Pennsylvania

David A. Chiriboga, Florida Mental Health Institute, University of South Florida

Andrew Christensen, University of California, Los Angeles

Rand D. Conger, University of California, Davis

Judith A. Feeney, University of Queensland, Australia

Diane Felmlee, University of California, Davis

Elaine Hatfield, University of Hawaii, Honolulu

Kristen Linnea Johnson, Andersen Consulting

Jean-Philippe Laurenceau, University of Miami

David T. Lykken, University of Minnesota, Minneapolis

Howard Markman, University of Denver

Patricia Noller, University of Queensland, Australia

Terri L. Orbuch, Oakland University, Rochester, Michigan

Catherine Pelachaud, Università di Roma

Paula R. Pietromonaco, University of Massachusetts at Amherst

Richard L. Rapson, University of Hawaii, Honolulu

Ronald D. Rogge, University of California, Los Angeles

Michael E. Roloff, Northwestern University

Susan Sprecher, Illinois State University

Scott Stanley, University of Denver

Rebecca M. Warner, University of New Hampshire

Jennifer Wheeler, University of Washington

Sarah Whitton, University of Denver

Marion C. Willetts, Illinois State University

Preface

When people think about personal relationships, questions about stability and change jump into mind. An individual's behavior in current relationships is often explained by invoking similar relationships from the past. Feelings about one's present-day relationships reflect not so much current circumstances as the manner in which those circumstances are perceived to have improved or deteriorated. Hopes, fears, fantasies, and goals for future relationships tend not to be conceived in a vacuum, but rather are couched in terms of the present and the past. Among the most common questions that we, as relationship researchers, get from our acquaintances and students are questions about how to avoid repeating the mistakes and misfortunes of past relationships in subsequent relationships (which probably accounts for the widespread appeal of this same question in popular media).

The compelling interest in questions about stability and change evidenced by the lay public is matched by researchers interested in the scientific study of personal relationships. It is not surprising, therefore, that when the International Society for the Study of Personal Relationships decided to sponsor a series of edited volumes on timely, cutting-edge theory and research, continuity and change in personal relationships were identified as a preeminent issue. The chapters collected in this volume testify to the intellectual vigor with which scholars have sought to unravel the complex processes and associations that contribute to relationship stability and change. Thus we believe that readers will find their appreciation of, and knowledge about, relationships stimulated, enlightened, challenged, inspired, provoked, and ultimately, we hope, raised to a new level of understanding.

If nothing else, this volume makes plain the fact that questions about stability and change are far more complex than they first appear. The chapters provide nuanced portrayals of how genetic, psychological, and social factors influence relationships, and how relational qualities, in turn, affect individuals and their social environments. The interaction among variables that occurs across these different levels of analysis represents one of the more fundamental themes throughout the volume. Most scholars agree that the causal influences between individuals and relationships are bidirectional – that is, that individual properties affect interactions and relationships and that relationship properties also affect individuals. Researchers also concur that properties and processes predictive at a given level of analysis may not be relevant at other levels of analysis. As is evident throughout this collection, then, questions about the perspective from which stability and change are examined, about the mechanisms associated with stability and change, and about the techniques used to measure stability and change are hotly debated.

In soliciting and organizing the contributions represented in this volume, we were guided by four propositions about relationships and how they function suggested by Sroufe and Fleeson (1986). The first proposition is that relationships are characterized by coherence and continuity. That is, even though relationships and relationship systems may be in a constant state of flux, relational processes often exhibit coherence across contexts and stability across transformations. There is, then, a seeming paradox: Relationships continually change, yet they do so in ways that are both patterned and often remarkably similar. Because relationships have structure, information about one component of the system may allow researchers to predict characteristics of other components. In other words, although relational processes and the behavioral manifestations of those processes may be dynamic and somewhat idiosyncratic, they are nonetheless intelligible. For instance, relationships that are headed toward dissolution may come apart at different times and at different rates, but existing research has identified some of the factors that contribute to dissolution processes and trajectories. Similarly, the interactions that occur between parents and children constantly change, yet scholars can forecast many of these changes before they occur.

Sroufe and Fleeson's second proposition is that individuals internalize (i.e., mentally represent) relationships. People know about relationships, particularly their own relationships. They believe that certain things are likely to happen in relationships and they evaluate their relationships in terms of those beliefs. Many popular theoretical systems – for example, attachment theory, object relations theory, and social cognitive theories – posit that internalized models of relationships exert potent influence on attention, perception, expectations, memory, emotion, judgment, and behavior (Reis & Downey, 1999). These mental representations, while often quite stable, are also open to change to varying degrees. A major life transition may compel individuals to reinvent their model of what a relationship is and ought to be. Furthermore, ordinary social life causes us to encounter people who possess alternative views of relationships, requiring that we cope with discrepancies between what we "know" about relationships and what others "know." This may happen in numerous ways. For example, individuals may accommodate diverse views, integrating differences within a more complex mental model; they may attempt to persuade the other person to change his or her views; or they may simply dismiss the differences. The tendency to change relationship beliefs depends to some extent, of course, on the roots of those beliefs. Some beliefs are emotionally charged, whereas others are dispassionate. Some beliefs are founded in personality and may reflect individuals' genetic legacy, whereas other beliefs are shaped primarily by experiences. The factors that affect differences in people's mental models about relationships and the ways that these models both reflect and cause stability and change in relationships are the foci of several chapters in this volume.

The third proposition is that representations of prior relationships are carried forward to new relationships. Thus, established relationship knowledge has consequences for subsequent cognition, affect, and behavior in social interaction (Baldwin, 1992; Berscheid, 1994). Assessments of others are profoundly influenced by expectations of what relationships should and should not be. Likewise, emotions, both positive and negative, reflect the correspondence between expectations and circumstances. Relationship knowledge is used to communicate with partners, to select among the various behavioral options available in any given situation, and to help interpret and then respond to others' behavior and communication. The "carrying forward" of relationship knowledge is based on more than personal development: The application of relational knowledge is situated within, and is influenced by, social, cultural, familial, and historical contexts that cue individuals about the relevance of different relational beliefs. Thus, relationship knowledge may influence future generations as knowledge, beliefs, values, myths, and secrets are transmitted from one generation to the next.

The fourth proposition described by Sroufe and Fleeson is that relationships are best considered as "wholes" (i.e., more than additive combinations of partner characteristics) and therefore should be examined in terms of the interrelation of their parts (i.e., their organization or structure; Reis, Collins, & Berscheid, 2000). In other words, relationships operate as interdependent systems of influence and constraint (Kelley, 1983). Thus, when one partner acts, the behavior of the other is necessarily affected. This may be evident, for example, in the tendency of a child to be hostile and reactive to one parent, yet warm and responsive to the other. Similarly, stability or change in one relational domain (i.e., financial contributions to the family) may facilitate or constrain the likelihood of change in another domain (i.e., parental roles). Chapters in this book clearly demonstrate that even a very focused change in one aspect of a relationship may have broad consequences for that relationship (and for the other relationships with which it is associated, as discussed in the next paragraph). The interconnected nature of relational systems presents a challenge for researchers and theorists who aim to understand and explain relational processes.

Relationship systems are characterized not only by the connections and relations between their components but also by the interactions between the dyad and its larger social environment. From birth, individuals and dyads contribute to systems or networks of relationships. As implied by the term "network," all relationships within a network influence one another to a greater or lesser degree. These influences in turn reflect back on the dyad and the development of the individual partners. The various levels of analysis inherent in this many-tiered system – individuals, dyads, families, groups, societies – are not discrete but rather coexist in a state of ongoing influence and interdependence (Reis et al., 2000). As is reflected in several chapters in this volume, relationship researchers often investigate these systems by examining some of their lower-level elements. For example, in examining family processes, the theorist may consider the mother–infant exchange as the focal point for analysis. Linking levels are feedback loops that amplify or dampen the effects of various interactions in the system.

ORGANIZATION OF THIS VOLUME

The field of personal relationships is multidisciplinary in large part because a proper understanding of personal relationships demands simultaneous focus on actors, behaviors, and contexts. Hence we have organized this volume according to these three important categories. The first section focuses on individuals as they enter, maintain, and dissolve relationships. These chapters turn the lens toward cognitive, emotional, and personality factors that undergird relational stability and change processes. In the second section, we move beyond the individual to examine what transpires between partners. These chapters describe dynamic processes of change that are revealed in interactions and interpersonal behaviors, as well the inferences that partners make about these behaviors. The third and final section considers how the processes of stability and change are embedded in social, cultural, and transhistorical contexts. This contextual perspective includes consideration of therapeutic interventions as well as new relationship variations that are emerging from contemporary technological innovations.

The chapters in this volume represent not so much a definitive declaration on the when, why, and how of stability and change but rather a portal between prior conceptualizations, which naively assumed that a correlation coefficient between two measures spanning a suitable interval would be all that was needed, and the future, in which, we believe, these and yet richer theoretical models will have been supported by empirical evidence. In other words, we hope this volume will do more than describe what is known about stability and change in relationships; we hope it will stimulate new research and new ideas into this perennially compelling topic.

REFERENCES

Baldwin, M. W. (1992). Relational schemas and the processing of social information. *Psychological Bulletin, 112,* 461–484.

Berscheid, E. (1994). Interpersonal relationships. *Annual Review of Psychology, 45,* 79–129.

Kelley, H. H. (1983). Analyzing close relationships. In H. H. Kelley, E. Berscheid, A. Christensen, J. H. Harvey, T. L. Huston, G. Levinger, E. McClintock, L. A. Peplau, & D. R. Peterson (Eds.), *Close relationships* (pp. 20–67). New York: Freeman.

Reis, H. T., & Downey, G. (1999). Social cognition in relationships: Building essential bridges between two literatures. *Social Cognition, 17,* 97–117.

Reis, H. T., Collins, W. A., & Berscheid, E. (2000). The relationship context of human behavior and development. *Psychological Bulletin, 126,* 844–872.

Sroufe, L. A., & Fleeson, J. (1986). Attachment and the construction of relationships. In W. W. Hartup & Z. Rubin (Eds.), *Relationships and development* (pp. 51–71). Hillsdale, NJ: Erlbaum.

PART ONE

ACTORS: THE SCAFFOLDING OF STABILITY AND CHANGE

A scaffold is a temporary structure built to support workers as they erect a new structure, or repair, reinforce, or demolish an existing one. Individuals and their distinctive personalities, emotions, and cognitions provide the scaffolding for change and stability in relationships. There is a continually evolving dynamic association between the factors that characterize individuals and those that define their relationships. The mental models, emotional history, and personality that individuals bring to their relationships create a context that promotes certain relational outcomes while discouraging others; these outcomes, in turn, affect the actors' personal qualities in numerous respects. Although the term "personality" is difficult to define, several contemporary approaches emphasize the characteristics that facilitate individuals' adaptation to the environment. Adapting to the social environment is, of course, one of life's most important and challenging tasks. Thus, studies of those dimensions of personality – and their manifestations in thoughts, feelings, and behavior – that regulate interpersonal relationships are likely to provide important insights into the processes of stability and change. The growing evidence that many genetically determined individual differences are designed to address common adaptive situations faced during human evolution (which, of course, prominently included interpersonal situations), and that other genetic differences interact with features of the environment in shaping the individual, testifies to the centrality of relationship-relevant personality factors in studying the processes of stability and change.

People's understanding of relationships is best considered as a work in progress, amenable to revision by experience, especially experience in current relationships. In other words, the "relationship outcomes" traditionally studied in research are not so much end states as they are way stations in an ongoing chain of relational states. Pietromonaco, Laurenceau, and Feldman Barrett provide an insightful discussion of processes that are associated with stability and change in representations of relationship knowledge. They describe existing literature on relationship knowledge representation and review evidence supporting representational stability. Then, having discussed several processes that help maintain stable relationship knowledge structures, they go on to propose how and when people's representations of relationships may change over time.

The effects of personality on people's interpersonal relationships are the focus of Asendorpf's contribution to this volume. Asendorpf begins by describing some of the difficulties researchers face in trying to establish causal links between personality and relationships. He then reviews studies that demonstrate effects of personality on relationships, including investigations of the influence of parents' and infants' personalities on infant attachment, and of the impact of children's aggressiveness and shyness on peer relationships. Asendorpf concludes with an insightful description of three mechanisms by which personality may affect relationships and speculations about future research concerning the strength of personality effects on relationships over the life span.

Next, Bryant and Conger take a developmental approach to understanding romantic relationships. They argue that the interpersonal competencies that influence the probability of success in romantic relationships can be traced back to interaction within individuals' family of origin. Building on current theories of intergenerational effects on relationships, Bryant and Conger propose an intergenerational conceptualization of romantic relationship development called the DEARR model (Development of Early Adult Romantic Relationships). This model offers relationship researchers a set of constructs for predicting how certain behavioral, cognitive, and emotional qualities in the family of origin may foster particular ways of relating to romantic partners. Bryant and Conger also present a preliminary test of their model that demonstrates the broad range of questions for which the DEARR model serves as a useful heuristic framework.

In the final chapter in this section, Lykken provides an intriguing account of "How Relationships Begin and End." Using twin research, he argues that mate selection is a largely fortuitous phenomenon. Lykken suggests, for example, that the well-documented finding of mate similarity occurs not because people prefer similar others as partners but rather because people choose partners from their pool of associates and those associates tend to share similar qualities. By contrast, Lykken argues that relationship disruption or divorce is strongly associated with partners' genetic characteristics, supporting this claim with such striking evidence as the 250% increase in the risk of divorce among monozygotic twins whose cotwin has experienced divorce. Lykken closes his chapter with several controversial suggestions about the initiation and dissolution of romantic relationships.

CHAPTER ONE

Change in Relationship Knowledge Representations

Paula R. Pietromonaco, Jean-Philippe Laurenceau, and Lisa Feldman Barrett

Over the past decade, researchers have begun to examine how people think about and construct their knowledge of close relationships. Little agreement exists about the nature of representations of relationship knowledge, although many theorists have proposed general definitions using concepts such as relational schemas (Baldwin, 1992, 1995; Miell, 1987; Planalp, 1987), internal working models (Bowlby, 1973; Collins & Read, 1994), prototypes (Bartholomew & Horowitz, 1991; Fehr & Baldwin, 1996; Klohnen & John, 1998), lay relationship theories (Fletcher & Thomas, 1996), interpersonal schemas (Safran, 1990), interpersonal scripts (e.g., Baldwin, 1992; Stern, 1985; Tomkins, 1979), and stories (Murray & Holmes, 1994; Sternberg, 1996). While these concepts differ somewhat in their underlying assumptions about the nature of the representation (for reviews, see Baldwin, 1992, 1995; Singer & Salovey, 1991), they are similar in two respects. First, relationship representations are thought to consist of well-organized, elaborated abstract knowledge about the self, others, and the interaction between the two that is derived from direct experiences. Second, relationship representations are assumed to be organized in some hierarchical fashion, including superordinate, abstract generalizations (e.g., "My mother is loving") at the higher levels and specific information (e.g., "She takes care of me when I'm sick") at the lower levels (e.g., Baldwin, 1992; Planalp, 1987).

Although theorists (e.g., Bowlby, 1969, 1979; Shaver, Hazan, & Bradshaw, 1988) often assume that relationship representations, like

---

Address correspondence to Paula R. Pietromonaco, Department of Psychology, Tobin Hall Box 37710, University of Massachusetts at Amherst, Amherst, MA 01002-7710. E-mail address: monaco@psych.umass.edu.

other kinds of representations (see Fiske & Taylor, 1991), tend to be stable over time and resistant to change, they leave open the possibility that revision and change can occur under some conditions. Few relationship theorists have delineated the process of change in relationship knowledge, but most would agree that the ability to change contributes to the quality and longevity of a relationship. The purpose of this chapter is to examine the processes that might underlie change in representations of relationship knowledge. To some extent, this task proved to be a creative one. Despite the richness of theory about relationship knowledge, little empirical evidence exists about the precise nature and organization of such representations (e.g., see Berscheid & Reis, 1998; Pietromonaco & Feldman Barrett, 2000), and even less is known about how relationship representations change over time.

As a consequence, we drew from various literatures to develop a series of proposals for how relationship representations might shift and change over time. The social-cognitive literature provided information about change in other kinds of knowledge representations (e.g., the self, attitudes, stereotypes), whereas the literatures on close relationships and marital intervention approaches provided information about change specifically in relationship knowledge. In particular, theory and research on marital interventions (e.g., cognitive-behavioral) that explicitly seek to change couples' beliefs, expectations, and goals about their relationship provided clues to the process of change. Taken together, the core idea is that change in relationship knowledge is a dynamic process that is closely tied to immediate and enduring life contexts.

RELATIONSHIP KNOWLEDGE REPRESENTATIONS

Before we discuss how relationship representations change, it is important to consider exactly what is known about the nature of the representations themselves. Researchers are far from specifying precisely how relationship knowledge is represented (see Berscheid & Reis, 1998). Although little direct evidence exists about the structure of relationship knowledge, we can extrapolate from social-cognitive work on mental representations. Theory and research on the representation of self-knowledge is especially relevant for understanding relationship representations. Relationship representations often are defined in terms of representations of self and significant others (e.g., see Markus & Cross, 1990), and they are thought to include distinct models of self and models of other (e.g., Baldwin, 1992; Bowlby, 1973) or representations of the self in relation to others (e.g., Andersen, Reznik, & Chen, 1997; Hinkley & Andersen, 1996; Ogilvie & Ashmore, 1991). Because representations of the self are considered to be an important component of relationship representations, research on the structure and stability of representations of the self can inform our understanding of relationship representations.

Relationship theorists (e.g., Baldwin, 1992; Bowlby, 1973; Collins & Read, 1994; Planalp, 1987), like self theorists (e.g., Markus & Wurf, 1987), have relied primarily on schema models, which include the related construct of "scripts" or event schemas. Schema models assume that representations have an internal structure (often hierarchical) and that they include abstract, generalized knowledge about a particular domain (e.g., about the self, another person, or an event). Schemas are thought to operate in a top-down manner, thereby shaping the construal of new information. Consistent with this view, attachment theorists (Bowlby, 1980; Bretherton, 1985; Collins & Read, 1994; Main, Kaplan, & Cassidy, 1985) have suggested that mental representations of attachment relationships are organized within a hierarchical structure, including abstract rules about attachment relationships at higher levels and knowledge about specific relationships and events at lower levels; these representations are assumed to guide how people perceive, interpret, and remember attachment-related information. Other theorists (Baldwin, 1992; Safran, 1990; Stern, 1985) have proposed that these representations include interaction scripts for a sequence of behaviors along with "if–then" contingencies (e.g., "If my partner demands attention, then I will withdraw") that guide such interaction patterns. Over all, relationship knowledge representations, like knowledge representations in general, typically are assumed to be well-organized structures in memory that guide the perception and interpretation of new information.

Although representations often are characterized as abstract structures that reside in memory, recent views (Markus & Wurf, 1987; Wilson & Hodges, 1992; for a review, see Smith, 1998) suggest that they also are flexible and dynamic, fluctuating in response to the situational context. Work on representations of self, for example, assumes that people hold a large array of knowledge about the self but, in any given situational context, only a subset of characteristics of the self, "the working self-concept," may be activated (Markus & Wurf, 1987). Similarly, relationship representations are likely to incorporate many different constructions of relationship knowledge, only some of which will be active in a given context (Baldwin, 1992; Baldwin, Keelan, Fehr, Enns, & Koh-Rangarajoo, 1996). The precise form of mental representations, including those for relationships, is not yet clear (see Smith, 1998), but it seems likely that relationship representations, like those for the self, will be complex, flexible, and dynamic.

STABILITY IN RELATIONSHIP REPRESENTATIONS

The social-cognitive literature (see Fiske & Taylor, 1991; Kunda, 1999), and especially work on the self, provides a starting point for understanding stability and change in relationship representations. Most of the social-cognitive literature emphasizes the stability of knowledge representations. People tend to confirm their expectations and beliefs by focusing on expectancy-consistent information, especially when they hold a long-standing expectation (Stangor & McMillan, 1992). People seek out and create environments that allow them to behave in a way that will confirm their beliefs about themselves (Swann, 1987), and they resist information that contradicts their self-views (Markus, 1977) or their prior expectations (Ross, Lepper, & Hubbard, 1975). People also bias their memory of events in a direction that is consistent with their current beliefs and expectations (Ross, 1989) and thereby create a sense of consistency over time. Stability in knowledge representations may serve the function of helping people to believe that the world is predictable and controllable (Fiske & Taylor, 1991).

Relationship representations, like other kinds of knowledge representations, show considerable stability (e.g., Fletcher & Kininmonth, 1992; Rothbard & Shaver, 1994). For example, longitudinal work examining attachment behavior, which serves as an indicator of underlying internal working models of attachment, demonstrates high levels of stability. The attachment classifications of young children show a high correspondence (73–96%) between behavior in the Strange Situation over several months (Main & Weston, 1981; Waters, 1978). Furthermore, attachment classifications in early childhood (12–18 months of age) predict other cognitive and behavioral indicators of internal working models in the same children at older ages (e.g., Grossman & Grossmann, 1991; Main et al., 1985; Waters, Wippman, & Sroufe, 1979; for a detailed review, see Rothbard & Shaver, 1994). Recent work (Waters, Merrick, Treboux, Crowell, & Albersheim, 2000) suggests that infants' attachment classifications (based on the Strange Situation) correspond highly with their attachment classification (based on the Adult Attachment Interview) in early adulthood. Indeed, 64% of the adults received the same attachment classification (i.e., secure, avoidant, or preoccupied) in infancy and 20 years later. Similarly, attachment in adulthood shows some stability (e.g., Kirkpatrick & Hazan, 1994; Klohnen & Bera, 1998; Scharfe & Bartholomew, 1994). For example, women's reports of attachment-related characteristics (e.g., interpersonal closeness, social confidence, emotional distance), which can be considered indicators of internal working models, were similar at ages 27, 43, and 52 years (Klohnen & Bera, 1998).

As with other knowledge, cognitive processes are likely to promote the stability of relationship knowledge. Information consistent with relationship beliefs is processed quickly and automatically (Fletcher, Rosanowski, & Fitness, 1994), facilitating the stability of relationship knowledge. Also, people reinterpret specific negative information that is inconsistent with their global positive views of the relationship (Murray & Holmes, 1993, 1994) in a way that leads them to maintain the stability of their positive views. Thus, relationship knowledge representations, like other knowledge representations, generally will show stability.

The literature on the self suggests that two fundamental motives underlie representational stability (see Fiske & Taylor, 1991; Linville & Carlston, 1994). First, people strive for consistency in their self-views, even if it means confirming a negative view of themselves (Swann, 1983, 1987). Second, most people desire positive, self-enhancing information (Taylor & Brown, 1988), which usually is consistent with their overall positive view of self. Goals toward consistency and self-enhancement create a push toward stability in self-views. Perceptions of relationships also appear to be guided by similar goals of consistency and relationship enhancement. People strive to maintain consistent views of their relationships, and they appear motivated to hold positive illusions about their relationships (Murray & Holmes, 1997; Murray, Holmes, & Griffin, 1996a,b), although this is likely to be true primarily for relationships characterized by more positive than negative interactions. These goals, like those for self, will promote stability in relationship views. Yet, people also are guided by a fundamental goal to seek accurate information about themselves and their social environment (Fiske & Taylor, 1991; Kunda, 1999), including their relationships. When accurate information conflicts with consistent or self-enhancing information, it may set the stage for change.

CHANGE IN RELATIONSHIP REPRESENTATIONS

Most theorists, while acknowledging the tendency toward representational stability, allow for the possibility that representations can change in response to new experiences, particularly when reality conflicts with prior expectations. In a similar vein, Bowlby (1969) argued that if working models of attachment relationships are to provide accurate predictions of the world, they must be revised when life circumstances change. Indeed, Bowlby (1969) chose the term "internal working models" to reflect the dynamic nature of knowledge about attachment relationships, and he proposed that such models can be updated, elaborated, or replaced in response to situational demands. Thus, although several processes operate to maintain stable relationship representations, some circumstances may initiate representational change.

Characteristics of Change

Change in relationship knowledge can be characterized along at least four dimensions: speed (slow or rapid), momentum (short-lived or enduring), breadth (local or global), and direction (positive or negative).* Furthermore, change can reflect both shifts in the accessibility of existing knowledge and the addition of new knowledge.

Speed of Change

Early work on schema change (Crocker, Fiske, & Taylor, 1984; Rothbart, 1981) focused, in part, on the speed at which changes in the abstract level of a schema occur. First, people might modify their knowledge gradually and incrementally, as if they were accumulating knowledge in a *bookkeeping* system. Second, they might experience sudden and dramatic change, or *conversion*, in the face of a traumatic or powerful event. Change in relationship knowledge could happen in either of these ways. Incremental change, or bookkeeping, might best describe changes that occur over a long period of time, from repeated exposure to similar events, or in response to gradual changes in life circumstances. For example, a woman may believe that romantic partners are unreliable and untrustworthy, but this view may change

---

* This chapter does not focus on representational changes that occur with age, but relationship representations are thought to become more abstract and elaborated as children develop cognitive abilities (e.g., see Main et al., 1985; Stern, 1985).

gradually as her partner repeatedly demonstrates both reliability and trustworthiness.

Conversion changes are likely to be triggered when unexpected relationship events are dramatically inconsistent with prior knowledge. A man who believes that his marriage is enduring, supportive, and happy is likely to be compelled to change his relationship beliefs when he learns that his wife has been unfaithful. Although earlier perspectives (Crocker et al., 1984; Rothbart, 1981) assumed that the structure of the abstract schema (e.g., number of levels of abstraction, number of subcategories) remains constant even following conversion change, other work (see Planalp & Rivers, 1996) suggests that the existing schema may be supplanted by entirely new knowledge. According to Planalp and Rivers (1996), in some situations (e.g., unexpected negative events), people must construct a new explanation or set of beliefs because a ready-made alternative does not exist; in these instances, people may strive to achieve explanatory coherence (see Miller & Read, 1991; Thagard, 1989, 1992) by creating a new framework for understanding the surprising events. This process may be similar to replacing "shattered assumptions" in the aftermath of victimization and trauma (Janoff-Bulman, 1992).

Momentum of Change

Some changes reflect immediate but short-lived responses to contextual constraints, whereas other changes persist over a longer time period as a result of repeated exposure to particular situational cues or in response to a major shift in life circumstances (e.g., a move, job change). These two broad classes of change have been identified in the literature on the self-concept (see Banaji & Prentice, 1994; Linville & Carlston, 1994). As Banaji and Prentice note, people are more likely to show temporary changes in their self-views after enacting a behavior in public versus in private (Tice, 1992), or when the immediate context (e.g., Kunda, Fong, Sanitioso, & Reber, 1993; McGuire & McGuire, 1988) increases the salience of a particular aspect of self. Banaji and Prentice also point out that people evidence more persistent change in their self-views in response to major life events, such as the birth of a child (Deutsch, Ruble, Fleming, Brooks-Gunn, & Stangor, 1988), or a traumatic experience (Janoff-Bulman, 1992).

Changes in relationship representations are likely to parallel those observed for the self. We can infer from the literature on the self that people are more likely to experience a change, at least momentarily, in their relationship representations when they can make inferences from behavior enacted in a public setting. Furthermore, the nature of the interaction context (e.g., a party with friends, at home with parents) may increase or decrease the salience and temporary accessibility of particular relationship knowledge. Likewise, significant, stable shifts in life circumstances should contribute to changes in relationship representations. Thus, some changes in relationship knowledge may be triggered by the immediate context, whereas others may derive from more enduring life contexts or significant life experiences.

Breadth of Change

Change can be broad or global, affecting the abstract, general level of a schema, or it can be narrower, affecting a more specific, lower level of a schema. Subtyping (Crocker et al., 1984; Rothbart, 1981) exemplifies a narrow form of change in which people attend to atypical instances and classify those separately as a *subtype* of the general case (e.g., Most teenagers are forgetful and make hasty decisions, but a few are very responsible.).

Some changes in relationship knowledge may occur via subtyping. For example, a woman might believe that most men will not be able to be responsive, reliable, and trustworthy romantic partners, but she might subtype as an exception the particular man with whom she is developing a relationship. Likewise, within a single relationship, partners might subtype particular behaviors as representative or not representative of the relationship as a whole. For example, a partner's irritable response might be subtyped as atypical, the result of a bad day or a temporary negative mood, rather than as an indicator of the partner's general behavior as a whole. In fact, the ability to subtype annoying behaviors might account for attribution differences noted in nondistressed versus distressed couples (Fletcher & Fincham, 1991). Nondistressed couples are able to attribute an uncivil comment or inconsiderate behavior to temporary variables, whereas distressed couples often attribute such responses to the offending partner's underlying personality. In the former case, partners may view the behavior as incongruent, and change in the relationship representation might occur via subtyping; in the latter case, partners may view the behavior as consistent and absorb it into the larger relationship representation, resulting in little or no change. Subtyping is a form of change that is in the interest of stability; it changes the representation by adding new information and a new category while preventing major change in the more general representation.

Direction of Change
Some research (e.g., Murray et al., 1996a,b) suggests that positive relationship representations are highly stable and resistant to change. Romantic partners are biased toward maintaining a positive view of their relationship and thus may be predisposed to attend to, interpret, and recall positive information and to reinterpret or transform potentially negative information (Murray & Holmes, 1993). Thus, positive relationship representations may be difficult to change, in part, because positive illusions help to promote stability. However, it is quite likely that positive illusions are maintained only against a backdrop of mostly positive interactions. When negative interactions increase in number, intensity, or extremity, they may be difficult to ignore or reinterpret. Once this threshold is crossed, negative interactions may exert a greater impact than comparable positive interactions.

A broad base of research suggests that negative information carries greater weight than positive information and thus may powerfully affect mental representations, including those about relationships. First, work on person perception (see Kanouse & Hanson, 1972) indicates that people weight negative information more heavily than positive information when making judgments about others (e.g., Fiske, 1980; Hamilton & Zanna, 1972). Consistent with this idea, happy marriages include about five times as many positive as negative interactions (Gottman & Levenson, 1992), providing indirect evidence that much more positive evidence is required to outweigh negative information. Furthermore, negative information receives more attention than positive information (Fiske, 1980; Pratto & John, 1991). The greater weighting and salience of negative information suggests that relationship representations may change more easily and more rapidly in a negative direction than in a positive direction. When change occurs rapidly, it is usually in response to highly negative events (Janoff-Bulman, 1992; Planalp & Rivers, 1996). Extreme negative events are most likely to undermine people's basic assumptions about themselves and the world (Janoff-Bulman, 1992). Indeed, it would be difficult to find extreme positive events that are as emotionally powerful as extreme negative ones. Second, work on emotion suggests that negative emotions are more differentiated than positive emotions (Averill, 1980; Ellsworth & Smith, 1988a,b; Schwarz & Clore, 1996; but see

Fredrickson, 1998). To the extent that emotions provide conceptual coherence in memory (Niedenthal, Halberstadt & Innes-Ker, 1999), negative representations may be more complex and differentiated than positive ones. If this is true, then negative representations not only may develop more rapidly but also may be slower to change.

Mechanisms of Change

Although variations in speed, momentum, breadth, and direction characterize the process of change in a general way, it is important to consider the precise mechanisms underlying change. We examine several possible mechanisms for change, triggered by either temporary or enduring situational contexts. We first consider temporary shifts in internal or external factors that change the accessibility of relationship knowledge. When these factors change in a more permanent way, they may produce more enduring changes in relationship knowledge. Although we discuss each mechanism separately, in many cases they may operate concurrently.

Influence of the Temporary Context

Internal or external changes in the immediate context (e.g., mood, goals, salient social information) can alter the accessibility of relationship knowledge, leading to variations in the current representation of a relationship. Mood, for example, can alter the way in which people think about others (for reviews, see Forgas, 1991, 1995). All other things being equal, people in a transient happy mood pay more attention to another person's positive qualities, whereas those in a transient negative mood pay more attention to negative qualities (Forgas & Bower, 1987). Similarly, people in a happy mood offer more positive attributions for the behavior of the self and others, although people in a sad mood make more negative attributions about themselves but not about others (Forgas, Bower, & Krantz, 1984; Forgas, Bower, & Moylon, 1990). Mood also affects attributions about close relationships, even when they are relatively long term (Forgas, 1994). People in a happy mood make more external, unstable, and specific attributions about serious conflicts in their relationship, whereas people in a sad mood make more internal, stable, and global attributions (Forgas, 1994). These mood-consistent attributions may lead people to view the relationship as a whole in a more favorable or unfavorable light.

Mood may produce transient change in relationship representations but, if a particular mood persists or recurs frequently, such changes may become a more readily accessible feature of the representation. Chronic dysphoria or depression, for example, may trigger repeated negative judgments of close relationships (e.g., Barnett & Gotlib, 1988), which, over time, may lead to changes in underlying relationship representations.

A variety of other contextual cues also can produce temporary shifts in relationship knowledge. Increasing the accessibility of a particular kind of relationship through visualization has been shown to temporarily alter the way in which people evaluate potential relationship partners (Baldwin et al., 1996). Contextual cues priming representations of significant others can lead individuals to apply existing relationship knowledge to a new partner (e.g., Andersen & Baum, 1994; Andersen & Cole, 1990). Other work (Hinkley & Andersen, 1996) has demonstrated that when people expect to interact with a new person who resembles a significant other, they adjust their self-descriptions to fit their views of themselves in relation to that particular significant other. All of these examples are consistent with the idea that relationship knowledge is dynamic and flexible, changing in response to the immediate context.

Relationship knowledge at any given moment in time also depends on current goals and the information available in the setting. Research by Murray and Holmes (1993) illustrates how motivation and situational cues might interact to change the way that people construe their relationships. Murray and Holmes propose that people generally are motivated to view their romantic partners in a positive light. When people are faced with the possibility that their partner has a fault (i.e., an immediate situational cue), they will restructure and reinterpret their relationship knowledge to fit their motivation to hold positive views of their partner. In one study, for example, when participants who reported low conflict in their relationship read a fictitious article about the importance of conflict in the development of intimacy, they constructed relationship stories that emphasized the positive role of conflict in their relationships (Murray & Holmes, Study 1). In this case, although the affect associated with the relationship representation remained stable, the interpretation and details of relationship events changed. Thus, this story construction process promotes stability of the positive affect associated with the relationship, while at the same time, the contextual cues appear to lead to shifts in the precise content of the active representation.

The degree to which temporarily primed knowledge or reconstructed information becomes an enduring part of a relationship representation remains an open question, but it is likely that repeated experience with similar contextual cues will increase the likelihood of the activation of similar representations. Furthermore, once information has been transformed, it is unlikely that the representation can return to its exact original form (see Smith, 1996).

How do the effects of accessibility map onto the change characteristics of speed, momentum, breadth, and direction? Temporary contextual cues are likely to produce rapid, short-lived, and narrow shifts in relationship representations, but, if similar contextual cues recur over time, particular representational patterns may be activated more easily and thus become more enduring and broad. Although this idea has yet to be tested empirically, it follows from social-cognitive work on the activation and accessibility of knowledge (Higgins, 1996). For example, a husband who experiences a temporary negative mood may more easily access instances in which his wife was unavailable or unresponsive, leading to a transient change in his current, active relationship representation, but this representation may become less accessible as he returns to a happier mood. In contrast, if the husband becomes depressed and therefore experiences a sustained negative mood, the more negative representation of his relationship may be activated repeatedly and thus become more long-lasting and general. In addition, temporary contextual cues (e.g., mood) should be able to move representations in either a positive or negative direction.

Several additional features may characterize change resulting from accessibility effects. Context cues may produce change only for less central aspects of relationship knowledge. This idea is supported by work on the self (see Kunda, 1999), suggesting that self-conceptions are more apt to shift along dimensions that are less central to the self (Markus, 1977). Also, people who have more diverse information about their relationship may be more responsive to situational cues, leading to greater variations in which knowledge is accessible in working memory. This pattern is analogous to the observation in the self-concept literature that people with more diverse self-conceptions show greater flexibility in their self-views from situation to situation (Kunda, 1999). For example, people who report greater variability in introversion–extraversion shift their self-conceptions in line with situational cues relevant to this dimension more than those who do not report such variability (Kunda, Fong, Sanitioso, & Reber, 1993).

Influence of the Enduring Context
When internal or external shifts in the immediate context persist over time, they may lead to more enduring changes in relationship representations. Most of the evidence for change in relationship representations comes from change associated with longer-term alterations in external circumstances, primarily in relation to attachment. Attachment behavior, and presumably the underlying internal working models, varies in response to fluctuations in the stability of the family environment (e.g., Easterbrooks & Goldberg, 1990) or in the quality of caregiving (e.g., Erickson, Sroufe, & Egeland, 1985). Recent work (e.g., Waters et al., 2000) provides further evidence that, under some circumstances, people appear to change their attachment patterns, especially when they undergo stressful experiences that may alter family dynamics (see Waters, Hamilton, & Weinfield, 2000).

Attachment patterns in adulthood, like those in childhood, also vary over time, suggesting that change may occur under some conditions (Baldwin & Fehr, 1995; Davila, Burge, & Hammen, 1997; Davila, Karney, & Bradbury, 1999; Fuller & Fincham, 1995). However, change in adulthood appears to be a complex process, tied to situational context, individual differences, and the interaction between the two (e.g., Davila et al., 1999). For example, Davila et al. found that newly married couples, who have experienced a major change in life context, typically become more secure, perhaps because the experience of staying in a marriage increases confidence that the spouse will remain available as a source of support. At the same time, women who evidenced stable individual differences in psychological vulnerabilities showed greater variations over time in their working models, suggesting that individual differences contribute to representational fluctuations. Although the mechanism underlying this effect remains to be determined, it may be that psychological vulnerabilities produce greater instability in women's reports of their attachment because of greater fluctuations in their moods, self-views, or responses to daily events. Over all, this work underscores the complex role of both environmental and person variables in understanding stability and change in attachment (see Rothbard & Shaver, 1994). Two mechanisms might explain, in part, how representations change in response to more permanent shifts in life context.

Reorganization of knowledge. Under some circumstances, people may reorganize and reframe their earlier experiences in a way that changes the quality of their relationship representations. Indirect evidence (see Hesse, 1999) for this idea comes from work focusing on individuals who report negative childhood attachment experiences during the Adult Attachment Interview (e.g., Main et al., 1985) but who evidence security in describing those relationships as adults. These adults, who appear to have changed their attachment representations and hence "earned security," present a coherent, thoughtful, and appropriately complex picture of their childhood attachment relationships, acknowledging negative experiences and the context in which they occurred. In contrast, adults who report negative childhood experiences and remain insecure often tell incoherent, disorganized stories about their childhood attachments. Furthermore, the responses of earned secures are similar to those with continuous security in the degree to which they show sensitivity and responsiveness in parenting their own children (Pearson, Cohn, Cowan, & Cowan, 1994; Phelps, Belsky, & Crnic, 1998). These individuals' responses during the Adult Attachment Interview suggest that they have reorganized their understanding of emotionally significant childhood events.[†] This process may be similar to the cognitive reorganization that appears to occur when people write about traumatic personal experiences (Pennebaker, 1989).

The marital intervention literature highlights the importance of reframing in changing relationship views. One approach, Integrative Couples Therapy (Christensen, Jacobson, & Babcock, 1995; Jacobson & Christensen, 1996), emphasizes the importance of reframing marital problems, particularly those related to partner behaviors that are unlikely to change. Spouses are encouraged to change some behavior but also to accept some undesirable behaviors of the partner by reframing their psychological meaning (Hayes, 1994). Acceptance is thought to reduce negative reactions and to facilitate the development of inti-

---

[†] Earned security is determined from participants' reports of their childhood experiences during the Adult Attachment Interview, leaving open the possibility that earned secures have not changed their relationship representations. Instead, they may inaccurately recall their early experiences or, because of underlying genetic predispositions, they may be more able to be resilient in the face of negative experiences (see Hesse, 1999). Whether earned security reflects change in working models remains to be determined in longitudinal studies.

macy (Jacobson & Christensen, 1996). Acceptance does not require new relationship knowledge, but rather, partners reorganize or reframe existing knowledge in a way that leads to more positive evaluations of the marriage. Interestingly, this reframing may be similar to the natural tendency of many individuals to construct positive illusions about their romantic partners (Murray & Holmes, 1993). Although the degree to which this form of therapy promotes reframing and relationship improvement remains an open question, a pilot study (Jacobson, Christensen, Prince, Cordova, & Eldridge, 2000) suggests that couples in Integrative Couples Therapy show a greater increase in marital satisfaction than those in a more traditional behavioral therapy.

Incorporation of new knowledge. Another way that relationship representations might develop and change as a result of major life events is through the incorporation of new information. For example, beginning a new romantic relationship or marriage is a major life event that might facilitate the integration of new knowledge. During such transitions, characteristics of a close other may become integrated into an individual's view of self (Aron & Aron, 1986, 1996). Consistent with this reasoning, spouses have been shown to respond more quickly when describing themselves on traits that are similar to those of their partner and more slowly for traits that are different, suggesting that overlap exists in their views of self and spouse (Aron, Aron, Tudor, & Nelson, 1991). Furthermore, longitudinal work (Aron, Paris, & Aron, 1995) has demonstrated that falling in love is associated with change and greater diversity in the content of the self. Although Aron and Aron describe this process as a way of expanding the self, it also could be conceptualized as a way of building (and changing) a relationship representation of the self in relation to a specific other. One explanation of these effects is that both spouses (Aron et al., 1991) and those newly in love (Aron, Paris, & Aron, 1995) have incorporated characteristics of their partner into their self-views, and these self–other units form part of the representation for that particular relationship.

Marital interventions often promote the incorporation of new relationship knowledge by providing alternatives to maladaptive beliefs and attributions (Baucom & Epstein, 1990), problematic behavioral scripts (Jacobson & Holtzworth-Munroe, 1986; Jacobson & Margolin, 1979) and distressing emotional responses (Greenberg & Johnson, 1988). These approaches attempt to increase the accessibility of alternative responses through deliberate, repetitive efforts to base responses on new information. However, most of these approaches also teach individuals to reorganize existing knowledge, making it difficult to determine whether changes in relationship knowledge result from the addition of new knowledge, reframing, or both.

Cognitive-behavioral interventions appear to produce some change in relationship knowledge. For example, distressed couples who participated in behavioral marital therapy with a cognitive restructuring component showed a decrease in dysfunctional cognitions, including relationship beliefs and attributions, in comparison with couples who participated in behavioral therapy alone (Baucom, Sayers, & Sher, 1990). However, as in other work (Baucom & Lester, 1986; Halford, Sanders, & Behrens, 1993), both groups were similar after completion of therapy on other measures of relationship adjustment. Thus, changing the cognitions of one's romantic partner will not necessarily alter relationship satisfaction in a linear fashion (for related work, see Karney & Bradbury, 2000). Although a primary goal of such interventions is to provide alternatives to maladaptive cognitions, methodological limitations make it difficult to pinpoint exactly where (e.g., which cognitions, what level of the representation) knowledge change occurred and exactly what process elicited change.

Some therapies focus on training individuals to engage in more constructive behaviors instead of problematic automatic behavioral sequences (Jacobson & Margolin, 1979; Stuart, 1980), which may be guided by underlying behavioral scripts. For example, many distressed couples evidence a demand–withdraw pattern in which one spouse approaches the partner in an attempt to discuss a conflict, while the partner attempts to withdraw from the interaction (Christensen & Heavey, 1993; Napier, 1978). Over time, this pattern becomes overlearned and readily accessible during future conflicts. Such maladaptive communication patterns are thought to arise from individual spouses acquiring "if–then" production rules or scripts about emotional and behavioral responses in conflict (Fitness, 1996; Scott, Fuhrman, & Wyer, 1991). For the approaching spouse, the production rule may be "If my partner communicates disinterest to me, then I should communicate anger to my partner," while for the withdrawing spouse, the production rule may be "If my partner communicates anger to me, then I should communicate disinterest to my partner." The task in behavioral marital therapy is to help couples to identify and replace maladaptive communication patterns that are strongly linked to relationship dissatisfaction (Gottman, 1994; Markman & Hahlweg, 1993). Although cognitive-behavioral marital therapy approaches reduce couple distress to a greater extent than no-treatment or wait-list control conditions (Baucom et al., 1998; Hahlweg & Markman, 1988; Jacobson & Addis, 1993), it is unclear whether the success results directly from behavioral and cognitive changes, from changes in the underlying interpersonal scripts, or from some other therapy-related process.

Emotionally focused therapy (Greenberg & Johnson, 1988), in contrast to some of the other therapies discussed, focuses explicitly on changing the emotions attached to relationship representations. This therapy, based on attachment theory, seeks to facilitate the recognition and expression of each partner's needs for closeness and security, and to invite responses that promote a secure bond and restructure negative internal working models. Thus, this therapy encourages constructive emotional responses while seeking to reduce responses promoting insecurity and distress, ultimately leading to the incorporation of new relationship knowledge by facilitating new relationship experiences. Several studies (Greenberg, Ford, Alden, & Johnson, 1993; Greenberg, James, & Conry, 1988) have examined the nature of change in emotionally focused therapy, including variables such as the expression of feelings and needs, emotional understanding, validation from the therapist and partner, and affiliation and independence. Although the studies generally have relied on small samples and self-reports, the findings are consistent with the idea that emotionally focused therapy increases partner accessibility and responsiveness through deepening affective experience, promoting self-disclosure, and changing negative interaction patterns to more adaptive patterns characterized by affiliation and independence. An underlying assumption is that these changes co-occur with a restructuring of affective experience and the content of internal working models, especially with respect to partner availability and responsiveness.

The influence of the enduring life context is likely to produce slow, gradual changes in relationship representations through knowledge reorganization and the addition of new knowledge. The degree to which such changes endure over time remains an open question. Although some marital interventions may alter relationship knowledge, few studies have examined directly how relationship knowledge (e.g., cognitions, attributions) evolves over time (e.g., over the course of therapy) or the duration of such changes after therapy is terminated. In addition, the direction of change usually examined in clinical intervention studies is from negative to positive, increasing the likelihood that change will occur slowly, if at all. Although shifts from positive representations to more negative or uncertain ones may happen rapidly, the process of rebuilding coherent representations proceeds gradually (Janoff-Bulman, 1992).

FURTHER CONSIDERATIONS

Several additional points need to be taken into account in understanding change in relationship knowledge. First, our conceptualization of change follows from schema models, but it is possible that other representational models (e.g., connectionist models) better capture the context-sensitive and dynamic nature of these representations. Second, implicit and explicit sources of relationship knowledge may have different trajectories of change. Third, relationship knowledge representations are likely to be highly charged with affect, suggesting that shifts in affect may mediate change. Each of these issues has implications for understanding the process of change.

Relationship Representations: Static or Dynamic?

The analysis presented here suggests that change is a dynamic process. However, schema models, along with other dominant approaches to knowledge structures (for a review, see Smith, 1998), characterize representations as "things" that are stored in memory in some form, implying a static, fixed entity. Theorists recently have suggested that connectionist models (or, parallel distributed processing models) offer an alternative and potentially useful framework for understanding knowledge representations (e.g., for detailed discussions, see Smith, 1996, 1998). In this type of model, knowledge representations are considered to be dynamic states that are sensitive to the immediate situational and personal context.

Several assumptions of connectionist models (see Smith, 1996, 1998) fit well with our view of dynamic change in relationship representations. Connectionist models assume that (a) representations are context-sensitive reconstructions, (b) representation and process are inseparable, (c) experience changes the representation by altering connection weights and hence the chronic accessibility of particular patterns, and (d) changes evoked by new experiences may be small and subtle, but they are irreversible. Furthermore, connectionist models are compatible with the notion of accessibility, suggesting that the more often a particular pattern is activated, the more likely it is to shape the processing of a new stimulus. Thus, a connectionist perspective implies two features of change that are consistent with our conceptualization. First, change occurs from moment to moment, with the ebb and flow of context. Second, change can be incremental, reflecting increases in accessibility with repeated similar experiences. When applied to relationship knowledge, this view suggests that relationship representations can include a wide array of information that shifts and changes with the nature of the context but, depending on previous learning experiences, some patterns will be more likely to emerge than others. It will be worthwhile for theorists to consider alternative representational models in constructing a theory of representational change, for such models may suggest somewhat different mechanisms of change. A more comprehensive understanding of the process of representational change will rest, in part, on identifying more precisely the nature of representational models.

Implicit versus Explicit Knowledge and Behavior
Knowledge representations contain both explicit and implicit knowledge, and it is possible that the two types of knowledge may have different profiles of change. Researchers usually infer change in relationship knowledge from people's conscious self-reports of their experiences, but many thoughts, feelings, and behaviors in relationships are guided by automatic, nonconscious processes (see Berscheid & Reis, 1998; Reis & Knee, 1996). Social-cognitive work has increasingly focused on social judgments and behavior that operate below conscious awareness (Bargh, 1997). Furthermore, theories of attitudes (Petty & Wegener, 1998), the self-concept (Epstein, 1990), and stereotyping (Greenwald & Banaji, 1995) suggest that people hold both implicit and explicit knowledge about the same domain, and that both kinds of knowledge can influence judgments and behavior. The implications for relationship representations are that people often may not be aware of at least a subset of their views of their relationship, and their implicit views may influence their subsequent thoughts, feelings, and behavior in the relationship. Within the attachment literature, theorists (Bowlby, 1980; Main, 1991) similarly have discussed that working models can come to function automatically, outside of conscious awareness. Furthermore, Bowlby (1980) proposed that people may have multiple models in which a particular aspect of reality is seen in ways that are contradictory (e.g., "My partner deeply loves me" and "My partner does not care about me and will desert me"). In Bowlby's view, one model may operate within conscious awareness, but the other may

operate primarily outside of awareness, protecting the person from a threat to self.

The distinction between implicit and explicit knowledge and behavior is important in evaluating whether representational change has occurred. When and how does representational change occur at the explicit, conscious level or at the implicit, less conscious level? Recent theorizing and research (Wilson, Lindsey, & Schooler, 2000) suggests that when an attitude about an object changes, the new attitude may not simply replace the old attitude; instead, people may hold dual attitudes – one that is implicit and one that is explicit. Wilson et al. (2000) argue that implicit attitudes are likely to affect processing when people have limited cognitive resources and motivation, whereas explicit attitudes will do so when adequate resources and motivation are available. Furthermore, implicit attitudes are apt to change slowly, whereas explicit attitudes may change more quickly (Wilson et al., 2000). This work suggests that change in relationship representations is complex, involving both explicit and implicit knowledge and processes. For example, marital interventions aim to detect and change couples' knowledge at both implicit and explicit levels. However, outcomes usually are assessed through self-report, a method that is likely to tap only explicit processes. Thus, whether such interventions are able to alter representations at the implicit level remains an open question.

Affect
Change in relationship knowledge is likely to be inextricably connected to affect. Relationships are a primary source of both pleasure and pain, and the most intense emotions are likely to be aroused in interactions with others. Yet most models of knowledge representations do not adequately incorporate affect. Most social-cognitive views of knowledge representations (e.g., Fiske & Taylor, 1991) consider affect to be a product of cognitive processes. But, as attachment theorists (e.g., Bowlby, 1980) and object relations theorists (e.g., Greenberg & Mitchell, 1983) have noted, relationship representations are likely to be affectively charged. This perspective suggests that affect is not merely an outcome of knowledge representations, but it is integral to the organization of knowledge, binding together information in knowledge representations (see Pietromonaco & Feldman Barrett, 2000). Work (Niedenthal et al., 1999) showing that people group together concepts that evoke similar emotional responses supports the view of affect as

the "glue" in mental representations. If this view is accurate, then change in relationship representations may require altering not only cold cognitions but also affect. Consistent with this view, recent evidence (Karney & Bradbury, 2000) suggests that changes in relationship cognitions are not always accompanied by corresponding changes in feelings about the relationship. Furthermore, this view implies that intervention methods will be more effective when they incorporate the restructuring of affective experience and expression (e.g., Greenberg & Johnson, 1988).

CONCLUSION

The aim of this chapter was to assess how change might occur in relationship representations. An integration of the literatures on social cognition, close relationships, and marital interventions suggests that relationship representations generally are stable, but that change can occur under some conditions. When change occurs, it is a dynamic process that is sensitive to temporary and enduring contextual cues. Change can vary along at least four dimensions (i.e., speed, momentum, breadth, direction) that may be closely connected to whether it results from temporary or enduring contextual cues. Furthermore, several processes may underlie representational change, including temporary shifts in the accessibility of relationship-relevant knowledge, the reorganization and reframing of relationship knowledge, and the incorporation of new knowledge and strategies.

Although our analysis provides some initial ideas about change in relationship representations, many pressing questions remain to be addressed. The characteristics and mechanisms of change depend on assumptions about the nature of mental representations. But, what is the best way of conceptualizing these representations? How is affect implicated in these representations and in the process of change? In what ways does implicit, less conscious processing contribute to change as compared to more explicit, conscious processing? How might relationship partners inhibit or facilitate change in relationship representations? Change in relationship cognitions is a reciprocal and dynamic process between two people and thus may be best revealed through investigations at both intrapersonal and interpersonal levels.

Although few empirical studies have focused on change in relationship knowledge, this topic is both theoretically rich and practically significant. Furthermore, the study of representational change crosses boundaries within social psychology (e.g., social cognition, close relationships) as well as between subareas of psychology (i.e., social, clinical, developmental, cognitive) and will benefit from integrative work among investigators in different areas. This endeavor also will require creative methodologies that combine longitudinal studies of stability and change in relationship knowledge with more microlevel laboratory studies of process (e.g., using social-cognitive methods). We hope that this chapter provides a framework from which researchers can begin to build a solid empirical base for understanding change in relationship knowledge.

REFERENCES

Andersen, S. M., & Baum, A. (1994). Transference in interpersonal relations: Inferences and affect based on significant-other representations. *Journal of Personality, 62,* 459–498.

Andersen, S. M., & Cole, S. W. (1990). "Do I know you?": The role of significant others in general social perception. *Journal of Personality and Social Psychology, 59,* 384–399.

Andersen, S. M., Reznik, I., & Chen, S. (1997). The self in relation to others: Motivational and cognitive underpinnings. In J. G. Snodgrass & R. L. Thompson (Eds.), *The self across psychology: Self-recognition, self-awareness, and the self-concept* (pp. 233–275). New York: New York Academy of Science.

Aron, A., & Aron, E. N. (1986). *Love as the expansion of self: Understanding attraction and satisfaction.* New York: Hemisphere.

——— (1996). Self and self-expansion in relationships. In G. J. O. Fletcher & J. Fitness (Eds.), *Knowledge structures in close relationships: A social psychological approach* (pp. 325–344). Mahwah, NJ: Erlbaum.

Aron, A., Aron, E. N., Tudor, M., & Nelson, G. (1991). Close relationships as including other in the self. *Journal of Personality and Social Psychology, 60,* 241–253.

Aron, A., Paris, M., & Aron, E. N. (1995). Falling in love: Prospective studies of self-concept change. *Journal of Personality and Social Psychology, 69,* 1102–1112.

Averill, J. R. (1980). On the paucity of positive emotions. In K. Blankstein, P. Pliner, & J. Polivy (Eds.), *Advances in the study of communication and affect. Vol. 6. Assessment and modification of emotional behavior* (pp. 7–45). New York: Plenum.

Baldwin, M. W. (1992). Relational schemas and the processing of social information. *Psychological Bulletin, 112,* 461–484.

——— (1995). Relational schemas and cognition in close relationships. *Journal of Social and Personal Relationships, 12,* 547–552.

Baldwin, M. W., & Fehr, B. (1995). On the instability of attachment style ratings. *Personal Relationships, 2,* 247–261.

Baldwin, M. W., Keelan, J. P. R., Fehr, B., Enns, V., & Koh-Rangarajoo, E. (1996). Social-cognitive conceptualization of attachment working models: Availability and accessibility effects. *Journal of Personality and Social Psychology, 71*, 94–109.

Banaji, M. R., & Prentice, D. A. (1994). The self in social contexts. *Annual Review of Psychology*, 297–332.

Bargh, J. A. (1997). The automaticity of everyday life. In R. S. Wyer (Ed.), *The automaticity of everyday life: Advances in social cognition* (Vol. 10, pp. 1–61). Mahwah, NJ: Erlbaum.

Barnett, P. A., & Gotlib, I. H. (1988). Psychosocial functioning and depression: Distinguishing among antecedents, concomitants, and consequences. *Psychological Bulletin, 104*, 97–126.

Bartholomew, K., & Horowitz, L. M. (1991). Attachment styles among young adults: A test of a four-category model. *Journal of Personality and Social Psychology, 61*, 226–244.

Baucom, D. H., & Epstein, N. (1990). *Cognitive behavioral marital therapy*. New York: Brunner/Mazel.

Baucom, D. H., & Lester, G. W. (1986). The usefulness of cognitive restructuring as an adjunct to behavioral marital therapy. *Behavior Therapy, 17*, 385–403.

Baucom, D. H., Sayers, S. L., & Sher, T. G. (1990). Supplementing behavioral marital therapy with cognitive restructuring and emotional expressiveness training: An outcome investigation. *Journal of Consulting and Clinical Psychology, 58*, 636–645.

Baucom, D. H., Shoham, V., Muser, K. T., & Daiuto, A. D. (1998). Empirically supported couple and family interventions for marital distress and adult mental health problems. *Journal of Consulting and Clinical Psychology, 66*, 53–88.

Berscheid, E., & Reis, H. T. (1998). Attraction and close relationships. In D. T. Gilbert, S. T. Fiske, & G. Lindzey (Eds.), *The handbook of social psychology* (pp. 193–281). Boston: McGraw-Hill.

Bowlby, J. (1969). *Attachment and loss: Vol. 1. Attachment*. New York: Basic.
(1973). *Attachment and loss: Vol. 2. Separation: Anxiety and anger*. New York: Basic Books.
(1979). *The making and breaking of affectional bonds*. London: Tavistock.
(1980). *Attachment and loss: Vol. 3. Loss: Sadness and depression*. New York: Basic Books.

Bretherton, I. (1985). Attachment theory: Retrospect and prospect. In I. Bretherton & E. Waters (Eds.), Growing points of attachment theory and research. *Monographs of the Society for Research in Child Development, 50*, (1–2, Serial No. 209), 3–35.

Christensen, A., & Heavey, C. L. (1993). Gender differences in marital conflict: The demand/withdraw interaction pattern. In S. Oskamp & M. Costanzo (Eds.), *Gender issues in contemporary society*. Newbury Park, CA: Sage.

Christensen, A., Jacobson, N. S., & Babcock, J. C. (1995). Integrative behavioral couples therapy. In N. S. Jacobson & A. S. Gurman (Eds.), *Clinical handbook of couples therapy*, 2nd ed. (pp. 31–64). New York: Guilford Press.

Collins, N., & Read, S. (1994). Cognitive representations of attachment: The structure and function of working models. In D. Perlman & K. Bartholomew (Eds.), *Advances in Personal Relationships* (Vol. 5, pp. 53–90). London: Jessica Kingsley.

Crocker, J., Fiske, S. T., & Taylor, S. E. (1984). Schematic bases of belief change. In J. R. Eiser (Ed.), *Attitudinal judgment* (pp. 197–225). New York: Springer-Verlag.

Davila, J., Burge, D., & Hammen, C. (1997). Why does attachment style change? *Journal of Personality and Social Psychology, 73,* 826–838.

Davila, J., Karney, B. R., & Bradbury, T. N. (1999). Attachment change processes in the early years of marriage. *Journal of Personality and Social Psychology, 76,* 783–802.

Deutsch, F. M., Ruble, D. N., Fleming, A., Brooks-Gunn, J., & Stangor, C. (1988). Information-seeking and maternal self-definition during the transition to motherhood. *Journal of Personality and Social Psychology, 55,* 420–431.

Easterbrooks, M. A., & Goldberg, W. A. (1990). Security of toddler–parent attachment: Relation to children's sociopersonality functioning during kindergarten. In M. T. Greenberg, D. Cicchetti, & E. M. Cummings (Eds.), *Attachment in the preschool years: Theory, research, and intervention* (pp. 221–244). Chicago: University of Chicago Press.

Ellsworth, P. C., & Smith, C. A. (1988a). From appraisal to emotion: Differences among unpleasant feelings. *Motivation and Emotion, 12,* 271–302.

(1988b). Shades of joy: Patterns of appraisal differentiating pleasant emotions. *Emotion and Cognition, 2,* 302–331.

Epstein, S. (1990). Cognitive-experiential self-theory. In L. A. Pervin (Ed.), *Handbook of personality: Theory and research* (pp. 165–192). New York: Guilford Press.

Erickson, J., Sroufe, L., & Egeland, B. (1985). The relationship between quality of attachment and behavior problems in preschool in a high-risk sample. In I. Bretherton & E. Waters (Eds.), Growing points of attachment theory and research. *Monographs of the Society for Research in Child Development, 50,* (1–2, Serial No. 209), 147–166.

Fehr, B., & Baldwin, M. (1996). Prototype and script analyses of laypeople's knowledge of anger. In G. J. O. Fletcher & J. Fitness (Eds.), *Knowledge structures in close relationships: A social psychological approach* (pp. 219–245). Mahwah, NJ: Erlbaum.

Fiske, S. T. (1980). Attention and weight in person perception: The impact of negative and extreme behavior. *Journal of Personality and Social Psychology, 38,* 889–906.

Fiske, S. T., & Taylor, S. E. (1991). *Social cognition.* New York: McGraw-Hill.

Fitness, J. (1996). Emotion knowledge structures in close relationships. In G. J. O. Fletcher & J. Fitness (Eds.), *Knowledge structures in close relationships: A social psychological approach* (pp. 195–217). Mahwah, NJ: Erlbaum.

Fletcher, G. J. O., & Fincham, F. D. (1991). Attribution processes in close relationships. In G. J. O. Fletcher & F. D. Fincham (Eds.), *Cognition in close relationships* (pp. 7–35). Hillsdale, NJ: Erlbaum.

Fletcher, G. J. O., & Kininmonth, L. (1991). Interaction in close relationships and social cognition. In G. J. O. Fletcher & F. D. Fincham (Eds.), *Cognition in close relationships* (pp. 235–255). Hillsdale, NJ: Erlbaum.

Fletcher, G. J. O., & Thomas, G. (1996). Close relationship lay theories: Their structure and function. In G. J. O. Fletcher & J. Fitness (Eds.), *Knowledge structures in close relationships: A social psychological approach* (pp. 3–24). Mahwah, NJ: Erlbaum.

Fletcher, G. J. O., Rosanowski, J., & Fitness, J. (1994). Automatic processing in intimate contexts: The role of close-relationship beliefs. *Journal of Personality and Social Psychology, 67*, 888–897.

Forgas, J. P. (1991). Affect and cognition in close relationships. In G. J. O. Fletcher & F. D. Fincham (Eds.), *Cognition in close relationships* (pp. 151–174). Hillsdale, NJ: Erlbaum.

(1994). Sad and guilty? Affective influences on the explanation of conflict in close relationships. *Journal of Personality and Social Psychology, 66*, 56–68.

(1995). Mood and judgment: The affect infusion model (AIM). *Psychological Bulletin, 117*, 39–66.

Forgas, J. P., & Bower, G. H. (1987). Mood effects on person perception judgments. *Journal of Personality and Social Psychology, 53*, 53–60.

Forgas, J. P., Bower, G. H., & Krantz, S. (1984). The influence of mood on perceptions of social interactions. *Journal of Experimental Social Psychology, 20*, 497–513.

Forgas, J. P., Bower, G. H., & Moylan, S. J. (1990). Praise or blame? Affective influences on attributions for success or failure. *Journal of Personality and Social Psychology, 59*, 809–819.

Fredrickson, B. (1998). What good are positive emotions? *Review of General Psychology, 2*, 300–319.

Fuller, T. L., & Fincham, F. D. (1995). Attachment style in married couples: Relation to current marital functioning, stability over time, and method of assessment. *Personal Relationships, 2*, 17–34.

Gottman, J. M. (1994). *What predicts divorce?* Hillsdale, NJ: Erlbaum.

Gottman, J. M., & Levenson, R. W. (1992). Marital processes predictive of later dissolution: Behavior, physiology, and health. *Journal of Personality and Social Psychology, 63*, 221–233.

Greenberg, J. R., & Mitchell, S. A. (1983). *Object relations in psychoanalytic theory.* Cambridge, MA: Harvard University Press.

Greenberg, L., James, P. L., & Conry, R. F. (1988). Perceived change processes in emotionally focused couples therapy. *Journal of Family Psychology, 2*, 5–23.

Greenberg, L. S., Ford, C., Alden, L., & Johnson, S. M. (1993). Change processes in emotionally focused couples therapy. *Journal of Consulting and Clinical Psychology, 61*, 78–84.

Greenberg, L. S., & Johnson, S. M. (1988). *Emotionally focused therapy for couples.* New York: Guilford Press.

Greenwald, A. G., & Banaji, M. R. (1995). Implicit social cognition: Attitudes, self-esteem, and stereotypes. *Psychological Review, 102*, 1–27.

Grossmann, K. E., & Grossmann, K. (1991). Attachment quality as an organizer of emotional and behavioral responses in a longitudinal perspective. In C. M. Parkes, J. Stevenson-Hinde, & P. Marris (Eds.), *Attachment across the life cycle* (pp. 93–114). London: Tavistock/Routledge.

Hahlweg, K., & Markman, H. J. (1988). Effectiveness of behavioral marital therapy: Empirical status of behavioral techniques in preventing and alleviating marital distress. *Journal of Consulting and Clinical Psychology, 56,* 440–447.

Halford, W. K., Sanders, M. R., & Behrens, B. C. (1993). A comparison of the generalization of behavioral marital therapy and enhanced behavioral marital therapy. *Journal of Consulting and Clinical Psychology, 61,* 51–60.

Hamilton, D., & Zanna, M. (1972). Differential weighting of favorable and unfavorable attributes in impression of personality. *Journal of Experimental Research in Personality, 6,* 204–212.

Hayes, S. C. (1994). Content, context, and the types of psychological acceptance. In S. C. Hayes, N. S. Jacobson, V. M. Follette, & M. J. Dougher (Eds.), *Acceptance and change: Content and context in psychotherapy* (pp. 13–32). Reno, NV: Context Press.

Hazan, C., & Shaver, P. R. (1987). Romantic love conceptualized as an attachment process. *Journal of Personality and Social Psychology, 52,* 511–524.

Hesse, E. (1999). The adult attachment interview: Historical and current perspectives. In J. Cassidy & P. R. Shaver (Eds.), *Handbook of attachment: Theory, research, and clinical applications* (pp. 395–433). New York: Guilford Press.

Higgins, E. T. (1996). Knowledge activation: Accessibility, applicability, and salience. In E. T. Higgins & A. W. Kruglanski (Eds.), *Social psychology: Handbook of basic principles* (pp. 133–168). New York: Guilford Press.

Hinkley, K., & Andersen, S. M. (1996). The working self-concept in transference: Significant other activation and self change. *Journal of Personality and Social Psychology, 71,* 1279–1295.

Jacobson, N. S., & Addis, M. E. (1993). Research on couples and couples therapy: What do we know? Where are we going? *Journal of Consulting and Clinical Psychology, 61,* 85–93.

Jacobson, N. S., & Christensen, A. (1996). *Integrative couple therapy: Promoting acceptance and change.* New York: Norton.

Jacobson, N. S., Christensen, A., Prince, S. E., Cordova, J. V., & Eldridge, K. (2000). Integrative Behavioral Couple Therapy: An acceptance-based, promising new treatment for couple discord. *Journal of Consulting and Clinical Psychology, 68,* 351–355.

Jacobson, N. S., & Holtzworth-Munroe, A. (1986). Marital therapy: A social-learning/cognitive perspective. In N. S. Jacobson & A. S. Gurman (Eds.), *Clinical handbook of marital therapy* (pp. 29–70). New York: Guilford Press.

Jacobson, N. S., & Margolin, G. (1979). *Marital therapy: Strategies based on social learning and behavior exchange principles.* New York: Brunner/Mazel.

Janoff-Bulman, R. (1992). *Shattered assumptions: Towards a new psychology of trauma.* New York: The Free Press.

Kanouse, D. E., & Hanson, L. R. (1972). Negativity in evaluations. In E. E. Jones, D. E. Kanouse, H. H. Kelley, R. E. Nisbett, S. Valins, & B. Weiner (Eds.), *Attribution: Perceiving the causes of behavior* (pp. 47–62). Morristown, NJ: General Learning Press.

Karney, B. R., & Bradbury, T. N. (2000). Attributions in marriage: State or trait? A growth curve analysis. *Journal of Personality and Social Psychology, 78,* 295–309.

Kirkpatrick, L., & Hazan, C. (1994). Attachment styles and close relationships: A four-year prospective study. *Personal Relationships, 1,* 123–142.

Klohnen, E. C., & Bera, S. (1998). Behavioral and experiential patterns of avoidantly and securely attached women across adulthood: A 31-year longitudinal perspective. *Journal of Personality and Social Psychology, 74,* 211–223.

Klohnen, E. C., & John, O. P. (1998). Working models of attachment: A theory-based prototype approach. In J. A. Simpson & W. S. Rholes (Eds.), *Attachment theory and close relationships* (pp. 115–140). New York: Guilford Press.

Kunda, Z. (1999). *Social cognition: Making sense of people.* Cambridge, MA: The MIT Press.

Kunda, Z., Fong, G. T., Sanitioso, R., & Reber, E. (1993). Directional questions direct self-perceptions. *Journal of Experimental Social Psychology, 29,* 63–86.

Linville, P. W., & Carlston, D. E. (1994). Social cognition of the self. In P. G. Devine, D. L. Hamilton, & T. M. Ostrom (Eds.), *Social cognition: Impact on social psychology.* San Diego, CA: Academic Press.

Main, M. (1991). Metacognitive knowledge, metacognitive monitoring, and singular (coherent) vs. multiple (incoherent) model of attachment: Findings and directions for future research. In C. M. Parkes, J. Stevenson-Hinde, & P. Marris (Eds.), *Attachment across the life cycle* (pp. 127–159). London: Tavistock/Routledge.

Main, M., & Weston, D. (1981). The quality of toddler's relationship to mother and to father: Related to conflict behavior and the readiness for establishing new relationships. *Child Development, 52,* 932–940.

Main, M., Kaplan, K., & Cassidy, J. (1985). Security in infancy, childhood, and adulthood: A move to the level of representation. *Monographs of the Society for Research in Child Development, 50* (1–2, Serial No. 209), 66–104.

Markman, H. J., & Hahlweg, K. (1993). Prediction and prevention of marital distress: A cross-cultural perspective. *Clinical Psychology Review, 13,* 29–43.

Markus, H. (1977). Self-schemata and processing information about the self. *Journal of Personality and Social Psychology, 35,* 63–78.

Markus, H., & Cross, S. (1990). The interpersonal self. In L. A. Pervin (Ed.), *Handbook of personality: Theory and research* (pp. 576–608). New York: Guilford Press.

Markus, H., & Wurf, E. (1987). The dynamic self-concept: A social psychological perspective. *Annual Review of Psychology, 38,* 299–337.

McGuire, W. J., & McGuire, C. V. (1988). Content and process in the experience of self. In L. Berkowitz (Ed.), *Advances in experimental social psychology* (Vol. 21, pp. 97–144). San Diego, CA: Academic Press.

Miell, D. (1987). Remembering relationship development: Constructing a context for interactions. In R. Burnett, P. McGhee, & D. D. Clarke (Eds.), *Accounting for relationships: Explanation, representation, and knowledge* (pp. 60–73). New York: Methuen.

Miller, L. C., & Read, S. J. (1991). On the coherence of mental models of persons and relationships: A knowledge structure approach. In G. J. O. Fletcher &

F. D. Fincham (Eds.), *Cognition in close relationships* (pp. 69–99). Hillsdale, NJ: Erlbaum.

Murray, S. L., & Holmes, J. G. (1993). Seeing virtues in faults: Negativity and the transformation of interpersonal narratives in close relationships. *Journal of Personality and Social Psychology, 65,* 707–722.

——— (1994). Storytelling in close relationships: The construction of confidence. *Personality and Social Psychology Bulletin, 20,* 650–663.

——— (1997). A leap of faith? Positive illusions in romantic relationships. *Personality and Social Psychology Bulletin, 23,* 586–604.

Murray, S. L., Holmes, J. G., & Griffin, D. (1996a). The benefits of positive illusions: Idealization and the construction of satisfaction in close relationships. *Journal of Personality and Social Psychology, 70,* 79–98.

——— (1996b). The self-fulfilling nature of positive illusions in romantic relationships: Love is not blind, but prescient. *Journal of Personality and Social Psychology, 71,* 1155–1180.

Napier, A. Y. (1978). The rejection-intrusion pattern: A central dynamic. *Journal of Marriage and Family Counseling, 14,* 5–12.

Niedenthal, P. M., Halberstadt, J. B., & Innes-Ker, A. H. (1999). Emotional response categorization. *Psychological Review, 106,* 337–361.

Ogilvie, D. M., & Ashmore, R. D. (1991). Self-with-other representations as a unit of analysis in self-concept research. In R. C. Curtis (Ed.), *The relational self: Theoretical convergences in psychoanalysis and social psychology* (pp. 282–314). New York: Guilford Press.

Pearson, J. L., Cohn, D. A., Cowan, P. A., & Cowan, C. P. (1994). Earned- and continuous-security in adult attachment: Relation to depressive symptomatology and parenting style. *Development and Psychopathology, 6,* 359–373.

Pennebaker, J. W. (1989). Confession, inhibition, and disease. In L. Berkowitz (Ed.), *Advances in experimental social psychology* (Vol. 22, pp. 211–244). San Diego: Academic Press.

Petty, R. E., & Wegener, D. T. (1998). Attitude change: Multiple roles for persuasion variables. In D. T. Gilbert, S. T. Fiske, & G. Lindzey (Eds.), *The handbook of social psychology* (pp. 323–390). Boston: McGraw-Hill.

Phelps, J. L., Belsky, J., & Crnic, K. (1998). Earned security, daily stress, and parenting: A comparison of five alternative models. *Development and Psychopathology, 10,* 21–38.

Pietromonaco, P. R., & Feldman Barrett, L. (2000). The internal working models concept: What do we really know about the self in relation to others? *Review of General Psychology, 4,* 155–175.

Planalp, S. (1987). Interplay between relational knowledge and events. In R. Burnett, P. McGhee, & D. D. Clarke (Eds.), *Accounting for relationships: Explanation, representation, and knowledge* (pp. 175–191). New York: Methuen.

Planalp, S., & Rivers, M. (1996). Changes in knowledge of personal relationships. In G. J. O. Fletcher & J. Fitness (Eds.), *Knowledge structures in close relationships: A social psychological approach* (pp. 299–324). Mahwah, NJ: Erlbaum.

Pratto, F., & John, O. P. (1991). Automatic vigilance: The attention-grabbing power of negative social information. *Journal of Personality and Social Psychology, 61,* 380–391.

Reis, H. T., & Knee, C. R. (1996). What we know, what we don't know, and what we need to know about relationship knowledge structures. In G. J. O. Fletcher & J. Fitness (Eds.), *Knowledge structures in close relationships: A social psychological approach* (pp. 169–191). Mahwah, NJ: Erlbaum.

Reis, H. T., & Shaver, P. (1988). Intimacy as an interpersonal process. In S. W. Duck (Ed.), *Handbook of personal relationships* (pp. 367–389). Chichester, England: Wiley.

Ross, M. (1989). Relation of implicit theories to the construction of personal histories. *Psychological Review, 96,* 341–357.

Ross, L., Lepper, M. R., & Hubbard, M. (1975). Perseverance in self-perception and social perception: Biased attribution processes in the debriefing paradigm. *Journal of Personality and Social Psychology, 32,* 880–892.

Rothbard, J. C., & Shaver, P. R. (1994). Continuity of attachment across the life span. In M. B. Sperling & W. H. Berman (Eds.), *Attachment in adults: Clinical and developmental perspectives* (pp. 31–71). New York: Guilford Press.

Rothbart, M. (1981). Memory processes and social beliefs. In D. Hamilton (Ed.), *Cognitive processes in stereotyping and intergroup behavior* (pp. 145–182). Hillsdale, NJ: Erlbaum.

Safran, J. D. (1990). Towards a refinement of cognitive therapy in light of interpersonal theory: I. Theory. *Clinical Psychology Review, 10,* 87–105.

Scharfe, E., & Bartholomew, K. (1994). Reliability and stability of adult attachment patterns. *Personal Relationships, 1,* 23–43.

Schwarz, N., & Clore, G. L. (1996). Feelings and phenomenal experiences. In E. T. Higgins & A. Kruglanski (Eds.), *Social psychology: A handbook of basic principles* (pp. 433–465). New York: Guilford Press.

Scott, C. K., Fuhrman, R. W., & Wyer, R. S., Jr. (1991). Information processing in close relationships. In G. J. O. Fletcher & F. D. Fincham (Eds.), *Cognition in close relationships* (pp. 37–67). Hillsdale, NJ: Erlbaum.

Shaver, P. R., Hazan, C., & Bradshaw, D. (1988). Love as attachment: The integration of three behavioral systems. In R. J. Sternberg & M. Barnes (Eds.), *The psychology of love* (pp. 68–99). New Haven, CT: Yale University Press.

Singer, J. L., & Salovey, P. (1991). Organized knowledge structures and personality: Person schemas, self schemas, prototypes, and scripts. In M. J. Horowitz (Ed.), *Person schemas and maladaptive interpersonal patterns.* Chicago: University of Chicago Press.

Smith, E. R. (1996). What do connectionism and social psychology offer each other? *Journal of Personality and Social Psychology, 70,* 893–912.

(1998). Mental representation and memory. In D. T. Gilbert, S. T. Fiske, & G. Lindzey (Eds.), *The handbook of social psychology* (pp. 391–445). Boston: McGraw-Hill.

Stangor, C., & McMillan, D. (1992). Memory for expectancy-congruent and expectancy-incongruent information: A review of the social and social developmental literatures. *Psychological Bulletin, 111,* 42–61.

Stern, D. N. (1985). *The interpersonal world of the infant: A view from psychoanalysis and developmental psychology.* New York: Basic Books.
Sternberg, R. J. (1996). Love stories. *Personal Relationships, 3,* 59–79.
Stuart, R. B. (1980). *Helping couples change: A social learning approach to marital therapy.* New York: Aronson.
Swann, W. B., Jr. (1983). Self-verification: Bringing social reality into harmony with the self. In J. Suls & A. G. Greenwald (Eds.), *Psychological perspectives on the self* (Vol. 2, pp. 33–66). Hillsdale, NJ: Erlbaum.
——— (1987). Identity negotiation: Where two roads meet. *Journal of Personality and Social Psychology, 53,* 1038–1051.
Taylor, S. E., & Brown, J. D. (1988). Illusion and well-being: A social psychological perspective on mental health. *Psychological Bulletin, 103,* 193–210.
Thagard, P. (1989). Explanatory coherence (and Commentaries). *Behavioral and Brain Sciences, 12,* 435–467.
——— (1992). *Conceptual revolutions.* Princeton, NJ: Princeton University Press.
Tice, D. M. (1992). Self-concept change and self-presentation: The looking glass self is also a magnifying glass. *Journal of Personality and Social Psychology, 63,* 435–451.
Tomkins, S. S. (1979). Script theory: Differential magnification of effects. In H. E. Howe & R. A. Dienstbier (Eds.), *Nebraska Symposium on Motivation, 1978, vol. 26.* Lincoln: University of Nebraska Press.
Waters, E. (1978). The reliability and stability of individual differences in infant–mother attachment. *Child Development, 49,* 483–494.
Waters, E., Hamilton, C. E., & Weinfield, N. S. (2000). The stability of attachment security from infancy to adolescence and early adulthood: General introduction. *Child Development, 71,* 678–683.
Waters, E., Merrick, S., Treboux, D., Crowell, J., & Albersheim, L. (2000). Attachment security in infancy and early adulthood: A 20-year longitudinal study. *Child Development, 71,* 684–689.
Waters, E., Wippman, J., & Sroufe, L. A. (1979). Attachment, positive affect, and competence in the peer group: Two studies in construct validation. *Child Development, 50,* 821–829.
Wilson, T. D., & Hodges, S. D. (1992). Attitudes as temporary constructions. In L. L. Martin & A. Tesser (Eds.), *The construction of social judgments* (pp. 37–65). Hillsdale, NJ: Erlbaum.
Wilson, T. D., Lindsey, S., & Schooler, T. Y. (2000). A model of dual attitudes. *Psychological Review, 107,* 101–126.

CHAPTER TWO

Personality Effects on Personal Relationships over the Life Span

Jens B. Asendorpf

Our personal relationships are shaped in part by our personality. Consider Jack, a single, outgoing, somewhat dominant, sometimes choleric man in his midtwenties, and Jill, a single, shy, sensitive, somewhat insecure, woman of the same age who would never drop an angry word about someone else. Each moves from the East Coast to the West Coast into a new position in the same company. How many new friends will each have after 1 month, and 5 years later? How will each one deal with parents and old friends who remain on the East Coast, after 1 month, and 5 years later? Will each find a love partner, and what will this relationship look like in 5 years? Readers will have no problems in generating expectations about the different social lives of Jack and Jill. For example, most would expect that Jack will report more new friends than Jill after 1 month, that Jack's friendships are less enduring than Jill's, and that Jack may be already divorced after 5 years whereas Jill may be still searching for a partner.

Thus, it is obvious that adults' personal relationships depend in part on their personalities. Although each individual relationship also depends on other factors – the personality of the relationship partner, external influences on the relationship, the intrinsic dynamics of the interaction history of the two, and not to forget simple chance – enduring personality characteristics such as temperament, IQ, and one's basic attitudes and values push each relationship in a particular direction at least slightly. These slight effects summate over time and different relationships, resulting in an overall relationship pattern

Address correspondence to Jens B. Asendorpf, Institut für Psychologie, Humboldt-Universität zu Berlin, Oranienburger Str. 18, 10178 Berlin, Germany. E-mail address: asen@rz.hu-berlin.de.

that is as characteristic of an adult as his or her knowledge or interests.

Less obvious is how this all begins in early life. To what extent does children's early personality shape their relationships with their parents, siblings, and playmates? Is the attachment of 12-month-olds to their mother influenced by their temperament? Is there evidence for opposite causal effects, that is, is children's personality, including their temperament, shaped by their prior close relationships? Do these causal effects from relationships to personality occur only in childhood, or are they still operating throughout adulthood? This chapter deals with these questions. The focus is on personality effects on relationships rather than vice versa, because relationship effects on personality are a traditional theme in research on personality (e.g., Kupersmidt, Coie, & Dodge, 1990; Sroufe, 1983).

The influence of enduring personality on relationships is one major stabilizing factor for personal relationships, from both a short-term and a long-term perspective. From a short-term perspective, the stability of each relationship partner's personality lends stability to their dynamic interaction. Imagine that you fell in love with someone who behaves completely unpredictably in similar situations – sometimes shy, sometimes aggressive, sometimes friendly. It would be impossible for you to establish the two key elements of a relationship with this person: a relationship schema (a stable mental representation of yourself and your partner in the relationship and of the relationship itself) and a stable interaction pattern in recurring situations.

From a long-term perspective, relationship stability is expected to increase with increasing stability of personality. For example, Roberts and DelVecchio (2000) found in a metaanalysis of the stability of personality traits that the six-year stability for such traits continuously increases (on average for many traits) from .35 in infancy to .75 at ages 50–60. Because some traits such as neuroticism, shyness, and aggressiveness influence relationships (see below), this long-term increase in the stability of personality is one of the reasons why relationships become more stable with increasing age.

FOUR OBSTACLES TO EMPIRICAL STUDIES OF PERSONALITY EFFECTS ON RELATIONSHIPS

Although causal questions about personality effects on relationships and vice versa are fundamental for understanding the codevelopment of personality and relationships, psychologically informed answers to these questions meet four main difficulties. First, early socialization research was dominated by either psychoanalytic or behavioristic approaches. Though different in many respects, both psychoanalysis and behaviorism assumed that personality is shaped by early social experiences, particularly with the parents. Therefore, early psychological socialization research focused on correlations between parenting styles and children's personality, and interpreted such correlations as causal effects that run from parent to child. This one-sided view of parent–child relationhips was first questioned by Bell (1968), but it took more than a decade until effects of children on parents were widely recognized (Bell & Harper, 1977; Lytton, 1990). This recognition opened the door for a dynamic-interactional, or transactional, view of socialization wherein children and parents, but also peers, continuously influence each other over time (Magnusson, 1990; Patterson, 1982; Sameroff, 1983).

Although this dynamic-interactional view has been widely accepted both in socialization and in relationship research, it developed only recently, and there is still a clear gap between theory and research practice. From a dynamic-interactional perspective, research on personality and relationship development should focus on the influence of personality on relationships *and* vice versa in order to compare the relative strength of these two influences. But decent studies of such reciprocal influences are demanding both in terms of time and effort and in terms of methodology. This is the second obstacle to serious answers about personality effects on relationships.

Cross-sectional studies that simply correlate personality and relationship characteristics at one point in time can only detect whether these two characteristics are linked, but they do not inform us about how such links came about. For example, a concurrent correlation between a child's aggressiveness and a conflictful relationship with the mother at age 10 may be due to (a) earlier effects of the child's aggressiveness on the relationship; (b) earlier effects of the conflictful relationship on the child's personality; (c) both (a) and (b); or (d) a "hidden variable" that influences both the child and the relationship, such as genes shared by mother and child, that dispose both for aggressiveness and therefore result in both child aggressiveness and a conflictful mother–child relationship.

These ambiguities of interpretation can be reduced only by much more costly longitudinal studies that assess personality and

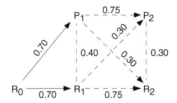

Figure 2.1. A spurious effect of personality on relationships caused by the continuation of an early relationship effect on personality: A fictitious example (see text).

relationships at different times in the same individuals. Because causality cannot act backwards, correlations between different time points seem to be more easily interpretable. For example, a predictive correlation between aggressiveness of the child at age 3 and a conflictful relationship with the mother at age 10 cannot be due to a causal effect of the later relationship on the earlier aggressiveness.

Although such causal interpretations are safer indeed, they are not safe enough because even predictive correlations can be due to spurious causality. Consider the example in Fig. 2.1. A personality trait at Time 1 (P_1, e.g., aggressiveness) shows a predictive correlation of .30 with a relationship quality at Time 2 (R_2, e.g., a conflictful relationship with the mother). However, when we consider the so-called *cross-lagged panel design*, that is, the whole pattern of possible correlations between P_1, P_2, R_1, and R_2, we will notice that the predictive correlation appears to be simply due to the fact that aggressiveness was associated with a conflictful mother–child relationship already existing at Time 1, and that this relationship quality was highly stable between Time 1 and Time 2. Path analysis (e.g., Kessler & Greenberg, 1981) and structural equation modeling (e.g., LISREL, EQS) are appropriate methods of distinguishing the *direct effect* $P_1 \rightarrow R_2$ from the *indirect effect* $P_1 \rightarrow R_1 \rightarrow R_2$. For each path in the full model, path coefficients are computed that measure the size (or strength) of the path independently from the size of all other paths in the model. Path analysis tells us in the example of Fig. 2.1 that the direct path from P_1 to R_2 is zero. Thus, the data show no influence of early personality on later relationships but simply a concurrent correlation between personality and a relationship quality at Time 1 that continues over time because both personality and the relationship quality are stable.

Personality Effects

The concurrent correlation between personality and relationship quality at Time 1, in turn, was in this example caused by an earlier relationship quality R_0 (e.g., insecure attachment to the mother at 12 months). Thus, the full story of the personality–relationship transaction is in this case that relationship quality affected personality whereas personality had no effects on the observed relationship qualities. Because of these nasty pitfalls in the interpretation of predictive correlations, it is important for the study of dynamic personality–relationship interactions that one rely not on correlations but on path coefficients that control for indirect effects.

However, it must be noted that even this method of detecting personality effects on relationhips cannot be perfectly trusted because the method controls only indirect effects of variables in the statistical model. It is always possible that "hidden variables" that are not included in the model cause a significant path in the model. But these are the limits of any correlational method. Ultimately, experimental variation of personality through an intervention is needed to show causal effects on relationships. For example, drug treatment of hyperactive children changes not only the child but also the child's relationship with the parents (e.g., Barkley, Karlsson, Pollard, & Murphy, 1985). But most such interventions and the necessary follow-up and control group studies are even more costly than cross-lagged panel designs.

The third obstacle for the study of personality effects on relationships is that in many studies both personality and relationship characteristics of the same individual are assessed through ratings from the same judge. Thus, parents are asked to rate both their infant's temperament and the infant's attachment to them, or spouses are asked to rate their own personality and their marital satisfaction. In these cases, both concurrent and predictive correlations may be inflated by shared method variance. Interindividual differences in judgment bias such as different tendencies for socially desirable descriptions or different usages of response scales induce spurious correlations between personality and relationships.

Again, a cross-lagged panel design is helpful here. Consider once more Fig. 2.1. If P and R are rated by the same judge, all *correlations* in Fig. 2.1 are biased by shared method variance. However, the *path coefficients* for $P_1 \to R_2$ and for $R_1 \to P_2$ control for the indirect paths $P_1 \to R_1 \to R_2$, and $R_1 \to P_1 \to P_2$, respectively. Because the indirect paths contain the full bias, the direct paths control for this bias at least in part.

The better solution is to assess personality and relationships through different methods. For example, infants' temperament may be judged by the mother, and their attachment to the mother may be observed in the Strange Situation Test.

The last obstacle to the empirical study of personality effects on relationships is that the effect sizes that can be expected cannot be high. This is due to the fact that a relationship is influenced by two different personalities plus interaction history (as far as it is not related to the personalities). Ahadi and Diener (1989) conducted Monte Carlo simulation studies on the maximum possible correlation between a predictor and an outcome when the outcome depends completely, and additively, on three independent predictors of similar strength. They found that the upper-bound predictor–outcome correlation was about .50 in this case. Thus, if we assume that the personalities of the two relationship partners are not correlated and that the interaction history is as important for the relationship as each partner's personality, the personality–relationship correlations cannot exceed .50. This is a serious constraint on the size of personality effects on relationships that has been rarely recognized in the personality and relationship literature.

EVIDENCE FOR PERSONALITY EFFECTS ON RELATIONSHIPS

Very few studies of personality effects on relationships have used cross-lagged panel or intervention designs. Therefore a review of the evidence for such effects that is based only on such strong designs would be extremely selective. Instead, I focus in this section on four examples of personality effects on relationships that refer to different ages over the life span and that offer fairly strong conclusions about personality effects on relationships, because these effects are relatively well researched with multiple methodologies.

Effects of Parents and Infants on Infant–Parent Attachment

According to traditional attachment theory, infants' attachment style to their parents is a function of the parent's sensitive responsiveness to the infant's needs, particularly in threatening situations (Ainsworth, Blehar, Waters, & Wall, 1978). Ainsworth et al. (1978) reported surprisingly high correlations above .70 between observed maternal sensitivity at 3 months and observed security of attachment of the infants in the Strange Situation Test at 12 months. In a recent metaanalysis of

21 nonclinical studies including more than 1,000 parent–infant pairs observed in the Strange Situation Test, DeWolff and van IJzendoorn (1997) estimated the true correlation between parental sensitivity and infants' attachment security (corrected for the unreliability of both measures) as being a modest .24. Thus, there is one well-established, modest link between parents' personality and infants' attachment that makes sense from the view of attachment theory.

Another link that has also been well supported is a correlation between parents' attachment security as assessed through the Adult Attachment Interview, and their infants' observed attachment security in the Strange Situation Test. In a metaanalysis of 18 studies including more than 1,000 parent–infant pairs, van IJzendoorn (1995) reported an agreement of 75% between the two classifications, which corresponds to a correlation of .47. Because parents' attachment security refers to an interview about the full history of the relationships with both parents, it is often considered as characterizing the personality of the parent rather than a concrete attachment relationship. Because this strong link between parents' personality and their infants' attachment security is not fully mediated by parental sensitivity (sensitivity correlated only .34 with parents' attachment security and only .24 with infants' attachment security), there are additional, yet unknown behavioral traits of parents that foster their infants' attachment security, or hidden third variables that drive both parents' and infants' attachment security.

Interestingly, the relatively strong correspondence between parents' and infants' attachment security is not weakened when only studies are considered that assessed parents' attachment security *before* their infants were born. Thus, in these cases (five studies including 392 parent–infant pairs) parents' security cannot be due to their infants' security, and we can be more sure that causality runs from parents' personality to the relationship with their infants.

Another argument supports this causal path even more strongly. In an intervention study with highly irritable (emotionally labile) infants, van den Boom (1994) tried to increase their mother's sensitive responsiveness through an extensive training when the infants were 6 and 9 months old. This training proved successful. The trained mothers had more secure children at 12, 18, 24, and 40 months than a control group of untrained mothers (van den Boom, 1995). For example, at 18 months there were only 26% secure children in the control group but 72% secure children in the intervention group.

This intervention study is interesting also from another perspective because the rate of secure children in the control group was unusually low. In nonrisk samples, the rate of secure children is approximately 65%. Thus, the 26% rate in the irritable group suggests that infants' early emotional lability – a temperamental trait – is related to their later attachment security. The literature is far from being consistent in this respect, however; most studies have failed to find significant correlations in unselected samples between infant temperament and attachment security as observed in the Strange Situation Test (see Thompson, 1998, for a review). The lack of an overall relation in the general population does not exclude the possibility, however, that extreme irritability *is* a risk factor for insecure attachment – as suggested by the van den Boom (1994, 1995) study.

Whereas it remains controversial whether infants' temperament influences their attachment security, modest relations have been reported between infants' temperament and the type of insecure attachment (anxious-ambivalent, C, versus avoidant, A). In an early metaanalysis, Goldsmith and Alansky (1987) reported a correlation of .16 between judgments of distress proneness and anxious-ambivalent attachment. Later studies have often, but not always, supported this relation. After correction for the unreliability of the measures, the estimated true correlation between distress proneness and type C attachment is similarly high as the true correlation of .24 between parental sensitivity and attachment security.

That the A versus C distinction may be more strongly related to infants' personality than the secure–insecure distinction is also suggested by Fox, Kimmerly, and Schafer (1991). Their metaanalysis of infant–mother versus infant–father attachment revealed that the consistency of infants' attachment style between the two parents was low for the insecure–secure distinction but high for the A versus C distinction. Thus, it seems that attachment security depends more on parental characteristics, whereas the infant's temperament influences more whether the infant becomes avoidant or anxious-ambivalent in the case of insecure attachment.

Together, these studies provide evidence that the personality of both the parent and the infant influence the attachment of the infant to the parent. The effects of the parents are better documented than the effects of the infants, and the effects of the parents are strong. Because the infants' personality measures mostly rely on parental judgments (a relatively weak assessment method), they may underestimate the true temperamental effects on attachment. Behavioral observations and physiological measures of temperament may yield stronger relations in the future although present findings are far from being consistent (see Rothbart & Bates, 1998).

Whereas the direction of causality for the personality → attachment effect is convincingly supported for parental personality by both the attachment interview studies and van den Boom's intervention study, the direction of causality is much less clear for the relation between infant temperament and attachment because of the lack of cross-lagged panel designs and the difficulty in modifying infants' temperament through intervention.

Effects of Children's Aggressiveness on Their Relationships

One of the most consistent findings in the peer relationship literature is that aggressive children are likely to be rejected by their peers. Not all aggressive children are rejected, to be sure, but aggressiveness in childhood is a strong and pervasive risk factor for peer rejection. This is true for preschool children, and it is true not only for peer ratings of aggressiveness (which pose problems of shared method variance) but also for teacher and parent ratings and for behavioral observations of aggressiveness (see Coie, Dodge, & Kupersmidt, 1990, for a review).

That this robust relation between aggressiveness and peer rejection is at least in part driven by personality effects on the peer relationships rather than vice versa is indicated by an intensive short-term longitudinal study on the emergence of peer rejection in newly formed peer groups. Dodge (1983) made up groups of unfamiliar second-grade boys that were not preselected for social status. They were observed in play groups of eight boys that met for eight almost daily sessions. After the last session, each of the eight boys in the group was asked in a sociometric interview to nominate group members that he liked and that he disliked. Those boys that were disliked by most of their peers, that is, the rejected boys, were observed before to hit other boys more often and to make more hostile comments than average-status boys.

Aggressive children evoke negative responses not only from peers but also from adults within a very short time. Anderson, Lytton, and Romney (1986) observed aggressive boys in interactions with mothers of nonaggressive and aggressive boys, and nonaggressive boys in interactions with mothers of nonaggressive and aggressive boys. Thus, they studied unrelated pairs of mothers and children. The aggressive boys evoked more negative reactions from both types of mothers than did nonaggressive boys, and the two types of mothers did not differ from each other in their negative reactions. Thus, the negativity of the interaction pattern was driven by the child, not by the mother. Although this short-term laboratory effect should not be overinterpreted, it is suggestive of similar effects of childhood aggressiveness on long-term parent–child relationships.

The detailed behavioral observations of Patterson and colleagues on the interaction of aggressive children with family members at home support this view. Compared to nonaggressive children in control families, aggressive children contribute to a vicious cycle of escalating aggression–counteraggression. Once being engaged in aggressive behavior, they are not stopped by the counteraggression of others but even enforced in their aggression. Therefore, the greatest difference between aggressive and nonaggressive children is not a higher rate of initial aggression but a longer sequence of aggression–counteraggression once the first aggressive act has occurred (the "coercive process," Patterson, 1982).

Analyses of the social cognition of aggressive children also support the idea that aggressiveness leads to negative relationships rather than vice versa. Aggressive children search social situations for fewer cues before they make attributional decisions, they are prone to interpret ambiguous behavior of others as hostile, are more likely to generate aggressive responses, and appear to believe that aggression will yield tangible rewards to solving interpersonal problems. Dodge (1986) and Crick and Dodge (1994) have integrated much of the existing evidence on the different social information processing of aggressive children in comprehensive and integrative models.

In later childhood and adolescence, a particular, well-studied effect of aggressiveness on peer relationships emerges that refers to the choice of friends. Although aggressive children face the risk of being rejected by their peers throughout childhood, this overall risk is somewhat decreasing in late childhood and adolescence, and, more importantly, the peer relationships of many aggressive children become strongly differentiated into rejecting and accepting peers. Beginning in early adolescence, aggressive-rejected children tend to join deviant cliques of similarly aggressive peers that value antisocial behavior (Dishion, Patterson, Stoolmiller, & Skinner, 1991). Unfortunately, acceptance by these peers reinforces their antisocial and aggressive tendencies instead of calming them down. Joining a deviant clique is a strong risk factor for engaging in criminal behavior (Patterson & Bank, 1989).

Recently, this personality effect on the social environment has been studied not only at the level of groups but also at the level of dyadic friendships. Hartup (1996) reviewed various studies on aggressive children's friendships and concluded that aggressive children tend to select other aggressive children as friends even for dyadic friendship.

Longitudinal studies have found long-term predictive correlations between aggressiveness in childhood and relationships even in adulthood. Caspi, Bem, and Elder (1989) discovered in a reanalysis of the longitudinal Berkeley Guidance Study that 50% of the men with a history of temper tantrums at ages 8 to 10 had divorced by age 40, compared with only 26% of the other men. Thus, childhood aggressiveness doubled the rate of divorce in midadulthood. Also, a strong path of .45 was found between childhood aggressiveness and occupational instability, controlling for the effects of both education and occupational status. This path appears to reflect problems with coworkers. Men with a history of ill-temperedness in childhood continued to be ill-tempered in adulthood, where it gets them into trouble with coworkers and supervisors.

In a different longitudinal study, Newman, Caspi, Moffitt, and Silva (1997) assessed the social relationships of the large sample of the New Zealand Dunedin Longitudinal Study at age 21 by both self- and informant reports. One comparison involved children who were observed to be either well adjusted or undercontrolled and aggressive at age 3. The undercontrolled-aggressive children 18 years later reported more interpersonal conflict at home and in their romantic relationships, had been fired more often from jobs, were more often victims of personal crimes, and scored higher on antisocial behavior; informants described them as less reliable and less cultured.

Together, numerous studies with very different methodologies have documented that aggressiveness in childhood has severe and long-lasting consequences on virtually all kinds of relationships: with parents, peers, spouses, and at work.

Effects of Shyness on Personal Relationships

Newman et al. (1997) also analyzed the Dunedin longitudinal sample for effects of observed inhibited-shy behavior at age 3 on social relationships at age 21. Compared to well-adjusted children, inhibited-shy children 18 years later reported lower levels of social support and were described by others as being less affiliative. However, unlike the undercontrolled-aggressive children, they were described as reliable in their relationships, and their close love and work relationships seemed to be unimpaired.

Also, Caspi, Elder, and Bem (1988) reanalyzed the Berkeley Guidance Study for long-term consequences of childhood shyness. They compared with the rest of the sample children that were identified at ages 8 to 10 in interviews with their mothers as being shy with strangers and emotionally inhibited. Interviews at ages 30 and 40 revealed that shy boys showed delayed relationship development. They had married 3 years later and had their first child 4 years later than nonshy boys. Shyness in girls was not related to these developmental milestones. Marital stability was unrelated to shyness in both men and women.

It seems that the shy women of this generation (they were born in 1928) better fit the traditional, passive female role than shy men fit the active male role in initiating relationships. A central feature of shyness in both childhood and adulthood is uneasiness in unfamiliar situations (Asendorpf, 1989; Asendorpf & van Aken, 1994). Shy men's uneasiness made it more difficult for them to get to know romantic partners and potential spouses and to initiate partnership and family relations. Shy women did not have these problems, given different societal expectations at this time, but it can be expected that the increasing social pressure on women to fulfill active, traditionally male roles may make the lives of shy women more difficult today.

Asendorpf and Wilpers (1998) detected a similar, short-term effect of shyness on young students' peer relationships when they entered the unfamiliar social world of the university. Various personality traits, including shyness, and all significant relationhips were assessed in a sample of 132 students aged 18–22 years simultanously seven times every three months, beginning in the first week at university. Thus, it was possible to analyze causal effects of personality on all important relationships in a strong cross-lagged panel design. Figure 2.2 illustrates the major finding with this design for the effect of shyness on the number of peer relationships (as defined by a relationship with a person aged 18–27 years).

At the beginning of students' experience at the university, there was a concurrent correlation of −.39 between shyness and the number of peer relationships. Thus, shy students initially reported fewer peers in their social network. As one might expect, shyness showed a high sta-

Personality Effects

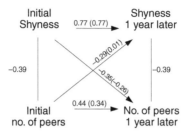

Figure 2.2. Shyness effect on the number of peer relationships and vice versa over the first year at university. Numbers indicate correlations; numbers in parentheses indicate path coefficients (data adapted from Asendorpf & Wilpers, 1998).

bility of .77 between the first and the second year at university. In contrast, the number of peer relationships was much less stable (only .44). Therefore, one might expect that the concurrent correlation between shyness and the number of peer relationships decreased over the first year at university because the peer relationships "developed away from shyness" due to a new factor that decreased their stability.

However, as Fig. 2.2 shows, the concurrent correlation between shyness and the number of peer relationships remained constant. This paradox is resolved by the significant path of −.26 between early shyness and later peer relationships. This path indicates that shyness at the beginning of students' university experience exerted an additional influence on the number of peer relationships above its initial correlation with this number. This additional influence kept the concurrent correlation between shyness and the number of peer relationships constant over time. It can be interpreted as a causal effect of early shyness on the development of peer relationships between the first and the second year of university.

Shyness not only had an effect on the number of relationships; it also had an effect on their quality. More specifically, shyness inhibited falling in love. To control for common method variance in the reports of shyness and love (an initial correlation of −.20 between shyness and love might have been be due simply to the fact that shy participants were more hesitant to identify a relationship as a love relationship), the analysis was restricted to those participants who did *not* report a love relationship at the first assessment. After 18 months, only 37% of the shy participants fell in love at least once, whereas 73% of the nonshy participants reported at least one love relationship.

Beyond shyness, this study found effects of agreeableness on the lack of interpersonal conflict and of conscientiousness on the frequency of interactions with family members. Also, all major findings were replicated in a diary study where a subsample of the participants reported all important social interactions over a period of 3 weeks in the middle of the first term and again 6 months later.

In addition to these findings of personality effects on relationships, our design also offered the rare opportunity to compare these effects directly with the opposite effects of relationships on personality. No evidence was found for such influences either in the relationship questionnaire or in the diary. For example, the path from the initial number of peers to shyness 1 year later was virtually zero (see Fig. 2.2). It may be argued that this asymmetry is not surprising, given the fact that personality was highly stable whereas social relationships changed a great deal during this life transition and therefore showed substantial instability of interindividual differences. Why should an unstable factor cause change in a much more stable factor?

More plausible indeed is a different effect of relationships on personality that is not captured by the relationship → personality paths. Consider again Fig. 2.2. If events occur that differentially change the number of peers *after* the initial assessment (e.g., a participant joins a student club and makes a lot of new friends, whereas another participant does not), and if this differential increase in the number of peers changes self-rated shyness, then there is an effect of relationship *change* on personality *change* that is not captured by the relationship → personality path. Instead, such an effect should induce a correlation between the change in the number of peers over the first year and the change in the shyness self-rating. Therefore, we also analyzed the correlations between relationship change and personality change. Again, these correlations were always close to zero. For example, the change in number of peers correlated −.01 with the change in shyness over the first year at university.

Together, this study resulted in a surprisingly clear picture of the causal influence of personality on relationships and vice versa in young adulthood. Various personality traits influenced the number and quality of various relationship types, but neither the number nor the quality of relationships nor relationship change exerted significant influence on personality. It seems that personality is already so crystalized in early adulthood that it is immune to new relationship experiences.

Two notes of caution are in order here. First, the findings referred only to self-rated personality traits. It may be that certain relationship experiences influenced students' behavioral tendencies in subtle ways that did not change their self-concept of personality. Second, the finding is constrained by the personality traits that were studied (the Big Five and subfactors of them); other personality characteristics such as attitudes and values may very well be influenced by relationship experiences (e.g., through confrontation with the attitudes and values of the fellow students).

Personality Effects on Marital Relationships

A considerable body of literature has evolved around the question of whether the quality of marital relationships (as assessed by marital satisfaction scales) and the stability of marital relationships (as assessed by the absence of divorce) are related to husbands' and wives' personality (see Karney & Bradbury, 1995, for a review). Although marital dissatisfaction predicts later divorce to some extent, marital quality and stability are not interchangeable because there are stable but unhappy marriages (Heaton & Albrecht, 1991). Also, marital satisfaction can vary between the spouses (the between-spouse correlation is about .65; that is, it is an individual variable), whereas marital stability is shared by both partners (it is a dyadic variable).

Findings of concurrent correlations between personality traits and marital satisfaction consistently show that neuroticism is the strongest personality correlate of unhappy marriage. This is true for both husbands and wives; correlations between self-rated neuroticism and self-rated marital dissatisfaction approximate .25 for both men and women (Karney & Bradbury, 1995). Because neuroticism correlates only weakly between husbands and wives, this well-supported finding indicates a strong correlation between the personality of both partners and their marital satisfaction. This correlation may be due to personality effects on marital dissatisfaction, to the fact that marital problems may lead the spouses to believe that they are neurotic, or to shared method variance. The personality → relationship interpretation is strengthened, however, by multiple additional findings.

First, the neuroticism–dissatisfaction correlation decreases only minimally when marital quality is assessed many years later than neuroticism (see Karney & Bradbury, 1995). For example, Kelly and Conley (1987) studied 237 couples and reported a correlation of .27 for husbands and .26 for wives when their neuroticism was assessed at the time of engagement, and marital dissatisfaction was assessed 20 years later. Although these authors did not analyze a full cross-lagged panel design, it seems highly plausible that neuroticism was more stable than marital dissatisfaction over this long period, so that a significant neuroticism → dissatisfaction path is expected.

Second, the Kelly and Conley (1987) study is one of the few where shared method variance can be excluded because neuroticism was rated not by the spouses themselves but by acquaintances. Third, neuroticism predicts not only marital dissatisfaction but also marital instability; neurotics more often get divorced than do emotionally stable persons (Kurdek, 1993; Karney & Bradbury, 1995). Because divorce is a real-life event that is not susceptible to judgmental biases, the neuroticism–divorce correlations cannot be due to shared method variance.

In the Kelly and Conley (1987) study, the neuroticism of both husbands and wives significantly predicted divorce not only within the next 20 years after engagement but also within the following 25 years. Thus, neuroticism in the twenties was a risk factor for divorce even in the sixties, that is, up to 45 years later. In light of this effect, the long-term neuroticism → dissatisfaction correlations reported by Kelly and Conley (1987) are even more remarkable because neurotics increasingly dropped out of the longitudinal sample, which restricts the variance in neuroticism in the remaining subjects and therefore the neuroticism → dissatisfaction correlation.

Personality traits other than neuroticism show weaker and less consistent effects on marital relationships. For example, in the Kelly and Conley (1987) study, lack of impulse control in men was a modest risk factor for late divorce and dissatisfaction after 45 years of marriage, but not for early divorce and dissatisfaction in the first 20 years of marriage, and lack of impulse control in women showed only a weak effect on dissatisfaction in late marriage. In a five-year longitudinal study, Kurdek (1993) found that wives', but not hubands', conscientiousness furthered marital stability. In contrast, the conscientiousness of gifted children and adolescents who were judged by their parents and teachers in 1927–1928 predicted marital stability over the following 60 years for both men and women (Tucker, Kressin, Spiro, & Ruscio, 1998).

Together these findings show consistent and enduring effects of personality on both marital satisfaction and stability. Because the interindividual variation in traits such as neuroticism and conscientiousness is partly due to genetic differences, these personality effects contribute to genetic effects on marital stability (see Lykken, Chapter Four of this volume). It should be noted, though, that personality mediates not only genetic effects on relationship quality and stability but also effects of the environment and of the gene–environment interaction.

MECHANISMS OF PERSONALITY EFFECTS ON RELATIONSHIPS

Buss (1987) proposed three key mechanisms through which personality becomes linked with the environment at large: selection, evocation, and manipulation. These concepts also can be used to classify personality effects on relationships. *Selection* in a narrow sense means that individuals select others for relationships with them on the basis of their own personality. The similarity of friends and spouses in many personality traits such as intelligence or openness to new experience is largely – but not exclusively – due to selection by both partners in the relationship. In a broader sense, selection also can refer to aggregates of relationships. Examples are the shyness effect on the number of peer relationships or the conscientiousness effect on family contact found by Asendorpf and Wilpers (1998). In these cases, personality traits exert similar effects on many relationships.

Evocation means that due to their personality, individuals unintentionally evoke responses from others that shape their relationships with them. For example, aggressive children often evoke peer rejection and a restrictive parenting style from their parents. Sometimes personality traits are even described in terms of evoked reactions, such as "charming," "trusted," or "provocative." In these cases, the distinction between personality and social response is blurred.

Manipulation means that individuals intentionally try to shape the course of a relationship on the basis of their personality. For example, a highly religious woman tries to convince a future spouse to share her beliefs in order to achieve a marriage that is accepted by the religious community, a Machiavellian employee in a large company tries to increase his chances for a better position by ingratiating himself with his boss, or a secure uncle tries to compensate for insecure parents of a nephew by offering a relationship in which the child can use him as a safe haven amid an unstable, stormy family.

CONCLUSIONS

The four reviewed examples of personality effects on relationships provide clear evidence that personality influences important relationships over the life span. The influences of personality are substantial, given the constraints on the effect of one individual on a dyadic relationship (correlations above .50 are unlikely to occur; see the section on methodological difficulties), and long-lasting (significant effects are detectable after 20 years and more; see the effects of childhood aggressiveness, shyness, and conscientiousness, and the effects of neuroticism on marital relationhips). The question of the direction of causality was discussed in each example, and multiple evidence was found for an interpretation of particular personality–relationship correlations in terms of personality → relationship effects rather than vice versa.

A notable exception was the infant temperament–attachment relation. Not only were the correlations themselves relatively weak and controversial, but also the direction of causality was less obvious. Because traditional attachment theory stresses the importance of early attachment experiences both for later relationships and for later personality (Bowlby, 1969), whereas advocates of a temperament perspective stress the importance of early temperamental traits for the development of attachment style (Fox et al., 1991), it is important to settle this point through appropriate longitudinal studies on the dynamic interaction between temperament and attachment.

Readers may wonder why I have not discussed an example of personality effects on relationships in old age. The reason is that there are no well-documented examples available (see Krause, Liang, & Keith, 1990; Lang, Staudinger, & Carstensen, 1998). In an attempt to study this question, Lang analyzed in a cross-lagged panel design the influence of neuroticism and extraversion on the social relationships of the at least 70-year-old participants in the Berlin Aging Study (Baltes & Mayer, 1999) over a time interval of 4 years. He found no significant paths from personality to social relationships (personal communication, August 1999). Unfortunately, important null findings such as this one are difficult to publish and therefore often go unnoticed.

The reason for this later independence of personality and relationships may simply be that most people have reached a close fit between their personality and their relationships at midadulthood (not always a healthy one as the examples of aggressives and neurotics show). Personality already has exerted its effects on the choice of social partners and the shaping of the quality of important relationships, and therefore few relationship changes due to personality differences occur in later adulthood, and vice versa. In addition, later life is characterized by having less time (and fewer options) left to develop new relationships. Therefore, personality may not exert many effects due to external reasons (such as reduced availability of others) and due to internal reasons (investing the remaining lifetime in those relationships that have already "proven to work well").

Because strongly designed studies on the codevelopment of personality and relationships are currently scarce, it is impossible to contrast personality effects on relationships and relationship effects on personality empirically and directly. As a consequence, strong conclusions cannot be made about the relative influence of personality on relationships and vice versa. My own intuition is that future studies may find an inverted U-shaped curve for the strength of personality effects on relationships with increasing age along with a gradual decrease of relationship effects on personality. Besides the research findings reviewed in the present chapter, I base this intuition on the common belief that the young become increasingly able to control their environment, including their personal relationships, to fit their needs and desires, and continue to work on that fit until it is reasonably good, whereas the old become more and more inflexible in their adjustment to new relationship partners. But empirical research is always good for surprises, and we must await future studies that test this hypothesis.

REFERENCES

Ahadi, S., & Diener, E. (1989). Multiple determinants and effect sizes. *Journal of Personality and Social Psychology, 56,* 398–406.

Ainsworth, M. D. S., Blehar, M. C., Waters, E., & Wall, S. (1978). *Patterns of attachment.* Hillsdale, NJ: Erlbaum.

Anderson, K. E., Lytton, H., & Romney, D. M. (1986). Mothers' interactions with normal and conduct-disordered boys: Who affects whom? *Developmental Psychology, 22,* 604–609.

Asendorpf, J. B. (1989). Shyness as a final common pathway for two different kinds of inhibition. *Journal of Personality and Social Psychology, 57,* 481–492.

Asendorpf, J. B., & van Aken, M. A. G. (1994). Traits and relationship status. *Child Development, 65,* 1786–1798.

Asendorpf, J. B., & Wilpers, S. (1998). Personality effects on social relationships. *Journal of Personality and Social Psychology, 74,* 1531–1544.

Baltes, P. B., & Mayer, K. U. (Eds.) (1999). *The Berlin Aging Study: Aging from 70 to 100.* Cambridge: Cambridge University Press.

Barkley, R. A., Karlsson, J., Pollard, S., & Murphy, J. V. (1985). Developmental changes in the mother–child interactions of hyperactive boys: Effects of two dose levels of Ritalin. *Journal of Child Psychology and Psychiatry, 26,* 705–715.

Bell, R. Q. (1968). A reinterpretation of the direction of effects in studies of socialization. *Psychological Review, 75*, 81–95.
Bell, R. Q., & Harper, L. V. (1977). *Child effects on adults*. Hillsdale, NJ: Erlbaum.
Bowlby, J. (1969). *Attachment and loss. Vol. 1. Attachment*. New York: Basic Books.
Buss, D. M. (1987). Selection, evocation, and manipulation. *Journal of Personality and Social Psychology, 53*, 1214–1221.
Caspi, A., Bem, D. J., & Elder, G. H., Jr. (1989). Continuities and consequences of interactional styles across the life course. *Journal of Personality, 57*, 375–406.
Caspi, A., Elder, G. H., Jr., & Bem, D. J. (1988). Moving away from the world: Life-course patterns of shy children. *Developmental Psychology, 24*, 824–831.
Coie, J. D., Dodge, K. H., & Kupersmidt, J. B. (1990). Peer group behavior and social status. In S. R. Asher & J. D. Coie (Eds.), *Peer rejection in childhood* (pp. 17–59). Cambridge: Cambridge University Press.
Crick, N. R., & Dodge, K. A. (1994). A review and reformulation of social-information processing mechanisms in children's social adjustment. *Psychological Bulletin, 115*, 74–101.
De Wolff, M. S., & van IJzendoorn, M. H. (1997). Sensitivity and attachment: A meta-analysis on parental antecedents of infant attachment. *Child Development, 68*, 571–591.
Dishion, T. J., Patterson, G. R., Stoolmiller, M., & Skinner, M. L. (1991). Family, school, and behavioral antecedents to early adolescent involvement with antisocial peers. *Developmental Psychology, 27*, 172–180.
Dodge, K. A. (1983). Behavioral antecedents of peer social status. *Child Development, 54*, 1386–1399.
  (1986). A social information processing model of social competence in children. In M. Perlmutter (Ed.), *Minnesota Symposia on Child Psychology* (Vol. 18, pp. 77–125). Hillsdale, NJ: Erlbaum.
Fox, N. A., Kimmerly, N. L., & Schafer, W. D. (1991). Attachment to mother/attachment to father: A meta-analysis. *Child Development, 62*, 210–225.
Goldsmith, H. H., & Alansky, J. A. (1987). Maternal and infant temperamental predictors of attachment: A meta-analytic review. *Journal of Consulting and Clinical Psychology, 55*, 805–816.
Hartup, W. W. (1996). The company they keep: Friendships and their developmental significance. *Child Development, 67*, 1–13.
Heaton, T. B., & Albrecht, S. L. (1991). Stable unhappy marriages. *Journal of Marriage and the Family, 53*, 747–758.
Karney, B. R., & Bradbury, T. N. (1995). The longitudinal course of marital quality and stability: A review of theory, method, and research. *Psychological Bulletin, 118*, 3–34.
Kelly, E. L., & Conley, J. J. (1987). Personality and compatibility: A prospective analysis of marital stability and marital satisfaction. *Journal of Personality and Social Psychology, 52*, 27–40.
Kessler, R. C., & Greenberg, D. F. (1981). *Linear panel analysis: Models of qualitative change*. San Diego, CA: Academic Press.

Krause, N., Liang, J., & Keith, V. (1990). Personality, social support, and psychological distress in later life. *Psychology and Aging, 5,* 315–326.

Kupersmidt, J. B., Coie, J. D., & Dodge, K. A. (1990). The role of poor peer relationships in the development of disorder. In S. R. Asher & J. D. Coie (Eds.), *Peer rejection in childhood* (pp. 274–305). Cambridge: Cambridge University Press.

Kurdek, L. A. (1993). Predicting marital dissolution: A 5-year longitudinal study of newlywed couples. *Journal of Personality and Social Psychology, 64,* 221–241.

Lang, F. R., Staudinger, U. M., & Carstensen, L. L. (1998). Socioemotional selectivity in late life: How personality does (and does not) make a difference. *Journal of Gerontology: Psychological Science, 53,* 21–30.

Lytton, H. (1990). Child and parent effects in boys' conduct disorder: A reinterpretation. *Developmental Psychology, 26,* 683–697.

Magnusson, D. (1990). Personality development from an interactional perspective. In L. A. Pervin (Ed.), *Handbook of personality: Theory and measurement* (pp. 193–222). New York: Guilford Press.

Newman, D. L., Caspi, A., Moffitt, T. E., & Silva, P. A. (1997). Antecedents of adult interpersonal functioning: Effects of individual differences in age 3 temperament. *Developmental Psychology, 33,* 206–217.

Patterson, G. R. (1982). *Coercive family process.* Eugene, OR: Castalia.

Patterson, G. R., & Bank, L. (1989). Some amplifying mechanisms for pathologic processes in families. In M. R. Gunnar & E. Thelen (Eds.), *The Minnesota Symposia on Child Psychology. Vol. 22: Systems and development* (pp. 167–209). Hillsdale, NJ: Erlbaum.

Roberts, B. W., & DelVecchio, W. F. (2000). The rank-order consistency of personality traits from childhood to old age: A quantitative review of longitudinal studies. *Psychological Bulletin, 126,* 3–25.

Rothbart, M. K., & Bates, J. E. (1998). Temperament. In W. Damon (Ed.), *Handbook of child psychology,* 5th ed. N. Eisenberg (Vol. Ed.), *Social, emotional, and personality development* (Vol. 3, pp. 105–176). New York: Wiley.

Sameroff, A. J. (1983). Developmental systems: Contexts and evolution. In W. Kessen (Ed.), *Handbook of child psychology, 4th ed. Vol. 1. History, theory, and methods* (pp. 237–294). New York: Wiley.

Sroufe, L. A. (1983). Infant–caregiver attachment and patterns of adaptation in preschool: The roots of maladaptation and competence. In N. Perlmutter (Ed.), *Minnesota Symposia on Child Psychology* (Vol. 16, pp. 41–83). Hillsdale, NJ: Erlbaum.

Thompson, R. A. (1998). Early sociopersonality development. In W. Damon (Ed.), *Handbook of child psychology,* 5th ed. N. Eisenberg (Vol. Ed.), *Social, emotional, and personality development* (Vol. 3, pp. 25–104). New York: Wiley.

Tucker, J. S., Kressin, N. R., Spiro, A., III, & Ruscio, J. (1998). Intrapersonal characteristics and the timing of divorce: A prospective investigation. *Journal of Social and Personal Relationships, 15,* 211–225.

van den Boom, D. C. (1994). The influence of temperament and mothering on attachment and exploration: An experimental manipulation of sensitive responsiveness among lower-class mothers with irritable infants. *Child Development, 65,* 1457–1477.

(1995). Do first-year intervention effects endure? Follow-up during toddlerhood of a sample of Dutch irritable infants. *Child Development, 66,* 1798–1816.

van IJzendoorn, M. H. (1995). Adult attachment representations, parental responsiveness, and infant attachment: A meta-analysis on the predictive validity of the Adult Attachment Interview. *Psychological Bulletin, 117,* 387–403.

CHAPTER THREE

An Intergenerational Model of Romantic Relationship Development

Chalandra M. Bryant and Rand D. Conger

"In conducting research on the quality of life of the American population, time and again we came to the conclusion that for most adults the cornerstone of a solidly constructed satisfying life free from overwhelming tensions is a happy and stable marriage" (Veroff, Douvan, & Hatchett, 1995, p. xiii). This quote underscores growing evidence that close social relationships promote personal well-being. Conversely, failure to establish or maintain such relationships in general, and romantic relationships in particular, predicts both physical and emotional distress (House, Landis, & Umberson, 1988; Simon & Marcussen, 1999; Wickrama, Lorenz, Conger, & Elder, 1997). Spouses and their children may experience negative emotional, physical, behavioral, social, or economic consequences as a result of either marital dissolution or ongoing marital conflict (Gottman, 1994; Halford, Kelly, & Markman, 1997; Harold & Conger, 1997; House et al., 1988; Simon & Marcussen, 1999).

Changes seen over the past few decades such as increases in divorce and remarriage, as well as the delaying of marriage, suggest that a large number of people experience the problems created by distress in relationships, while others lack the health-promoting benefits of satisfying

---

During the past several years support for this research has come from multiple sources including the National Institute of Mental Health (MH00567, MH19734, MH43270, MH48165, MH51361), the National Institute on Drug Abuse (DA05347), the Bureau of Maternal and Child Health (MCJ-109572), the MacArthur Foundation Research Network on Successful Adolescent Development among Youth in High-Risk Settings, and the Iowa Agriculture and Home Economics Experiment Station (Project No. 3320). Requests for reprints should be addressed to Chalandra M. Bryant, Institute for Social and Behavioral Research, Iowa State University, 2625 North Loop Drive, Suite 500, Ames, Iowa 50010-8296.

romantic ties. Findings indicate that people who are able to establish and maintain a stable and happy romantic union experience a significant health advantage, compared to those who cannot. Despite the acknowledged importance of competence in intimate relationships, little is known about the developmental roots of the ability to successfully initiate and sustain such relationships (Christensen, 1998; Parke, 1998). The formation of intimate relationships, in other words becoming a couple and maintaining an identity as a couple, is a developmental process; however, many researchers begin their study of these relationships with marriage. While legally, marriage marks a crucial turning point in a relationship, intimate relationships begin before the wedding. Therefore, designating the starting point of the study at the couple's first meeting, first date, or the time at which cohabiting began may make more sense if one is interested in the development of competence in romantic relationships (Christensen, 1998). For example, research suggests that dysfunctional patterns of interactions develop before marriage (Leonard & Roberts, 1998; Noller & Feeney, 1998; O'Leary & Cascardi, 1998). Thus, to understand the development of relationships and the partners involved requires that an investigation begin prior to marriage. Moreover, the development of close relationships may or may not include marriage, as marriage is conceptualized as an event, not unlike other events that take place over the course of relationships (Christensen, 1998).

As noted, a developmental approach to understanding romantic ties requires an examination of prerelationship predictors of relationship characteristics, consistent with several current theoretical models (e.g., Bradbury, Cohan, & Karney, 1998; Huston & Houts, 1998; Tallman, Burke, & Gecas, 1998). For example, Huston and Houts (1998) suggest, through a perpetual problems model, that problems existing in the early years of marriage can be traced back to courtship. We argue that problems can be traced back farther than courtship. Indeed, the processes involved in any given marital outcome can be linked to premarital circumstances and interactions, including relationship-promotive or -inhibiting experiences in the family of origin. In this chapter we argue that the competencies that promote an individual's success in establishing a stable and satisfying adult romantic relationship can be traced to family experiences during childhood and adolescence.

To our knowledge, no prospective, longitudinal studies have been published that examine the connection between characteristics of the family of origin and specific interpersonal skills or competencies predicted to influence the probability of success in early adult romantic relationships. One study of over 120 individuals – interviewed during adolescence and later as young adults – revealed that self-reports of family interactional characteristics during adolescence predicted adult reports of happiness or problems in romantic relationships (Feldman, Gowen, & Fisher, 1998). However, specific adult competencies that might shed light on the association between earlier relationships in the family of origin and later experiences with romantic partners were not examined in this study. The association between adults' marital quality and the marital quality of their parents (when these adults were adolescents) was prospectively examined in a similar study; however, the findings were inconclusive (Feng, Giarrusso, Bengston, & Frye, 1999). That study also failed to include measures of specific skills or competencies that might explain the link between experiences in the family of origin and subsequent relationships with intimate partners. In yet another prospective study, evidence of marital quality across generations was discovered; yet, as was the case with previous studies, specific skills and competencies were not assessed (Amato & Booth, 1997).

Although these and similar studies do not provide direct evidence for the influence of the family of origin on interpersonal skills or competencies in early adult romantic relationships, the research on interpersonal violence and divorce does provide some information. Such work suggests that individuals from divorced or separated families are significantly more likely to end their own marriages through divorce or separation than are individuals from two-parent homes; they are also more likely to have nonmarital ties that are unstable and distressed (Amato & Booth, 1997; Amato & Keith, 1991; Sanders, Halford, & Behrens, 1999). In addition, children raised in families fraught with interpersonal violence are more likely to exhibit physical aggression toward a romantic partner (O'Leary & Cascardi, 1998). These findings imply that the quality and course of adult romantic relationships may be shaped by the interactional characteristics of the family of origin. The earliest findings for this intergenerational influence, however, are limited to more extreme developmental histories involving divorce or violence.

To help address the gap in current understanding, we propose a model that predicts how specific behavioral, cognitive, and emotional characteristics in the family of origin might prime young adults to behave in certain ways with romantic partners. The model also predicts the types of feelings about the relationship those learned behaviors should elicit from romantic partners, as well as the implications of those responses for the success of the union. This chapter proceeds by first presenting an intergenerational conceptualization of romantic relationship development which we refer to as the DEARR model (Development of Early Adult Romantic Relationships). We then provide a preliminary test of a specific portion of the model.

THE THEORETICAL MODEL

The DEARR model proposes that characteristics in the family of origin will, over time, affect the development of early adult romantic relationships through their influence on the youth's (a) social and economic circumstances and (b) individual characteristics (see Fig. 3.1). The model also proposes a possible direct influence of experiences in the family of origin on attributes of the couple relationship. The model then links those attributes to the young adult's relationship success. The following discussion considers the elements of the model and their interrelationships.

The Family of Origin

The first set of variables in the DEARR model are labeled *Relationship-Promoting vs. -Inhibiting Experiences in the Family of Origin* (Fig. 3.1). These variables include the emotions, behaviors, and cognitions of multiple family members, both parents and children. In the analyses presented later in this chapter, we identify a target child from each family who is followed into early adulthood and a sibling. Thus, unlike much of the previous work in this area, our model of the family of origin extends beyond parent–child or parent–parent relationships to include relationships with siblings. Siblings play a crucial role in the development of children's understanding of interpersonal relationships (Buhrmester & Furman, 1990; von Salisch, 1997). This is not surprising given that children spend more time interacting with their siblings than with their parents (Dunn, 1984). These sibling interactions provide an avenue through which individuals exhibit numerous behaviors and express a range of emotions that typically are of greater intensity than those exhibited in other relationships (Katz, Kramer, & Gottman, 1992). Children also develop an understanding of relationships and the complex emotions driving those relationships by observing parent–sibling

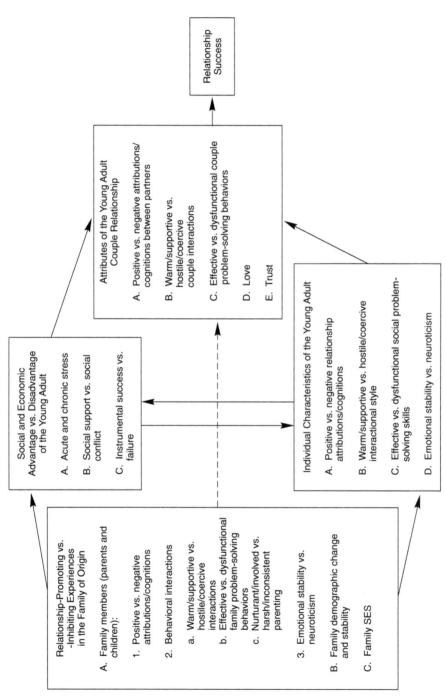

Figure 3.1. Model for the Development of Early Adult Romantic Relationships (DEARR).

behavioral interactions (Parke & O'Neil, 1997). As shown in Fig. 3.1, the model proposes several behavioral, cognitive, and emotional characteristics in the family of origin that should influence early adult romantic relationship development either directly or indirectly.

Family Members' Positive versus Negative Attributions or Cognitions about Relationships

Cognitions form the template individuals use to process events in intimate relationships. Relationship-related cognitions may include attributions about the causes of others' behaviors as well as beliefs about marriage or divorce. These cognitions may also include beliefs about the trustworthiness or dependability of romantic partners in general. Especially important, the DEARR model proposes that these cognitions are learned, in part, through experiences in the family of origin. For example, the experience of parents' marital separation may lead children from divorced families to think differently about relationships than do individuals from two-parent families. Dostal and Langhinrichsen-Rohling (1997) argue that "relationship-specific cognitions are one mechanism by which a predisposition toward divorce is passed from one generation to the next" (p. 103). Their model suggests that adults whose parents divorced maintain different cognitions about relationships than do adults from two-parent homes. It is possible that these cognitions develop as a result of experiencing family interactions surrounding the divorce; that is, those interactions may impart a set of assumptions about interpersonal relationships (Bedrosian & Bozicas, 1994). For example, quarrels between parents who eventually divorce and their statements of disillusionment about their marriages and relationships in general should lead children to have more negative perceptions about marriage and romance (e.g., Greenberg & Nay, 1982).

This suggests that cognitions are shaped by experiences in the family of origin. These experiences include not only the divorce itself, but also the negative sentiments expressed by parents regarding romantic ties. As we consider the cognitions behind injunctions such as "Don't be close" (because intimacy with others is risky), even more light is shed on the issue. Silvestri (1992) explored the "Don't be close" injunction in male adults from both two-parent and divorced homes. Male adults from divorced homes sanctioned this cognition at a higher rate than those from two-parent homes. Silvestri argued that the "Don't be close" view is a precursor to creating distance in interpersonal relationships, which decreases intimacy and relationship satisfaction, thereby making divorce more likely. Similarly, Rozendal and Wells (1983), using a sample of college-aged adults from divorced and two-parent families, explored assumptions regarding the concept of "family." Their findings indicated that the divorced group rated concepts of mother, father, marriage, and family less favorably than the two-parent group. These findings suggest that family members from divorced homes are more likely to (a) accept divorce as a reasonable way to deal with marital discord; (b) make more negative evaluations about family and marriage; and (c) approach intimate relationships with caution. The experience of divorce and the sentiments expressed by parents during the process of separation illustrate one pathway through which the family-of-origin has an impact on the relationship cognitions of adults, consistent with the DEARR model, as indicated by the arrow leading from *Experiences in Family of Origin* to *Individual Characteristics*.

The example of the influence of divorce on relationship cognitions is, of course, only one illustration of how processes in the family of origin might influence cognitive development. According to attachment theory, for example, conflicts or lack of dependability in parent–child and parent–parent relationships may lead children to have negative cognitive representations of relationships; they may think of relationships or partners as being undependable and untrustworthy (Bowlby, 1969, 1973, 1980; Hazan & Shaver, 1987; Main, Kaplan, & Cassidy, 1985; Taylor, Parker, & Roy, 1995). For instance, earlier work shows that individuals reporting problems and conflict in their own romantic relationships also report unhappiness in their parents' marriages (Amato & Booth, 1991; Booth & Edwards, 1990). Individuals who remember positive relationships with their parents tend to report better marital quality after the birth of a child than do those individuals whose recollections are not as positive (Belsky & Isabella, 1985). It may also be the case that individuals develop a positive or negative attributional style in the family of origin regarding the causes of another's behavior in close relationships (Matthews & Conger, under review). That is, according to the DEARR model, positive or negative sentiments expressed about relationships or about the causes of one another's behaviors in early family relationships will predict a similar cognitive and attributional style in later adult romantic relationships, as indicated by the broken line in Fig. 3.1.

Behavioral Interactional Processes and Parenting in the Family of Origin

As noted, the DEARR model proposes that interactional processes in the family of origin may affect the way that individuals think about relationships. In addition, the model predicts that the quality of interpersonal exchange in the family of origin will have an independent influence on later romantic relationship development (Fig. 3.1). The model proposes three dimensions of behavior that should be especially important. First, a large body of research now indicates that negative, hostile, or coercive behaviors in intimate relationships are positively associated with relationship instability and dissatisfaction; whereas positive, warm, and supportive interactions are positively related with stable and satisfying unions (Conger, Rueter, & Elder, 1999; Gottman, 1994; Matthews, Wickrama, & Conger, 1996). Second, there is increasing evidence that romantic partners who have good problem-solving skills are more capable of avoiding distress in their relationships than are those without such skills (e.g., Conger et al., 1999). Third, parents who are nurturant and involved in their children's lives and who avoid harsh and inconsistent parenting have offspring who are more successful in extrafamilial relationships (e.g., Conger et al., 1992, 1993a). The model in Fig. 3.1 indicates that all of these dimensions of early family experience will affect early adult romantic relationship development. We propose several mechanisms by which this process might operate.

Regarding hostile versus supportive interactional styles and effective versus dysfunctional problem-solving skills, we expect that observational learning will occur such that the child carries forward what he or she observes in interactions (a) between parents, (b) between parents and siblings, and (c) between other siblings. That is, the child should emulate the types of interactional styles prevalent in his or her family of origin (Sanders et al., 1999). We call this the *observational learning hypothesis*. A child also may be socialized to behave along these dimensions through a process of direct interaction with siblings or parents. Thus, the model implies either a *sibling or parent socialization hypothesis*. Parental socialization regarding appropriate behavior in general, however, should involve nurturant/involved rather than harsh/inconsistent parenting. Children who have caregivers who train them to behave appropriately toward others should be more skillful in their later interactions with romantic partners, whereas children treated harshly and inconsistently should be more impulsive and less skillful in such interactions (Capaldi & Clark, 1998; Simons, Lin, & Gordon, 1998).

The model also suggests, however, that these various behavioral traits may reflect continuity in the child's interactions from the family of origin to a young adult romantic partner. That is, behaviors between members of the family of origin are influenced by the child (as well as the reverse), who eventually becomes involved in a relationship (e.g., Rueter & Conger, 1998). Thus, carryover of interactional style from the family of origin to early adult romantic relationships may reflect relatively stable behavioral traits already present during childhood and adolescence. We call this the *behavioral continuity hypothesis*. The DEARR model proposes that observational learning, sibling socialization, parent socialization, and behavioral continuity may all operate in linking family of origin experiences to the development of early adult romantic relationships.

Emotional Stability versus Neuroticism

Bradbury and his colleagues (e.g., Bradbury et al., 1998; Karney & Bradbury, 1995) have suggested that neuroticism is a relatively stable trait that may adversely affect the course of romantic relationships. Neuroticism encompasses dispositions toward irritability and depressed mood. Presumably, emotions counter to neuroticism, such as joy and good humor, would promote more satisfying romantic relationships. Important for present purposes, there is increasing evidence that the neurotic symptoms of one family member tend to exacerbate the same emotions in other family members (e.g., Ge, Conger, Lorenz, Shanahan, & Elder, 1995). Thus, the DEARR model proposes that family members tend to influence one another's positive and negative emotional dispositions. These affective styles are predicted to carry forward and eventually to influence the development of early adult romantic relationships. Highly neurotic individuals are expected to have more troubled romantic relationships, whereas those with more optimistic and agreeable dispositions are expected to have greater relationship success.

Family of Origin Demographic Characteristics and Socioeconomic Status

The *DEARR* model also includes family demographic history as well as family socioeconomic status, which we argue can have a direct effect on both individual characteristics of the target and the social and economic situation of the target young adult. Previous research indicates, for instance, that improvements in parents' financial situations are associated with offspring experiencing less marital conflict; likewise, parental unemployment is associated with less marital happiness for their children (Amato & Booth, 1997). Presumably, these linkages occur because economically disadvantaged parents are unable to provide the kinds of resources for their children that enable a reasonably successful transition to early adulthood. Thus, family of origin resources have an impact on an individual's relationship trajectories in young adulthood. Divorce usually has negative effects on families' financial situations, which often leads to a decrease in children's education and achievement opportunities (Brandwein, Brown, & Fox, 1974). As a result, these children tend to become economically disadvantaged early and their economic plight continues – if interventions are not implemented – through adulthood. Children in these situations therefore tend to experience financial strains in their marriage and that can lead to marital problems and even dissolution (Dostal & Langhinrichsen-Rohling, 1997). This is represented in Fig. 3.1 by the path from *Experiences in the Family of Origin* to *Social and Economic Advantage versus Disadvantage*.

Studies show that individuals from high-resource families tend to delay marriage longer than do those from low-resource families (Amato & Booth, 1997; Goldscheider & Goldscheider, 1993; Thornton, 1991). Individuals from high-resource families are marrying later in order to first complete college and begin their careers (Amato & Booth, 1997). Thus, they may have happier marriages because they are entering these unions with greater advantages and lower stress. They tend to have more education and higher incomes than do their counterparts from low-resource families. They are therefore less likely to experience acute or chronic stress caused by economic hardship (Conger et al., 1992, 1993b). The resources provided in their families of origin afforded them the opportunity to further their education, which, in turn, increased their income-earning potential. In other words, resources provided by their families of origin had a positive influence on their own social and economic situations. Economic strain in the family of origin not only decreases the ability of the family to provide financial assistance to their offspring as adolescents seek to further their education, but it also decreases the ability of the family to provide financial assistance once their offspring are married. Economic hardship can affect offspring in another way. It can increase the risk of marital conflict and subsequent marital distress (Conger et al., 1999). Children's exposure to parent–parent conflict and hostility may then influence their behavioral and emotional dispositions (Conger, Ge, Elder, Lorenz, & Simons, 1994). We argue that those dispositions then predict the course of offspring's romantic relationships years later.

The DEARR model, then, proposes an array of characteristics in the family of origin that are predicted to influence a child's level of competence or dysfunction in relation to the development of early adult romantic relationships. As shown in Fig. 3.1, these family of origin effects are expected to influence later relationship success through three interrelated mediating processes: (a) the social and economic advantage or disadvantage of the young adult; (b) the general emotional, behavioral, and cognitive characteristics of the young adult; and (c) attributes of the young adult's couple relationship(s). We now turn to discussion of these mediational domains.

Mediators of Family of Origin Influences

The first set of mediators involves *Social and Economic Advantage versus Disadvantage*, such as acute and chronic stress, social support versus conflict, and instrumental success versus failure. There is increasing evidence that the social and economic circumstances of the family of origin affect the social and economic circumstances of children as they transition to early adulthood. Elder and Conger (2000) showed, for example, that the children of families with the greatest social and economic resources were more likely to experience social and economic success and less likely to experience ongoing stresses and strains as young adults than children from less advantaged families. Figure 3.1 proposes that these family-related advantages and disadvantages should affect the general characteristics of the young adult and specific attributes of the couple relationship. For example, the model suggests that, just as stress caused by economic hardship increases conflict between parents, so too may it lead to conflict in the early adult's romantic relationship(s), because similar dynamics are at work. Negative events such as economic hardship also can have dire effects on individual characteristics such as negative emotions, by increasing depression or sadness, or interpersonal behaviors, by increasing hostile, antisocial, or angry-coercive actions (Conger et al., 1992, 1993a; Conger et al., 1993). Not only do material resources and economic support provided by the family of origin affect adolescents, so too does emotional or social support. Individuals receiving greater support for their relationships report greater commitment and score higher on other measures of dyadic formation as well (Bryant & Conger, 1999; Sprecher & Felmlee, 1992). Moreover, individuals who experience instrumental success in education or work should feel less stress and strain and be less prone to emotions or behaviors that would negatively affect relationship processes.

A second set of mediating variables in the model involves *Individual Characteristics of the Young Adult* such as cognitions, behaviors, and emotions that carry forward from the family of origin. These variables include the intrapersonal or personality characteristics of the early adult as demonstrated in social relations in general and not just in romantic relationships. The same behaviors, cognitions, and emotional dispositions that partners exhibit premaritally seem to predict later success or failure in their marriages, suggesting that the characteristics partners bring to their relationships have a significant impact on the development of said relationships over time (Huston & Houts, 1998; Leonard & Roberts, 1998; Noller & Feeney, 1998). For example, personality characteristics such as neuroticism – defined as a stable tendency to report negative feelings and dissatisfaction over time, regardless of the situation – are associated with marital quality (Karney & Bradbury, 1995). Thus, these emotional, behavioral, and cognitive characteristics of the early adult are predicted to directly influence specific attributes of early adult couple relationships. The set of double paths in Fig. 3.1 indicate that although *Social and Economic Advantage versus Disadvantage* may influence *Individual Characteristics*, *Individual Characteristics* may also influence *Social and Economic Advantage versus Disadvantage*, as such characteristics may, for example, impact young adults' stress and their ability to elicit support. Feelings of social efficacy can lead to more supportive relations with others (Bandura, 1997).

A third set of mediating variables in the model involves *Attributes of the Young Adult Couple Relationship*, such as the quality of the young partners' attributions about one another, their behavioral interactions (warmth, hostility, problem solving), as well as their trust in and love for one another. Partners' attributions about their relationships or about their significant others appear to influence the probability of relationship dissolution (Karney & Bradbury, 1995). Thus, the manner in which partners assess their relationships may affect the course of those relationships (Gottman, 1994; Matthews et al., 1996). The DEARR model proposes that these attributions are significantly influenced by the attributional and cognitive styles regarding relationships learned in the family of origin and carried forward in the individual characteristics of the young adult.

We also expect that current social stresses and strains will negatively impact couples' attributions about one another (Matthews et al., 1996). Similarly, attributional style and beliefs about the dependability of romantic partners are predicted to affect feelings of trust and love. Trust is a belief in the integrity of another. It increases partners' sense of security in their relationships. Love is the degree to which partners feel a sense of closeness and belonging to each other. The concept of trust has been linked to attributions – in particular, individuals' attributions concerning their partners' benevolence, honesty, or motivation (Altman & Taylor, 1973; Phillips & Metzger, 1976). According to the model, the more positive an individual's attributions regarding a partner and the more positive his or her beliefs about romantic relationships in general, the greater the likelihood that the individual will have a positive view of a specific relationship and subsequently rate the relationship as being successful. In the same fashion, behaviors associated with the stability and quality of romantic relationships, such as problem solving and expressed emotions by partners, are expected to result from the earlier predictors in the model.

Relationship Success

The final set of variables in the model focus on *Relationship Success*. Does the relationship survive? In other words, are the partners committed to the relationship? Commitment refers to the intent to continue a relationship over time; it is based upon partners' intentions for the future of their relationships (Johnson, 1991; Rusbult, 1980). Are both partners in the relationship satisfied and happy? To the extent that a relationship is reported by partners to be highly satisfying and stable, it is defined as highly successful (Glenn, 1990). Notice that the final set of mediators involving couple attributes is proposed to entirely account for the link between earlier predictors and relationship success. This proposition suggests that the interpersonal competencies acquired in the family of origin influence relationship success as reported by either the target youth or the romantic partner. That is, the model proposes that competencies brought to the relationship by the partners, via the pathways described in Fig. 3.1, will determine the eventual success of the union. We call this the *interpersonal competence hypothesis*. The final variable in the model requires that both partners assess the success of the relationship. Thus, the final component of the DEARR model is dyadic in nature.

TESTING A PORTION OF THE DEARR MODEL

To complete the present discussion, we test several predictions from the model. The most potent research design for evaluating the DEARR model is a prospective, longitudinal, multiinformant study extending from childhood or adolescence to the early adult years. Unfortunately, most earlier research has been limited in this regard. First, much of the earlier research in this area was cross-sectional in nature, and consequently the results of such work cannot be used to make definitive statements about the temporal ordering of proposed causal relationships. Second, much of the research was retrospective, particularly with regard to relationships of offspring with their parents. Such retrospective accounts are biased by current moods and circumstances. Third, many of the samples used were derived from universities or clinical settings and may not represent processes operating in community populations. Fourth, earlier research relied heavily on self-reports of behavioral interactions. Self-reported behaviors may reflect moods and dispositions more than actual interactions. Fifth, reports of parent–parent and parent–child conflict were obtained from only one source, the young adults, which again may bias findings. Sixth, the focus was on only parents and the targeted young adult, with no mention of the influence of siblings living in the home. Lastly, targets' romantic partners were not included as part of the sample. (See, for example, Dostal & Langhinrichsen-Rohling, 1997; Feldman et al., 1998; Taylor et al., 1995) Because of the multiinformant and longitudinal nature of the community study used for the following analyses, we overcome these limitations in the present report.

In the present test of a portion of the DEARR model (see Fig. 3.2), we focus on family members' behaviors toward one another and ask how the environment created by such behaviors shapes a target family member's behaviors toward romantic partners. The target family member entered the research in 1989 as a seventh-grader and was followed into early adulthood. Following from the predictions in Fig. 3.1, we hypothesize that high warmth and low hostility in the family of origin, assessed over a period of four years (1989 through 1992), will predict the same behaviors by target young adults toward

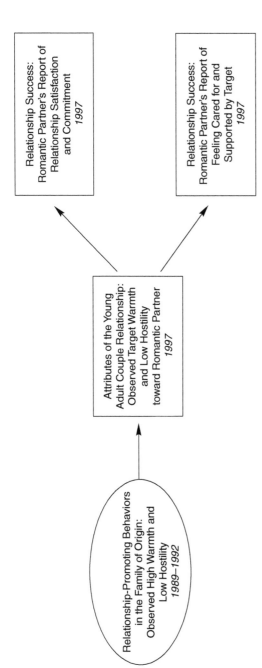

Figure 3.2. Predictions from the DEARR model to be empirically tested.

their romantic partners five years later (1997). We expected that these relationship-promoting behaviors in the family of origin would be directly related to an important couple attribute, namely, the way the target young adults treat their romantic partners. We further hypothesized that targets' behaviors toward romantic partners would predict dimensions of relationship success as assessed by their partners' reports of the quality of the relationship.

The data for these analyses come from a study of 451 rural white families that began in 1989. At that time the median age was 39 years for husbands and 37 years for wives. Spouses' median education level was 13 years. To participate in the study, families had to have one child in the seventh grade (the "target" child for the study) and another child within 4 years of age of this child. The average age of the target was 13 years in 1989. For the present study, Time 1 (1989–1992) represents the early adolescent years of the target child. In 1997 (Time 2), 418 of the original target adolescents participated in the study and 199 of them were involved in a romantic relationship. Those 199 targets (88 males and 111 females) reported having either a spouse, cohabiting partner, or boyfriend/girlfriend in 1997. At that time, the average age of targets was 21 years.

From 1989 through 1992, families completed questionnaires and a series of structured videotaped discussion tasks. In 1997, adolescents in the study families, now young adults, completed a similar battery of questionnaires and were videotaped with their romantic partners. For the videotaped discussion tasks, family members were given a set of questions on cards that interviewers instructed them to read and discuss. The tasks were designed to stimulate family interactions in order to obtain information regarding social skills and emotional affect. Trained observers coded the videotapes using a global rating system assessing behavioral exchanges based on a 9-point scale, ranging from 1, *the behavior is not at all characteristic of the person being rated* to 9, *the behavior is mainly characteristic of the person being rated* (Melby et al., 1993). The system taps into nonverbal and verbal behaviors.

Family of Origin Behavioral Interactions, 1989 to 1992: Observer Ratings

High warmth. The environment of warmth in the household was assessed by measuring behavioral interactions indicative of both high warmth and low hostility. The high-warmth construct was a composite of five scales that rated (using the 9-point rating system) behaviors

Romantic Relationship Development

directed by one family member toward another (e.g., mother to target, target to mother, and so on). The five scales included in the composite were (a) warmth/support, assessing expressions of care; (b) communication, assessing the ability to clearly express points of view; (c) assertiveness, assessing the ability to express points of view in a self-confident, nonthreatening manner; (d) prosocial behavior, assessing helpfulness and sensitivity; and (e) listener responsiveness, assessing attention to others. The mean of these five scales (data for which were collected over four years, 1989 to 1992) were used to ascertain the degree of warmth among each combination of dyads in the family. Parents' behavior to target and to sibling also included one additional scale: positive reinforcement. Positive reinforcement is a scale assessing the degree to which parents respond positively to children's appropriate behavior. Reliabilities (internal-consistency coefficients) ranged from .91 to .95. For example, the reliability for sibling-to-parent and parent-to-sibling warmth was .92.

Low hostility. The low-hostility construct was a composite of three scales that rated behaviors directed by one family member toward another. The three scales included in the composite were (a) hostility, assessing angry, critical behavior; (b) angry coercion, assessing threatening control attempts; and (c) antisocial behavior, assessing insensitivity. The scales were reverse-scored to reflect low hostility. The means of those ratings represent sibling–parent/parent–sibling, parent–target/target–parent, target–sibling/sibling–target, father–mother/mother–father behavioral interactions over the course of four years, 1989 to 1992.

The Young Adult Couple – Five Years Later

Target warmth toward romantic partner: Behaviors indicative of high warmth and low hostility. Target high warmth toward romantic partner was assessed by calculating the mean of the five scales (warmth, communication, assertiveness, prosocial behavior, and listener responsiveness) previously mentioned. Target low hostility toward partner was assessed by reverse-scoring and calculating the mean of the three scales (hostility, angry coercion, and antisocial behavior) previously mentioned. These data were collected in 1997. The reliabilities for high warmth and low hostility were .91 and .92, respectively.

Romantic partner's feelings of relationship satisfaction and commitment. Romantic partners included spouses/partners and boyfriends/girlfriends. In 1997 (Time 2), targets' romantic partners responded to four items rated on Likert scales, which assessed their satisfaction with and commitment to their relationship. Means were computed. The reliability for spouses/partners was .85 and for boyfriends/girlfriends, .84.

Romantic partner's feeling cared for and supported by target. In 1997 (Time 2), targets' romantic partners responded to four items asking how often during the past month did the target (a) "let you know she/he ... cares?" (b) "act loving ... toward you?" (c) "let you know that she/he appreciates you ... ?" and (d) "act supportive ... ?" Means were computed. The reliability for spouses/partners was .94 and for boyfriends/girlfriends, .92.

Results

A latent variable structural equation model (SEM) was used to examine the empirical credibility of the proposed associations among constructs. Maximum likelihood estimates of the model coefficients were obtained using AMOS (Arbuckle, 1997). We controlled for parents' education. The SEM evaluates whether family warmth and low hostility at Time 1 predict the manner in which targets behave toward romantic partners five years later, at Time 2, when they are young adults. The model further evaluates whether targets' behavior toward their partners influences their partners' judgments of relationship success (Fig. 3.2). Male and female targets were analyzed together. Analyses not reported here demonstrated that there were no significant differences in the findings as a function of the young adult's gender.

Prior to estimating the SEM, we evaluated the correlations among study constructs. Those correlations were consistent with expectations (Table 3.1). The observed environment of warmth in the family of origin correlated significantly with targets' observed warmth to romantic partners, $r = .48$. Targets' observed warmth to partners significantly correlated with partners' reports of satisfaction as well as with partners' reports of feeling cared for and supported by targets. These promising correlations indicated the potential value of estimating the proposed SEM.

As shown in Fig. 3.3, the environment of warmth in the family of origin was estimated through a secondary factor analysis yielding two latent constructs: high warmth and low hostility. Each of those constructs had four indicators representing the behavior of each of the studied family members toward the other. All error variances except those between sibling–parent/parent–sibling high warmth and

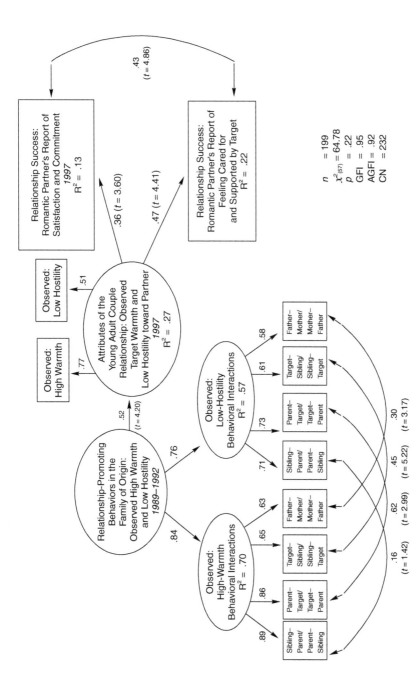

Figure 3.3. Observed behaviors in the family of origin predicting targets' observed behaviors toward romantic partners, which in turn predict romantic partners' self-reports regarding relationships with targets; female and male targets analyzed together; standardized path coefficients.

Table 3.1. Correlations Among Constructs; Male and Female Targets Analyzed Together

	1	2	3	4	5
1. Parents' education	1.00				
2. Observed: Environment of warmth in family of origin	.41*	1.00			
3. Observed: Target's warmth to romantic partner	.31*	.48*	1.00		
4. Romantic partner's report of relationship satisfaction and commitment	.10	.20*	.34*	1.00	
5. Romantic partner's report of feeling cared for and supported by target	.11	.22*	.47*	.53*	1.00

* $p < .05$.

sibling–parent/parent–sibling low hostility (.16, t = 1.42) were significantly correlated.

The standardized regression coefficient reveals that the environment of warmth in the family of origin significantly predicted targets' warmth toward romantic partners five years later. Targets' warmth toward romantic partner significantly predicted (a) romantic partners' reports of relationship satisfaction and commitment and (b) romantic partners' reports of feeling cared for and supported by targets. Error variances between the two outcome variables were significantly correlated with one another.

The direct path from the environment of warmth in the family of origin to romantic partner report of satisfaction and commitment, without target warmth toward partner included, was significant (.19, t = 2.18). That path was not significant when target warmth toward partner was included in the model (.03, t = .27). Similarly, the direct path from the environment of warmth in the family of origin to romantic partner report of feeling cared for and supported, without target warmth toward partner included, was significant (.22, t = 2.43). That path was not significant when target warmth toward partner was included (–.02, t = –.17). This suggests that target warmth toward romantic partner mediates the relationship between experiences in the family of origin and romantic partners' reports about relationship success, consistent with predictions from the DEARR model.

Discussion

The DEARR model proposes that a set of characteristics in the family of origin will, over time, influence the competence of a child in early adult romantic relationships. The model predicts that family of origin experiences will influence attributes of the early adult couple relationship either directly or indirectly through (a) early adult socioeconomic circumstances and (b) individual attributes of a young adult. The model hypothesizes that either directly or through these developmental pathways the family primes youth to behave, think, or feel in specific ways about intimate relationships and romantic partners. These relationship attributes, in turn, predict relationship success. This model is especially significant in that it addresses specific skills or competencies that help explain the link between experiences in the family of origin and subsequent close relationships.

An optimal assessment of the DEARR model entails the use of a prospective, longitudinal, multiinformant research design. Just such a design was used to provide a preliminary test of a portion of the model. In that test, we hypothesized that behavioral interactions in the family of origin, assessed over a period of four years (1989–1992), would predict like behaviors 5 years later (1997) by target young adults toward their romantic partners. In addition, we further hypothesized that targets' behaviors toward romantic partners would influence dimensions of relationship success as assessed by their partners. The correlations (Table 3.1) and structural equation model (Fig. 3.3) provide support for our hypothesized associations. Moreover, analyses also indicated that the association between experiences in the family of origin and partners' feelings of relationship satisfaction and commitment, as well as feelings of being cared for and supported by target, were mediated by warm and supportive behaviors toward the partner. These findings were remarkably consistent with the DEARR model, which predicts that *Relationship-Promoting Experiences in the Family of Origin* influence *Relationship Success* through *Attributes of the Young Adult Couple Relationship* (Fig. 3.1). To our knowledge, this study provides the first longitudinal, prospective information regarding connections between the family of origin and markers of success in early adult romantic relationships.

Although this particular test of a portion of the DEARR model has suggested its utility, the present analyses suggest more questions than they answer. These questions can provide important guidelines for future research. First, despite the fact that the sample was recruited from the community at large, it was a rural white sample. We do not know if the same or similar results would be obtained using an urban white sample, or a rural minority sample. Thus, the utility of the model needs to be investigated across various populations (e.g., samples representing various cultures, family structures, sexual orientations, etc.).

Several questions also are suggested by the strategy with which the latent constructs were developed. Because the goal of this test of the DEARR model was to examine the behavioral environment of the family as a whole, we did not clearly distinguish between behaviors that the target may have simply observed (e.g., parent–sibling behaviors) and those in which the target was directly involved (such as parent–target interactions). Instead, we used all such behaviors as indicators – essentially combining them to create our latent construct. This measurement strategy leaves open the question of whether the associations observed here reflect, for example, the impact of direct socialization, or observational learning, or both, on the development of early adult romantic relationships. The DEARR model suggests that these influences should be additive, each contributing to the development of relationship competence. It may be, however, that only some of these proposed causal processes account for the findings reported here. This issue should be addressed in future research.

Using the DEARR model (Fig. 3.1) as a template, many more questions can be posed. How do parents' cognitions about marriage (*Family of Origin*) affect targets' cognitions about relationships in general (*Individual Characteristics of Young Adult*)? What impact does that then have on targets' cognitions about their specific partners (*Attributes of Young Adult Couple Relationship*), and in turn, how does that influence relationship success? How does harsh/inconsistent parenting (*Family of Origin*) affect targets' emotional stability (*Individual Characteristics of the Young Adult*), and how does that then affect targets' ability to trust romantic partners (*Attributes of Young Adult Couple Relationship*)? Questions such as these in each new study would support a developmental approach to understanding the course, stability, and quality of early adult romantic relationships. As one considers the numerous combinations of paths that can be tested, it becomes clear that a notable advantage of using the DEARR model is that it facilitates a *systematic* test of the effects of the family of origin on early adult romantic relationships.

REFERENCES

Altman, I., & Taylor, D. (1973). *Social penetration: The development of interpersonal relationships.* New York: Holt, Rinehart and Winston.

Amato, P., & Booth, A. (1991). Consequences of parental divorce and marital unhappiness for adult well-being. *Social Forces, 69,* 895–914.

———. (1997). *A generation at risk: Growing up in an era of family upheaval.* Cambridge, MA: Harvard University Press.

Amato, P., & Keith, B. (1991). Parental divorce and adult well-being: A meta-analysis. *Journal of Marriage and the Family, 53,* 43–58.

Arbuckle, J. (1997). *AMOS users' guide: Version 3.6.* Chicago: SPSS.

Bandura, A. (1997). *Self-efficacy: The exercise of control.* New York: W. H. Freeman.

Bedrosian, R., & Bozicas, G. (1994). *Treating family of origin problems.* New York: Guilford Press.

Belsky, J., & Isabella, R. (1985). Marital and parent–child relationships in family of origin and marital change following birth of a baby: A retrospective analysis. *Child Development, 56,* 342–349.

Booth, A., & Edwards, J. (1990). Transmission of marital and family quality over the generations: The effect of parental divorce and unhappiness. *Journal of Divorce, 13,* 41–58.

Bowlby, J. (1969). *Attachment and loss. Vol. 1: Attachment.* New York: Basic Books.

———. (1973). *Attachment and loss. Vol. 2: Separation: Anxiety and anger.* London: Hogarth.

———. (1980). *Attachment and loss. Vol. 3: Loss: Sadness and depression.* New York: Basic Books.

Bradbury, T., Cohan, C., & Karney, B. (1998). Optimizing longitudinal research for understanding and preventing marital dysfunction. In T. N. Bradbury (Ed.), *The developmental course of marital dysfunction* (pp. 279–311). Cambridge: Cambridge University Press.

Brandwein, R., Brown, C., & Fox, E. (1974). Women and children last: The social situation of divorced mothers and their families. *Journal of Marriage and the Family, 36,* 498–514.

Bryant, C., & Conger, R. (1999). Marital success in domains of social support in long-term relationships: Does the influence of network members ever end? *Journal of Marriage and the Family, 61,* 437–450.

Buhrmester, D., & Furman, W. (1990). Perceptions of sibling relationships during middle childhood and adolescence. *Child Development, 61,* 1398–1387.

Capaldi, D., & Clark, S. (1998). Prospective family predictors of aggression toward female partners for at-risk young men. *Developmental Psychology, 34,* 1175–1188.

Christensen, A. (1998). On intervention and relationship events: A marital therapist looks at longitudinal research on marriage. In T. N. Bradbury (Ed.), *The developmental course of marital dysfunction* (pp. 377–392). Cambridge: Cambridge University Press.

Conger, R., Conger, K., Elder, G., Lorenz, F., Simons, R., & Whitbeck, L. (1992). A family process model of economic hardship and adjustment of early adolescent boys. *Child Development, 63,* 526–541.

(1993a). Family economic stress and adjustment of early adolescent girls. *American Psychological Association, 29,* 206–219.

Conger, R., Ge, X., Elder, G., Lorenz, F., & Simons, R. (1994). Economic stress, coercive family process, and developmental problems of adolescents. *Child Development, 65,* 541–561.

Conger, R., Lorenz, F., Elder, G., Simons, R., & Ge, X. (1993b). Husband and wife differences in response to undesirable life events. *Journal of Health and Social Behavior, 34,* 71–88.

Conger, R., Rueter, M., & Elder, G., Jr. (1999). Couple resilience to economic pressure. *Journal of Personality and Social Psychology, 76,* 54–71.

Dostal, C., & Langhinrichsen-Rohling, J. (1997). Relationship-specific cognitions and family-of-origin divorce and abuse. *Journal of Divorce and Remarriage, 27,* 101–120.

Dunn, J. (1984). *Sisters and brothers.* London: Fontana Paperbacks.

Elder, G., Jr., & Conger, R. (2000). *Children of the land: Adversity and success in rural America.* Chicago: University of Chicago Press.

Feldman, S., Gowen, L., & Fisher, L. (1998). Family relationships and gender as predictors of romantic intimacy in young adults: A longitudinal study. *Journal of Research on Adolescence, 8,* 263–286.

Feng, D., Giarusso, R., Bengston, V., & Frye, N. (1999). Intergenerational transmission of marital quality and marital instability. *Journal of Marriage and the Family, 61,* 451–463.

Ge, X., Conger, R., Lorenz, F., Shanahan, M., & Elder, G. (1995). Mutual influences in parent and adolescent psychological distress. *Developmental Psychology, 31,* 1–14.

Glenn, N. (1990). Quantitative research on marital quality in the 1980s: A critical review. *Journal of Marriage and the Family, 52,* 818–831.

Goldscheider, F., & Goldscheider, C. (1993). *Leaving home before marriage: Ethnicity, familism, and generational relationships.* Madison: University of Wisconsin Press.

Gottman, J. (1994). *What predicts divorce? The relationship between marital processes and marital outcomes.* Hillsdale, NJ: Erlbaum.

Greenberg, E., & Nay, W. (1982). The intergenerational transmission of marital instability reconsidered. *Journal of Marriage and the Family, 44,* 335–347.

Halford, G., Kelly, A., & Markman, H. (1997). The concept of a healthy marriage. In W. K. Halford & H. J. Markman (Eds.), *Clinical handbook of marriage and couples intervention* (pp. 3–12). New York: Wiley.

Harold, G., & Conger, R. (1997). Marital conflict and adolescent distress: The role of adolescent awareness. *Child Development, 68,* 333–350.

Hazan, C., & Shaver, P. (1987). Romantic love conceptualized as an attachment process. *Journal of Personality and Social Psychology, 52,* 511–524.

House, J., Landis, K., & Umberson, D. (1988). Social relationships and health. *Science, 241,* 540–545.

Huston, T., & Houts, R. (1998). The psychological infrastructure of courtship and marriage: The role of personality and compatibility in romantic relationships. In T. N. Bradbury (Ed.), *The developmental course of marital dysfunction* (pp. 114–151). Cambridge: Cambridge University Press.

Johnson, M. (1991). Commitment to personal relationships. In W. H. Jones & D. Perlman (Eds.), *Advances in personal relationships* (pp. 117–143). London: Jessica Kingsley.

Karney, B., & Bradbury, T. (1995). Longitudinal research on marriage. *Psychological Bulletin, 118*, 3–34.

Katz, L., Kramer, L, & Gottman, J. (1992). Conflict and emotions in marital, sibling, and peer relationships. In C. U. Shantz & W. W. Hatrup (Eds.), *Conflict in child and adolescent development* (pp. 122–152). Cambridge: Cambridge University Press.

Leonard, K., & Roberts, L. (1998). Marital aggression, quality, and stability in the first year of marriage: Findings from the Buffalo Newlywed Study. In T. N. Bradbury (Ed.), *The developmental course of marital dysfunction* (pp. 44–73). Cambridge: Cambridge University Press.

Main, M., Kaplan, N., & Cassidy, J. (1985). Security in infancy, childhood, and adulthood: A move to the level of representation. *Monographs of the Society for Research in Child Development, 50*, 66–104.

Matthews, L., & Conger, R. (under review). Intergenerational transmission of relationship attributions.

Matthews, L., Wickrama, K., & Conger, R. (1996). Predicting marital instability from spouse and observer reports of marital interactions. *Journal of Marriage and the Family, 58*, 641–655.

Melby, J. N., Conger, R. D., Book, R., Rueter, M., Lucy, L., Repinski, D., Ahrens, K., Black, D., Brown, D., Huck, S., Mutchler, L., Rogers, S., Ross, J., & Stavros, T. (1993). *The Iowa Family Interaction Rating Scales* (4th ed.) Unpublished manuscript. Center for Family Research in Rural Mental Health, Iowa State University, Ames.

Noller, P., & Feeney, J. (1998). Communication in early marriage: Responses to conflict, nonverbal accuracy, and conversational patterns. In T. N. Bradbury (Ed.), *The developmental course of marital dysfunction* (pp. 11–43). Cambridge: Cambridge University Press.

O'Leary, D., & Cascardi, M. (1998). Physical aggression in marriage: A developmental analysis. In T. N. Bradbury (Ed.), *The developmental course of marital dysfunction* (pp. 343–374). Cambridge: Cambridge University Press.

Parke, R. (1998). A developmentalist's perspective on marital change. In T. N. Bradbury (Ed.), *The developmental course of marital dysfunction* (pp. 393–409). Cambridge: Cambridge University Press.

Parke, R., & O'Neil, R. (1997). The influence of significant others on learning about relationships. In S. Duck (Ed.), *Handbook of personal relationships: Theory, research, and interventions* (pp. 29–59). Chichester: Wiley.

Phillips, G. M., & Metzger, N. J. (1976). *Intimate communication.* Boston: Allyn and Bacon.

Rozendal, F., & Wells, J. (1983). Use of the semantic differential to evaluate long-term effects of loss of parent on concepts of family. *The Journal of Genetic Psychology, 143*, 269–278.

Rueter, M., & Conger, R. (1998). Reciprocal influences between parenting and adolescent problem solving behavior. *Developmental Psychology, 34*, 1470–1482.

Rusbult, C. (1980). Commitment and satisfaction in romantic associations: A test of the investment model. *Journal of Experimental Psychology, 16,* 172–186.

Sanders, M., Halford, W., & Behrens, B. (1999). Parental divorce and premarital couple communication. *Journal of Family Psychology, 13,* 60–74.

Silvestri, S. (1992). Marital instability in men from intact and divorced families: Interpersonal behavior, cognitions, and intimacy. *Journal of Divorce and Remarriage, 18,* 79–108.

Simon, R., & Marcussen, K. (1999). Marital transitions, marital beliefs, and mental health. *Journal of Health and Social Behavior, 40,* 111–125.

Simons, R., Lin, K., & Gordon, L. (1998). Socialization in the family of origin and male dating violence: A prospective study. *Journal of Marriage and the Family, 60,* 467–478.

Sprecher, S., & Felmlee, D. (1992). The influence of parents and friends on the quality and stability of romantic relationships: A three-wave longitudinal investigation. *Journal of Marriage and the Family, 54,* 888–900.

Tallman, I., Burke, P., & Gecas, V. (1998). Socialization into marital roles: Testing a contextual, developmental model of marital functioning. In T. N. Bradbury (Ed.), *The developmental course of marital dysfunction* (pp. 312–342). Cambridge: Cambridge University Press.

Taylor, L., Parker, G., & Roy, K. (1995). Parental divorce and its effects on the quality of intimate relationships in adulthood. *Journal of Divorce and Remarriage, 24,* 181–202.

Thornton, A. (1991). Influence of marital history of parents on the marital and cohabitational experiences of children. *American Journal of Sociology, 96,* 868–894.

Veroff, J., Douvan, E., & Hatchett, S. (1995). *Marital instability: A social and behavioral study of the early years.* Westport, CT: Praeger.

von Salisch, M. (1997). Emotional processes in childbearing relationships with siblings and friends. In S. Duck (Ed.), *Handbook of personal relationships: Theory, research, and interventions* (pp. 61–80). Chichester: Wiley.

Wickrama, K. A. S., Lorenz, F. O., Conger, R. D., & Elder, G. H., Jr. (1997). Marital quality and physical illness: A latent growth curve analysis. *Journal of Marriage and the Family, 59,* 143–155.

CHAPTER FOUR

How Relationships Begin and End
A Genetic Perspective

David T. Lykken

In modern societies around the world, most romantic relationships begin when two people meet and fall in love. Authorities (e.g., Walster & Walster, 1978), as well as most long-married couples, agree that the affection between mated partners occurs in two forms: romantic love, which normally comes first and then, if all goes well, is followed by the even stronger bond of companionate love and commitment. The initial or infatuation stage often starts surprisingly soon after the first meeting. When the infatuation is mutual, as it must usually be for a relationship to ensue, it is characterized both by delight and by a sense of wonderment. "Is it not remarkable that the one person I was meant to love has crossed my path and, more wonderful still, that my lover loves me too?" Romantic love blossoms early but, like the rose, it also in most cases languishes and dies too soon. The world over, for example, the modal period between marriage and divorce, if divorce occurs, is about four years (Fisher, 1991). In those relationships that last, however, infatuation's span is sufficient to permit the maturation of companionate love, a slower growing but much more enduring plant, which is based on shared experiences and shared investments and on a gradual intertwining of habit patterns, needs, and understandings.

When companionate love fails to develop, when one or both partners come to find the relationship too onerous to bear, or when either partner is afflicted by a new infatuation for some third party, then relationships commonly end through separation or divorce. In this chapter I shall review the evidence, most of it from twin research done by my

---

Address correspondence to David T. Lykken, Emeritus Professor of Psychology, University of Minnesota, Minneapolis, MN 55455. E-mail address: dlykken@tfs.psych.umn.edu.

colleagues and myself at the University of Minnesota, showing that the risk for relationship disruption or divorce is very strongly dependent upon the genetic characteristics of the partners while, paradoxically, infatuation and initial mate selection – the beginning of the relationship – seems to be determined primarily by chance.

ROMANTIC LOVE AND MATE SELECTION

My colleague Auke Tellegen and I investigated the bases of mate selection in a large sample of middle-aged twins from the Minnesota Twin Registry (Lykken & Tellegen, 1993). Our findings, that infatuation is largely unpredictable either on genetic or environmental grounds, have to my knowledge never been critiqued in print and certainly they have not been empirically refuted. Neither, however, have they been generally accepted except, perhaps, by poets. Psychologists assume as a consensual predicate that behavior is lawful and that important human responses are in principle predictable. Lovers, also, at least while walking down the aisle, assume that their mutual attraction was inevitable for a host of reasons that are obvious, at least to themselves.

The Similarity Model

There is extensive and well-replicated evidence that people tend to resemble their own spouses on nearly every dimension that has been studied. Modest positive spousal correlations have been reported for anthropometric variables (.10 to .30: Plomin, DeFries, & Roberts, 1977), for IQ (.37: Bouchard & McGue, 1981), somewhat stronger ones for physical attractiveness (.38 to .52: Murstein, 1972; White, 1980) and educational attainment (.46: Plomin et al., 1977). Spousal similarity in personality, measured by self-report or other-rated, is weak, with correlations ranging from −.23 to .47 but averaging about .15 (Buss, 1984), while correlations for personal values are slightly higher, .20 to .58 (Jensen, 1978; Caspi, Herbener, & Ozer, 1992). The unwed biological parents of adopted-away children have been found to be about as similar to one another as are spousal pairs in more committed relationships (Plomin et al., 1977).

It is a curious fact that by far the strongest and best replicated psychological similarity between spouses is to be found in the cluster of traits that includes religiosity (Waller, Kojetin, Bouchard, Lykken, & Tellegen, 1990), conservatism (Martin et al., 1986), and authoritarianism

(Altemeyer, 1996); spousal correlations on these correlated dimensions range from .40 to nearly .70. We have replicated and extended some of this research on assortative mating in our studies of Minnesota-born middle-aged twins and their families (Lykken & Tellegen, 1993, p. 56).

We had collected biographic and inventory data from a large sample, based on birth records of middle-aged twins, born from 1936 through 1955, and from many of their spouses, a sample that is demographically representative of the general population of the north central United States (Lykken, Bouchard, McGue, & Tellegen, 1990). Five inventories, totaling 623 items concerned with personality, self-rated talents, occupational and recreational interests, and attitudes on 14 controversial topics, were mailed to these twins and their spouses. The return rate was 74% overall; completed inventories were returned by both members of 901 pairs of married twins, by 1,052 of their spouses, and by the spouses of both twins in 269 of these pairs. The battery was also completed by 133 pairs of the parents of the younger participant twins.

Personality traits were assessed using the Multidimensional Personality Inventory (MPQ: Tellegen & Waller, 1994). In addition to the 14 Attitude items and the 14 scales of the MPQ, the inventory items generated 18 Talent and Self Rating factors (e.g., Good Looks, Mental Ability, Probity), 19 Recreational Interest factors (e.g., Intellectual Pursuits, Gambling, Hunting, Religious Activities), and 18 Occupational Interest Factors (e.g., Blue Collar, Personal Service, Farming or Ranching, Selling or Trading; see Waller, Lykken, & Tellegen, 1995). Adding age, height, weight, ponderal index, foot length, and years of education makes up a total of 89 variables, all of which (except for age itself) were corrected for quadratic regression on age (McGue & Bouchard, 1984), separately by sex, before correlations were computed. Although we did not choose this set of variables for the purpose of studying spousal similarity, it does constitute a broad and varied collection of measures, many of which would be of interest to prospective mates.

The wide age range of the sample made it possible to investigate whether spousal similarity increases with years married, the question being: Are the observed similarities due to assimilation or are they already in place when couples decide to marry? In this sample of 1,052 twin–spouse and 133 parental couples, absolute within-pair differences on all variables except for age were correlated with years married, to determine, for each variable, whether spousal similarity increases with cohabitation. The correlations between absolute within-pair differences

Table 4.1. The 11 (of 89) Variables That Yielded the Highest Spousal Correlations. Within-Pair Correlations for MZ and DZ Twins Are Provided for Comparison.

Variable	Spousal Correlation	Twin Correlations MZs	DZs
N of Pairs	1,185	512	389
Age	.82	1.00	1.00
Interest in Church Activities	.57	.59	.33
Years of Education	.56	.74	.55
Attitude toward Abortion	.49	.53	.35
MPQ Traditionalism	.48	.62	.34
Interest in Nightlife, Flirting	.37	.43	.21
Interest in Gambling	.36	.51	.37
Interest in Hunting and Fishing	.36	.55	.30
Interest in Camping and Hiking	.34	.54	.25
Attitudes: Conservative vs. Liberal	.33	.39	.28
Attitude toward Defense Spending	.33	.35	.09

and years married ranged from −.09 to +.12; the mean correlation was −.006. The most plausible inference is that these couples were about as similar on these variables when they married as they were when assessed. This result corroborates previous reports (Buss, 1984; Caspi et al., 1992).

Husband–wife correlations within the 1,185 spousal pairs then were computed for each of these 89 variables. The 11 variables yielding the largest spousal correlations are listed in Table 4.1. Seven of these 11 variables comprise a higher-order factor that can be labeled Traditional Values. People high on this factor enjoy church activities and have high scores on the MPQ's Traditionalism scale; they oppose abortion, favor a strong national defense, and are politically conservative; they do not enjoy gambling, visiting nightclubs, or flirting. This is plainly the dimension of religiosity-conservatism previously noted as being second only to age in strength of spousal resemblance. A second dimension is educational attainment. Finally, the spousal pairs correlated .34 to .36 in their interests in hunting, fishing, camping, canoeing, hiking, and so on. Every one of the 89 spousal correlations was positive although 47 were less than .20 and only the 11 listed in Table 4.1 were greater than .30.

Thus, we know from many sources that partners in relationships tend to resemble one another at least slightly in nearly every measurable characteristic whether physical, psychological, or demographic. If people tend to mate with partners similar to themselves, can this similarity model then explain who mates with whom? This model fades in plausibility as soon as we contemplate a pair of lovers, each delighted in her or his one and only choice. Poets do not celebrate their loved ones' resemblance to themselves. Because we were psychologists, however, Tellegen and I resorted to a statistical test of the similarity model. We discovered that, even if we could find five mutually orthogonal variables, each of which showed spousal correlations as high as .50, then this would narrow down the field of choices for the average mate-seeker only by about 14%, leaving 86% of all adults of the appropriate gender as eligible candidates. The fact seems to be, not that we choose mates who are similar to ourselves, but rather that the mates we choose tend to be from among our associates and (most of) our associates tend to be people rather like ourselves.

The Idiographic Model

Our second hypothesis was that mate choice is idiographic, that each person has individual mating criteria that reflect his or her own tastes and interests, likes and dislikes. Our test of this model was based on the assumption that monozygotic (MZ) twins, who share an identical genetic blueprint as well as a common rearing environment, must also have very similar mating criteria. We knew (and later verified on our own sample) that MZ twins have very similar tastes, interests, and attitudes and tend to make very similar choices in clothes, recreational activities, friends, and occupations. This is true even for MZ twins who had been separated in infancy and reared apart (MZA twins) as Bouchard, Lykken, McGue, Segal, and Tellegen (1990) have demonstrated. As documented in detail by William Wright (1998), MZA twins tend to use the same brand of cigarettes or toothpaste, to have similar hobbies and similar fears, to wear similar clothing and jewelry, to have similar personalities, even to select similar names for their pets and children.

Tellegen and I therefore assumed that the spouses of MZ twins should prove to be similar as well, more similar to one another at least in some respects than they are to their twin spouses. They should also be more similar than the spouses of dizygotic (DZ), or fraternal, twins who, like ordinary siblings, share on average just half of their polymorphic genes. DZ twins, in turn, we expected to choose spouses who are more similar than random pairs of persons of the same age and sex. The fact that mates do in fact somewhat resemble one another also predicts that the spouses especially of MZ twins will tend to be more alike in most respects than spouses of random pairs of people. But the idiographic model predicts that MZ twins are likely to select mates who are *very* similar in that subset of features that happen to be criterional to that twin pair.

We tested this prediction on 152 pairs of spouses of MZ twins and 117 pairs of spouses of DZ twins, using 74 of the 89 variables listed above (the Attitude variables were single Likert-type items and did not have sufficient range of variation for this purpose). The average spouse–spouse correlations were small (.14 and .11 for MZ and DZ spouses, respectively) and not significantly different. But the idiographic model only requires that spouses of MZ twins be similar in respect to a subset of variables, those that happened to seem important to their MZ-twin mates. To test this, we plotted, for MZ and DZ spouse-pairs and for same-sex spouses randomly paired, the cumulative number of variables having mean absolute within-pair differences ranging from 0.05 SDs to 6.4 SDs. The idiographic model predicts that spouses of MZ twins will be more similar on more variables than spouses of DZ twins. In fact, however, the curves for MZ, DZ, and for random pairs of spouses were virtually coincident. At least with this wide-ranging set of 74 variables, the idiographic model cannot be supported.

In the United States, there should be some 8,000 married couples where both spouses are MZ twins. For each of these couples, there is *at least* a 25% chance that both cotwins would have been themselves unattached when they first met, yielding at least 2,000 possible instances of MZ pairs married to other MZ pairs. If infatuation is lawfully determined by those characteristics of the pair that are determined either genetically or through experiences shared with the respective MZ cotwin, then there should be *at least* a 50% chance that the best man and the maid of honor at the first wedding should become the bride and groom at a subsequent wedding – there ought to be at least 1,000 MZ married pairs in the United States. We don't know the actual count, but in 30 years of twin research I have heard of only two or three cases. But this surely is a surprising result. If MZ twins reared together, who employ very similar criteria for their other life choices, do not do so when they make the most important choice of all, what could be going on? Tellegen and I decided to collect some more data.

Twins' Evaluations of Their Cotwins' Choices

A new questionnaire, prominently labeled "Confidential," was mailed to 100 pairs each of male and female MZ and DZ twins in the Minnesota Registry. The questionnaire included five items. The first two asked each twin to compare his or her own with the cotwin's choices of clothing and of household furnishings and decoration. The alternatives for the clothing item were: "(1) Our choice in clothes is almost identical; (2) is quite similar; (3) is as similar as two friends; (4) is not very similar; (5) is very different, contrasting; (6) I can't answer this question." Alternatives for the Household item were similar. Items 3 and 4 asked the twin to indicate how he or she would feel about taking the kind of vacations that the cotwin took or about having the kind of job the cotwin had. The alternatives provided were "(1) Would hate it; (2) Ho-hum; (3) Okay; (4) Would like it; (5) Would love it; (6) Can't answer."

The final, mate-selection item was identified as the "most important choice that most of us ever make" and the strict confidentiality of our individual records was once again emphasized. The respondent twin was asked to think back to when the cotwin first decided to marry and to describe his or her feeling at that time about the twin's choice of mate. The alternatives were "(1) I felt that I'd rather stay single than marry my twin's fiancée; (2) I would not have chosen my twin's fiancée; (3) I had no strong feeling one way or the other; (4) I really liked my twin's fiancée; (5) I could have fallen for my twin's fiancée; (6) I just can't answer this question." Completed questionnaires were returned by 120 MZ men, 109 DZ men, 168 MZ women, and 150 DZ women.

The data show that, for both sexes, twins approve of their cotwins' choices of wardrobe, household furnishings, vacation activities, and jobs and this similarity in choice behavior is significantly greater for MZ than for DZ twins. "On the crucial question of mate selection, however, a very different picture emerges. About as many twins of both sexes and both twin types *disliked* as *liked* their cotwins' choice of fiancée (i.e., the number who reported more negative feelings than the neutral alternative, 'no strong feeling one way or the other,' about equaled the number reporting more positive feelings). The MZ twins did not approve of their cotwins' choices significantly more than did the DZ twins" (Lykken & Tellegen, 1993, p. 63).

Thus, recalling when they first met the person with whom their identical twin had fallen in love and proposed to marry, our MZ twins produced a distribution of reactions that was about what one would expect had we asked them how they felt about the spouse of their next-door neighbor. Before concluding, however, that one's choice of mate is wholly unrelated either to one's genes or one's upbringing, we need to consider an alternative hypothesis. The relationship between, especially MZ, cotwins is usually quite close. Is it possible that those twins who say that they regarded their cotwins' fiancée with an indifferent or a jaundiced eye were actually looking at that person as a rival for their twin's affection?

This idea would not explain why none of the 46 MZ twins in our sample whose cotwin had married a twin had formed a relationship with that spouse's twin. Nevertheless, we sent similar questionnaires to the nontwin spouses of twins, asking, in the case of MZ spouses, how they felt about the near-clone of their beloved when they first met him or her. The results were the same as before, a distribution ranging from "I could have fallen for that person myself" to "I would rather have stayed single than marry that person" and centered on indifference. The husbands of the female MZ twins were somewhat inclined toward a positive reaction to their lover's clone, but this can probably be attributed to the well-established finding that, in many different cultures, men attach more importance to physical appearance than do women (Buss, 1989). Because these husbands found their lovers to be physically attractive, they would be likely to react to their lovers' MZ cotwins in the same way. Yet fully 25% of these husbands actually disliked the cotwin and only 13% said that they "could have fallen for her myself."

These data, based on large and representative samples, strongly support the surprising conclusion indicated earlier: The fact that MZ twins are not biased in favor of their cotwins' choice of mate indicates that mate choice is not generally predictable from the chooser's genetic tendencies nor from the values and traits that twins acquire from their common rearing environment. The fact that the spouses of MZ twins are not generally attracted to the clone of their own choice of mate indicates that mate choice also is not generally predictable from the characteristics of the chosen. Taken together, these facts seem to imply that mate choice is generally unpredictable. It may be, in fact, that whom one falls in love with is determined merely by whom one happens to be standing next to when Cupid's arrow strikes!

Evolutionary psychology provides a plausible explanation for this curious state of affairs. Unlike many species of birds and mammals, the common ancestors of the modern great apes and of ourselves did not pair-bond. Infant chimps can soon cling to their mother's fur as she moves through the pantry of the forest. Their unidentifiable fathers are needed only, in company with the other males, to help protect the troop from outside danger. But, when the early hominids began to produce babies with large brains who were much slower to develop after birth, single motherhood became very chancy. Feeding and protecting those altricial infants during their first few years of life came to require more than just one adult caretaker.

Natural selection had rather quickly to devise a solution to this problem, and pair-bonding, the solution that had already worked so well for loons and foxes, was the one selected. When random mating was gradually replaced by pair-bonding, it became possible for fathers to know their own child and to be especially protective and nurturant toward this agent of their own genetic immortality. But how could pair-bonding be effected? Presumably the glue that bonded the mated pairs together in ancestral times was the same glue that does that job today, infatuation. It seems very likely that our many-great-grandparents fell in love with one another. But we are still left with our original question: If love's choice depends neither on the chooser or the chosen, how is it determined? My colleague, Tellegen, suggested what seems to me to be a plausible, albeit partial, answer.

Goslings and the young of other precocial birds mature quickly and can wander from the nest in all directions soon after hatching. Natural selection has provided the mothers of such chicks with an invaluable assistant – imprinting. Goslings imprint on the first moving and reasonably gooselike object they see once they hatch and then become tied to it by an invisible bond. These bonds enable the mother goose to lead her imprinted brood to food or to safety.

Tellegen's suggestion was that hominid pair-bonding may be similar to imprinting in geese. Goslings do not imprint on their mother because she embodies for them all things lovable; if a neighbor goose, or a gander, or even Konrad Lorenz (1952) happens to be the first large, moving object that they see after hatching, they will follow her or him instead. Similarly, one can become infatuated with almost any person who is enough like one's self to feel comfortable with. Perhaps, like goslings, people become imprinted on almost any such broadly suitable individual simply because that individual is there, at the right time and place, and perhaps also because he or she does something then that mysteriously triggers one's affection. One possible trigger is an indication that one's love might be reciprocated, as in: "I think I could love someone madly, if someone would only love me." Tellegen's hypothesis seems plausible to me but clearly there are mysteries that remain to be investigated.

THE GENETICS OF DIVORCE

Relationships end for a wide variety of reasons. Partners may grow apart rather than together. One partner may prove to be abusive or may become infatuated in a new direction. One or both partners may slide into mental illness or some incapacitating addiction. I have a friend who became infatuated with a girl younger than his own children, divorced his wife, married the girl, and then, when the infatuation lifted after several years, he discovered that his princess was a child with whom he had nothing in common and could not even like. Could an eventuality that takes so many forms and has so many possible causes have genetic roots? Is it possible that Risk for Divorce is like a trait, distributed in some bell-shaped curve across the population, so that each of us possesses it in some degree, and that the strength of that trait might be in part inherited?

Matt McGue and I decided to investigate this problem, using again the middle-aged participants of the Minnesota Twin Registry as our research subjects (McGue & Lykken, 1992). A questionnaire was prepared to assess each twin's marital history as well as that of the respondent's parents, the respondent's current and former spouse, if any, and the marital history also of the parents of the current and former spouses. Completed questionnaires were returned by both members of 1,516 same-sex twin pairs (275 male MZ pairs, 447 female MZ pairs, 288 male DZ pairs, and 506 female DZ pairs) in which both twins had been married at least once (about 7% of the Registry twins had never married). These respondents ranged in age from 34 to 53 years. Some 20.3% of these twins had been divorced at least once, compared to 12.2% of their parents and 14.3% of the parents of the twins' spouses. This lower divorce rate for the parental group reflects both the secular increase in the divorce rate and also the lower divorce rate that is observed for couples who have had children.

Table 4.2. Risk of Divorce for MZ and DZ Twins as a Function of Whether the Cotwin or the Parents Had Ever Divorced.

DZ Twins Cotwin's Status:	Parents Divorce Status (%)		Increase (%)
	Not Divorced	Divorced	
Not Divorced	18.6	26.6	42.0
Divorced	28.8	38.6	45.5
Increase	54.8	45.1	
MZ Twins **Cotwin's Status:**			
Not Divorced	12.1	17.6	45.5
Divorced	43.2	53.1	22.9
Increase	257.0	201.7	

We found first that risk for divorce increased by about 50% if either the twin's or the spouse's parents had ever been divorced. Moreover, these parental contributions were independent and additive; the risk that the twin's marriage will end in divorce goes up the same amount if the spouse's parents were divorced, whether or not the twin's own parents were divorced. Secondly, we found that the risk of divorce of a DZ twin increases by the same amount (about 50%) if the DZ cotwin has divorced as if the twin's parents have divorced. As shown in Table 4.2, the increase in risk for DZ twins is about the same whether the cotwin or the parents have divorced. Moreover, these effects also are additive, with the risk going up about 44% if the parents divorced and then up another 50% if the cotwin divorces.

Finally, we found that the risk of divorce for an MZ twin increases by fully 250% if the MZ cotwin has gone through a divorce! Table 4.2 shows that, if the cotwin is still married, parental divorce increases the risk for the target twin about 45% for both MZ and DZ twins. But if the MZ cotwin is divorced, then divorce of the parents increases risk only about half as much, because it provides less new information. The cotwin's experience tells us that someone with the genome of the target twin was involved in a divorce, but was it the cotwin's genome or the spouse's genome (or both) that led to that result? The fact that the twins' parents got divorced increases the probability that it was the cotwin's genome (identical to the target's), rather than the spouse's,

Table 4.3. Data from the Minnesota Study of Twins Separated in Infancy and Reared Apart.

	MZA Pairs	DZA Pairs
Number of pairs where both had married	57	48
Pairs concordant for no divorce	36	20
Pairs concordant for divorce	10	5
Pairs discordant for divorce	11	23
Risk if cotwin not divorced	11/(72 + 11) = 13%	23/(40 + 23) = 37%
Risk if cotwin is divorced	20/(20 + 11) = 65%	10/(10 + 23) = 30%

that led to the breakup of the cotwin's marriage. McGue and I argued that these data obviously show that divorce risk is very strongly genetic in origin. Like crime, divorce is heterogeneous; people get divorced for many different reasons, but most of them involve traits of temperament – impulsiveness, aggression, danger-seeking, and so on – all traits that themselves have strong genetic roots.

But a clever radical environmentalist could easily generate a different post hoc interpretation. If I am having problems in my marriage, as everyone does from time to time, then if my parents had solved *their* problems by divorce, that option might seem more plausible and acceptable to me. If my DZ cotwin or sibling had gone through a divorce, then once again my resistance to marriage dissolution might be weakened. And everyone knows how close MZ twins tend to be, how they expect to react the way their cotwin does, to like the same movies or vacations, and so on. Surely it is not surprising that my inclination toward any given course of action will be considerably increased if my MZ cotwin has made a similar choice. Could it be that Matt and I were premature in claiming we had demonstrated a genetic basis for risk for divorce?

Since the McGue and Lykken paper was published, T. J. Bouchard, Jr., has allowed us to analyze the marital status of his large sample of twins who were separated in infancy and reared apart (Bouchard et al., 1990). These people were unacquainted with their biological parents or with their cotwins when they first married and when they first split, if they did. In considering the results, shown in Table 4.3, it is interesting to imagine that, unbeknown to you, you have an MZA or reared-apart twin out there somewhere, whom you've never met (it is possible)! That twin was married and may, or may not, have also been divorced and the data show that whether he or she did or did not divorce might make a considerable difference in the risk we must predict for your own marriage.

Among the 57 MZA pairs in the Bouchard sample, where both twins had married, if the cotwin had never divorced, the risk for the target twin's marriage was only about 13%. **But,** if the cotwin *had* divorced, then that risk leaps up to 65%. The corresponding data for the 48 pairs of DZA twins were 37% and 30%, a trivial difference and in the "wrong" direction. These data do not fit the environmentalist conjecture but they do not agree with McGue and Lykken either. These data seem to indicate that risk for divorce is an emergenic trait (Lykken, 1982; Lykken, Bouchard, McGue, & Tellegen, 1992), that it is strongly genetic but also configural so that it runs weakly if at all in families.

We can reconcile these results with those of McGue and Lykken by acknowledging that there is in fact considerable family influence on risk of divorce and that this explains the effect of parental or sibling divorce. Behavior geneticists have been insisting for some time that it is very hard to find *any* evidence for a significant effect of shared family environment. But if parental or sibling divorce raises one's own risk of divorce by 50% – and if this is unlikely to be due to shared genes, since divorce risk seems to be emergenic – then that is assuredly a significant shared-family effect. It would be interesting to collect divorce data on adoptees. Suppose your divorce risk goes up substantially if your adoptive parents divorced while you are growing up, or if your unrelated, adoptive sibling gets divorced later on – that would clinch the argument for a strong shared-environment effect.

What would be left to explain is why the risk for MZA twin marriages is more strongly predictable from the fate of the reared-apart cotwin even than it is for twins reared together. For MZ twins reared together, the risk goes from 12% to 45% when the cotwin divorces while, for MZA twins, it goes from 13% to 65%. This difference at the high end may not be statistically significant, but it does make sense. MZ twins reared together need to learn to differentiate themselves from one another. They develop from necessity the ability to see themselves as individuals, not bound to follow one another's path. We know of a pair of male MZs, for example, who were so similar as to be uncanny. They were attending a small Lutheran college in Iowa during the Vietnam War when the parents received simultaneous letters from each of them, a surprise to the parents because these twins usually wrote a joint letter. The first letter said: "I've been thinking that it's time for me to learn how to get along on my own, so I've decided to enlist in the Marines." The second letter said: "Billy and I can't do everything together all our lives, so I've decided to enlist in the Marines." When they discovered that they both had made the same decision, the twins flipped a coin to see who would go first and who would wait three months so that they would not end up in the same company.

Your divorce risk will go from about 13% to about 65% if your MZA cotwin turns out to have divorced, a stronger effect than if you and your twin had been reared together, because you have never practiced trying to be independent of or different from your cotwin and you therefore are inclined to let your genetic steersman make your decisions for you.

WHAT IS ONE TO DO?

So relationships begin with the blind unpredictability of infatuation and they end with the apparent biological inevitability of genetic determination. This is a bleak picture indeed. Yet in truth it is not quite so bleak as it appears at first glance. This nihilistic notion of biological determinism is probably the most dispiriting; let us examine that dark question more closely and see if we can find a way to let a little sunlight in.

If Your MZ Twin Gets Divorced, Is Your Own Marriage Doomed?

Do one's genes determine one's mind, and therefore one's behavior, in the same biological and ineluctable way that they determine one's height or the five fingers on one's hand? I have considered this question in another place, beginning as follows:

We cannot yet begin to trace the many steps that intervene between the protein-making activities in which the genes are directly engaged and their ultimate influence upon individual differences in complex psychological traits. We assume that behavioral differences are associated with nervous system differences. Some of the latter undoubtedly are "hard-wired" biological differences. We can imagine, for example, that some brains work faster or more consistently than others or that the inhibitory mechanisms that enable focused concentration are biologically stronger or more reliable in some brains than in others. It is probable that the brain mechanisms responsible for the feelings of happiness and satisfaction are more easily activated in some people than in others and that the same thing is true of those mechanisms involved in the negative emotions that inhibit well-being. But surely many of the brain differences that account for differences in personality, interests, and attitudes are differences in the "software," and are the result of learning and experience. Yet, if nurture or experience is the proximal cause of individual differences in these traits, how can one explain the strong association between these differences and genetic variation (i.e., nature)? (Lykken, 1999, pp. 52–53)

Psychologists for too long have thought about this problem in terms of the misleading formula "Nature *vs.* Nurture," which implies that, for example, your personality is *either* shaped (somehow) directly by your genes, *or* it is fashioned by your experience through learning. A much more accurate formula would be "Nature *via* Nurture" because, in spite of our still great ignorance about how the genes create the brain, we can be confident that the ways in which the genes affect the mind are largely indirect, by influencing the kinds of experiences we tend to have, and the kinds of environments that we seek out.

One sees this in the nursery where responsive, happy infants elicit from the best of parents different responses than do fretful, unresponsive babies. The toddler who, at 2 or 3, is exploring, climbing, falling down, knocking things over, pulling things out, has very different experiences and elicits different reactions from his caretakers than does her less adventurous, more sedentary sibling. In the neighborhood and at school, children with different appearance and especially different inherent temperaments evoke different responses from their peers, teachers, and other adults. In pace with the child's mobility and freedom, he or she can seek out environments that are compatible with his or her interests and temperament. We, all of us, not only learn from our experiences but also choose them, or, in some cases, they choose us.

Thus, what we become depends in large measure on what we have experienced, just as the radical environmentalists have always said. But what we experience depends, also in large measure, upon what we are like genetically, upon how we appear, how we react, and on what kinds of companions and what sorts of environments we innately tend to gravitate toward. But there is a world of difference between habit patterns acquired through experience, however much those experiences are biased or fomented by genetic inclination, and hard-wired instincts that are mysteriously but biologically determined like the web-building instincts of the barn spider. Your child's innate temperament may incline him to resist when you tell him to stop doing this or start doing that. If you reward him for resisting by backing off, by not taking the trouble to enforce your injunction, then he may learn to respond coercively to any interference with his free will and autonomy, and his risk of divorce, once he is grown, may be significantly increased. If you instead take the trouble to consistently ensure obedience to your instruction, and to let the child know that compliance is both admirable and lovable, then he will learn a different lesson. If your own innate tendency, when your mate disappoints or offends you, is to stay mad until he or she sees the error of his or her ways and apologizes, then your own risk for divorce may become dangerously high – that is, if you habitually give in to this tendency.

We each of us have our own genetic steersman and, if we let him steer our course according to his lights, then we shall reach whatever destination can be predicted from the careers of our four grandparents. But the genetic steersman usually can be resisted, sometimes countermanded altogether. If your mate offends or disappoints you then, if you just bite your tongue and let it go, nine times out of ten it will no longer seem important by next morning or next week. Sometimes, with mates as with your offspring, it is necessary to put your foot down but – with mates more than with offspring – it is often best to let it go. Your genetic steersman is not always wrong, but he's not always right either, and it is your life, after all.

Learning that you have a genetic risk for marriage failure is like learning the same thing about your chances of acquiring heart disease or cancer. In all three cases, a sensible person will take steps to counteract or minimize the risk. If you are by nature an impulsive risk-taker, then one hopes that you take care to monitor yourself while driving in traffic. Those same traits contribute to risk of divorce and therefore you should stay alert, when interacting with an attractive stranger at a party, for example. Your genetic steersman is unlikely to apply the brakes, so you must accept that responsibility yourself. If experience tells you that your steersman will probably dominate in these instances, then you can avoid divorce by not forming a serious relationship in the first place.

If Love Is Blind, Can One Avoid the Rocks?

Suppose one has drawn up a carefully considered list of the attributes one wishes in a spouse. The evidence indicates that, when love's arrow strikes, the elf that shot that arrow will not have consulted one's list. What one can do, however, is to try to limit one's associates to the kinds of people who at least roughly meet that list's criteria. Then the person one is standing next to when the arrow strikes will be easier to cleave to when the delirium abates. At the singles bar, however, one is taking a real gamble.

If, from the onset of infatuation until its all-too-soon conclusion, one pays attention only to the rockets and the bells, then one may one day awake to find that one is living with a stranger. Infatuation is like a three-year trial period in which the two apprentices are expected to learn the business, to learn to live together amicably, and to really get to know and value one another. Many psychotherapists discover that, by getting to know their patient intimately, they discover and can admire the unique and extraordinary complexity of even damaged human beings. By really trying to get to know one's mate, the differences as well as the similarities, the weaknesses as well as the strengths, I think one maximizes the chances for romance to grow into respect and for infatuation to mature into a partnership of enduring deep affection.

I have lived in the house in which I write these words for more than 30 years. My wife and I have made some changes, corrected some defects. The house still is not perfect but it is *our* house, full of our shared memories; we are accustomed to it and we are comfortable here. I am more important to my wife than any house, but the analogy is useful. She has corrected some of my defects and accommodated to the others. Her roots have intertwined with mine. We share many interests and attitudes, but we have learned to respect each other's rights to disagree. We are independent entities, but we are clearly partners in living. "The pillars of the temple stand apart, yet they quiver to the same music."

THE PURPOSE OF RELATIONSHIPS

The reason that we humans seek and form romantic relationships is that our early ancestors acquired through natural selection the tendency to pair-bond. And they acquired that tendency in order to maximize the chances that the offspring of their mating would survive to become productive members of their band or tribe and pass along their genes unto succeeding generations. *Children* are the raison d'être of human romantic relationships. When a love relationship produces children but then breaks down before those children have matured, I think that a crime has been committed against society at large but also and especially against those children. John Stuart Mill, that great liberal, thought so too:

The fact itself, of causing the existence of a human being, is one of the most responsible actions in the range of human life. To undertake this responsibility

– to bestow a life which may be either a curse or a blessing – unless the being on whom it is to be bestowed will have at least ordinary chances of a desirable existence, is a crime against that being. (*On Liberty*, p. 124)

In spite of recent and much publicized decreases, the violent crime rate in the United States now is four times what it was in 1960. Other social pathologies, including school drop outs, teen-age pregnancy, child abuse, teen-age runaways, juvenile delinquency, and also single-parenthood have increased concurrently and in similar degree. More than two-thirds of incarcerated delinquents, of high school dropouts, of teenage runaways, of abused or murdered babies, and of juvenile murderers were reared without their biological fathers. A boy reared without his father is *seven times* more likely to become delinquent than boys reared by both biological parents. I have examined this problem at some length in recent years (Lykken, 1993, 1995a,b, 1996, 1997a,b, 1998, 1999, 2000) and I will not repeat the arguments here. The conclusion that they inexorably lead to is that most crime and social pathology is caused by parental mis-, mal-, or nonfeasance.

Child psychiatrist Jack Westman (1994) has proposed that parents wishing to produce and rear a child should be required first to obtain a license. Similar proposals had been made earlier by Sir Francis Galton in the 19th century, by juvenile and family court judge, Benjamin Lindsey (Lindsey & Evans, 1927), and by Margaret Mead (1974), but Westman's appraisal of the problem is by far the most comprehensive. The requirements for licensure would be similar to those commonly required of persons wishing to adopt someone else's baby. The would-be parents ought to be mature, married to each other, self-supporting, and not incapacitated by mental disease or defect.

The cited papers provide compelling evidence that children reared by the unlicensable parents would (and do) evidence a much higher rate of delinquency and other social pathology than do children born to mature, married, and self-supporting parents. Those who oppose parental licensure should suggest another social policy that would mitigate this metastasizing social problem. For the sake of the children, we have to find a solution. There is much to think about.

REFERENCES

Altemeyer, B. (1996). *The authoritarian specter.* Cambridge, MA: Harvard University Press.

Bouchard, T. J., Jr., & McGue, M. (1981). Familial studies of intelligence: A review. *Science, 212*, 1055–1059.

Bouchard, T. J., Jr., Lykken, D. T., McGue, M. M., Segal, N., & Tellegen, A. (1990). The sources of human psychological differences: The Minnesota Study of Twins Reared Apart. *Science, 250*, 223-228.

Buss, D. M. (1984). Marital assortment for personality dispositions: Assessment with three different data systems. *Behavior Genetics, 14*, 111–123.

— (1989). Sex differences in human mate preferences: Evolutionary hypotheses tested in 37 cultures. *Behavioral and Brain Sciences, 12*, 1–49.

Caspi, A., Herbener, E. S., & Ozer, D. J. (1992). Shared experiences and the similarity of personalities: A longitudinal study of married couples. *Journal of Personality and Social Psychology, 62*, 281–291.

Fisher, H. (1991). Monogamy, adultery, and divorce in cross-species perspective. In M. H. Robinson & L. Tiger (Eds.), *Man and beast* (pp. 95–126). Washington, DC: Smithsonian Institution Press.

Jensen, A. R. (1978). Genetic and behavioral effects of nonrandom mating. In J. H. F. van Abeelen (Ed.), *Human variation: The biopsychology of age, race, and sex* (pp. 51–105). San Diego: Academic Press.

Lindsey, B., & Evans, W. (1927). *The companionate marriage*. New York: Boni & Liveright.

Lorenz, K. (1952). *King Solomon's ring*. New York: Crowell.

Lykken, D. T. (1982). Research with twins: The concept of emergenesis. Presidential Address, 21st Annual Meetings of the Society for Psychophysiological Research, Washington, DC, 1981; *Psychophysiology, 19*, 361–373.

— (1993). Predicting violence in the violent society. *Applied and Preventive Psychology, 2*, 13–20.

— (1995a). Antisociality equals incompetent parents times difficult genetic temperament. *Behavioral and Brain Sciences, 18*, 563–564.

— (1995b). *The antisocial personalities*. Mahwah, NJ: Erlbaum.

— (1996). Giving children a chance in life. *The Chronicle of Higher Education*, February 6, B1–2.

— (1997a). Incompetent parenting: Its causes and cures. *Child Psychiatry and Human Development, 27*, 129–137.

— (1997b). Factory of crime. *Psychological Inquiry, 8*, 261–270.

— (1998). The case for parental licensure. In T. Millon, E. Simonsen, & M. Birket-Smith (Eds.), *Psychopathy: Antisocial, criminal, and violent behaviors* (pp. 122–143). New York: Guilford Press.

— (1999). *Happiness*. New York: Golden Books.

— (2000). The causes and costs of crime and a controversial cure. *Journal of Personality, 68*, 559–605.

Lykken, D. T., & Tellegen, A. (1993). Is human mating adventitious or the result of lawful choice?: A twin study of mate selection. *Journal of Personality and Social Psychology, 65*, 56–68.

Lykken, D. T., Bouchard, T. J., Jr., McGue, M., & Tellegen, A. (1990). The Minnesota Twin Registry: Some initial findings. *Acta Geneticae Medicae et Gemellologiae, 39*, 35–70.

(1992). Emergenesis: Genetic traits that may not run in families. *American Psychologist, 47,* 1565–1577.

Martin, N. G., Eaves, L. J., Heath, A. C., Jardine, R., Feingold, L. M., & Eysenck, H. J. (1986). Transmission of social attitudes. *Proceedings of the National Academy of Sciences, 83,* 4364–4368.

Mead, M. (1974). Marriage in two steps. In R. E. Winch, & G. B. Spanier (Eds.), *Selected studies in marriage and the family,* 4th ed. (pp. 507–510). New York: Holt, Rinehart & Winston.

McGue, M., & Bouchard, T. J., Jr. (1984). Adjustment of twin data for the effects of age and sex. *Behavior Genetics, 14,* 325–343.

McGue, M., & Lykken, D. T. (1992). Genetic influence on risk of divorce. *Psychological Science, 3,* 368–373.

Murstein, B. I. (1972). Physical attractiveness and marital choice. *Journal of Personality and Social Psychology, 22,* 8–12.

Plomin, R., & DeFries, J. C. (1980). Genetics and intelligence: Recent data. *Intelligence, 4,* 15–24.

Plomin, R., DeFries, J. C., & Roberts, M. K. (1977). Assortative mating by unwed biological parents of adopted children. *Science, 196,* 449–450.

Tellegen, A., & Waller, N. (1994). Exploring personality through test construction: Development of the Multidimensional Personality Questionnaire. In S. R. Briggs & J. M. Cheek (Eds.), *Personality measures: Development and evaluation* (Vol. 1, pp. 133–161). Greenwich, CT: JAI Press.

Vandenberg, S. G. (1972). Assortative mating, or who marries whom? *Behavior Genetics, 2,* 127–157.

Waller, N. G., Kojetin, B. A., Bouchard, T. J., Jr., Lykken, D. T., & Tellegen, A. (1990). Genetic and environmental influences on religious interests, attitudes, and values: A study of twins reared apart and together. *Psychological Science, 1,* 1–5.

Waller, N. G., Lykken, D. T., & Tellegen, A. (1995). Occupational interests, leisure time interests, and personality: Three domains or one? Findings from the Minnesota Twin Registry. In R. Dawes & D. Lubinsky (Eds.), *Assessing individual differences in human behavior: New methods, concepts and findings* (pp. 233–259). Palo Alto, CA: Davies-Black.

Walster, E., & Walster, G. W. (1978). *Love.* Reading, MA: Addison-Wesley.

Westman, J. (1994). *Licensing parents.* New York: Insight Books.

White, G. L. (1980). Physical attractiveness and courtship progress. *Journal of Personality and Social Psychology, 39,* 660–668.

Wright, W. (1998). *Born that way.* New York: Knopf.

PART TWO

BEHAVIORS: THE PROCESSES OF STABILITY AND CHANGE

Relationships, as defined by Robert Hinde (1979), consist of "intermittent interaction between two people, involving interchanges over an extended period of time." This definition highlights the importance of examining the behaviors that comprise social interaction, as well as the cognitive and emotional processes that underlie and give meaning to these behaviors. The chapters in this section explore processes involved in interaction between relationship partners and the effects of these processes. Although often bypassed by researchers who instead focus on partners' self-reported affects and cognitions, behavior is nevertheless the linchpin of the relational system because it is through the processes of interacting and communicating that individuals *relate* to each other. Communication, one class of interaction behavior with special importance for ongoing relationships, is emphasized in several chapters. As readers will see, although all communication is behavior, not all behavior involves communication.

In the first chapter, Roloff and Johnson offer a new twist on an oft-studied behavior: arguing. They begin by noting that although researchers typically treat couples' arguments as limited in scope and duration, many arguments reoccur and may extend over lengthy intervals. These extended conflict episodes are referred to as "serial arguments." Drawing on previous research to theorize about the antecedents and consequences of serial arguing, Roloff and Johnson lay a foundation for further studies by first defining serial arguments and then explicating their key elements. The authors' careful synthesis of the literature demonstrates the value of examining stability and change in couples' disagreements.

Noller and Feeney next provide a fascinating review of longitudinal studies spanning the early years of marriage. They begin by describing some problems commonly found in longitudinal research and clarifying the potential of such investigations for uncovering patterns of stability and change in relationships. They further use their own findings, as well as those of other researchers, to illuminate links between relationship satisfaction and communication patterns, attachment-related concerns, and perceptions of social support. Noller and Feeney's analysis makes plain the centrality of communication to relationships as well as the inextricable ties between patterns of communication and both cognitive and affective variables.

Research and theory on sacrifice is the focus of Whitton, Stanley, and Markman's chapter. These authors propose a compelling rationale for examining sacrifice in romantic relationships and explore several definitions that have been offered in the literature. They then discuss and explain connections between sacrifice and relationship variables such as stability, commitment, and satisfaction. Their review serves as the foundation for an innovative theoretical framework for studying sacrifice in romantic relationships.

Chiriboga's chapter centers on the role of relationship stability in people's lives. To a cursory reading, research and theory in gerontology and behavioral health seem to support a relatively straightforward conclusion: that increased relationship stability is associated with better physical and mental well-being. However, Chiriboga's in-depth analysis, bolstered by data from a longitudinal study of normative transitions, shows that this association is considerably more complex and multifaceted than it initially appears. He suggests that stability and change have different implications for individuals and the relationships in which they participate, depending on the context and partners' desires.

Warner's chapter takes a methodological bent to illustrate that the techniques researchers use to examine individuals' and couples' behavior influence the types of conclusions that may be drawn from a study. Warner focuses on the utility of microanalytic methods for understanding stability and change, showing that the microanalytic "breakdown" of interactive behavior offers potentially telling insights into social contexts and personal relationships. To provide readers with a notion of the conceptual terrain associated with microanalytic techniques, Warner reviews existing literature and discusses some of the controversies associated with the diverse ways that researchers define social behavior patterns. She then goes on to describe how choices made in collecting and analyzing microanalytic data (e.g., participant characteristics, the particular context examined) may affect not only the utility of a study, but also the findings themselves.

In the final chapter of this section, Rogge and Bradbury develop a comprehensive framework for understanding change in relationships. They note that traditional analyses emphasize *how* couples change. Rogge and Bradbury's framework expands this traditional focus to three sets of questions. First, who changes over time? Examining issues associated with this question provides a basis for discussing risk factors and moderating variables for change. Second, what changes in relationships? The concerns raised by this question suggest the need to broaden the list of outcome and process variables typically used in marital research. Third, when does change take place? Asking this question promotes a much-needed developmental view of relationships. Rogge and Bradbury's multifaceted perspective provides a suitable coda for this section in raising several important questions for all who are interested in relational stability and change.

REFERENCE

Hinde, R. A. (1979). *Toward understanding relationships*. London: Academic Press.

CHAPTER FIVE

Serial Arguing over the Relational Life Course
Antecedents and Consequences

Michael E. Roloff and Kristen Linnea Johnson

Individuals who believe that disagreements are healthy and resolvable are more satisfied with their relationships than are those who do not have such a perspective (Crohan, 1992). Unfortunately, remaining optimistic can be difficult. Marital arguing is linked to negative moods (Bolger, DeLongis, Kessler, & Schilling, 1989) and marital instability (McGonagle, Kessler, & Gotlib, 1993). Because arguing is an inevitable part of intimate relationships, researchers have investigated how individuals might conduct their disagreements so as to avoid negative by-products. Although research provides useful insights, the methods typically employed yield a restricted view of arguing. With the development of sophisticated methods for studying interaction, researchers have increasingly focused their attention on the behaviors that occur during an argumentative encounter. Often couples enact an argument that is recorded, coded, and statistically scrutinized for patterns. This methodology affords a rigorous way to identify the behaviors occurring during an encounter, but the observed pattern could be limited to the specific interaction that was analyzed. In particular, focusing on a single argumentative encounter may provide little information about the developmental course of the disagreement (i.e., those processes that occurred prior to or after an argumentative episode).

Although treating arguments as though they are of limited duration accurately characterizes some disagreements, this approach does not capture the essence of others. Relational disagreements about a given

Address correspondence to Michael E. Roloff, Department of Communication Studies, Northwestern University, 1881 Sheridan Rd., Evanston, IL 60208. (847) 491-5834. E-mail address: m-roloff@nwu.edu. Or address to Kristen Linnea Johnson, Andersen Consulting, Houston, TX 77024. (713) 837-2067. E-mail address: kristen.l.johnson@ac.com.

issue can extend beyond single encounters (Benoit & Benoit, 1987). When this is the case, relational partners engage in serial arguing during which their argumentative episodes about a given issue reoccur and are linked (Trapp & Hoff, 1985). Repeated arguments can have negative consequences for both individuals and relationships. Although individuals become less emotionally reactive to many ongoing stressors, spouses report that their mood becomes significantly worse as an argument extends over several days (Bolger et al., 1989), and frequent arguing about relational power is linked to declining satisfaction (Kurdek, 1994) with the relationship.

Unfortunately, the underlying processes of serial arguing have not been fully explicated. To fill this void, we offer a framework from which to understand serial arguing. We first explicate the construct and then discuss its antecedents and effects.

THE NATURE OF SERIAL ARGUING

Serial arguing involves argumentative episodes focused on a given issue that occur at least twice. Therefore, serial arguing has three key elements: argumentative episodes, issue-focus, and reoccurrence.

Argumentative Episodes

Jacobs and Jackson (1981) conceive of an argument as the "disagreement-relevant expansion of speech acts" (p. 122). An argument occurs when conversationalists withhold desired speech acts from each other and instead, engage in acts that are not preferred. Instead of agreeing with an expressed complaint, the perpetrator may choose to challenge its veracity. Thus, the expression of opposition is the hallmark of having an argument and disagreement is a primary characteristic that individuals believe differentiates their verbal conflicts from nonconflictive interactions (Resick et al., 1981).

Opposition occurs in three segments of an argumentative episode. First, a disagreement begins with a challenge to another's behavior, self-concept, statements, or significant others (Vuchinich, 1987). Individuals sometimes engage in simple negation in which they provide no indication of the basis for the opposition (Vuchinich, 1984). Alternatively, conversationalists may express the basis of their resistance by attacking the truthfulness of each other's position or by questioning its appropriateness (Jackson & Jacobs, 1980). Finally, communicators may indirectly negate each other's positions through implication or negative labeling (Vuchinich, 1984). Although necessary, a single challenge is insufficient to start an argument. To be an argument, a second form of opposition must be present; the challenged party must oppose the challenge (Vuchinich, 1987). In his analysis of family quarrels, Vuchinich (1987) found that 64% of the initial oppositional moves were challenged. In the remaining cases, the person who was initially opposed either complied with the challenge or ignored it. Finally, opposition may extend beyond the initial challenge and its counterattack. After an initial challenge sequence, conversationalists may expand the argument by adding new material that is aimed at buttressing their initial positions (Jackson & Jacobs, 1980). Indeed, oppositional moves can be recycled throughout the interchange (Vuchinich, 1986).

The aforementioned analysis suggests that an argumentative episode begins when opposition is initiated and continues until expressed opposition ends. However, that does not mean that the point of disagreement has been resolved. Studies conducted on relational conflict indicate that individuals often end their argumentative episodes without agreement. Benoit and Benoit (1987) found that roughly 40% of the everyday argumentative episodes reported by college students ended when the interactants simply stopped arguing or when one person left the scene. Similarly, Lloyd (1987) discovered that 32% of the disagreements reported by dating couples ended with the partners mutually agreeing to stop the discussion and another 16% ended with one partner leaving the scene or refusing to further discuss the issue. In an observational study of family dinner table quarrels, Vuchinich (1990) reported that 66% ended in a standoff in which the participants implicitly agreed to disagree and moved on to other activities and 2% ended with one party leaving the scene or refusing to argue anymore. In a study of sibling conflicts, Raffaelli (1992) found that 37% of the quarrels ended without agreement, and Montemayor and Hanson (1985) found that adolescents reported that 50% of their arguments with parents or siblings ended with the parties withdrawing from the interaction without resolving the issue.

If argumentative episodes end without resolution, they may reoccur. Indeed, almost half of the college students in Benoit and Benoit's (1987) research reported that they had the same argument with the same person fairly often. This implies that individuals can identify a specific issue upon which recurring argumentative episodes are focused.

Issue-Focus

Because serial arguing is focused on a particular issue, we must understand the nature of an issue. An issue is an event, object, behavior, or concept about which individuals hope that they can bring their viewpoints and/or behavior into alignment. One's understanding of an issue is affected by how broadly it is defined. At their broadest, issues can be construed as general areas of conflict. For example, Kurdek (1994) asked gay, lesbian, and heterosexual newlyweds to indicate how frequently they argued with their partners about relational issues. A factor analysis yielded the following conflict areas: (a) power, (b) social issues, (c) personal flaws, (d) distrust, (e) intimacy, and (f) personal distance. Kurdek reasoned that power and intimacy are the areas of greatest interdependency (one partner's outcomes are heavily influenced by the other partner) and conflict about them should be especially common and problematic. Indeed, disagreements about power and intimacy were the most frequent and damaging conflict areas across all types of relationships.

Although conceiving of issues as broadly defined clusters of topics has merit, such an approach ignores important variation among instances within each of the clusters. For example, asking parents how often they argue about their children does not highlight which of many aspects of parenting is the focus of the ongoing disagreement. In a study of parental conflict between custodial parents and the partners from whom they were separated, Schaeffer (1989) focused on four different types of interparent conflict: (a) where the children should live, (b) how they should be raised, (c) frequency of visitations, and (d) discipline. On average, disagreements were more frequent for the last three issues than for the first one, but the frequency of disagreements about living arrangements, visitation, and discipline had a more negative impact on the friendliness of the parental relationship than did the frequency of disagreement about child rearing.

Furthermore, using broad-based categories overlooks subissues that are associated with an issue that may be especially important. For example, dating couples report that they often have serial arguments about a specific behavior that violated an expectation (Johnson & Roloff, 1998). In such cases, they might argue about whether or not the behavior in question actually occurred, who is responsible for the problem, how much harm resulted from the behavior, or how to resolve the issue. Two individuals might disagree on any or all of these

Serial Arguing

subissues. For example, Johnson and Roloff (2000b) found that the person who typically initiated an episode of a serial argument was more likely than those who were the targets to believe that the issue required urgent action. With increasing frequency of episodes, targets became more pessimistic that the issue could be resolved, whereas initiators became somewhat more optimistic.

Unfortunately, research does not inform us as to the best way to understand the issues involved in serial arguing. Using open-ended questions, we have asked individuals to describe the issue of their serial arguments (Johnson & Roloff, 1998). Their responses vary in the level of abstraction (e.g., power, cigarette smoking). In part, this may reflect genuine differences in how individuals conceive of relational problems. For some, an issue may be an isolated behavior (e.g., not listening), but for others, an issue constitutes a label that implies a cluster of similar but unspecified behaviors (e.g., insensitivity implies not listening, being critical). Perhaps in the early stages of serial arguing, the issue is tied to a specific action, but as the disagreement continues, it is relabeled to include other similar actions. Indeed, the reoccurring nature of a serial argument could cause a variety of argumentative features to change.

Reoccurrence

Over time, serial arguments may vary in pattern, form, and participant roles.

Pattern

Pattern refers to the amount of time that separates argumentative encounters. Many serial arguments are composed of dispersed clusters of argumentative episodes (i.e., several episodes occurring within a short time frame, but the clusters of episodes are dispersed over a larger unit of time). For example, Trapp and Hoff (1985) reported a husband and wife who characterized their serial argument as short, 3- to 5-minute episodes dispersed over several days, and two friends who described a serial argument in which short clusters occurred over two and a half months. This pattern may reflect attempts to manage the disruption resulting from repeated arguing. If unchecked, serial arguing could become all consuming and detract from other activities. For example, based on observations of family quarrels, Vuchinich (1986) argued that individuals follow a conversational rule that attenuates the number of speaking turns involved in a given argument. By keeping an argument brief, individuals can focus their attention on other important activities and also may reduce the likelihood of conflict escalation. Indeed, Trapp and Hoff (1985) observed that individuals involved in an argumentative episode often become more verbally aggressive as the episode continues and after the episode "flares up," the interactants disengage so as to "cool off." After the partners calm down, they often reengage each other about the issue. Trapp and Hoff (1985) noted that this pattern of "flare up, and cool off, try again" may occur a number of times.

This attenuation principle may also limit the cluster of episodes that occur within a given time unit. Although a given argumentative episode ends when the individuals quit talking with each other about the issue, relational partners may continue to experience the episode after the discussion is over. After a conflict, individuals often spend considerable time mulling about what had transpired (Cloven & Roloff, 1991) and often replay the negative aspects of the conflict in their minds (Zagacki, Edwards, & Honeycutt, 1992). Such cognitive activity does not seem to help individuals to better understand the dispute and actually seems to make them feel worse (Cloven & Roloff, 1991). Indeed, the extent to which individuals mentally replay an episode of serial argument is positively correlated with believing that the dispute will never be resolved (Johnson & Roloff, 1998). Should such thoughts become intrusive, they could negatively impact other areas of the partners' lives. Hence, individuals may be motivated to bring a cluster of episodes to an end with the hope of returning to "normalcy."

Although individuals may close off a cluster of episodes, the issue may emerge at some later point and another cluster of episodes may be enacted. Because the issue is left unresolved, the conditions that led to the argument may remain unchanged and may reoccur. Indeed, individuals report that the onset of an episode of serial arguing can be predicted from situational cues and a partner's transient mood (Johnson & Roloff, 1998). If so, then the time interval between clusters will depend upon how soon the provoking situational cue or mood reemerges.

Although we believe that most serial arguments follow a pattern of dispersed clusters, there may be great variation with regard to the form of the clusters.

Form

Form refers to the content of the communication occurring across episodes. Although serial arguments are focused on a single issue across episodes, the specific content of each episode could vary. At least three forms may be enacted. The first reflects stagnation as relational partners repeat similar statements with sufficient frequency across episodes that their comments seem predictable. Some individuals in dating relationships report that they can predict what they and their partners will say in an episode (Johnson & Roloff, 1998) and some reconstruct what they believe to be a script of a typical episode (Johnson & Roloff, 2000a). Although research does not verify whether the speech acts occurring during argumentative episodes match those in the cognitive script, it is likely that repetitive statements do occur and they cause relational partners to become pessimistic about whether the argument can be resolved (Johnson & Roloff, 1998).

Second, relational partners may escalate their argument across episodes through issue expansion. Kelley (1979) speculated that conflict escalation results from expanding the focus of an argument from a specific undesirable behavior to the underlying dispositions that produced the action. During initial episodes, complaints may be tied to a specific instance. However, should one encounter resistance or if the person remains noncompliant after promising to change, argumentative episodes become focused on the target's character rather than on the specific behavior. Although such a shift could reflect the greater tendency of complainers than targets to analyze the problem (Sagrestano, Christensen, & Heavey, 1998), it also could be an attempt by complainers to buttress the legitimacy of their claims by citing multiple instances of a provocation (Kelley, 1979). Regardless of the motive, the person who is complained against may respond by defending his or her character or by pointing out that the complainer shares responsibility for the problematic behavior. Moreover, the target may broaden the issue by pointing out a deficiency in the complainer's behavior or character. By countercomplaining (Gottman, Markman, & Notarius, 1977), the target may shift the issue from his or her own alleged deficiencies to those of the partner. However, the self-reported use of countercomplaining during argumentative episodes is negatively related to believing that a serial argument can ever be resolved (Johnson & Roloff, 1998).

Although our analysis implies that issue expansion is an undesirable aspect of serial arguing, it may not always be. To resolve an issue, individuals may need to discuss a variety of topics. Hence, a third form of a serial argument may reflect an exploratory discussion of many aspects of a particular issue as individuals try to find a mutually acceptable solution. In such cases, rather than escalating the conflict through character attacks, individuals try to stay focused on developing a solution. Indeed, the degree to which individuals report that their typical argumentative episode involves open discussion of feelings, attempts to understand each other's viewpoints and consideration of alternative solutions is positively correlated with being optimistic that their serial argument can be resolved (Johnson & Roloff, 1998).

Thus, serial arguments are composed of clusters of linked episodes that are dispersed over time and whose form may vary. The roles the partners play within episodes may also vary over time.

Participant Role

Arguments begin because one person challenges another's behavior and the target of the complaint resists. This implies that there are two roles within a serial argument; the initiator, who desires that his or her partner change, and the resistor, who does not wish to change. Indeed, the accounts of serial arguments indicate that one partner plays the role of initiator who demands change, while the other is the resistor who withdraws or becomes defensive (Johnson & Roloff, 2000b).

However, a person's role in a serial argument may not be static. For example, an individual who is complained against may conclude that his or her behavior is not problematic and instead believe that the initiator's preferred behavior is much worse or that the initiator's complaining is more egregious than is the behavior that is the focus of the original complaint. Consequently, the resistor may initiate argumentative episodes aimed at changing his or her complaining partner. Indeed, Caughlin and Vangelisti (1999) found that the degree to which individuals want their partners to change with regard to a specific issue is positively related to having interactions in which the individuals demand that the partners alter their behavior and the partners withdraw and also to having interactions in which the partners demand that the individuals modify their actions and the individuals withdraw. Although this study was not focused on serial arguing, it could indicate that on a given issue, the argumentative role that a person plays shifts across episodes.

We now explore the antecedents and consequences of serial arguing through the life course of a relationship.

SERIAL ARGUING ACROSS THE LIFE COURSE OF A RELATIONSHIP

Our perspective views serial arguing as embedded within a larger negotiation process. Hence, we highlight the interrelationship between negotiation and serial arguing before analyzing antecedents and consequences.

Negotiation

Sawyer and Guetzkow (1965) define negotiation as "a process through which two or more parties – be they individuals, groups, or larger social units – interact in developing potential agreements to provide guidance and regulation in their future behavior" (p. 466). The primary aim of negotiation is to create an agreement that will guide future conduct. These agreements help to establish social order (Strauss, 1978) by filling in the gaps in rules of conduct. While such processes are evident in formal organizations (Strauss, 1978), intimate relationships also evidence negotiated order. Although social rules that guide relationships can be identified (Argyle & Henderson, 1985), they are typically cast in a rather broad fashion that could render problematic attempts to apply them in a given situation. Hence, in order to clarify role expectations and to coordinate their actions, relational partners negotiate what each should do in a given circumstance. In most cases, negotiations occur without incident. Partners make direct requests of one another, which are typically honored (e.g., Witteman & Fitzpatrick, 1986) and many criticisms are accepted without opposition (e.g., Vuchinich, 1987). Thus, the existing social order is maintained and there is little need for arguing.

Although social order often is maintained without incident, changed circumstances may threaten the adequacy of the negotiated order and when they do, individuals attempt to restore a sense of certainty. This implies that the potential for serial arguing should be greatest at times when a relationship is undergoing change. However, change is insufficient to prompt serial arguing. Only when relational partners have fundamentally different interests or views should relational change prompt serial arguing.

Although individuals vary with regard to their tolerance for relational uncertainty, continued serial arguing and the resulting absence of a relatively stable negotiated order could eventually erode relational quality. When individuals are committed to their relationships, they accommodate their partner's negative behavior by remaining loyal and voicing complaints (Rusbult, Verette, Whitney, Slovik, & Lipkus, 1991). At some point, though, protracted arguing may undercut commitment and individuals may become neglectful of the relationship or choose to exit from it. If the issue of disagreement is important to the individuals, then commitment may erode, and even an issue that was initially of minor consequence could become of major importance. Indeed, Steinmetz (1977) found that spouses often fight over "picky, everyday, annoying things" that to an outsider seem of little consequence. However, the degree to which an individual perceives his or her spouse to have irritating and annoying habits predicts divorce within a 12-year span (Amato & Rogers, 1997). As a result, to prevent relational damage, partners may engage in behaviors that serve to attenuate negative by-products resulting from ongoing disagreement.

We believe that relational transitions constitute an important antecedent to serial arguing and that unless controlled, serial arguing could have negative consequences for a relationship.

Antecedents of Serial Arguing

Close relationships inherently involve a degree of interdependency and intimate relationships have higher degrees of interdependency than do less intimate ones. Thus, an intimate's actions, roles, and personality have consequences not only for him- or herself but also for his or her partner. When those consequences are of different valence for each partner, a serial argument can result as individuals attempt to negotiate a new order that will prevent or minimize harm (Braiker & Kelley, 1979). Changing relational circumstances can threaten particular aspects of interdependency and serve as antecedents of serial arguing. We will illustrate our point by briefly examining scholarship focused on conflict during courtship, the transition to marriage, child rearing, and divorce.

Courtship Conflict

Although changing in form over the years, most Americans go through a process of dating or courtship prior to marrying. Based on the retrospective accounts of married couples, as a courting relationship moves toward greater involvement, partners generally engage in more activities together (Surra, 1985), talk more about their relationship (Braiker & Kelley, 1979), and become more in love (Braiker & Kelley, 1979). Conflict also increases as couples move from casual to serious dating but remains stable through engagement to marriage (Braiker & Kelley, 1979). Couples whose relationships ended before marriage report that conflict increased in a linear fashion as they moved from (a) casual dating to being "a couple," (b) being "a couple" to becoming committed to the relationship, and (c) being committed to the relationship to feeling uncertain about wanting to continue it, but that it leveled off after partners became certain that they did not wish to be in the relationship (Lloyd & Cate, 1985). Although the aforementioned studies only included general measures of conflict, it is likely that some involved serial arguments. Johnson and Roloff (1998) found that daters reported that on average they had over two ongoing serial arguments, and Lloyd (1990) reported in a longitudinal study that individuals whose dating relationships ended experienced more ongoing disagreement over a given issue than did those whose relationships continued.

However, none of the aforementioned studies have tied serial arguing to changes in the interdependent nature of the relationship. We believe that it is possible to do so. As dating relationships become more intimate, the amount of joint activity increases. Although engaging in joint activities enhances relational satisfaction and stability in dating relationships, increases in some activity levels can lead to both frequent disagreement and reduced levels of relational satisfaction (Surra & Longstreth, 1990). Specifically, among women, the greater the frequency of sexual intercourse, the greater the reported amount of arguing about the activity and the lower the relational satisfaction. Among men, the greater the amount of joint relational maintenance activity (self-disclosure and nonsexual physical affection), the greater the amount of reported disagreement about the activity and the lower the relational satisfaction. Importantly, these statistical associations remained significant even after controlling for individual and partner preferences for each activity as well as the degree to which the two partners had similar preferences. This implies that disagreements do not always flow directly from different preferences for an activity but instead reflect something about the activity itself. With regard to sexual activity, it is possible that as frequency increases, disagreement could occur over any number of subissues. For example, Long,

Cate, Fehsenfeld, and Williams (1996) found that among the most frequently mentioned subissues were disagreements about (a) the kinds of sexual acts to be performed, (b) who initiates sexual activity, (c) the number of previous sexual partners, (d) one partner not being in the mood for sex, and (e) the rejection of a sexual initiation. The same process could explain why relational maintenance becomes a problem. Part of relational maintenance includes self-disclosure and as relational partners disclose more about themselves, there is greater likelihood that one or both partners discover undesirable things about the other. Indeed, Johnson and Roloff (1998) found that about a third of the serial arguments reported by daters focused on conflicting beliefs and values.

Our analysis suggests that serial arguing during courtship arises from behavioral interdependency but it is possible that it also emerges from issues related to the direction of the relationship. As courtship continues, individuals may actively begin to consider whether or not the relationship might lead to marriage. When broaching this subject, they may find that they have fundamentally different outlooks, and serial arguing may result, which could lead to relational termination. Hill, Rubin, and Peplau (1976) found that 43% of women and 29% of men reported that their dating relationship ended because of different ideas about marriage and over half of men and women reported that the breakup resulted from either party's desire to be independent.

Transition to Marriage

After marriage, serial arguing could change in two ways. First, serial arguing about some issues may become less frequent. Assuming that courtship serves as a screening process, those daters who have intractable arguments should be less like to marry. Furthermore, public commitment to marriage may alleviate some concerns that existed during courtship and especially with regard to sexual activity. For example, Buss (1989) interviewed courting couples and newlyweds about how frequently they upset each other. The following six were less common among newlyweds than among daters: (a) males acting jealous or dependent, (b) females acting neglectful or rejecting, (c) both males and females being unfaithful, (d) both males and females showing sexual interest in the opposite sex, and (e) both males and females being sexually aggressive. However, marrying can create new problems. Some couples will be living together for the first time and may discover incompatible daily routines. Moreover, with the end of courtship, they may pay less attention to each other. All of this could create greater tension and even abusive behavior. Buss found the following problems were reported more frequently by newlyweds than by daters: (a) both male and female moodiness, (b) males being inconsiderate, (c) males appearing disheveled, and (c) both male and female physical and verbal abuse.

Furthermore, as a new marriage progresses, problems may change in priority. In a longitudinal study, Sternberg and Beier (1977) found that the top three topics of marital conflict reported by newlywed husbands were (1) politics, (2) religion, and (3) money, but one year later they were (1) money, (2) politics, and (3) sex. Among newlywed wives, the rank order was (1) friends, (2) politics, and (3) money, but one year later, the order was (1) money, (2) friends, and (3) sex. Two patterns are evident from the rank orders. During a year's time, money became the primary topic of arguing, and disagreement about sex emerged.

Vangelisti and Huston (1994) examined how satisfaction with marital domains differed over a two-year span starting from being a newlywed through to the second anniversary. During that time, satisfaction with finances did not differ, but spouses became less satisfied with the quality of their marital communication, influence over decisions, sex life, personal leisure time, and time spent together as a couple and with friends and family. For newlywed wives, marital happiness was primarily a function of their satisfaction with the time they spent with their husbands and with their family and friends, but at the beginning of the second year, the key predictors were satisfaction with the quality of their marital communication and sex life, and at the beginning of the third year, the critical predictors were satisfaction with marital communication, influence over decision making, and division of household tasks. Marital happiness of newlywed husbands was not significantly related to satisfaction with any of the domains, but at the start of the second year, husbands' happiness was positively related to the quality of marital communication, and influence over decision making, and at the beginning of the third year it was positively related to satisfaction with marital communication quality.

Although complicated, our analysis suggests that the issues of serial arguing change as couples make the transition from courtship to marriage and that some issues become more salient over the first few years of marriage, although their importance may vary across years and by spouse. Thus, we expect ebb and flow with regard to the frequency of clusters of argumentative episodes as well as who might initiate them.

Child Rearing

The introduction of children into a marriage should impact the nature of the interdependency between spouses and therefore the negotiated order. Spouses with children must develop and enact parental roles that are mutually acceptable, and those responsibilities may impact their enactment of spousal roles. Unfortunately, this negotiation is not always easy. Self-reported marital problems with decision making, child rearing, relatives, money, and expression of affection are greater among parents living with preschool and school-age children relative to those whose older children are beginning to or have moved from the house (Swensen, Eskew, & Kohlhepp, 1981). Similarly, cross-sectional studies find that marital satisfaction decreases with the introduction of children and does not start to improve until they begin the process of leaving the home (e.g., Rollins & Cannon, 1974). Marital arguing also seems to increase with the introduction of children. Crohan (1996) found that relative to couples who remained childless, parents experienced more marital conflict in the years after a child was born than they did prior to the birth. Moreover, the frequency of marital arguing decreases as children become older, and the ability to resolve arguments seems to increase, although there is a slight decrease when the child enters adolescence (Steinmetz, 1977).

Although several factors could explain the increase in marital arguing after the introduction of children, one factor is conflict associated with the distribution of housework and child-care responsibilities. Cross-sectional studies indicate that satisfaction with the division of household labor is significantly related to marital arguing and satisfaction is lowest among wives when there are preschool, school-age, or teenage children living in the house relative to when there are no children or the children have moved away (Suitor, 1991). In part, this may arise from mothers performing more child care than they had expected and their husbands doing less than expected (Ruble, Fleming, Hackel, & Stangor, 1988). However, this relationship is complex. When wives are committed to prebirth expectations for a relatively equal division of labor, doing proportionally more child care and housework than expected has a negative effect on marital satisfaction, but among wives who endorse traditional roles, doing proportionally more of the aforementioned than expected increases marital satisfaction (Hackel & Ruble, 1992). In the same vein, MacDermid, Huston, and McHale (1990) found that marital arguing after the birth of a child was greatest among husbands and wives who had traditional sex role attitudes but whose postpartum division of family labor was more equal. If these patterns translate into serial arguing, wives with less traditional sex role orientations may initiate serial arguments when they are doing more child care and housework than expected, but women who have more traditional sex role orientations may actually initiate more serial arguments when they are sharing duties with their husbands.

As noted earlier, the negative by-products associated with having children lessen with time and especially after the children leave the house (Orbuch, House, Mero, & Webster, 1996). However, adult children sometimes return home to live, and when they do, serial arguing could begin anew, but for different reasons. Although parents who have an adult child residing in the house do not report significantly more disagreement than do those who are living with no children at home, within the former households there is a positive correlation between the amount of parent–child disagreement and spousal disagreement (Suitor & Pillemer, 1987). This could reflect parent–child disputes spilling over into the marriage. Although the generational disagreement is not great, the return of an adult child to the parents' house can create parent–child conflict (Clemons & Axelson, 1985). Relative to sons, daughters report more frequent disputes with their parents about significant others, staying out late, and getting along with the family, whereas sons report that disagreements about money and substance use are more common than do daughters (Ward & Spitze, 1996). It is possible that one parent could side with the child against the other parent on any of these issues, which might produce marital discord. Thus, although the return home of an adult child to live might not increase the amount of discord, it could shift the topics of disagreement to those associated with parent–child relations.

Divorce

Some individuals divorce because of conflict. In an analysis of complaints that caused couples to divorce, Kitson and Sussman (1982) found that couples often mentioned joint conflict over gender roles, disagreements over spending and control of money, conflict over the children, and arguing about everything. This implies that couples who are divorcing might experience a linear increase in arguing through the divorce, but that arguing should fall off once the divorce legally reduces their interdependency. However, for some couples, the pattern might be different. For example, some couples may reduce their level of arguing prior to a formal decision to divorce. Courtright, Millar, Rogers, and Bagarozzi (1990) found that among couples going through counseling, those who ultimately divorced were more avoidant and less involved in an argumentative episode than were those who ultimately repaired their marriage. Thus, when relational commitment falls to low levels, partners may decide that continued arguing serves no purpose and they may avoid conflict in anticipation of a formal end to the relationship.

In addition, some divorced couples might continue to argue after the divorce is finalized. A divorce decree might leave intact some aspects of their interdependency, and a divorced couple might still come into contact in social situations. Continued contact could lead to conflict. In a sample of divorced couples, Masheter (1991) found that the overall frequency of postdivorce quarreling was relatively low, but was significantly greater among those who had children than among those who did not. Also, Masheter found that the frequency of quarreling was negatively related to postdivorce well-being, but that attitude toward the spouse was not. In part, the latter may result from individuals who have hostile attitudes toward their former spouses, choose to avoid them, and hence, have no opportunity for arguing (Masheter, 1991). However, former spouses with children have more frequent contact, which paradoxically is positively correlated with both their friendliness and their frequency of arguing (Masheter, 1991). These patterns may reflect differences in couples (former parents who get along vs. those who don't) or may indicate that frequent contact due to children increases arguing about the logistics of child care but also creates a basis for ongoing cooperation that reduces hostility. Regardless, serial arguing may continue even after a marriage has been legally terminated and is likely to be centered in areas of ongoing interdependency.

Our review has been brief but highlights how issues involved in serial arguing might change as a relationship evolves. Now we turn to the consequences of serial arguing.

Relational Consequences

Repetitious arguing could lead to the conclusion that the issue cannot be resolved and it is impossible to restore the negotiated order. As a result, individuals become dissatisfied with their relationship and disengage. However, the vulnerability of a relationship to the harmful side effects of serial arguing may lessen as a relationship matures. First, as relationships develop, partners could become more psychologically, emotionally, and financially invested in them. As such, they become more committed to the continuation of the relationship if only to prevent the loss of their financial assets (cf. Orbuch et al., 1996) and social rewards (e.g., Heaton & Albrecht, 1991). When this is the case, dissatisfaction arising from a serial argument may need to surpass a higher threshold before it threatens a more developed relationship (cf. White & Booth, 1991).

Second, as relationships develop, couples may have fewer important issues about which to argue. Spouses who have been married for a longer time report fewer marital problems (Swensen et al., 1981) and the topics of marital conflicts are less salient (Zietlow & Sillars, 1988) than for those who have been married for a shorter time. Because conflicts over less salient issues are less confrontational and more cordial, older couples may be better able to resolve most issues in a single episode or perhaps leave them permanently unresolved (Zietlow & Sillars, 1988). This does not mean that serial arguments will never occur. Indeed, wives in more established marriages report more difficulty resolving disagreements than do those in younger ones (Vaillant & Vaillant, 1993). Moreover, when discussing a highly salient, unresolved issue, retired couples are more likely to become locked into a mutual confrontational pattern, whereas young and middle-aged couples deescalate such conflicts by engaging in more analytical behavior (Zietlow & Sillars, 1988). Even so, serial arguments in mature relationships may be less frequent and may not harm relational quality.

Third, as relationships develop, partners may learn to avoid the conditions that prompt argumentative episodes. Although individuals in marriages of longer duration report that they are less tolerant of their partner's unpleasant characteristics than are those in younger marriages (Swenson et al., 1981), that does not mean that they confront their partner every time they observe a provocative behavior. Steinmetz (1977) noted that many of the spouses in her study of marital conflict indicated that they had "learned to keep their mouths shut" as their marriage matured. Indeed, partners may agree to declare an ongoing topic taboo as a means of reducing its frequency and harm (cf., Roloff & Ifert, 1998).

Finally, as a relationship matures, individuals may be better able to confront one another in a less harmful manner. Disagreement inherently involves a degree of negative affect, but some couples temper it with positive affect, which serves to deescalate their negative expressions and increase their relational satisfaction and stability (Gottman, Coan, Carrere, & Swanson, 1998). Interestingly, research indicates that during discussion of relational problems, more affection is expressed by older couples as compared to middle-aged couples (Carstensen, Gottman, & Levenson, 1993). This affection may help offset expressed negativity.

Thus, although serial arguing may be common across the life course of a relationship, its nature may change as partners confront new challenges to their negotiated order. Partners' ability to withstand the negative consequences of repeated disagreement may increase as the relationship matures. It is important to note, however, that most of our analysis is speculative. Because so little research has been conducted on serial arguing, we cited studies that did not directly measure repeated disagreement and subsequent research may find them wanting. We also recognize that because of the difficulty of observing ongoing relational disputes, research conducted on serial arguing has employed self-report methodologies that are subject to inaccuracy and bias. Attempts to blend self-reports with behavioral observations of argumentative episodes are necessary. We hope that our essay stimulates interest among researchers on the causes and consequences of serial arguing.

REFERENCES

Amato, P. R., & Rogers, S. J. (1997). A longitudinal study of marital problems and subsequent divorce. *Journal of Marriage and the Family*, 59, 612–624.

Argyle, M., & Henderson, M. (1985). The rules of relationships. In S. Duck & D. Perlman (Eds.), *Understanding personal relationships: An interdisciplinary approach* (pp. 63–84). Thousand Oaks, CA: Sage.

Benoit, W. J., & Benoit, P. J. (1987). Everyday argument practices of naive social actors. In J. W. Wentzel (Ed.), *Argument and critical practices* (pp. 465–473). Annandale, VA: Speech Communication Association.

Bolger, N., DeLongis, A., Kessler, R. C., & Schilling, E. A. (1989). Effects of daily stress on negative mood. *Journal of Personality and Social Psychology, 57,* 808–811.

Braiker, H., & Kelley, H. H. (1979). Conflict in the development of close relationships. In R. L. Burgess. & T. L. Huston (Eds.), *Social exchange in developing relationships* (pp. 135–168). San Diego, CA: Academic Press.

Buss, D. M. (1989). Conflict between the sexes: Strategic interference and evocation of anger and upset. *Journal of Personality and Social Psychology, 56,* 735–747.

Carstensen, L. L., Gottman, J. M., & Levenson, R. W. (1993). *Emotional behavior in long-term marriages.* Manuscript submitted for publication.

Caughlin, J. P., & Vangelisti, A. L. (1999). Desire for change in one's partner as a predictor of the demand/withdraw pattern in marital communication. *Communication Monographs, 66,* 66–89.

Clemens, A. W., & Axelson, L. J. (1985). The not-so-empty nest: The return of the fledgling adult. *Family Relations, 34,* 259–264.

Cloven, D. H., & Roloff, M. E. (1991). Sense-making activities and interpersonal conflict: Communicative cures for the mulling blues. *Western Journal of Speech Communication, 55,* 134–158.

Courtright, J. A., Millar, F. E., Rogers, L. E., & Bagarozzi, D. (1990). Interaction dynamics of relational negotiation: Reconciliation versus termination of distressed relationships. *Western Journal of Speech Communication, 54,* 429–453.

Crohan, S. E. (1992). Marital happiness and spousal consensus on beliefs about marital conflict: A longitudinal investigation. *Journal of Social and Personal Relationships, 9,* 89–102.

(1996). Marital quality and conflict across the transition to parenthood in African American and white couples. *Journal of Marriage and the Family, 58,* 933–944.

Gelles, R. J. (1972). *The violent home: A study of physical aggression between husbands and wives.* Thousand Oaks, CA: Sage.

Gottman, J. M., Coan, J., Carrere, S., & Swanson, C. (1998). Predicting marital happiness and stability from newlywed interactions. *Journal of Marriage and the Family, 60,* 5–22.

Gottman, J. M., Markman, H., & Notarius, C. (1977). The topography of marital conflict: A sequential analysis of verbal and nonverbal behavior. *Journal of Marriage and the Family, 39,* 461–477.

Hackel, L. S., & Ruble, D. N. (1992). Changes in the marital relationship after the first baby is born: Predicting the impact of expectancy disconfirmation. *Journal of Personality and Social Psychology, 62,* 944–957.

Heaton, T. B., & Albrecht, S. L. (1991). Stable unhappy marriages. *Journal of Marriage and the Family, 53,* 747–758.

Hill, C. T., Rubin, Z., & Peplau, L. A. (1976). Breakups before marriage: The end of 103 affairs. *Journal of Social Issues, 32,* 147–168.

Jacobs, S., & Jackson, S. (1981). Argument as a natural category: The routine grounds for arguing in conversation. *Western Journal of Speech Communication, 45,* 118–132.

Jackson, S., & Jacobs, S. (1980). Structure of conversational argument: The pragmatic bases for the enthymeme. *Quarterly Journal of Speech, 66,* 251–265.

Johnson, K. L., & Roloff, M. E. (1998). Serial arguing and relational quality: Determinants and consequences of perceived resolvability. *Communication Research, 25,* 327–343.

— (2000a). Correlates of the perceived resolvability and relational consequences of serial arguing in dating relationships: Argumentative features and the use of coping strategies. *Journal of Social and Personal Relationships, 17,* 677–687.

— (2000b). The influence of argumentative role (initiator vs. resistor) on perceptions of serial argument resolvability and relational harm. *Argumentation, 14,* 1–15.

Kelley, H. H. (1979). *Personal relationships: Their structures and processes.* Hillsdale, NJ: Erlbaum.

Kitson, G. C., & Sussman, M. B. (1982). Marital complaints, demographic characteristics, and symptoms of mental distress in divorce. *Journal of Marriage and the Family, 44,* 87–101.

Kurdek, L. A. (1994). Areas of conflict for gay, lesbian, and heterosexual couples: What couples argue about influences relationship satisfaction. *Journal of Marriage and the Family, 56,* 923–934.

Lloyd, S. A. (1987). Conflict in premarital relationships: Differential perceptions of males and females. *Family Relations, 36,* 290–294.

— (1990). A behavioral self-report technique for assessing conflict in close relationships. *Journal of Social and Personal Relationships, 7,* 265–272.

Lloyd, S. A., & Cate, R. M. (1985). The developmental course of conflict in dissolution of premarital relationships. *Journal of Social and Personal Relationships, 2,* 179–194.

Long, E. C. J., Cate, R. M., Fehsenfeld, D. A., & Williams, K. M. (1996). A longitudinal assessment of a measure of premarital sexual conflict. *Family Relations, 45,* 302–308.

MacDermid, S. M., Huston, T. L., & McHale, S. M. (1990). Changes in marriage associated with the transition to parenthood: Individual differences as a function of sex-role attitudes and changes in the division of household labor. *Journal of Marriage and the Family, 52,* 475–486.

Masheter, C. (1991). Postdivorce relationships between ex-spouses: The roles of attachment and interpersonal conflict. *Journal of Marriage and the Family, 53,* 103–111.

McGonagle, K. A., Kessler, R. C., & Gotlib, I. H. (1993). The effects of marital disagreement style, frequency, and outcome on marital disruption. *Journal of Social and Personal Relationships, 10,* 385–404.

Montemayor, R., & Hanson, E. (1985). A naturalistic view of conflict between adolescents and their parents and siblings. *Journal of Early Adolescence, 5,* 23–30.

Orbuch, T. L., House, J. S., Mero, R. P., & Webster, P. S. (1996). Marital quality over the life course. *Social Psychology Quarterly, 59,* 162–171.

Raffaelli, M. (1992). Sibling conflict in early adolescence. *Journal of Marriage and the Family, 54,* 652–663.

Resick, P. A., Barr, P. K., Sweet, J. J., Kieffer, D. M., Ruby, N. L., & Speigel, D. K. (1981). Perceived and actual discriminators of conflict from accord in marital communication. *The American Journal of Family Therapy, 9*, 58–68.

Rollins, B. C., & Cannon, K. L. (1974). Marital satisfaction over the family life cycle: A reevaluation. *Journal of Marriage and the Family, 36*, 271–282.

Roloff, M. E., & Ifert, D. (1998). Antecedents and consequences of explicit agreements to declare a topic taboo in dating relationships. *Personal Relationships, 5*, 191–206.

Ruble, D. N., Fleming, A. S., Hackel, L. S., & Stangor, C. (1988). Changes in the marital relationship during the transition to first time motherhood: Effects of violated expectations concerning division of household labor. *Journal of Personality and Social Psychology, 55*, 78–87.

Rusbult, C. E., Verette, J., Whitney, G. A., Slovik, L. F., & Lipkus, I. (1991). Accommodation processes in close relationships: Theory and preliminary empirical evidence. *Journal of Personality and Social Psychology, 60*, 53–78.

Sagrestano, L. M., Christensen, A., & Heavey, C. L. (1998). Social influence techniques during marital conflict. *Personal Relationships, 5*, 75–89.

Sawyer, J., & Guetzkow, H. (1965). Bargaining and negotiation in international relations. In H. C. Kelman (Ed.), *International behavior: A social-psychological analysis* (pp. 466–520). New York: Holt, Rinehart and Winston.

Schaeffer, N. C. (1989). The frequency and intensity of parental conflict: Choosing response dimensions. *Journal of Marriage and the Family, 51*, 759–766.

Steinmetz, S. K. (1977). *The cycle of violence: Assertive, aggressive, and abusive family interaction*. New York: Praeger.

Sternberg, D. P., & Beier, E. G. (1977). Changing patterns of conflict. *Journal of Communication, 27*, 97–103.

Strauss, A. (1978). *Negotiations: Varieties, contexts, processes, and social order*. San Francisco, CA: Jossey-Bass.

Suitor, J. J. (1991). Marital quality and satisfaction with the division of household labor across the family life cycle. *Journal of Marriage and the Family, 52*, 221–230.

Suitor, J. J., & Pillemer, K. (1987). The presence of adult children: A source of stress for elderly couples' marriages? *Journal of Marriage and the Family, 49*, 717–725.

Surra, C. A. (1985). Courtship types: Variations in interdependence between partners and social networks. *Journal of Personality and Social Psychology, 49*, 357–375.

Surra, C. A., & Longstreth, M. (1990). Similarity of outcomes, interdependence, and conflict in dating relationships. *Journal of Personality and Social Psychology, 59*, 501–516.

Swensen, C. H., Eskew, R. W., & Kohlhepp, K. A. (1981). Stage of family life cycle, ego development, and the marriage relationship. *Journal of Marriage and the Family, 43*, 841–853.

Trapp, R., & Hoff, N. (1985). A model of serial argument in interpersonal relationships. *Journal of the American Forensic Association, 22*, 1–11.

Vaillant, C. O., & Vaillant, G. E. (1993). Is the U-curve of marital satisfaction an illusion? A 40-year study. *Journal of Marriage and the Family, 55*, 230–239.

Vangelisti, A. L., & Huston, T. L. (1994). Maintaining marital satisfaction and love. In D. J. Canary & L. Stafford (Eds.), *Communication and relational maintenance* (pp. 165–186). San Diego, CA: Academic Press.

Vuchinich, S. (1984). Sequencing and social structure in family conflict. *Social Psychology Quarterly, 47*, 217–234.

——— (1986). On attenuation in verbal family conflict. *Social Psychology Quarterly, 49*, 281–293.

——— (1987). Starting and stopping spontaneous family conflicts. *Journal of Marriage and the Family, 49*, 591–601.

——— (1990). The sequential organization of closing in verbal family conflict. In A. D. Grimshaw (Ed.), *Conflict talk: Sociolinguistic investigations of arguments in conversations* (pp. 118–138). Cambridge: Cambridge University Press.

Ward, R. A., & Spitze, G. (1996). Gender differences in parent–child coresidence experiences. *Journal of Marriage and the Family, 58*, 718–725.

White, L. K., & Booth, A. (1991). Divorce over the life course: The role of marital happiness. *Journal of Family Issues, 12*, 5–21.

Witteman, H., & Fitzpatrick, M. A. (1986). Compliance-gaining in marital interaction: Power bases, processes, and outcomes. *Communication Monographs, 53*, 130–143.

Zagacki, K. S., Edwards, R., & Honeycutt, J. M. (1992). The role of imagery and emotion in imagined interaction. *Communication Quarterly, 40*, 56–68.

Zietlow, P. H., & Sillars, A. L. (1988). Life-stage differences in communication during marital conflict. *Journal of Social and Personal Relationships, 5*, 223–245.

CHAPTER SIX

Communication, Relationship Concerns, and Satisfaction in Early Marriage

Patricia Noller and Judith A. Feeney

Longitudinal studies are undoubtedly critical to understanding the developmental course of marriage (Bradbury, 1998; Karney & Bradbury, 1995; Kurdek, 1998). This type of research can provide a more accurate and sensitive assessment of relationship functioning over time, with each couple being used as their own controls. Further, as Bradbury notes, longitudinal studies "have the potential to *explain* how marriages succeed and fail rather than simply *describe* the differences between couples who are already distressed and those who are not" (p. 3).

Several groups of researchers have carried out longitudinal studies of marriage, focusing primarily on the link between communication and relationship satisfaction. In these studies, however, communication has often been measured at only one point in time, with satisfaction being measured at several other times. A study by Huston and Vangelisti (1991) is an exception to this pattern, as they assessed both socioemotional behaviors and relationship satisfaction at all three waves; however, self- and partner reports were obtained by telephone interview, rather than by observing actual communication patterns. Researchers' claims that communication patterns are stable over time have often been made on the basis of indirect evidence; for example, the extent to which communication at one point in time can predict satisfaction at a later time.

Some longitudinal studies have also been prone to a range of other criticisms, such as not distinguishing between first and second marriages or between childless couples and parents, or failing to analyze

Address correspondence to Patricia Noller, School of Psychology, University of Queensland, Queensland, 4072, Australia. Electronic mail may be sent to *pn@psy.uq.edu.au*.

the data separately for husbands and wives (Karney & Bradbury, 1995; Kurdek, 1998). Most studies have used only self-report measures and only two assessment times, limiting the possibility of detecting complex patterns of change. In several studies, many of the variables measured on the first occasion have not been administered again at subsequent times.

Recently, Karney and Bradbury (1995) reviewed the theories, methods and findings of 115 longitudinal studies of marriage. Based on this review, these researchers suggested improvements to longitudinal research that would provide more definitive answers about the development of marital relationships over time. These suggestions include the need to study couples across the transition to marriage (not just after the marriage), the need to use homogeneous samples (e.g., couples married for a similar length of time), the need to assess all measured variables at all waves of the study, the need to look at the data cross-sectionally as well as longitudinally, and the need to focus on broad inclusive constructs.

LONGITUDINAL EXPLORATION OF THE EARLY YEARS OF MARRIAGE

Longitudinal studies may be particularly important to charting the early stages of marriage, given that marriage can be regarded as a major transition point in couple relationships, especially if the partners have not lived together prior to the marriage. In addition, many marriages end within the first few years, and couples often date the demise of their marriages to problems experienced in the first couple of years (Burns, 1980).

There are two broad issues concerning the early stages of marriage that can be explored particularly effectively using longitudinal designs. First, it is possible to assess the extent of *change in relationship variables* during this formative time. It is important to know, for example, whether conflict patterns generally become more or less destructive after marriage, and whether relationship development is accompanied by increases or decreases in the extent to which couples understand one another and perceive each other's behavior accurately. Second, longitudinal designs allow an exploration of *changing patterns of association* among relationship variables. In particular, it is possible that certain responses to conflict differ in their concurrent and predictive links with relationship satisfaction. For example, the tendency to withdraw from conflict may reduce couples' anxiety about tackling difficult issues as they arise, but increase the potential for further conflict in the long term, because issues are not resolved (Gottman & Krokoff, 1989).

In this chapter we will discuss these two broad issues using data from our own laboratory, as well as from other researchers who have conducted longitudinal studies of marriage. Most of these studies have focused heavily on the links between communication and satisfaction. It is not surprising that this area of research has proved fruitful, given that communication is the means by which couples share thoughts and emotions, make decisions, and resolve problems; that is, communication is at the very heart of any relationship.

Our goal in this chapter, however, is to view marital relationships in a broader context that considers not only couple communication but also partners' more general relationship concerns. Specifically, we want to explore the implications of couples' attachment-related concerns and perceptions of social support for their relationships at this formative stage of marriage. Pierce, Sarason, and Sarason (1990) suggest that relationship events need to be understood in terms of their meanings for the individual, and that these meanings are a product of both intrapersonal and interpersonal contexts. In other words, relationship events are interpreted in the light of the individual's inner working models of self, others, and close relationships (the intrapersonal context), and the quantity and quality of supportive relationships (the interpersonal context). This perspective implies that variables tapping attachment style and perceptions of social support have a great deal of relevance for couple functioning.

Our Own Longitudinal Study

As noted earlier, we will explore patterns of change in relationship variables, using both our own work and the work of other researchers. Given the broad focus of our discussion, our aim is not to provide an exhaustive review of all the available literature, but rather, to present key findings. The main focus in our own work is on a longitudinal study of early marriage, which has provided a comprehensive assessment of relationship processes and outcomes (Feeney, Noller, & Callan, 1994; Noller & Feeney, 1994, 1998; Noller, Feeney, Bonnell, & Callan, 1994). Because this study is quite complex, it is first necessary to provide a brief overview of the methodology employed.

Table 6.1. Summary of Measures.

Construct Assessed	Instrument	Measures
Relationship satisfaction	Quality Marriage Index (Norton, 1983)	Total satisfaction
Quantity and quality of conversation	Marital Communication Inventory (Noller & Feeney, 1994)	Quantity (frequency and initiation of talk) Quality (disclosure, recognition, satisfaction)
Experience of conflict	Marital Communication Inventory	Frequency of conflict
	Communication Patterns Questionnaire (Christensen & Sullaway, 1984)	Positivity, negativity, disengagement, demand– withdraw, destructive process, postconflict distress
	Conflict strategies	Strategies coded from interactions: reason, assertion, support, coercion, manipulation, avoidance
Nonverbal accuracy	Marital Communication Scale (standard content messages)	Accuracy of decoding for positive, negative, and neutral messages
Attachment	15 items derived from Hazan and Shaver (1987)	Comfort with closeness Anxiety over relationships
Social support	Social Support Inventory (Procidano & Heller, 1983)	Support from friends Support from family

Couples were seen on three occasions: 4 to 6 weeks before marriage, 12 months after marriage, and about 21 months after marriage (33 couples completed all phases of the study). Although relationship satisfaction and communication were important foci of the study, we also included measures of broader relational dimensions: attachment and social support (see Table 6.1 for a summary of measures used and variables assessed). Two major aspects of communication were assessed using questionnaires: the quantity and quality of conversations, and the nature of conflict (frequency of conflict, and ways of dealing with conflict). Quantity and quality of conversations were assessed using the Marital Communication Inventory. Quantity scores reflect the amount of talk across 12 different topics, whereas Quality scores reflect the constructiveness of communication processes, as perceived by the couple. Frequency of conflict was assessed in terms of the extent of differences of opinion over the same 12 topic areas, and couples' characteristic ways of dealing with conflict were assessed using the Communication Patterns Questionnaire, which was scored for six scales (see Table 6.1).

Couples also engaged in two interaction tasks. The first task involved couples discussing an issue salient to their relationship, and then identifying all those points at which they were aware of using a particular strategy in dealing with the conflict situation. These responses were transcribed for content analysis, resulting in the identification of three positive and three negative strategies (again, refer to Table 6.1). To assess the extent to which couples understood each other's communications, the second interaction task involved spouses sending each other a set of ambiguous messages, with the listener being asked to indicate which of three possible meanings was intended. Accuracy scores were defined as the number of communications correctly decoded.

CHANGE IN RELATIONSHIP FUNCTIONING OVER TIME

As we noted earlier, the first important issue in the study of early marriage concerns the extent to which relationship variables change systematically over time. Our discussion of this issue will focus on three main areas: change in levels of relationship satisfaction, change in patterns of communication, and change in broader relationship concerns.

Change in Satisfaction

A recent longitudinal study of couples extended over the first six years of marriage (Kurdek, 1998). Kurdek found that, for both husbands and wives, marital satisfaction gradually decreased over the first six years, with the largest change occurring between the first and second years. In another long-term study, Lindahl, Clements, and Markman (1998) studied couples across the first nine years of marriage and found that satisfaction declined over the first three years, before plateauing. Similarly, these researchers found that the intensity of reported problems peaked about three years into the marriage, and then declined. Several other studies have also shown small declines in satisfaction early in marriage, with Leonard and Roberts (1998) showing a decrease over the first year, and Huston and Vangelisti (1991) showing a decrease over the first two years. These findings support the suggestion that the first two to three years of marriage may be critical for the future satisfaction and stability of couple relationships. In our own longitudinal study described above, however, there were no significant changes over time in relationship satisfaction.

Over all, then, research seems to point to declines in satisfaction during the early years of marriage. It is important to note, however, that the declines reported are generally quite small. Further, the lack of significant change over time in our own study is partially consistent with interview data from long-term married couples, showing that it is not unusual for couples to report close, positive relationships throughout their marriage, although not without some ups and downs (Weishaus & Field, 1988).

Change in Communication Patterns

As we noted earlier, communication is critical to the quality of couple relationships. For this reason, it is important to understand how communication develops over the early years of marriage. For example, do couples lose their initial intimacy and enthusiasm for talk? Do differences of opinion get resolved, or do they tend to intensify over time? Do responses to conflict become more constructive, or more embittered?

Quantity and Quality of Communication

The notion that couples in recent marriages spend a considerable amount of time conversing with each other is supported by diary studies, showing that young married couples report spending about 14 hours a week in direct communication with one another (Dickson-Markman & Markman, 1988; Noller & Feeney, 1998). The relevance of couples' day-to-day interactions is underlined by a diary study that showed that happy couples spent more time together than unhappy couples, as well as more time talking, more time discussing personal topics, and less time arguing (Kirchler, 1989). This is an important point, given that many researchers have focused specifically on couples' conflict-centered communication rather than on their general patterns of communication.

In their study of the first two years of marriage, Vangelisti and Huston (1994) found that both husbands and wives became less satisfied with the quality of their communication. However, some of their data collection involved retrospective reports, which may have increased the likelihood of contrast effects. In our own study, which did not rely on retrospective reports, the conversational measures showed no change over time in the quantity of communication, but a gradual increase in quality. That is, spouses tended to report increased levels of disclosure, recognition, and satisfaction for both self and partner, although the differences over time were small. These findings seem to suggest that early marriage may be a time for honing communication skills, at least for couples who are happy with their relationships.

Frequency of Conflict
According to Leonard and Roberts (1998), the early years of marriage may be the period in which marital conflict is most frequent and intense. This argument is supported indirectly by the finding that levels of aggression are higher in younger than in older spouses (Suitor, Pillemer, & Straus, 1990). In further support of this argument, several researchers have reported substantial rates of interpersonal aggression at the premarital stage, and similar levels continuing throughout the first year of marriage (Leonard & Roberts, 1998; O'Leary et al., 1989). A study by Huston and Houts (1998) also showed relatively high levels of conflict in the first two years of marriage, but unlike the other studies just mentioned, suggested an increase in conflict from courtship to marriage. Finally, in our own longitudinal study, we found no evidence of change over time in the reported frequency of conflict across the diverse topics of discussion canvassed.

The relative stability in frequency of conflict reported by most researchers seems to indicate that the conflicts and differences of opinion reported after marriage are generally present beforehand. Further, given that studies have frequently relied on self-report measures, it is clear that couples are more or less aware of those differences. This point is particularly interesting given the suggestion that couples enter marriage with unrealistically positive views of their relationship (Vangelisti & Huston, 1994). It appears that partners may be reasonably realistic in terms of their awareness of differences between them but less realistic in terms of their ability to resolve these differences. This point brings us to the next question, concerning couples' ways of dealing with conflict situations.

Dealing with Conflict

Responses to conflict have been assessed in various ways. For example, Huston and Houts (1998) assessed spouses' negativity toward each other in terms of specific partner behaviors, such as criticizing and dominating. They found that the frequency of these behaviors remained relatively stable and occurred at generally low levels during the first two years of marriage. In their longitudinal study, Lindahl et al. (1998) used two approaches to assess responses to conflict: a summary measure of negative behaviors that was obtained at each point in the study, and measures of withdrawal and verbal aggression that were first included when the couples had been married for three years. These researchers found that withdrawal and verbal aggression declined from that three-year mark, but that the overall level of negative communication increased over time. This increase in negativity occurred, however, in the context of a parallel increase in positive (supportive) communication. Hence, there is some evidence that, with time, partners become more willing to vocalize complaints, but also more able to resolve disagreements constructively.

There was no change over time on the scales of the Communication Patterns Questionnaire in our study, suggesting that the conflict patterns that were used two years into these marriages were very similar to those used premaritally. In other words, destructive patterns of dealing with conflict tended to be present quite early, in at least some of these couple relationships. Again, as for the frequency of conflict, it is interesting to note that these results are based on self-reports, which means that some couples were aware of using these destructive behaviors even before marriage.

Although there was no *overall* change over time for the conflict strategies that couples in our study identified from their interaction task, complex changes over time were obtained for spouses low in relationship satisfaction. In terms of negative strategies, these less satisfied spouses decreased their use of manipulation and conflict avoidance at Time 2 (12 months after marriage), but increased these behaviors again at Time 3 (21 months after marriage). Further, in terms of positive strategies, less satisfied husbands increased their use of reason and logic from Time 1 to Time 2, but reduced it again at Time 3; less satisfied wives increased their expression of support for the partner at Time 2, but decreased it very markedly at Time 3 (see Table 6.1).

These findings add to the knowledge gained from studies using more global measures of responses to conflict, such as negativity.

Specifically, the interaction-based findings consistently suggest that less happy spouses make a concerted effort over the first year or so to create a more constructive climate of marital interaction. By the time two years of marriage have passed, however, they seem to revert to the more destructive patterns they used earlier. It is interesting to speculate as to whether the high use of reason by unhappy husbands may actually be counterproductive and serve to polarize the couple; his emphasis on reasonableness and rationality is likely to be at odds with her tendency to become emotional (Bandler, Grinder, & Satir, 1976). Bandler et al. discuss four strategies of communicator stance that people adopt under stress. One of these is the "computer" or ultrareasonable individual, who appears calm, cool, and collected but feels quite vulnerable on the inside.

Nonverbal Accuracy
Although there has been considerable research exploring the nature of conflict in the early stages of marriage, there has been little longitudinal research assessing spouses' perceptions of one another, or their ability to understand each other. Acitelli, Douvan, and Veroff (1997) examined spouses' perceptions of each other in terms of actual similarity, perceived similarity, and understanding; these variables were assessed separately for constructive and destructive behaviors employed during the couple's most recent disagreement. They found very little evidence of change in these measures of spousal perceptions from the first to the third year of marriage.

In our study, we were interested in obtaining a more general measure of spousal understanding. For this reason, we used the standard content paradigm mentioned earlier, which assesses couples' ability to decode the nonverbal aspects of each other's communications. This methodology has been used by Noller (1980, 1981), who showed that distressed spouses were less accurate than nondistressed spouses at decoding each other's nonverbal messages, that wives were more accurate message senders than husbands, and that the husbands' communication skill was more strongly linked to the marital satisfaction of the couple than was the skill of wives.

In our more recent study (Noller & Feeney, 1994), we found that accuracy of decoding increased for all three message types (positive, neutral, and negative), suggesting that nonverbal accuracy in newlyweds increases with increasing exposure to one another's communication. Although it is possible that practice at the experimental task contributed to the increase in scores, two findings support the view that practice effects were likely to be minimal. First, improvement over time varied across message types, being greater for negative and neutral messages than for positive ones. Second, the time lag between testing sessions was at least 9 months, making it unlikely that specific messages or behaviors would be remembered across this time frame.

Changes in Relationship Concerns

Because it is likely that generalized perceptions of relationships are important to pair bonds, we chose to include measures of working models of attachment and perceptions of social support in our study. According to attachment theory, working models of attachment may be revised in response to powerful relationship experiences (Bowlby, 1973). For this reason, it is important to assess whether couples' early experiences of married life have systematic effects on key attachment dimensions. For example, does marriage tend to reduce individuals' anxieties about possible loss and abandonment? Does marriage highlight concerns about trust, closeness, and dependence? In addition, as couple relationships develop, there may be changes in perceptions of closeness to, and support from, family and friends. Do these changes take a predictable form?

Attachment

Although there has been a great deal of discussion about the stability and instability of measures of adult attachment, there has been much less investigation of systematic patterns of change over time. In an 8-month longitudinal study of young couples in dating and marital relationships, Scharfe and Bartholomew (1994) found no evidence of systematic shifts toward security or insecurity, regardless of whether attachment was assessed by self-report, partner report, or interview. Similarly, in a 4-year follow-up of Heller and Shaver's (1987) adult sample, Kirkpatrick and Hazan (1994) reported little evidence of systematic change overall, although respondents who described themselves as anxious-ambivalent at Time 1 were more likely to change to avoidant than to secure attachment.

Among the couples in our study, the two attachment scales showed a marginal degree of change over time, which was significant only for the comfort with closeness scale. Couples in this sample reported becoming somewhat *less* comfortable with closeness and dependence during the second year of their marriage, although it is again important to note that the change was small. While this result was unexpected, it may reflect a reaction to the intensity of early marriage, with spouses coming to desire somewhat more autonomy and independence. This finding fits with Noller, Feeney, and Blakeley-Smith's (forthcoming) study of dialectical contradictions in marriage, in which 36% of the couples reported that one or both partners had moved toward more autonomy during the course of their relationship, whereas only a small percentage had moved toward more connectedness.

Social Support

A recent longitudinal study has provided evidence that life transitions such as full-time employment and marriage tend to bring young people closer to their families (Aquilino, 1997). Similarly, longitudinal data gathered across the transition from late adolescence to early adulthood indicate that, as young people begin to adopt adult roles, their relationships with their parents increase in respect, affection, understanding, and mutuality (Thornton, Orbuch, & Axinn, 1995). Parents also tend to have more positive attitudes toward their adult children who are married with offspring of their own, and to worry more about those who are single or divorced (Aldous, 1987).

Consistent with these findings, perceptions of family support increased over the course of our study, with spouses reporting substantially higher levels of family support after marriage than before. A gender difference in family support also increased over time: Husbands and wives reported similar levels of family support premaritally, but only wives reported steadily increasing levels of support. This finding may explain the tendency, in Western cultures, for married women to stay more in touch with their families of origin than married men. Perhaps daughters, but not sons, develop more mature relationships with their parents once they marry and leave home, and the quality of the parent–adult child relationship improves as a result. It is also possible that the role of "spouse" is more salient to parents' perceptions of daughters than of sons. It is important to note that we found no change over time in perceived support from friends, for either gender.

Summary of Findings for Change over Time

Over all, the available evidence suggests that there is little change in levels of conflict across the early years of marriage, indicating that at least some of the problems that occur in the first few years are already present premaritally. Further, it seems that destructive ways of dealing with conflict, as indexed by global measures of negativity, are either stable over time or increase only slightly. The more specific measure of conflict strategies used in our study suggests the presence of an interesting dynamic in the interactions of less satisfied couples. In the first year of marriage, these couples seem to make a serious attempt to improve the emotional climate of their interactions. Unfortunately, our data suggest that these attempts may be relatively short-lived, perhaps because the partner's response is generally not reinforcing.

Despite the limited evidence for change over time in levels of conflict and responses to conflict, it seems that a number of aspects of the marital relationship tend to show improvement over the first two years. First, Lindahl et al. (1998) reported a gradual increase in levels of supportive communication. Similarly, data from our own research point to perceptions of increasing quality of day-to-day communication.

Second, there appears to be an increase in partners' understanding of each other, as reflected in our measure of nonverbal accuracy. This finding might appear to conflict with that of Acitelli et al. (1993, 1997), who reported no change in understanding over the first three years of marriage. As we have already noted, however, their measure focused on perceptions of spouse behavior during couples' most recent disagreement. Hence, what appear to be discrepant findings may be explained by the different methods used to assess understanding between partners.

Third, as suggested by Aquilino (1997), there is evidence that marriage may bring about increased closeness to parents, at least for wives. Provided that the parents are supportive of the young couple's relationship, this increased closeness is likely to have a positive impact on the quality of their relationship.

CHANGING PATTERNS OF ASSOCIATION WITH RELATIONSHIP FUNCTIONING

Although it is important to know how relationship functioning changes during the first few years of marriage, another broad issue concerns changing patterns of association among relationship variables. Given the central role of couples' own evaluations of their relationships, concurrent and predictive links with relationship satisfaction are of particular interest. What variables reliably predict couples' satisfaction with their relationship? And how do these levels of satisfaction impact on later interactions?

Associations with Communication Patterns

It is generally agreed that constructive communication is associated with greater satisfaction, when these variables are measured at the same point in time. Although these associations seem to be robust across stage of marriage (Feeney, 1994), there is some debate as to whether communication measures predict later satisfaction, and also whether they are influenced by earlier satisfaction.

Quantity and Quality of Communication

As we have already noted, a large number of studies suggest that communication is related to concurrent satisfaction. For example, in their study of early marriage, Vangelisti and Huston (1994) used a global measure of communication ("the way you and your partner have been communicating with one another"), and found that communication and relationship satisfaction were correlated at both one and two years after marriage for both husbands and wives. These researchers commented that spouses' evaluations of their marriage were consistently related to the quality of their day-to-day interactions, and much less consistently related to demographic and personality variables.

In our study, relationship satisfaction was generally unrelated to concurrent reports of the quantity of conversation, although women who reported more couple conversation premaritally reported higher satisfaction. In contrast, the *quality* of conversation showed fairly consistent links with concurrent satisfaction. Happy spouses generally reported higher levels of disclosure, recognition, and satisfaction with discussion. This finding supports a large body of literature showing the importance of communication to relationship functioning (Noller & Fitzpatrick, 1990).

Longitudinal studies also suggest that premarital communication is related to *later* satisfaction (Julien, Markman, & Lindahl, 1989; Lindahl et al., 1998; Smith, Vivian, & O'Leary, 1990). For example, Vangelisti and Huston (1994) reported that patterns of spousal communication and influence predicted later levels of love and satisfaction. White (1983), on the other hand, found that predictive relations were evident only in the direction of earlier satisfaction predicting later levels of couple interaction.

For our couples, there were no predictive relations between satisfaction and the quantity or quality of communication, in either direction. Given the consistent concurrent relations that we obtained, it seems that these particular measures of communication tend to be linked with immediate feelings about the relationship rather than long-term satisfaction. It seems surprising that there are no links between quality of communication and later satisfaction, given the centrality of communication to relationship development. As we discuss next, however, it is important to distinguish between conversation on everyday topics, as assessed here, and conflictual interactions.

Frequency of Conflict

It is reasonable to expect that couples who experience high levels of conflict will be less satisfied with their relationship than other couples. Consistent with this argument, a large body of literature shows that distressed spouses report more conflict than nondistressed spouses (Christensen & Walczynski, 1997). Similarly, our study revealed moderate to strong correlations between frequency of conflict and concurrent relationship satisfaction at all times and for both genders. Hence, it seems likely that the differences of opinion experienced by these couples have a pervasive effect on their evaluations of their relationship, even at this early stage of marriage.

Frequency of conflict also seems to be relevant to the prediction of later satisfaction. For example, Kelly, Huston, and Cate (1985) found that premarital conflict was the best predictor of later conflict and dissatisfaction. In our own study, however, the direction of predictive relations between satisfaction and frequency of conflict was gender specific. For husbands, later satisfaction was predicted by premarital reports of frequency of conflict; this association was quite strong, even after controlling for initial levels of satisfaction. For wives, premarital satisfaction was inversely related to the frequency of later conflict. Hence, for women, low satisfaction early in the relationship may be related to the development of negative attitudes to the partner, which may then lead to higher probability of conflict and disagreement. This proposition fits with other literature indicating that respect for the partner is an important component of marital quality (Feeney, Noller, & Ward, 1997).

Dealing with Conflict

Despite the evidence that frequency of conflict has important implications for how couples evaluate their relationships, it is also important to consider the processes and outcomes of conflict interactions. For example, a critical issue is the extent to which couples avoid versus engage conflict (e.g., Gottman & Krokoff, 1989). Fitzpatrick (1988) and Gottman (1994), in separate attempts to develop typologies of marriage, found that this dimension was crucial in discriminating between couples.

With regard to conflict avoidance and engagement, there is also evidence that men and women tend to take different roles in conflict interactions. Ball, Cowan, and Cowan (1995) found that women tended to raise issues for discussion but that husbands tended to control the content and the outcome of the discussion. Christensen and Heavey (1990) also have explored gender differences in patterns of dealing with conflict, but their focus has been on the demand–withdraw pattern of interaction. In this pattern, women again tend to be the ones who raise issues and pressure for change, whereas men tend to be the ones who withdraw. Various explanations have been offered for this widespread pattern, including men's physiological arousal in the presence of marital conflict (Gottman & Levenson, 1988) and the power structures in society, which favor men (Christensen & Heavey, 1990). Given that these latter researchers found that husbands were more likely to withdraw during discussion of their wives' conflict issues than during discussion of their own issues, withdrawing may be a way of husbands maintaining power and avoiding changes in their own behavior. However, it is important to recognize that this pattern has been associated with lower relationship satisfaction (Christensen & Heavey, 1990).

Another response to conflict that is generally related to lower levels of concurrent satisfaction is negativity of affective expression (Gottman & Krokoff, 1989; Huston & Vangelisti, 1991; Smith et al., 1990). It is interesting to note that the detrimental effects of negativity have been known for some time, with Terman and his colleagues (1938) commenting on the effects of "unhappy temperament" on couple relationships.

In our study, concurrent relations between the interaction-based measure of conflict strategies and relationship satisfaction were scattered. The strongest concurrent links between satisfaction and the questionnaire measure of conflict patterns occurred for wives at the initial assessment, whereas for husbands, concurrent links between conflict patterns and satisfaction were evident only at the two later times. It is interesting to speculate about why the link between satisfaction and conflict patterns was strong for wives premaritally, whereas for husbands, it strengthened over time. Men may generally be less sensitive than women to communication patterns (Tannen, 1990) and may see them as less important to couple relationships (Feeney et al., 1997). It could be argued, then, that the reality of married life makes husbands more aware of the important role that responses to conflict play in marriage and more sensitive to their impact over time.

Several groups of researchers have studied the various responses to conflict and their impact on later satisfaction. Markman, Silvern, Clements, and Kraft-Hanak (1993) carried out a longitudinal study of a small group of couples who were assessed before marriage and on several occasions afterward. Although coded videotapes of marital interaction revealed no gender differences in problem solving or conflict behaviors premaritally, these variables seemed to be more important for husbands' satisfaction than for that of wives. This effect was present concurrently (both before and after marriage) and when premarital communication was used to predict satisfaction six years later. Men's satisfaction at the later time was negatively related to their own premarital appeasement and avoidance and to partners' premarital retaliation and negative communication.

Other studies have supported the importance of premarital responses to conflict. Smith et al. (1990) showed the importance of premarital disengagement, with such disengagement being negatively related to marital satisfaction after 18 and 30 months of marriage. Newton and Kiecolt-Glaser (1995) showed that hostility expressed by newlywed husbands was associated with linear decreases in their own and their wives' reports of marital quality, even after controlling for the correlated variable of neuroticism.

In our own study, predictive relations between the interaction-based measure of conflict strategies and relationship satisfaction were again scattered. Our questionnaire-based measure of conflict patterns predicted later satisfaction for wives only. Satisfaction, on the other hand, predicted later conflict patterns for both husbands and wives. Husbands tended to respond to lower satisfaction with more disengagement and withdrawal at later times, whereas wives tended to respond with higher levels of negativity and other destructive conflict behaviors. These findings support those of Christensen and Heavey (1990) concerning the gendered nature of the demand–withdraw pattern.

Nonverbal Accuracy

To our knowledge, there has been no previous longitudinal research assessing the implications of couples' nonverbal accuracy. Given the finding that men tend to have a negative bias in interpreting their spouses' communication (Gaelick, Bodenhausen, & Wyer, 1985; Noller, 1980), it is not really surprising that in our study concurrent satisfaction was related only to husbands' accuracy at decoding positive and neutral messages from their wives. It may be that an important skill for husbands is being able to accept a positive message as positive and a neutral message as neutral. This suggestion is supported by a study showing that errors in husbands' decoding were related to the extent to which they attributed negative intentions to their wives (Noller & Ruzzene, 1991).

Similarly, in terms of prediction over time, husbands' premarital satisfaction predicted greater accuracy of husbands' decoding their wives' messages at the later times, for all message types. For wives, on the other hand, premarital satisfaction was *inversely* related to accuracy for negative messages. In other words, wives who were happier with their relationships early on tended to be less accurate decoders of negative messages from their husbands later in the marriage. Perhaps their satisfaction creates a bias to perceive even negative messages more positively than intended. This result fits with Noller's (1980) finding that wives tend to have a positive bias in decoding their husbands' messages, whereas husbands tend to have a negative bias in decoding their wives' messages. The current finding that positivity bias may be greater for happy wives also fits with the argument that satisfaction levels create "sentiment override" (Weiss, 1984), which colors perceptions of many aspects of the relationship.

Associations with Relationship Concerns

A large body of research now attests to the importance of individual differences in attachment for the functioning of couple relationships. The key dimensions underlying attachment style, comfort with closeness and anxiety over relationships, have been linked with communication processes and relationship satisfaction, but the direction of causal relations remains largely unresolved. Relationships with friends and family may also impact on the development of the couple bond. However, there is some evidence that the effect of relationships with others may depend on variables such as gender and marital quality (Dickson-Markman & Markman, 1988). Again, the nature of these effects is not fully understood.

Attachment

Cross-sectional data indicate that comfort with closeness is associated with self-disclosure and other indices of intimacy (Collins & Read, 1990; Mikulincer & Nachshon, 1991). Further, anxiety over relationships is associated with a higher frequency of couple conflict and with distress, anger, and hostility in response to conflict (e.g., Rholes, Simpson, & Stevens, 1998).

In our study, as expected, anxiety over relationships showed strong negative correlations with concurrent relationship satisfaction for both husbands and wives. In contrast, comfort with closeness was related to concurrent satisfaction for husbands only, and the correlations were moderate in size. The fact that comfort with closeness and marital satisfaction were linked only for husbands also fits with previous studies (e.g., Kirkpatrick & Davis, 1994). This finding has been explained in terms of sex role socialization: Men tend to be encouraged in dominance and competition, whereas women are encouraged in affiliation and cooperation. Hence, concerns about intimacy may be more salient for men in the context of a close relationship like marriage.

Measures of adult attachment also predict relationship outcomes (relationship status, satisfaction, and commitment) at later points in time (Feeney & Noller, 1992; Kirkpatrick & Davis, 1994; Shaver & Brennan, 1992). Some researchers have suggested, however, that this predictive power stems mainly from the relative stability of adult attachment style. In other words, prediction may be weak, when initial scores on attachment are controlled (e.g., Kirkpatrick & Hazan, 1994).

On the other hand, there is also some evidence that measures of adult attachment are predicted by relationship experiences, suggesting a complex pattern of causal influence. For example, Scharfe and Bartholomew (1994) found that the absolute amount of change in interview ratings of attachment security was related to the number of positive interpersonal events experienced during the course of their study, for both males and females. In addition, Kirkpatrick and Hazan (1994) reported that, for respondents initially describing themselves as secure in attachment, relationship breakup was associated with a shift toward insecurity.

Data from our longitudinal study revealed predictive relations between attachment and marital satisfaction for husbands only. Husbands' anxiety over relationships predicted their lower satisfaction later in the marriage, and their earlier satisfaction predicted high comfort with closeness and low anxiety over relationships. The latter finding fits with attachment theory, which proposes that experiences in close relationships can impact on working models of self and others. It is not clear why the predictive relations were restricted to husbands. Perhaps patterns of sex role socialization are again relevant. That is, because there is less emphasis on young men developing intimate relationships, experiences in the early years of marriage may be particularly formative for them.

Social Support

Kurdek's (1998) longitudinal study showed that overall satisfaction with social support at Year 1 was positively related to concurrent and later marital satisfaction for both spouses. Our own research showed that concurrent relations between social support and marital satisfaction were relatively scattered. For example, after a year of marriage, husbands' perceptions of support from friends and family were positively correlated with their marital satisfaction. In terms of predictive relations, the only significant result was the positive effect of husbands' premarital support from both friends and family on later satisfaction. The consistency of this effect suggests that those men who have good relationship skills premaritally, and across a range of relationships, develop the most satisfying and intimate couple bonds. One reason for this positive effect may be the tendency for at least some of these relationships to involve high levels of approval of, and support for, the couple bond (Spanier & Lewis, 1980).

PUTTING IT ALL TOGETHER

It seems clear from the literature that some aspects of marital relationships are more prone to change than others. For example, slight declines in satisfaction seem to be found in many studies, but little change is found in conflict patterns. This lack of change in responses to conflict seems to suggest that "premarital communication patterns may set the stage for later problems in a relationship" (Hill & Peplau, 1998, p. 239). Results for change over time are not completely conclusive, however, and may depend on the way that constructs are conceptualized and assessed; for example, as we noted earlier, "negativity" has been assessed in a variety of ways.

When predictive relations are considered, the situation is even more complex. For example, it seems that relationship satisfaction predicts later nonverbal accuracy, but that the reverse pattern does not hold. In contrast, there is evidence of bi-directional links between satisfaction and responses to conflict. These findings highlight the need for researchers to be more specific in their language and avoid glibly using such generic terms as "communication" and "conflict," which can have many meanings. In our study, for instance, the predictive links with satisfaction were very different for conflict patterns and for quantity and quality of conversation. (The conversational measures showed no predictive links with satisfaction in either direction.)

Further, responses to conflict can be assessed using either global or more specific measures. Our interaction-based measure of conflict strategies yielded only scattered correlational findings, but showed a clear and consistent picture of change over time. In contrast, the questionnaire measures of conflict patterns and frequency of conflict showed many links with satisfaction, but no change over time. These findings suggest that global self-reports may be less sensitive to change over time than measures that are specific to one interaction and based on immediate and behaviorally based reports of conflict. The importance of using both types of measures in studying marital conflict is underlined by these results.

Adding to the complexity is the fact that predictors of later satisfaction are often gender specific. In fact, in our study, husbands' later satisfaction was predicted by anxiety over relationships, support from family and friends, and frequency of conflict. For wives, in contrast, later satisfaction was predicted by levels of disengagement, negativity, and destructive process, and by the extent of manipulation in the conflict interaction. The use of destructive responses to conflict early in the relationship seems to be more predictive of later dissatisfaction for wives than for husbands. Perhaps wives, who are generally more aware of the importance of communication skills, react more strongly to problems in dealing with conflict. On the other hand, the frequency of conflict seems to be most salient for husbands, who may generally find conflict aversive and overarousing (Gottman & Levenson, 1988).

It is interesting to note that although women react with dissatisfaction to maladaptive conflict processes early in the relationship, and although they seem to be aware of these processes, they are not necessarily deterred from going ahead with the marriage. Why do couples not heed these warning signals? One factor is likely to be the rosy glow of courtship, which may lead to an unrealistic optimism about the future of the relationship. The sense of investment in the relationship, and in the wedding itself, may also prevent couples from acting on any doubts they may be experiencing about their relationship. In addition, prewedding jitters tend to be treated as a normal part of the transition to marriage, rather than as a warning sign of potential relationship difficulties.

Despite the optimism of young couples, it seems that destructive conflict patterns are very important to the developmental course of relationship functioning. Throughout the literature, there is considerable support for the concept of premarital determinism (Hill & Peplau, 1998; Olson, 1990). That is, the quality of the premarital relationship is highly predictive of marital success or failure. This issue is not completely resolved, however, with researchers such as Whyte (1990) concluding that premarital experiences have minimal impact on marital success.

Most longitudinal studies of marriage have not included measures tapping general relationship concerns, such as attachment and social support. For this reason, it is particularly interesting to note that both of these variables showed predictive relations with satisfaction, in both directions, but only for men. Attachment security and perceptions of social support are thought to reflect internalized representations of one's own self-worth and of others' responsiveness (Pierce et al., 1990). Perhaps these internalized representations are important to men's satisfaction in their primary relationship because men, unlike women, are not strongly encouraged to be affiliative, or to act as the caretakers of relationships. Given this general lack of relationship training, men's ability to develop strong intimate bonds may be affected quite powerfully by specific relationship experiences and the resulting models of close relationships.

It is interesting to note that recent research has provided some support for mediational models of relationship quality. Specifically, it appears that the effect of attachment security on relationship satisfaction may be explained, in part, by its association with variables such as self-disclosure, emotional expression, and constructive responses to conflict (Feeney, Noller, & Roberts, 1998). Such patterns of mediation offer the possibility of developing more integrative models of predictive relations.

Further research into stability and change over time is likely to have important implications for both premarital and marital counseling. A relevant question, for example, concerns the way in which a particular behavior, such as avoidance, comes to be seen so much more negatively later in relationships. In this regard, Felmlee's (1998) work on relationship disenchantment has begun to suggest specific processes by which partner "virtues" come to be seen as "vices." Hence, although it is crucial for counselors working with premarital couples to assess communication patterns and teach more constructive responses to conflict, they also may need to highlight for couples the potential difficulties that destructive conflict patterns may create later on. This is especially important given that overlearned patterns of communication tend to be relied on in times of severe stress, when couples are most vulnerable.

Partners' patterns of communication are undoubtedly driven, to a large extent, by cognitive and affective variables, including working models of self, others, and social relationships. Our findings suggest that these variables are important to the study of early marriage, both in terms of charting relations with members of the social network over time and in terms of clarifying the predictors of relational satisfaction. Further research needs to focus not just on communication behaviors or on cognitive and affective processes in isolation, but on the interplay between these two sets of variables.

There has been a strong tradition for counselors working with distressed couples to focus on changing their overt communication patterns, using Behavioral Marital Therapy. Although the techniques used in this type of therapy have clear benefits, it would seem equally important for practitioners to explore the expectations and interpretations of behavior that may contribute to destructive styles of communication. Such an approach is likely to produce some resolution of underlying issues, rather than being restricted to symptomatic behaviors. In terms of research, an integrative approach that considers both communication behaviors and working models of relationships has the potential to increase our understanding of the course of early marriage. In particular, it may move us beyond a primarily descriptive endeavor to one that focuses on the complex dynamics of close relationships.

REFERENCES

Acitelli, L. K., Douvan, E., & Veroff, J. (1993). Perceptions of conflict in the first year of marriage: How important are similarity and understanding? *Journal of Social and Personal Relationships, 10,* 5–19.

(1997). The changing influence of interpersonal perceptions on marital well-being among black and white couples. *Journal of Social and Personal Relationships, 14,* 291–304.

Aldous, J. (1987). New views on the family life of the elderly and the near-elderly. *Journal of Marriage and the Family, 49,* 227–234.

Aquilino, W. S. (1997). From adolescent to young adult: A prospective study of parent–child relations during the transition to adulthood. *Journal of Marriage and the Family, 59,* 670–686.

Ball, F., Cowan, P., & Cowan, C. (1995). Who's got the power? Gender differences in partner's perceptions of influence during marital problem-solving discussions. *Family Process, 34,* 303–321.

Bandler, R., Grinder, J., & Satir, V. (1976). *Changing with families.* Palo Alto, CA: Science and Behavior Books.

Bowlby, J. (1973). *Attachment and loss: Vol. 2. Separation: Anxiety and anger.* New York: Basic Books.

Bradbury, T. N. (1998). Introduction: The developmental course of marital dysfunction. In T. N. Bradbury (Ed.), *The developmental course of marital dysfunction* (pp. 1–8). Cambridge: Cambridge University Press.

Burns, A. (1980). *Breaking up: Separation and divorce in Australia.* Melbourne: Nelson.

Christensen, A., & Heavey, C. L. (1990). Gender, power and marital conflict. *Journal of Personality and Social Psychology, 59,* 73–81.

Christensen, A., & Sullaway, M. (1984). Communication Patterns Questionnaire. Unpublished questionnaire, University of California, Los Angeles.

Christensen, A., & Walczynski, P. (1997). Conflict and satisfaction in couples. In R. Sternberg & M. Hojjat (Eds.), *Satisfaction in close relationships* (pp. 249–275). New York: Guilford Press.

Collins, N. L., & Read, S. J. (1990). Adult attachment, working models and relationship quality in dating couples. *Journal of Personality and Social Psychology, 58,* 644–663.

Craddock, A. (1980). The impact of social change on Australian families. *Australian Journal of Sex, Marriage and the Family, 1,* 4–14.

Dickson-Markman, F., & Markman, H. J. (1988). The effect of others on marriage: Do they help or hurt? In P. Noller & M. A. Fitzpatrick (Eds.), *Perspectives on marital interaction* (pp. 294–322). Clevedon: Multilingual Matters.

Feeney, J. A. (1994). Attachment style, communication patterns, and satisfaction across the life cycle of marriage. *Personal Relationships, 1,* 333–348.

Feeney, J. A., & Noller, P. (1992). Attachment style and romantic love: Relationship discussion. *Australian Journal of Psychology, 44*, 69–74.

(1996). *Adult attachment*. Thousand Oaks, CA: Sage.

Feeney, J. A., Noller, P., & Callan, V. J. (1994). Attachment style, communication and satisfaction in the early years of marriage. In K. Bartholomew & D. Perlman (Eds.), *Advances in personal relationships* (Vol. 5, pp. 269–308). London: Jessica Kingsley.

Feeney, J. A., Noller, P., & Roberts, N. (1998). Attachment and close relationships. In C. Hendrick & S. Hendrick (Eds.), *Close relationships: A sourcebook* (pp. 185–201). Thousand Oaks, CA: Sage.

Feeney, J. A., Noller, P., & Ward, C. (1997). Marital satisfaction and spousal interaction. In R. J. Sternberg & M. Hojjat (Eds.), *Satisfaction in close relationships* (pp. 160–189). New York: Guilford Press.

Felmlee, D. H. (1998). Fatal attraction. In B. H. Spitzberg & W. R. Cupach (Eds.), *The dark side of close relationships* (pp. 3–33). Mahwah, NJ: Erlbaum.

Fitzpatrick, M. A. (1988). *Between husbands and wives: Communication in marriage*. Newbury Park, CA: Sage.

Gaelick, L., Bodenhausen, G., & Wyer, R. (1985). Emotional communication in close relationships. *Journal of Personality and Social Psychology, 49*, 1246–1265.

Gottman, J. M. (1994). *What predicts divorce? The relationship between marital processes and marital outcomes*. Hillsdale, NJ: Erlbaum.

Gottman, J. M., & Krokoff, L. J. (1989). Marital interaction and satisfaction: A longitudinal view. *Journal of Consulting and Clinical Psychology, 57*, 47–52.

Gottman, J. M., & Levenson, R. W. (1988). The social psychophysiology of marriage. In P. Noller & M. A. Fitzpatrick (Eds.), *Perspectives on marital interaction* (pp. 182–200). Clevedon: Multilingual Matters.

Heller, C., & Shaver, P. (1987). Romantic love conceptualised as an attachment process. *Journal of Personality and Social Psychology, 52*, 511–524.

Hill, C., & Peplau, L. (1998). Premarital predictors of relationship outcomes: A 15 year follow-up of the Boston couples study. In T. Bradbury (Ed.), *The developmental course of marital dysfunction* (pp. 237–279). Cambridge: Cambridge University Press.

Huston, T. L., & Houts, R. (1998). The psychological infrastructure of courtship and marriage: The role of personality and compatability in romantic relationships. In T. Bradbury (Ed.), *The developmental course of marital dysfunction* (pp. 114–152). Cambridge: Cambridge University Press.

Huston, T. L., & Vangelisti, A. (1991). Socioemotional behavior and satisfaction in marital relationships: A longitudinal study. *Journal of Personality and Social Psychology, 61*, 721–733.

Julien, D., Markman, H., & Lindahl, K. (1989). A comparison of a global and a microanalytic coding system: Implications for future trends in studying interactions. *Behavioral Assessment, 11*, 81–100.

Karney, B. R., & Bradbury, T. N. (1995). The longitudinal course of marital quality and stability: A review of theory, method and research. *Psychological Bulletin, 118*, 3–34.

Kelly, C., Huston, T. L., & Cate, R. (1985). Premarital relationship correlates of the erosion of satisfaction in marriage. *Journal of Social and Personal Relationships, 2,* 167–178.

Kirchler, E. (1989). Everyday life experiences at home: An interaction diary approach to assess marital relationships. *Journal of Family Psychology, 2,* 311–336.

Kirkpatrick, L. A., & Davis, K. E. (1994). Attachment style, gender and relationship stability: A longitudinal analysis. *Journal of Personality and Social Psychology, 66,* 502–512.

Kirkpatrick, L. A., & Hazan, C. (1994). Attachment styles and close relationships: A four year prospective study. *Personal Relationships, 1,* 123–142.

Kurdek, L. (1998). Developmental changes in marital satisfaction: A 6-year prospective longitudinal study of newlywed couples. In T. N. Bradbury (Ed.), *The developmental course of marital dysfunction* (pp. 180–204). Cambridge: Cambridge University Press.

Leonard, K. E., & Roberts, L. J. (1998). Marital aggression, quality and stability in the first year of marriage: Findings from the Buffalo Newlywed Study. In T. N. Bradbury (Ed.), *The developmental course of marital dysfunction* (pp. 44–73). Cambridge: Cambridge University Press.

Lindahl, K., Clements, M., & Markman, H. J. (1998). The development of marriage: A 9-year perspective. In T. N. Bradbury (Ed.), *The developmental course of marital dysfunction* (pp. 205–236). Cambridge: Cambridge University Press.

Markman, H. J. (1979). The application of a behavioral model of marriage in predicting relationship satisfaction for couples planning marriage. *Journal of Consulting and Clinical Psychology, 47,* 743–749.

(1981). Prediction of marital distress: A 5-year follow-up. *Journal of Consulting and Clinical Psychology, 49,* 760–762.

(1984). The longitudinal study of couples' interactions: Implications for understanding and predicting the development of marital distress. In K. Hahlweg, & N. Jacobson (Eds.), *Marital interaction: Analysis and modification* (pp. 253–281) New York: Guilford Press.

Markman, H. J., Floyd, F., Stanley, S. M., & Storaasli, R. (1988). The prevention of marital distress: A longitudinal investigation. *Journal of Consulting and Clinical Psychology, 56,* 760–762.

Markman, H. J., Silvern, L., Clements, M., & Kraft-Hanak, S. (1993). Men and women dealing with conflict in heterosexual relationships. *Journal of Social Issues, 49,* 107–125.

Mikulincer, M., & Nachshon, O. (1991). Attachment style and patterns of self-disclosure. *Journal of Personality and Social Psychology, 61,* 321–331.

Newton, T. L., & Kiecolt-Glaser, J. K. (1995). Hostility and erosion of marital quality during early marriage. *Journal of Behavioural Medicine, 18,* 601–619.

Noller, P. (1980). Misunderstandings in marital communication: A study of couples' nonverbal communication. *Journal of Personality and Social Psychology, 39,* 1135–1148.

(1981). Gender and marital adjustment level differences in decoding messages from spouses and strangers. *Journal of Personality and Social Psychology, 41,* 272–278.

Noller, P., & Feeney, J. A. (1994). Relationship satisfaction, attachment and nonverbal accuracy in early marriage. *Journal of Nonverbal Behavior, 18*, 199–221.

Noller, P., Feeney, J. A., Bonnell, D., & Callan, V. J. (1994). A longitudinal study of conflict in early marriage. *Journal of Social and Personal Relationships, 11*, 233–252.

Noller, P., & Feeney, J. A. (1998). Communication in early marriage: Responses to conflict, nonverbal accuracy and conversational patterns. In T. Bradbury (Ed.), *The developmental course of marital dysfunction* (pp. 11–43). Cambridge: Cambridge University Press.

Noller, P., & Fitzpatrick, M. A. (1990). Marital communication in the 1980s. *Journal of Marriage and the Family, 52*, 832–843.

Noller, P., & Ruzzene, M. (1991). The effects of cognition and affect on marital communication. In G. J. O. Fletcher & F. D. Fincham (Eds.), *Affect and cognition in close relationships* (pp. 203–233). Hillsdale, NJ: Erlbaum.

Noller, P., Feeney, J., & Blakeley-Smith (in press). Handling pressures for change in marriage. In V. Manusov & J. H. Harvey (Eds.), *Attribution, communication behaviour and close relationships*. Cambridge: Cambridge University Press.

Noller, P., & Venardos, C. M. (1986). Sending emotional messages in marriage: Nonverbal behavior, sex and communication clarity. *Journal of Social and Personal Relationships, 3*, 31–42.

Norton, R. (1983). Measuring marital quality: A critical look at the dependent variable. *Journal of Marriage and the Family, 45*, 141–151.

O'Leary, K., Barling, J., Arias, I., Rosenbaum, A., Malone, J., & Tyree, A. (1989). Prevalence and stability of physical aggression between spouses: A longitudinal analysis. *Journal of Consulting and Clinical Psychology, 57*, 263–268.

Olson, D. (1990). Marriage in perspective. In F. D. Fincham & T. N. Bradbury (Eds.), *The psychology of marriage* (pp. 402–419). New York: Guilford Press.

Pierce, G., Sarason, B., & Sarason, I. (1990). Integrating social support perspectives. In S. Duck & R. C. Silver (Eds.), *Personal relationships and social support* (pp. 173–189). Newbury Park, CA: Sage.

Procidano, M. E., & Heller, K. (1983). Measures of perceived social support from friends and from family: Three validation studies. *American Journal of Community Psychology, 2*, 1–24.

Rholes, W. S., Simpson, J. A., & Stevens, J. G. (1998). Attachment orientations, social support and conflict resolution in close relationships. In J. A. Simpson & W. S. Rholes (Eds.), *Attachment theory and close relationships* (pp. 166–188). New York: Guilford Press.

Scharfe, E., & Bartholomew, K. (1994). Reliability and stability of adult attachment patterns. *Personal Relationships, 1*, 23–43.

Shaver, P., & Brennan, K. (1992). Attachment styles and the "big five" personality traits: Their connections with each other and with romantic relationship outcomes. *Personality and Social Psychology Bulletin, 18*, 536–545.

Smith, D. A., Vivian, D., & O'Leary, K. D. (1990). Longitudinal prediction of marital discord from premarital expressions of affect. *Journal of Consulting and Clinical Psychology, 58*, 790–797.

Spanier, G. B., & Lewis, R. A. (1980). Marital quality: A review of the seventies. *Journal of Marriage and the Family, 42,* 825–839.
Suitor, J., Pillemer, K., & Straus, M. (1990). Marital violence in a life course perspective. In M. A. Straus & R. J. Gelles (Eds.), *Physical violence in American families: Risk factors and adaptations to violence in 8,145 families* (pp. 305–320). New Brunswick, NJ: Transaction Publishers.
Tannen, D. (1990). *You just don't understand.* New York: William Morrow.
Terman, L. M., Buttenweiser, P., Ferguson, L. W., Johnson, W. B., & Wilson, D. P. (1938). *Psychological factors in marital happiness.* New York: McGraw-Hill.
Thornton, A., Orbuch, T. L., & Axinn, W. G. (1995). Parent–child relationships during the transition to adulthood. *Journal of Family Issues, 16,* 538–564.
Vangelisti, A. L., & Huston, T. L. (1994). Maintaining marital satisfaction and love. In D. Canary & L. Stafford (Eds.), *Communication and relational maintenance* (pp. 165–186). San Diego, CA: Academic Press.
Weishaus, S., & Field, D. (1988). A half century of marriage: Continuity or change? *Journal of Marriage and the Family, 50,* 763–774.
Weiss, R. L. (1984). Cognitive and behavioral measure of marital interaction. In K. Hahlweg & N. S. Jacobson (Eds.), *Marital interaction: Analysis and modification* (pp. 232–252). New York: Guilford Press.
White, L. (1983). Determinants of spousal interaction: Marital structure or marital happiness. *Journal of Marriage and the Family, 45,* 571–579.
Whyte, K. (1990). *Dating, mating and marriage.* New York: Aldine de Gruyter.

CHAPTER SEVEN

Sacrifice in Romantic Relationships
An Exploration of Relevant Research and Theory

Sarah Whitton, Scott Stanley, and Howard Markman

Sacrifice is a construct that has received very little attention in research and theory on intimate relationships. One reason for this neglect may be the controversial nature of sacrificing for one's personal relationships; how sacrifice relates to relationship factors and individual well-being is highly disputed. On one hand, some individuals (ranging from clinicians to feminists to individuals who simply have experience in romantic relationships) display strong negative opinions of sacrifice in the context of intimate relationships, suggesting that it is harmful to the individual and associated with "codependency." Followers of feminist theory go so far as to state that sacrifice is one of the major causes of depression and relationship dissatisfaction in females (Jack, 1991; Lerner, 1988). On the other hand, researchers have recently been reporting the positive role of sacrifice in relationships (Van Lange et al., 1997; Stanley & Markman, 1992). Further, some marital and family theorists (Bahr & Bahr, 1997) have emphasized the need to begin including the concept of sacrifice in marital and family theories because of the crucial, positive role it plays in those relationships. How do we reconcile these different views of sacrifice? Is sacrificing for one's relationship related to positive or negative factors of the relationship? What are its effects at the individual level?

In this chapter, we will explore the existent research and theory surrounding sacrifice, focusing on the question of how sacrifice relates to relationship stability, commitment, and satisfaction. Further, various theoretical speculations about why sacrifice is associated with these

Address correspondence to Sarah Whitton, Department of Psychology, University of Denver, 2155 S. High Street, Denver, CO 80208. E-mail addresses: Sarah Whitton, *swhitton@nova.psy.du.edu*; Scott Stanley, *smstanley@aol.com*.

relationship factors will be explored. We will conclude by proposing a theory on how these differing speculations can be reconciled into one comprehensive, testable framework for understanding and studying sacrifice in romantic relationships.

WHY LOOK AT SACRIFICE IN INTIMATE RELATIONSHIPS?

Research from the altruism literature (Bar-Tal, 1976) reveals that self-sacrifice in extreme and nonextreme situations is seen most often between family members, and in decreasing amounts as the kinship connection becomes more distant. For example, Ma (1993) found that the tendency to sacrifice one's life for another decreases in the following order of relationships: close relatives, best friends, very weak young or socially elite strangers, common strangers, and enemies. Further, Bahr and Bahr (1997), in a review of Tzvetan Todorov's 1996 book, *Facing the Extreme: Moral Life in the Concentration Camps*, note that sacrifices in the camps were most often made for the benefit of a family member, usually a husband, wife, parent, or child. Such findings suggest that the more closely a person is related to another, the more likely he or she is to give up something, or sacrifice, in order to help that person. Although it would be quite interesting to explore the reasons behind this association between closeness of relation and sacrifice, including the evolutionary advantage of performing altruistic acts for one's closest genetic relatives, the point here is that the existence of such an association renders it very important to look at sacrifice in the closest of personal relationships – marriage and the nuclear family. As Bahr and Bahr ask, "if most often it was family members who exhibited such self-sacrifice, then how can we claim to understand family processes [while we] lack a theoretical lens that brings self-sacrifice into focus?" (p. 18).

In addition, although it is scarcely talked about in current social science, Noller (1996) found that people in the community identified sacrifice, along with caring, trust, respect, and loyalty, as part of their conception of what "love" means. Further, Pam, Plutchik, and Conte (1973) found that altruism is one of the unique aspects of love that differentiates it from friendships. It is important to note that while these findings indicate that sacrifice is an important, defining feature of romantic relationships, this does not mean that individuals actually perceive their actions within a love relationship as sacrificial. Rather, it is likely that being in love involves willingly giving up immediate desires for the sake of the relationship or partner, without perceiving those actions as sacrifices.

Finally, Interdependence theory (Kelley & Thibault, 1978; Kelley, 1979) emphasizes the impact that sacrifice has on the health of close relationships. Kelley and Thibault suggest that romantic partners frequently are forced to choose between sacrificing for their relationship or acting in self-interest, because situations in which partners' interests differ are commonly experienced in romantic relationships. When individuals' interests conflict with those of their partners, the individuals' options include ending the relationship, selfishly pursuing self-interest, or sacrificing, by forgoing self-interest to benefit the partner or maintain peace in the relationship. Which option partners choose in resolving these situations is crucial for maintaining healthy functioning. In fact, much evidence from the marital literature points to the importance of how partners handle conflicts in determining the longevity and happiness of their relationships (e.g., Gottman, 1993; Gottman & Krokoff, 1989; Markman, Stanley, & Blumberg, 1994; Notarius & Markman, 1993). Since sacrifice is one of the behaviors by which partners can resolve their conflicts, it may play a powerful role in mediating the linkages between differences or disagreements and relationship quality and stability.

Definition of Sacrifice

Given the numerous – and highly differing – common conceptions of what "sacrifice" means, it is first important to clearly define the concept. The *Random House College Dictionary*, revised edition (1982), offers as one definition of *sacrifice*, "the surrender or destruction of something prized or desirable for the sake of something considered as having a higher or more pressing claim." This definition unifies specific definitions of sacrifice, such as religious sacrifice and sports-related sacrifice. Whether one sacrifices an animal to a god or a fly ball to the right fielder of the other team, a crucial point is that the sacrifice is made with the aim of obtaining something more valued – in these examples, god's grace or a run scored for your baseball team.

Within the area of marital research, only two definitions of *sacrifice* were found. These appeared in the work of Stanley and colleagues (Stanley & Markman, 1992; Stanley, 1998) and Van Lange and colleagues (1997). Stanley's definition (1998) builds on the idea of giving up something for something else more prized; he writes that "sacrifice is giving up something for a greater good. In marriage, one of the 'greater goods' is the needs of your mate. The other is the needs of your marriage" (p. 184). Similarly, Van Lange and colleagues define sacrifice in intimate relationships as "[forgoing] immediate self-interest in order to promote the well-being of a partner or relationship" (p. 1374). Thus, there appears to be a consensus among interested researchers that, in the context of romantic relationships, the term *sacrifice* is used to describe acts in which individuals give up some immediate desire in the interest of bettering their relationship or benefiting their partner.

It is also important to stress what is *not* considered a sacrifice in romantic relationships. Stanley (1998) makes the crucial point that sacrificing is different from martyring oneself, in the popular sense of the word. Acting as a martyr implies giving in order to put the other in debt and thereby benefit the self. In sharp contrast, sacrifice entails freely giving of the self for the benefit of the partner or the relationship. That is, if Jane agrees to go with her husband, Bob, to a business party that she finds unpleasant, intending to then make him feel guilty for how much she gives up for him, this is martyrdom, not sacrifice.

Further, Van Lange and colleagues (1997) make the important distinction between sacrifice for the relationship and *costs* of the relationship, which are defined as psychological experiences of dissatisfaction due to the relationship. Specifically, these authors point out that sacrifice and costs differ along two dimensions. First, costs refer to the *feeling or perception* that something associated with the relationship is unpleasant, while sacrifice refers to *behaviors*. That is, costs can be nonbehavioral (e.g., a consequence of an action, an undesirable attribute of the partner, or a negative situation resulting from participation in the relationship). For example, Bob may experience as a cost of his relationship that his friends do not like his wife, Jane, so that he can not spend time with them and Jane simultaneously. In contrast, sacrifices necessarily involve an *act* of forgoing self-interest with the intention of furthering positive goals. Thus, it would be a sacrifice in this case if Bob were to give up going to the baseball game with his friends so that he could spend the evening with Jane – an act that he knows will lead to Jane being more happy and their relationship running more smoothly.

The second distinction between sacrifices and costs is that while costs are by definition experienced as unpleasant, sacrifice may or may not be unpleasant. For example, some individuals will feel pleasure in being able to do something special for their partner. In fact, Stanley and Markman (1992) measure the degree to which individuals feel satisfied with sacrificing for their partners as part of their overall measure of dedication in romantic relationships. In our example, Bob may not be very upset that he opts for an evening with Jane over a game with the boys, but rather feel happy that he is able to show her how important she is to him. This latter distinction becomes crucial in the later discussion of *why* individuals in relationships sacrifice.

EMPIRICAL EVIDENCE FOR THE BENEFITS OF SACRIFICE IN ROMANTIC RELATIONSHIPS

Although very little research has investigated sacrifice within romantic relationships, the existing evidence shows that sacrifice is, in fact, one of the things that partners in successful relationships are both more willing to do and report more satisfaction in doing than partners in less committed healthy and satisfying relationships.

Van Lange and colleagues (1997) conducted a series of six studies investigating the role of willingness to sacrifice, or the "propensity to forgo immediate self-interest to promote the well-being of a partner or relationship" (p. 1374) in dating and marital relationships. These researchers measured willingness to sacrifice by pitting self-interest (operationalized as the three or four most important activities in one's life outside of the relationship) against the interest of the relationship. Participants, presented with the scenario that they could not continue their most important life activities *and* maintain their romantic relationship, reported the degree to which they would consider sacrificing, or giving up, the valued activity in order to maintain the relationship. Each of these studies provided support for the hypothesis that willingness to sacrifice is associated with healthier and more stable relationships; willingness to sacrifice was positively associated with higher levels of dyadic adjustment, strong commitment, high relationship satisfaction, and higher odds of the relationship persisting.

Our team (Stanley & Markman, 1992) has investigated another attitude toward sacrificing – satisfaction with sacrifice – which is defined as "the degree to which people feel a sense of satisfaction in doing things that are largely or solely for their partner's benefit" (p. 596). Our findings show that satisfaction with sacrifice, as measured by self-report, is positively related to relationship quality and all other measures associated with dedication in personal relationships (e.g., priority of the relationship, couple identity, and desiring the relationship to last; Stanley & Markman, 1992). Satisfaction with sacrifice was also strongly correlated with relationship satisfaction, level of disclosure in the relationship, the degree to which individuals feel they would be worse off without their spouse, and several measures of commitment.

In fact, based on these findings, we have asserted that satisfaction with sacrifice is so integrally related to commitment that it is one of the means through which we tap into level of commitment present in a given relationship (Stanley & Markman, 1992). This brings up an interesting issue in the study of sacrifice: Is sacrifice merely one component of commitment? Or is it a separate, but correlated, construct that functions in different ways? If it is in fact simply one part of the construct of commitment, then it seems tautological to assert the relationship between the two. However, we believe that sacrifice can be viewed *either* as part of dedication *or* as a mechanism that is correlated with but distinct from the construct of commitment. In fact, one of the justifications for creating the measure of commitment which taps into, but keeps separate, the many underlying dimensions of the construct is that it is crucial to be able to separately assess the subconstructs of commitment when examining relationship dynamics, as is the case in the present discussion.

Van Lange et al.'s (1997) results show that when commitment is narrowly defined as "the degree to which an individual experiences long term orientation toward a relationship" (p. 1374) and sacrifice is viewed as a separate construct, willingness to sacrifice exerts effects on dyadic adjustment in the relationship beyond those accounted for by commitment. Further, Stanley and Markman (1992) found that satisfaction with sacrifice relates in quite differing ways to individuals' religiosity and the stage of relationship than other subconstructs of commitment, such as long-term orientation to the relationship. Thus, separating the factors of long-term orientation and attitudes toward sacrificing for the relationship from one another, either by defining commitment more narrowly or separating the subconstructs of commitment, allows interesting and informative dynamics involved in committed relationships to be uncovered. Given this, the present chapter will treat sacrifice as a separate mechanism that is related to commitment rather than a component of commitment.

In summary, recent empirical evidence suggests that individuals' willingness to sacrifice for their relationship and their satisfaction with sacrificing for the relationship are associated with their perception of positive characteristics of the relationship, including higher commitment, higher satisfaction with the relationship, and healthier couple functioning. In addition, individuals' willingness to sacrifice is associated with reduced chances of relationship breakup. It is important to note that these studies do not just find that a person's sacrifice is good for the relationship; rather, they suggest that sacrifice also is associated with positive individual factors for the one doing the giving. That is, sacrifice is associated with the sacrificer's *own perceptions* of having a more committed and healthily functioning relationship, and his or her greater satisfaction with the relationship. This is important to recognize, as it is strong evidence against the argument that sacrifices that better the relationship somehow come at the expense of the individual doing the sacrificing.

Examples of Sacrifice: Accommodation and Editing

There is much research on a particular behavior frequently seen between romantic partners during conflicts that fits the definition of sacrifice. This behavior has been labeled by different researchers as either *accommodation* or *editing*, and refers to an individual choosing to say something constructive (rather than to retaliate) following a destructive or negative communication by the partner. In our opinion, this behavior is a great example of sacrificing; that is, it involves forgoing immediate self-interest for the sake of the relationship or the partner in the specific context of communication between partners about a conflict.

Rusbult and colleagues (Rusbult, Verette, Whitney, Slovik, & Lipkus, 1991), in their work on accommodation, have shown that in response to a partner's negative behavior, individuals' fundamental, self-centered instinct is to respond negatively. However, individuals frequently do not act on this instinct, but instead transform the situation into one in which reacting constructively leads to more highly valued outcomes. That is, individuals consider the broader and more long-term goals and characteristics of the partner and the relationship and choose to act in a way that will benefit those long-term goals. In this way, accommodation is a form of sacrifice; individuals forgo their own immediate self-interest in order to serve the interests of the partner or maintain a healthy relationship.

Similarly, Gottman, Markman, and Notarius (1977) have studied editing, or the ability to recognize a negative partner behavior yet not respond in kind. This is objectified within couple interactions when a listener displays negative affect to the speaker's communication, but then responds nonnegatively in his or her next speaker turn. Notarius and colleagues (1989) note that editing "implies the operation of a cognitive process operating between the subjective receipt of a partner's message and a spouse's behavioral response" (p. 41), which resonates with Van Lange and colleagues' description of how committed individuals consider their long-term goals for the relationship before acting. This cognitive process allows individuals to make the choice to sacrifice the self-benefiting behavior (responding negatively) for the greater good of their relationship goals.

The positive influence of accommodation and editing on relationships has been well documented in the literature. In a research review of couples' interactions, Weiss and Heyman (1997) list as one of the four well-established characteristics of happy couples a tendency "to respond positively even when their partner is being negative to them" (p. 24). Specifically, researchers note that the negative escalation cycles that occur when couples *are not* accommodating or editing are powerful discriminators between distressed and nondistressed couples (Gottman, Coan, Carrere, & Swanson, 1998; Gottman & Levenson, 1986; Lindahl, Clements, & Markman, 1998). Thus, forgoing one's own immediate preference to retaliate when faced with destructive comments by the partner – which may be called accommodation, editing, or sacrifice – is associated with happy and nondistressed relationships. This provides support for the positive influence of sacrificing behaviors on intimate relationships.

THEORY ON THE POSITIVE ROLE OF SACRIFICE IN RELATIONSHIPS

Although the link between attitudes toward sacrifice, as measured by satisfaction with sacrifice and willingness to sacrifice, and positive relationship factors, including commitment, satisfaction, and level of couple functioning appears to be established, the question remains as to why this link exists. One way of framing this question is to ask what internal motivations associated with more satisfying and committed relationships give rise to willingness to sacrifice or satisfaction with sacrifice. Van Lange and colleagues (1997) note that this question has yet to be empirically studied, and they recommend that future research on sacrifice in intimate relationships "obtain more direct and valid evidence regarding the internal events that accompany willingness to forgo self-interest" (p. 1392). Understanding these underlying internal workings is the next step to understanding the link between sacrifice and positive relationship factors.

Interdependence theory (Kelley & Thibault, 1978) offers a theoretical framework through which to examine the factors influencing whether individuals are likely to sacrifice. They theorize that as partners become more interdependent, they begin to take into account long-term goals for the relationship, stable dispositions of the self and partner, and norms of the relationship. Based on these thoughts, they tend to depart from acting on the basis of their own self-interest and instead tend to act based on broader goals associated with the relationship. This process has been termed the "Transformation of Motivation" (Kelley & Thibault, 1978; Kelley, 1979). The individual who goes through this transformation of motivation is then more likely to forgo self-interest and act in accordance with what would be best for both members of the couple or for the relationship as a whole, or sacrifice. For example, as Bob begins to think about the long-term goals of his relationship with Jane, about how she is a very giving and kind person, and about how the two of them normally work to enhance the relationship, he is more likely to skip going to the baseball game (his immediate desire) in order to keep harmony in the relationship and please Jane. Thus, Interdependence theory suggests that higher commitment and interdependence should be linked with greater tendencies to sacrifice for the relationship.

Several theorists have moved beyond this general link, speculating on how two *specific* developments concomitant with increased interdependence and commitment are associated with more positive attitudes toward sacrificing for one's relationship or partner (Stanley & Markman, 1992; Stanley, 1998; Van Lange et al., 1997). These two developments are the growth of a long-term view of the relationship and the increase in a sense of couple identity.

Long-Term View

Researchers and theorists interested in romantic relationships consistently define commitment in terms of a long-term view of the relationship, or the dedication to continue the relationship over an

Sacrifice in Romantic Relationships

extended period of time (Johnson, 1982; Levinger, 1980; Rusbult 1980, 1983; Stanley & Markman, 1992). A long-term view of one's relationship is hypothesized to be integrally related to one's motivations to sacrifice for that relationship. If a couple views their relationship as short-term, what they get out of it immediately is all that is important. However, when a couple has a long-term view of their relationship, the partners are able to tolerate some sacrifice on behalf of the other in the belief that things even out over time (Stanley, 1998). Thus, individuals who expect their relationship to continue for some time are able to delay their own needs or desires with the knowledge that they eventually will be fulfilled.

Similarly, Van Lange and colleagues (1997) state that "commitment involves long-term orientation; committed individuals look beyond the here and now, considering not only the current non-correspondence problem but also anticipating future non-correspondent situations.... Thus, acts of sacrifice may represent a conscious or unconscious means to maximize long-term self-interest" (p. 1375). That is, when individuals have a sense that their relationship will go on for some time into the future, it becomes less essential that they immediately get out of it equal to what they are putting in. Instead, they have two potential motivations for sacrificing.

First, they are able to anticipate that the sacrifice they make now in the interest of the partner may be reciprocated in the form of later sacrifice by the partner. In our example, Bob may find it easier to sacrifice a night out with the boys to be with Jane since he anticipates that next weekend she may forgo her own wish to spend the evening with her girlfriends in order to have special time with Bob. Second, they personally will benefit from their sacrifice by the higher level of relationship quality in the future created by that sacrificial act. After Bob's decision to decline the invitation to the ballgame, Jane is more satisfied with her relationship, which she expresses verbally and by showing more affection toward Bob in the following week. Stanley (1998) elaborates on this second motivation, suggesting that it is the long-term view of a relationship that makes investing in the relationship worthwhile, and that sacrifice can be viewed as one type of investment. In other words, it is the knowledge that one will reap the benefits of current sacrifices through increased future quality of the relationship that, in part, makes one want to sacrifice.

In contrast, consider a couple in marital therapy where one partner is not sure of whether he or she wants to stay in the marriage. This lack of a committed, long-term view of the relationship hinders progress in the treatment because neither partner is willing to make the sacrifices that are necessary to make the relationship stronger. Specifically, one crucial component of treatment is often to communicate and process through difficult issues between the partners. This type of discussion is fitting with the definition of sacrifice, as it is often quite unpleasant and emotionally draining but is in the interest of improving the quality of the relationship. However, in this scenario, both partners resist because they simply are not confident that the relationship will last long enough for that kind of investment in the relationship – a sacrifice for the relationship – to pay off.

These theoretical speculations asserting the expectation of long-term personal benefit as a motivation for sacrifice bring up some of the complexities inherent in studying the construct. Some might state that when individuals' actions are motivated by self-interest, whether the benefit to self is immediate or delayed, those actions cannot by definition be considered sacrifices. That is, if individuals are behaving in a manner that they know will benefit themselves in the long run, then they are not truly acting in a selfless way. This argument, although thought-provoking, seems to come down to the age-old philosophical issue of whether people ever really behave in ways that cannot be somehow traced to personal gain. In fact, in the altruism literature, it is commonly recognized that most altruistic behaviors lead to self-rewards, including feelings of satisfaction or pride for having done a good deed. It is virtually impossible for a given behavior to meet the strict definition of altruism, which dictates that the behavior is carried out without expectation of reward. Therefore, several researchers have suggested that unless altruism is to be studied as a hypothetical construct, this constriction on the definition must be loosened (Bar-Tal, 1976, p. 7).

Similarly, we feel that the definition of sacrifice in relationships cannot be limited to those behaviors that are motivated by absolutely no personal benefit. Instead, we will simply look to the qualitative difference between behaviors that are strictly self-serving and those behaviors that are based on long-term thinking about what will benefit both the self and the partner, as well as the relationship. The delayed personal gain suggested by theorists to be part of sacrifice is in the form of individual benefits that are associated with having a healthier relationship. This seems a far cry from the self-oriented motivation behind martyrdom that is either unrelated or negatively related to the partner's interest. Recall the example of Jane going to a party with Bob so that she could deliberately make him feel guilty for it. Jane's motivations clearly are to benefit herself at Bob's expense (whether in the short or long run) and are not concerned with positively influencing the relationship. Compare this to Bob's act of spending the evening with Jane rather than going to the ballgame, motivated in part by the knowledge that this action will allow him and his wife to get along better in the near future. Bob is motivated by the prospect of pleasing his wife and contributing to a happier relationship, both of which are likely to also bring him positive effects. While both behaviors may eventually benefit the one performing them, they are qualitatively very different in the immediacy with which they benefit the self and the way that they affect the partner and relationship. Therefore, we will consider all acts which forgo immediate self-interest and benefit either the partner or relationship as consistent with the definition of sacrifice, whether or not they also contribute to later personal gain.

Couple Identity

Various researchers and theorists have described the formation of commitment as a shift in thinking from what's best for the self to what's best for the couple. As described above, Interdependence theory (Kelley & Thibault, 1978) emphasizes the transformation of motivation, or the process of moving from concern with self-interested preferences to concern with joint outcomes for self and the partner, which goes along with increasing commitment. Levinger (1979) describes this process this way: "... as interpersonal involvement deepens, one's partner's satisfactions and dissatisfactions become more and more identified with one's own" (p. 175). In other words, as relationships become more committed, they become less exchange oriented and closer to what Clark and Mills (1979) describe as communal; the members become increasingly concerned with the other's welfare and responsive to the other's needs. More recently, we (Stanley & Markman, 1992) have described this process as the development of a *couple identity*, defined as "the degree to which an individual thinks of the relationship as a team, in contrast to viewing it as two separate individuals, each trying to maximize individual gains" (p. 596). We have found that the strength of one's couple identity is strongly correlated with relationship commitment.

This association between increased commitment and a stronger sense of couple identity seems particularly relevant for the notion of sacrifice. Stanley (1998) points out that when couples have that strong sense of teamwork and oneness, things that one partner wants are easily perceived as something that is good for the couple as a whole, because the sense of oneness is so strong. Individuals who have such a strong sense of couple identity that they don't differentiate between what is good for them and what is good for the couple should find it less of a deviation from self-interest to act in accordance with what is best for the relationship, even when it departs from their immediate, self-oriented desires. Van Lange and colleagues (1997) similarly suggest that partners can become "linked, to the extent that a departure from self-interest that benefits the partner may not be experienced as a departure from self-interest" (p. 1375). For example, since Bob cares more about the well-being of his relationship with Jane than he does about his own desire to go to the baseball game, it does not feel to him that it is against his self-interest to sacrifice going to the game in order to make Jane happy and their relationship run more smoothly.

Indirect evidence for the influence of this shift toward a couple identity on sacrifice comes from Stanley and Markman (1992), who found that satisfaction with sacrifice for one's relationship is associated with the presence of a couple identity. However, the mere correlation between the two does not substantiate the claim that it exists because the sacrifice feels like less of a sacrifice to the individual partners. Our current research (described later) is designed to directly examine this claim by measuring the degree to which behaviors that the average person would describe as representing sacrifice are *perceived* as detrimental to the self by the individual performing them, as well as how these perceptions are related to relationship stability, commitment, and satisfaction.

THEORY AND EVIDENCE FOR THE NEGATIVE EFFECTS OF SACRIFICE IN RELATIONSHIPS

The research and theory discussed so far address general trends across populations of individuals in romantic relationships, and therefore cannot capture the individual differences in how levels of sacrificing influence relationship factors or individual well-being. One potentially crucial individual difference involves the level or amount of sacrifice that one performs. Can an individual sacrifice for the relationship *too much*, so that the consistent subordination of his or her own needs and desires to that of the partner or relationship becomes, in fact, detrimental to the well-being of the individual or of the relationship? It seems logical to suggest that if one partner gives to the relationship repeatedly and without appropriate concern for his or her own well-being, both the individual and the relationship will be less healthy. This line of thinking implies that the association between sacrifice and relationship factors such as satisfaction and level of couple functioning is not linear. Rather, when levels of sacrifice for the relationship exceed a certain threshold, the association should weaken or, in the extreme case, reverse, indicating a curvilinear relationship. It is important to determine whether or not this is the case if research on sacrifice is to be used in informing clinical practice. Blindly educating romantic partners that forgoing their own interest for that of the partner or relationship will be good for the relationship in all cases – the more the better – could potentially be quite damaging to those individuals who already are giving too much, or to those who take this advice so seriously that they begin to sacrifice at what are unhealthy levels. The next sections will review attachment theory and feminist theory, each of which offers a perspective on how sacrificing too much can have negative consequences.

Attachment Theory

Some evidence for an association between extremely high levels of sacrifice and negative relationship and individual outcomes can be found in the attachment literature (e.g., Bartholomew, 1990; Kunce & Shaver, 1994). According to attachment theory, adults classified into the three groups of secure, preoccupied, and dismissing attachment styles, should approach giving for the relationship quite differently. Bartholomew (1990; Bartholomew & Horowitz, 1991) makes the theoretical claim that preoccupied individuals have internal working models that involve negative perceptions of the self and positive views of the partner. Another feature of the preoccupied attachment style is a concern over abandonment (Feeney, 1994). Together, these characterizations of preoccupied individuals suggest a propensity to sacrifice at very high levels, even to the extent of damaging the self. That is, since they view the partner more positively than they view the self, it would be congruent with their working model to forgo self-interest in an effort to benefit the partner. Further, to quell their anxiety of being abandoned, preoccupied persons theoretically should be driven to sacrifice in order to maintain the relationship, even in situations where giving is detrimental to the self.

This is in contrast to securely attached individuals, who Bartholomew suggests have positive models of both self and partner. We would therefore expect secure persons to be willing to sacrifice in order to benefit the partner and relationship, but not when it would negatively impact the self in a serious way. That is, this theory suggests that secure individuals are likely to show a balance between benefiting the relationship or partner and benefiting the self, thereby exhibiting moderate levels of sacrifice. Finally, dismissing individuals, who are hypothesized by Bartholomew to have positive views of the self and negative views of the partner, would be expected to exhibit very low levels of sacrifice for the partner.

There is some empirical evidence for these theoretical speculations that preoccupied individuals will show the highest levels of sacrifice for the relationship or partner. Kunce and Shaver (1994) found that subjects who were preoccupied about their attachments reported the highest level of "compulsive caregiving" or the tendency to not be able to stop themselves from taking care of their partner "too much." Also, preoccupied individuals tend, more than secure and dismissing persons, to engage in indiscriminate and overly intimate self-disclosure (Mikulincer & Nachshon, 1991), often trying to "give" of the self in order to establish intimacy with the other.

If the relationship between sacrifice and relationship satisfaction, healthiness, and persistence is linear, then it is these preoccupied partners who should report the most positive relationship factors. However, this does not appear to be the case. Several studies show that preoccupied individuals report less positive and less satisfying relationships than do securely attached people (e.g., Pistole, 1989; Simpson, 1990). Kirkpatrick and Hazan (1994) found that although preoccupied women paired with avoidant men tend to have relationships that are as long-lasting as those of two secure individuals, they report the least satisfaction with their relationships. One reason for this may be that indiscriminate and excessive sacrifice, although aimed at generating intimacy and reciprocation from the partner, is ineffective in achieving these goals. Rather, immoderate giving of the self may be perceived as overwhelming or smothering by the partner, who then is motivated to establish distance in the relationship. Based on this dynamic, the preoccupied partner's expectations are not met and he or she feels dissatisfied with the relationship.

In summary, the attachment literature offers a theoretical basis for harmful effects of sacrificing for one's relationship at very high levels. In addition, it provides indirect evidence that extremely high levels of sacrifice, or indiscriminate sacrifice for the relationship, are related to negative, rather than positive, relationship factors.

Feminist Theory

In the past two decades, there has been an abundance of feminist theory describing the harmful effects of sacrifice, or at of least sacrificing too much, on women. Most of this work has stemmed from Carol Gilligan's model (1982) that women are more relationship-oriented than men, and that women have a pattern of moral development that is rooted in the ethics of caring and connection. Based on qualitative studies, many writers have supported the notion that women evidence greater relationship orientation than do men (e.g., Chodorow, 1978; Gilligan, 1982; Rubin, 1983), and Bilsker, Schiedel, and Marcia (1988) found that females' identities are more rooted in interpersonal relationships. Related to sacrifice, this theory suggests that because women are more relationship focused, they are more invested in having and maintaining relationships and are therefore willing to give up more in order to do so.

Feminist theorists also suggest that there are feminine imperatives of *how* a woman should act to cultivate and maintain relationships. Harriet Lerner (1985, 1988) suggests that women feel that they *must* sacrifice in order to maintain their relationships; they are socialized to believe that if they did not do so, any subsequent relationship difficulties or failures would be the result of their not adhering to this gender role. Lerner points out that excessive sacrifice occurs when "too much of the self (one's beliefs, values, wants, priorities, ambitions) becomes negotiable under relationship pressures"(p. 227). That is, when a woman begins to sacrifice even those components of the self that are crucial to her self-identity for the sake of the relationship, it often leads to her experiencing a loss of her self.

Similarly, Dana Crawley Jack's (1991) model of female depression posits that many women have gender-specific cognitive schemas about how to form and maintain intimate relationships. These schemas, which include the expectation that women must put the needs of others in front of the needs of the self in order to secure relationships, lead women to silence many of their thoughts, feelings, and actions.

Prolonged and repeated self-negation aimed at meeting the requirements for schemas of appropriate feminine behavior in the context of relationships contributes to a reduction in self-esteem and feelings of a "loss of self." This low self-esteem and sense of loss are then influential in the development of depression.

While conceptually compelling, there is little empirical evidence for these theories. Two studies failed to empirically validate the putative expectations for women's behavior in romantic relationships. Jerold Heiss (1991) investigated men's and women's definitions of the roles that men and women should adhere to when in a romantic relationship. Contrary to the hypothesis that women are expected to meet idealized other-oriented standards in their relationship by subordinating their own needs and interests to those of their partners, Heiss found that women prescribed *less* sacrifice for women in relationships than men prescribed for men when in love. Further, men did not require more other-oriented behavior from women than women required of men. However, women actually prescribed *more* other-oriented behavior for men than they did for women. Furthermore, Hammersala and Frease-McMahan (1990) found no gender differences in willingness to sacrifice goals such as education or career for one's relationship. When forced to choose either their relationship or a particular life goal, women were no more likely to choose the relationship than were men. The findings from both studies clearly oppose the hypothesis that women are expected (by themselves or by the men with whom they have relationships) to subordinate their desires to those of their male partners. However, it must be noted that these studies were both conducted with college students, who are quite likely to be less traditional than the population as a whole in their conceptions of gender roles. Further, even if there is not a prevalence of expectations that women sacrifice more than men for their romantic relationships, this does not rule out the possibility that individual differences in the degree to which people hold such expectations are associated with differences in levels of sacrificing behaviors, perceptions of sacrifice as detrimental to the self, or mental health outcomes.

Dana Crawley Jack (Jack, 1991; Jack & Dill, 1992) has studied these individual differences. Based on her model of female depression described above, she developed the "Silencing the Self Scale" (STSS), which targets the degree to which an individual subscribes to the traditional "rules" of the feminine role in relationships. The scale is aimed at tapping the extent to which a woman believes that she should act in certain prescribed ways to create or maintain her romantic relationship, even when this is detrimental to her self. The scale includes four subscales rationally derived to reflect the key dimensions of women's self-schemas: Externalized Self-perception, Care as Self-sacrifice, Silencing the Self, and The Divided Self. Participants indicate their extent of agreement with such items as "Caring means choosing to do what the other person wants, even when I want to do something different" and "I don't speak my feelings in an intimate relationship when I know they will cause disagreement." She has found, in three samples of women, that more endorsement of these traditional gender schemas is associated with more depressive symptomatology (Jack & Dill, 1992). However, it should be noted that the Care as Self-sacrifice Subscale, which is most relevant to our examination of the role of sacrifice in relationships, was not significantly correlated with depression in one of the samples of women, and in the other it showed a smaller correlation with depression than did the other subscales. This could be evidence that viewing sacrifice as part of what caring in a romantic relationship means is not as predictive of depression in women as are the other scales (silencing of one's self or a perception of the self as divided), which tap more harmful gender-based schemas. In fact, some females may have bought into the romantic ideology (e.g., Cancian, 1987), which includes caring and self-sacrifice for the other as an integral component of love, to such an extent that they do not perceive the sacrifices they make for their partners as harmful to the self. Under these circumstances, acts of sacrifice should not be linked with diminished mental health.

Other support for the influence of individual differences on sacrifice comes from Hammersala and Frease-McMahan's study (1988). Despite their findings that gender itself does not influence willingness to sacrifice a personal goal for a relationship, they found that individual differences in sex-role orientation do influence choices between relationships and goals. More typically feminine persons are likely to choose the relationship over the goal, while the most typically masculine individuals are likely to choose the personal goal. However, this study does not address the outcomes of such choices.

THE ROLE OF PERCEPTIONS IN SACRIFICE

Thus far, we have presented theories and empirical evidence from the general psychological literature, attachment theorists and researchers, and feminist theorists and researchers, all of which seem to present contrasting views on how sacrifice relates to relationship commitment and satisfaction and individual well-being. However, upon closer examination, it becomes apparent that all of these theories have a common theme running through them. Whether from the psychological researchers positing sacrifice as a positive relationship factor, or from feminist theorists suggesting that female sacrifice often leads to depression, these theories essentially place their evaluation of sacrifice on *how it is perceived by the individual making the sacrifice*. Thus, we propose a theory that integrates and reconciles these theories by focusing on the crucial role that one's *perceptions* of one's sacrifices in a relationship plays in determining the outcome of those sacrifices. First, we will explore the role of the perceptions surrounding one's sacrifices in each of the theories we have thus far explored.

Interdependence theorists (e.g., Van Lange et al., 1997) and commitment theorists (Stanley, 1998) speculate that the link between sacrifice and commitment occurs in part due to the change in perceptions of how harmful the sacrifice is to the self that goes along with increased commitment. For those individuals who have a strong sense of couple identity, and are therefore more interested in the well-being of the couple unit than their own individual gains, it is theorized that acts of sacrifice will be easier *because they do not feel like they are as much of a sacrifice* (Whitton, Stanley, & Markman, 2000). That is, since the couple's outcome is so important to the individual, giving personally for the good of the relationship or partner is, in effect, serving to benefit what that individual values. Hence, such relational partners may give more in the way of "sacrificial behavior" but actually *perceive* that these actions are less sacrificial; that is, less detrimental to self-interest. Similarly, individuals who have a long-term view of the relationship are predicted by this theory to perceive acts that forgo immediate self-interest for the benefit of the partner as less of a sacrifice per se, since they can be reasonably confident that their action will benefit themselves in the future, either through a happier relationship or reciprocated sacrificial acts from the partner. Thus, individuals who have more of a long-term view of their relationship and a stronger sense of couple identity are hypothesized to be less likely to *perceive* acts of forgoing their immediate self-interest *as* sacrifices than will those with less of a long-term view and couple identity (Whitton et al., 2000).

Although feminist theory, in stark contrast to the commitment-based theories discussed above, tends to focus on the potential negative effects of sacrifice in relationships, it also suggests that how individuals perceive their sacrifices is very important in determining the outcome of the sacrifice. In fact, the basis of feminist theory's criticism of sacrifice lies in the detrimental effects posited to be related to women *perceiving* their sacrifices to be harmful to their own self. A woman's perception that she has given up something important to her sense of self or perhaps even given up so much that she feels she has "lost" her self are the key to the development of depression, not the sacrificial acts themselves. In contrast, for females who have bought into the feminine romantic ideology to such an extent that they no longer perceive their acts of giving to their husbands as sacrifices at all, the sacrificial acts are not likely to be associated with depression.

This convergence between theories points to the importance of individuals' *perceptions* of their sacrifice for relationships in determining the associations sacrifice will have with relationship factors (commitment and satisfaction) as well as individual factors (sense of self and depression). Based on this review of different theories and empirical evidence regarding sacrifice in romantic relationships, we put forth the comprehensive theory that behavioral sacrifice can be positive or negative for individuals or their relationship, depending on how sacrificers perceives it (Whitton et al., 2000). Do individuals perceive their act of giving to the partner as detrimental to the self? Or as an action done in the interest of the person they love and the relationship they value? Remember that sacrifice is defined as the giving up of one thing for another thing considered to be of greater value. When individuals perceive their actions according to this conception of sacrifice, it can be a powerful positive influence on the relationship and one's sense of self. However, when many small actions are perceived as losses to the self that are not performed in the interest of a greater good, such as the betterment of a relationship or loved one, sacrifice may be harmful, leading to negative relationship and mental health consequences.

Preliminary Evidence Supporting the Crucial Role of Perceptions

We have specifically focused on how perceptions of one's sacrifices within a relationship are associated with relationship commitment and satisfaction and individual mental health (e.g., Whitton & Stanley, 1999; Whitton et al., 2000). In this work, a new measure of perceptions of sacrifice within relationships was developed. Experts in the field of romantic relationships generated items that are representative of the typical sacrificial behaviors that individuals in romantic relationships perform on a day-to-day basis. The 40 most commonly cited and theoretically important items were selected to comprise the new measure. For each item (describing one behavior seen by experts as a "sacrifice"), participants indicated how frequently in the last month they had performed the behavior on a four-point Likert scale (0 = Never, 3 = Very often). Then, for each item that participants indicated having performed at least once in the past month, they reported the extent to which performing the behavior felt like it was harmful to their self-interest on a four-point Likert scale (0 = Not at all, 3 = Very harmful). The preliminary sample consisted of 171 cohabiting (married or unmarried) individuals.

Consistent with hypotheses, results indicated that individuals with more of a long-term view of their relationship perceived acts of forgoing self-interest to be *less* harmful to the self, as did individuals who reported greater relationship quality. However, an increase in reported couple identity was negatively related to perceptions of sacrifice as harmful to the self only for males. For females, this correlation was nonsignificant. These results suggest that both a long-term view of the relationship and overall relationship quality play important roles in determining how harmful to the self individuals perceive their sacrifices to be, while couple identity is only influential for males. Why couple identity does not appear to influence perceptions of sacrifice for females is unclear; however, it may be due to a tendency of females to have a strong sense of couple identity regardless of other relationship factors. In addition, perceptions of sacrifice as harmful to the self were positively related to level of depression for both genders, explaining variance beyond that accounted for by overall relationship quality. Thus, the more harmful individuals perceive their sacrifices to be to the self, the more likely they are to exhibit depressive symptoms.

These findings provide preliminary evidence in support of our comprehensive model of sacrifice in intimate relationships. First, there is clear support for the proposed association between commitment dynamics (long-term view of the relationship for both genders, couple identity for males only) and the perception of sacrifices as harmful (or not) to the self. Second, there is support for the hypothesis that increased depressive symptomatology is associated with individuals perceiving themselves to be making sacrifices that are harmful to self-interest. Neither the commitment-based literature nor the feminist theory alone could account for both of these findings. However, our comprehensive framework, which focuses on the importance of how people sacrificing perceive their sacrifices to affect self-interest, accounts for the possible associations of sacrifice to positive relationship factors as well as diminished mental health.

Other Influences on How Sacrifices Are Perceived

Even among individuals with similar levels of commitment, perceptions of how harmful sacrificing is to the self varies. Therefore, the next aspect of our research program will be determining what factors, other than overall commitment, influence whether individuals see their sacrifices as detrimental to the self or as meaningful actions performed in the interest of the relationship. There are several likely candidates for such factors, briefly reviewed here.

First, Rusbult (personal communication, 1998) believes that being frequently called upon to sacrifice is harmful because it is experienced as a cost of the relationship. Thus, the raw number of situations in which a partner sacrifices may be an important influence on how the acts of sacrifice are perceived. Also important is the perceived reciprocity of sacrifice within relationships. We already have proposed (in the context of discussing the importance of a long-term view of the relationship) that the expected reciprocation of sacrifice is important to individuals' perception that acts of sacrifice are not so harmful to the self. We hypothesize that, even for committed individuals, knowing that the partner is not likely to reciprocate sacrifices will have an effect similar to that of not having a long-term view. That is, a lack of perceived reciprocity will be associated with perceptions that one's sacrifices are harmful, even in committed relationships.

Bahr and Bahr (1997) suggest that the reason feminist theory has portrayed sacrifice as negative is "largely because it has been seen as a behavior required more of women, and especially of mothers, than of men" (p. 7). By being *required* to sacrifice more often, one may have the negative perception that sacrifice is not within one's own locus of control. This lack of choice in whether or not to sacrifice may well be linked with experiencing sacrifice as harmful to the self.

The extent to which people are able to give deeper meaning to their acts of sacrifice also may be important in determining how their sacrifices are perceived to affect the self. If, according to individuals' personal value system, sacrifice is the proper behavior to exhibit in times of conflict of interest with the partner, they will be less likely to perceive the sacrifice as meaningless or as detrimental to the self, even when the more tangible results are not positive. This echoes Bar-Tal's (1976) conclusion from a review of altruistic behaviors that sacrificial acts that are consistent with one's norms and beliefs may actually give pleasure to the self, regardless of the response of the other, if there is meaning in the act on the part of the one giving the sacrifice. Thus, sacrificial behaviors that are performed under conditions where they are frequently called upon, unilateral, required, or lacking in higher meanings are those we would presume to be seen as the most detrimental to the self.

CONCLUSION

Based on this review of sacrifice in romantic relationships, it is clear that sacrifice is a concept integrally related to intimate relationships, and one that warrants further study. Although feminist theory has provided strong critiques against the hypothesis that sacrifice is always good for both the relationship and the individual, this does not suggest that sacrifice should be completely rejected as having a positive role in intimate relationships. Rather, it points to the importance of investigating the conditions under which sacrifice is beneficial rather than harmful. Here, we have presented strong theoretical support and preliminary empirical evidence for the crucial role that perceptions of one's sacrifices play in determining the outcome of those sacrifices. Future research should focus on testing this new framework by empirically examining the influence of these perceptions (of sacrifice as more or less harmful to the self) on the levels of sacrifice seen in relationships, as well as the effects of those sacrifices on individual and relationship factors. It will also be important to explore the putative factors – commitment and otherwise – that influence how individuals perceive their sacrifices, to determine how to best target negative perceptions of sacrifice shown by distressed couples in clinical interventions.

REFERENCES

Bahr, K. S., & Bahr, H. M. (1997). Another voice, another lens: Making a place for sacrifice in family theory and family process. Virgnia F. Cutler Lecture, College of Family, Home, and Social Sciences, Brigham Young University, November 13.

Bar-Tal, D. (1976). *Prosocial behavior*. Washington, DC: Hemisphere.
Bartholomew, K. (1990). Avoidance of intimacy: An attachment perspective. *Journal of Social and Personal Relationships, 7*, 147–178.
Bartholomew, K., & Horowitz, L. M. (1991). Attachment styles among young adults: A test of a four-category model. *Journal of Personality and Social Psychology, 61*, 226–244.
Bilsker, D., Schiedel, D., & Marcia, J. (1988). Sex differences in identity status. *Sex Roles, 18*, 231–236.
Cancian, F. M. (1987). *Love in America*. Cambridge: Cambridge University Press.
Chodorow, N. (1978). *The reproduction of mothering*. Berkeley, CA: University of California Press.
Clark, M. S., & Mills, J. (1979). Interpersonal attraction in exchange and communal relationships. *Journal of Personality and Social Psychology, 37*, 12–24.
Cook, K. S., & Emerson, R. M. (1978). Power, equity and commitment in exchange networks. *American Sociological Review, 43*, 721–739.
Feeney, J. A. (1994). Attachment style, communication patterns, and satisfaction across the life cycle of marriage. *Personal Relationships, 1*, 333–348.
Gilligan, C. (1982). *In a different voice*. Cambridge, MA: Harvard University Press.
Gottman, J. M. (1993). A theory of marital dissolution and stability. *Journal of Family Psychology, 7*, 57–75.
 (1994). *What predicts divorce? The relationship between marital processes and marital outcomes*. Hillsdale, NJ: Erlbaum.
Gottman, J. M., & Krokoff, L. J. (1989). Marital interaction and satisfaction: A longitudinal view. *Journal of Consulting and Clinical Psychology, 57*, 47–52.
Gottman, J. M., & Levenson, R. W. (1986). Assessing the role of emotion in marriage. *Behavioral Assessment, 8*, 31–48.
Gottman, J. M., Coan, J, Carrere, S., & Swanson, C. (1998). Predicting marital happiness and stability from newlywed interactions. *Journal of Marriage and the Family, 60*, 5–22.
Gottman, J. M., Markman, H. J., & Notarius, C. I. (1977). The topography of marital conflict: A sequential analysis of verbal and non-verbal behavior. *Journal of Marriage and the Family, 39*, 461–478.
Hammersala, J. F., & Frease-McMahan, L. (1990). University students' priorities: Life goals vs. relationships. *Sex Roles, 23*, 1–14.
Heiss, J. (1991). Gender and romantic-love roles. *Sociological Quarterly, 32*, 575–591.
Jack, D. C. (1991). *Silencing the self: Women and depression*. Cambridge, MA: Harvard University Press.
Jack, D. C., & Dill, D. (1992). The Silencing the Self Scale: Schemas of intimacy associated with depression in women. *Psychology of Women Quarterly, 16*, 97–106.
Johnson, M. P. (1982). The social and cognitive features of the dissolution of commitment to relationships. In S. Duck (Ed.), *Personal relationships: Dissolving personal relationships* (pp. 51–73). New York: Academic Press.
Kelley, H. H. (1979). *Personal relationships: Their structures and processes*. Hillsdale, NJ: Erlbaum.

(1983). Love and commitment. In H. H. Kelley, E. Berscheid, A. Christensen, J. H. Harvey, T. L. Huston, G. Levinger, E. McClintock, L. A. Peplau, & D. R. Peterson (Eds.), *Close relationships* (pp. 265–314). New York: Freeman.

Kelley, H. H., & Thibaut, J. W. (1978). *Interpersonal relations: A theory of interdependence.* New York: Wiley.

Kirkpatrick, L. A., & Hazan, C. (1994). Attachment styles and close relationships: A four-year prospective study. *Personal Relationships, 1,* 123–142.

Kunce, L. J., & Shaver, P. R. (1994). An attachment-theoretical approach to caregiving in romantic relationships. In K. Bartholomew & D. Perlman (Eds.), *Attachment processes in adulthood. Advances in personal relationships, Vol. 5.* (pp. 205–237). London: Jessica Kingsley.

Lerner, H. G. (1985). *The dance of anger: A woman's guide to changing the patterns of intimate relationships.* New York: Harper & Row.

(1988). *Women in therapy.* Northvale, NJ: Jason Aronson.

Levinger, G. (1979). A social exchange view on the dissolution of pair relationships. In R. L. Burgess & T. L. Huston (Eds.), *Social exchange in developing relationships* (pp. 169–193). New York: Academic Press.

(1980). Toward the analysis of close relationships. *Journal of Experimental Social Psychology, 16,* 510–544.

Lindahl, K., Clements, M., & Markman, H. (1998). The development of marriage: A nine-year perspective. In T. N. Bradbury (Ed.), *The developmental course of marital dysfunction* (pp. 205–236). Cambridge: Cambridge University Press.

Ma, H. K. (1993). The relationship of altruistic orientation to human relationships and situational factors in Chinese children. *Journal of Genetic Psychology, 154,* 85–96.

Markman, H. J. (1981). Prediction of marital distress: A 5-year follow-up. *Journal of Consulting and Clinical Psychology, 49,* 760–762.

Markman, H. J., Stanley, S. M., & Blumberg, S. (1994). *Fighting for your marriage: Positive steps for a loving and lasting relationship.* San Francisco, CA: Jossey Bass.

Mikulincer, M., & Nachshon, O. (1991). Attachment styles and patterns of self-disclosure. *Journal of Personality and Social Psychology, 61,* 321–331.

Noller, P. (1996). What is this thing called love? Defining the love that supports marriage and family. *Personal Relationships, 3,* 97–115.

Notarius, C. I., & Markman, H. J. (1993). *We can work it out: Making sense of marital conflict.* New York: Putnam.

Notarius, C. I., Benson, P. R., Sloane, D., Vanzetti, N. A., & Hornyak, L. M. (1989). Exploring the interface between perception and behavior: An analysis of marital interaction in distressed and nondistressed couples. *Behavioral Assessment, 11,* 39–64.

Pam, A., Plutchik, R., & Conte, H. (1973). Love: A psychometric approach. *Proceedings of the Annual Convention of the American Psychological Association,* 159–160.

Pistole, C. (1989). Attachment in adult romantic relationships: Style of conflict resolution and relationship satisfaction. *Journal of Social and Personal Relationships, 6,* 505–510.

Rubin, L. B. (1983). *Intimate strangers: Men and women together.* New York: Harper & Row.
Rusbult, C. E. (1980). Commitment and satisfaction in romantic associations: A test of the investment model. *Journal of Experimental Social Psychology, 16,* 172–186.
——— (1983). A longitudinal test of the investment model: The development (and deterioration) of satisfaction and commitment in heterosexual involvements. *Journal of Personality and Social Psychology, 45,* 101–117.
Rusbult, C. E., Verette, J., Whitney, G. A., Slovik, L. F., & Lipkus, I. (1991). Accommodation processes in close relationships: Theory and preliminary empirical evidence. *Journal of Personality and Social Psychology, 60,* 53–78.
Simpson, J. A. (1990). Influence of attachment styles on romantic relationships. *Journal of Personality and Social Psychology, 59,* 971–980.
Stanley, S. M. (1998). *The heart of commitment: Compelling research that reveals the secrets of a lifelong, intimate marriage.* Nashville: Thomas Nelson.
Stanley, S. M., & Markman, H. J. (1992). Assessing commitment in personal relationships. *Journal of Marriage and the Family, 54,* 595–608.
Todorov, Tzvetzan (1996). *Facing the extreme: Moral life in the concentration camps.* New York: Metropolitan Books.
Van Lange, P. A. M., Rusbult, C. E., Drigotas, S. M., Arriaga, X. B., Witcher, B. S., & Cox, C. L. (1997). Willingness to sacrifice in close relationships. *Journal of Personality and Social Psychology, 72,* 1373–1395.
Weiss, R. L., & Heyman, R. E. (1997). A clinical-research overview of couples interactions. In W. K. Halford & H. J. Markman (Eds.), *Clinical handbook of marriage and couples intervention* (pp. 13–41). New York: Wiley.
Whitton, S. W., & Stanley, S. M. (1999). *Sacrifice in romantic relationships: The role of perceptions.* Poster presented at the Convention of the American Psychological Society, Denver, CO.
Whitton, S. W., Stanley, S. M., & Markman, H. J. (2000). *Sacrifice in romantic relationships.* Manuscript in preparation, University of Denver.

CHAPTER EIGHT

Stability and Change in Social Relations
Perspectives from Gerontology and Stress Research

David A. Chiriboga

In this chapter the stability of social relationships is considered, with special attention paid to research and theory emanating from the fields of gerontology and stress. Gerontology from its very beginnings has identified social relationships as vital to the well-being of older persons. Stress research generally has been more circumscribed in its treatment of social relationships. The latter have been studied primarily for their role as potential mediators in the basic stress paradigm. This paradigm includes three elements: (a) stressors, which are the acute and chronic events and situations that impact on individuals; (b) mediators, such as social supports, that may moderate or shape the potential impact of stressors; and (c) outcomes, generally cast in terms of physical and psychological.

Despite the attention paid to social supports in studies of aging and stress, the significance of stability in relationships has received little direct attention. However, literally hundreds of studies have investigated one particular form of relational instability: social losses resulting from bereavement or divorce or relocation.

After examining a number of issues related to stability, a final section of the chapter evaluates the stability of relationships on the basis of data from a longitudinal study of normative transitions. In this latter study, subjects were followed up periodically over a 10-year period. The results provide evidence of the multiple forces associated with the stability of social activities.

Address correspondence to David A. Chiriboga, Florida Mental Health Institute, University of South Florida, 13301 Bruce Br Downs Boulevard, Tampa, Florida. E-mail address: dchiriboefmhi.usf.edu

BACKGROUND

General Considerations Concerning Social Relationships and Well-Being

The study of social relationships has intrinsic worth but also has significance for the very pragmatic reason that such relationships have repeatedly been associated with higher morale, life satisfaction, fewer symptoms of depression, and even reduced risk of death (e.g., Myers, 2000; Zimmer, Hickey, & Searle, 1995). Interest in social relationships and well-being can be traced back to Emile Durkheim's classic essays on the association between social integration and suicide and to Leo Srole's work on anomie. Today there is general recognition that social relations have profound and complex effects. Indeed, there are indications that a strong and stable social network may even help prevent functional decline in the elderly (e.g., Unger, McAvay, Bruce, Berkman, & Seeman, 1999).

In the field of gerontology, two theories, known respectively as Activity Theory and Disengagement Theory, provided an early focus on the contributions of social involvements to well-being. These theories did not specifically address relationships per se but instead focused more generally on differing levels of involvement in social activities. Activity Theory, as described by Havighurst (1957), suggested that in later life, and indeed at any stage of life, people who were more active were more satisfied with their lives. A stable set of social relationships might therefore be an asset at higher levels; change in the direction of more social relationships would also be of benefit.

Disengagement Theory (Cumming & Henry, 1961) presented an alternative based on the premise that in later life persons had potentially greater choice over their levels of activity. In Disengagement Theory there was a focus on not only level of activity but the context of the activity: (a) whether the individual wished to be high or low on activity, and (b) whether society wished the individual to be high or low on activity. Take for example the case of a worker approaching the retirement years: Does the worker wish to remain at work or retire, and does the employer wish the worker to remain at work or retire? A similar example might be made for a married couple: Does the wife wish to remain married or not, and does the husband wish to remain married or not? In both instances, life satisfaction or morale is theoretically associated with situations reflecting congruence: Self and society want the self to remain involved or to become less involved. The implications of stability in social relationships would therefore depend on whether the individual and society desired stability or change.

One lesson to be learned from these early studies, indeed, is that stability and instability may have differing implications, depending on context and personal desires. The desired and expected loss of a job (and association with fellow workers) as a result of retirement is quite different from job and relational loss resulting from being fired or retiring due to ill health. Changes in relationships resulting from the so-called empty nest transition of middle age have been characterized as including lower levels of interaction but a sustained closeness. Such changes are often greeted with relief, not despair, by the parents (Fiske & Chiriboga, 1990). The death of a close friend or family member in contrast is greeted almost universally with sadness.

Reasons Why Social Relationships May Promote Well-Being

Before questions concerning the significance of stability of social relations can even begin to be addressed, it may be helpful to review the significance of social relations in general. The actual mechanisms by which social relationships influence well-being are multiple and little understood. From an evolutionary point of view, it has been proposed that since survivability was historically enhanced by the availability of friends who were willing to make sacrifices on your behalf, the presence of such "deep friendships" creates a sense of protectedness and comfort (Bush, 2000; Tooby & Cosmides, 1996). Similarly, Baumeister and Leary (1995) theorize that out of our social evolution has come a need for belongingness. Reis and colleagues (Reis, Sheldon, Gable, Roscoe, & Ryan, in press) have postulated that relatedness represents one of a small set of psychological processes that, depending on how well they are expressed, lead to well-being or its opposite. Instability in relationships might therefore create a threat to relatedness.

A less evolutionary perspective than those described above can be found in most current research on why relationships promote well-being. It has been proposed, for example, that social relationships increase opportunities to enhance personal development and self-esteem (Lemon, Bengtson, & Peterson, 1972; Zimmer et al., 1995). According to Zimmer et al., the key ingredients of social activities are the frequency of participation and the level of intimacy associated with the activity. These twin ingredients create opportunities that foster wellness. Moreover, the same team found evidence that social activity, but not solitary or physical activity, was linked to well-being. Others report that social relationships can improve the physical health and functional capacities of older persons, especially those whose health is compromised (e.g., Unger et al., 1999). As will be noted in a later section dealing with relations as social supports, the suggested mechanisms center on social relationships providing instrumental and emotional help in times of need.

A Question of Gender
There is evidence that social networks may have a greater influence on the well-being of males, possibly because of the latter's typically more sparse social networks. In a longitudinal study of marital separation and divorce, Chiriboga, Catron, and Associates (1991) found that increases in the number of friends was related to positive outcomes, but only for men. Further analyses revealed that the effect was most evident among men whose social networks immediately after marital separation were relatively small. Among these men, increases in the size of their social networks was associated with improved psychological well-being at a 3-year follow-up interview. Seeman's (1996) extensive review of the literature also found evidence of a more protective effect of social relations for men. The generally larger social networks of women may create a reserve strength that can be drawn upon in emergencies.

A Question of Age
There is evidence that the importance of social relationships is accentuated among the elderly. For example, compared to younger adults, 17-year all-cause mortality rates in one large hospital system were more strongly associated with smaller social networks for persons aged 60 and over (Seemen, Kaplan, Knudsen, Cohen, & Guralnik, 1987). The reason for this greater importance may be that, as people age, their coping resources gradually erode as a result of functional decline, reduced income, and reduced social network due to deaths and relocation increases. As their available coping resources diminish, their support system becomes one of the key factors in coping with adversity, even though this system is itself being diminished (Fiske & Chiriboga, 1990; Unger et al., 1999). Among the elderly the stability of one's relational network may be a key factor in maintaining both physical and mental well-being.

A Question of Self-Esteem

For many years, the literature has explored the possibility that social relationships can provide a buffer against threats to self-esteem. This interpretation is most often encountered in the stress literature, where it is hypothesized that social relations can minimize a stress condition's capability of affecting the individual's self-esteem (e.g, Pearlin, 1999; Thoits, 1999). The loss of self-esteem, it is hypothesized, can increase the risk of depression and even health problems (Cohen, Doyle, Skoner, Rabin, & Gwaltney, 1997). One reason is that friends can perform such actions as reassuring individuals that they are not bad, that they are capable, that the problem does not reflect on who and what they are. Such an idea is entirely congruent with a hypothesis posed by Rosenberg (1979) a number of years ago. According to Rosenberg, "mattering" is critical to feelings of well-being. If individuals feel that they matter to someone, then their self-worth and esteem are enhanced and maintained.

Overall, there is evidence that reductions in social relationships, as well as a chronically sparse set of relationships, have serious implications for the well-being of individuals. Social loss has a strong and usually negative effect on people at any age (e.g., Carnelley, Wortman, Kessler, 1999). Low levels of social support not only are linked to the development of health problems, but also to mortality (e.g., Berkman, Leo-Summers, & Harwitz, 1992; Sarason, Sarason, Irwin, & Gurung, 1997; Williams & Chesney, 1993). However, it should also be pointed out that individuals with long and stable histories of living in voluntary isolation may actually be protected from one major stressor: the loss of significant others.

Social Relationships over Time

While children and young adults may not have much of a "history" of social relationships, by the time individuals reach middle and later life they not only have developed characteristic social likes and dislikes but also have usually one or more long-term relationships. The length of these relationships may not simply be due to age. A long time ago, Neugarten (1968) concluded on the basis of a study of 100 highly successful men and women that the middle years of life are marked by an increased awareness of oneself and one's preferences and abilities, including those related to the interpersonal. More recent research has provided some substantiation of Neugarten's conclusion. Carstensen,

Gross, and Fung (1997), for example, found evidence that in the later years people are more knowledgeable and selective in their social relationships. This selectivity may lead to greater stability, but also greater investment in relationships. For example, Chiriboga, Catron and Associates (1991) found that middle-aged and older persons were much harder hit by marital separation than were young adults.

Recognizing that individuals have a history of social relationships, many of which have endured for years if not decades, Antonucci and Akiyama (1995) developed the concept of a social convoy that accompanies the individual over the life course. According to Antonucci and Akiyama, the stability of one's social relationships over the life course is an important area of study. A related approach is to consider the "career" or trajectory of an individual's social relationships over time (Chiriboga, 1994). The career model suggests that there is a gradual evolution or change in relationships in general. In other instances, such as in a caregiving or work-focused relationships, there may even be distinct stages that are linked to changes in the health of the care recipient or changes in job status.

Evidence for and about Stability in Social Relationships

Much of the available information on stability actually comes from the literature on instability: Studies of bereavement and other social disruptions have a long history in the behavioral sciences. A growing number of these studies, however, are addressing relationship stability. Curiously, the very mundane factor of travel time has emerged as critical in studies of relational stability, especially among older persons. In one longitudinal study of over 2,000 older subjects, Klein, Ikkink, and van Tilburg (1999) showed that relationships are more likely to be continued if they are more intense, involve close family, and involve less travel time. Results from the 95 remaining subjects in the 16th year of the Bangor Longitudinal Study of Aging indicated that the confidants had changed for a majority of respondents, with the changes being due primarily to disabilities and death (Wenger & Jerrome, 1999). Less travel time was again implicated as a major factor in retention of a confidant.

This centrality of travel time among older friendship systems may arise in part because mobility is more likely to be compromised with age and in part because aging is associated with a host of physical, social, and economic needs that are more difficult to address if friends and relatives are more distant. Among younger persons and those of all ages who are free of health and economic constraints, the Internet, phones, and various modes of transportation may reduce the salience of geographic proximity or travel time.

The Nature of Instability

While instability often is presented as a problematic feature in social relations, it also may create new opportunities and challenges. The stress literature often treats social loss as a stressor, but it also provides evidence that individuals can grow from the challenges posed by these losses (e.g., Bowlby, 1980). One longitudinal study of the divorce process found that in their social activities as well as morale, middle-aged subjects were initially more disrupted than younger subjects by marital separation but generally fared better than younger subjects some three to four years later (Chiriboga et al., 1991).

It has already been noted that when individuals have an impoverished or minimal social network, gains to one's social network can provide benefit (Chiriboga et al., 1991; Peek & Lin, 1999). Interestingly, there is also evidence that individuals with ample networks are more likely to report changes in the network (Klein, Ikkink, & van Tilburg, 1999). Reductions in smaller networks, such as those more characteristic of the elderly and males of all ages, may, however, have greater implications for well-being than instability in larger networks.

Social Support: An Integral Component of Social Relationships

One vigorous line of research focuses on social relations as resources that help individuals deal with acute and chronic stress conditions. In this type of research, relationships are evaluated specifically in terms of their social support characteristics, and the focus of attention frequently is on how resources help one individual rather than on the reciprocal exchange of help. As mentioned at the beginning of this chapter, stress researchers have examined the role social relationships play as mediators and buffers during stressful circumstances. Despite the attention that has been paid to this issue, however, what is meant by the term *social support* remains ambiguous since it can refer to multiple conditions and circumstances.

Among health professionals, a distinction is commonly made between informal and formal support systems. Informal supports are those provided by family, friends, acquaintances, and other non-professionals. One of the earliest gerontological studies of informal supports found that even contacts with seemingly peripheral persons like grocery store clerks or bank tellers may provide a buffer against the impact of stressors (Lowenthal & Haven, 1968). Formal supports, in contrast, are those provided by professional and semiprofessional individuals and groups such as visiting homemaker or nurse programs, suicide hotlines, and the clergy. Since formal supportive relationships are costly to society, a great deal of attention has been paid to how to make informal supports more able to sustain the burden of care.

Social supports generally arise from interpersonal relationships marked by feelings of positive regard, commitment, and personal valuation. Researchers often define the notion of social support in terms of behavior that provides someone with emotional, instrumental, self-esteem enhancing, or informational support (Martire, Schulz, Mittelmark, & Newsom, 1999; Unger et al., 1999). The actual or perceived adequacy of the support system is also important (e.g., Oxman & Berkman, 1990), regardless of whether it is composed of one other person or an entire social network (e.g., Antonucci & Akiyama, 1995). It may be helpful to bear in mind that the adequacy of informal support activities depends heavily on characteristics of the network (Lin, 1999; Thoits, 1999). Stability is one such characteristic.

Caregiving as a Very Specific Type of Supportive Relationship
From the point of view of social relationships, the support literature is informative since it provides information on how and when social relationships are beneficial or detrimental for all of us. Caregiving research is even more focused. The literature draws attention to relationships involving the sustained provision of care to a person who is unable to reciprocate, and it typically focuses on the care provider rather than the care recipient (e.g., Montgomery, 1999). There is general agreement that caregiving represents a multidimensional construct involving such factors as amount of support required, gender of support provider and recipient, past relationship of provider and recipient, and even personality (e.g., Dyck, Short, & Vitaliano, 1999). The stability of the caregiving relationship has not been evaluated systematically, but it can be hypothesized that instability in the caregiver relationship might have immediate and at times costly implications for the well-being of both provider and recipient. The caregiving relationship also shifts over

time, as dependencies change and as the experience of the caregiver and care recipient evolve (Chiriboga, 1994).

Support: Who Provides It?
Studies generally have suggested that families provide the bulk of social support for the elderly. Contrary to popular opinion, most elderly maintain frequent contact with family and provide at least as much support as they receive. Also of interest is that in the area of support certain minority groups may have an advantage. The family support system often is more extensive among those of Hispanic or African American heritage, and other individuals or groups may also play an important role (Hogan & Spencer, 1993; Jackson & Antonucci, 1992). For example, people associated with church may figure prominently in the social network of African Americans (McRae, Thompson, & Cooper, 1999). Instability in these larger networks of potential caregivers may have fewer negative consequences due to redundancies of the network.

Support as a Mediator of Stress
Literally hundreds of studies have investigated the role of family and friends as mediators or "buffers" against the impact of stress conditions. In part, buffering may result from the direct provision of needed resources, be they emotional or financial support, services, or information (House, Umberson, & Landis, 1988). There is a suggestion that when people feel part of a social group, they act in a more socially responsible manner or take better care of themselves. Less obvious is that the presence of social supports may work to counteract the deleterious impact of stress upon functioning of the immune system (Cohen et al., 1997; Kiecolt-Glaser, 1999).

While it is true that in stress research social relationships are primarily considered in terms of their potential role as mediators, new directions are emerging. These new directions include studies of the negative consequences of supports and relationships, caregiving as a specific instance of support provision, and the mechanisms by which social relationships become supportive. As mentioned earlier, the stability of relationships is rarely examined in the stress literature except for instances where someone close to the subject of study dies. This specific instance of instability is generally examined from the perspective of the loss being a stressor in itself, rather than as an instance of a more general phenomenon of relational instability.

A LONGITUDINAL STUDY OF TRANSITIONS

In this section several research questions related to some of the issues that have been discussed in preceding sections are explored. The data used to answer the questions come from a longitudinal study of individuals undergoing periods of transition. The questions do not address all the issues but are intended simply to focus attention on several that deal with issues of stability in social relationships. The first question is: How stable are social activities over time, and how does the stability of these activities compare to that manifest by other qualities of individuals? The second questions asks: Is there any evidence that social activities are related to the self-concept of individuals, and is this relationship maintained over time? The third and fourth questions ask whether social stressors might act as a destabilizing force in social activities and in the self-concept.

Background Information

Begun in late 1968, the focus of this life span study was what happened to four groups of average, community-dwelling people over time. Each group was facing a major normative transition. The two youngest groups consisted of: (a) high school seniors who were facing graduation and entry into adult status, and (b) men and women whose first marriage was less than one year old and who would presumably be dealing with issues of parenting within the next few years. Two groups at earlier and later stages of middle age were also included: (c) men and women whose youngest child was a high school senior and who therefore were likely to face the proverbial "empty nest," and (d) men and women who either were expecting to retire within five years or who had a spouse about to retire.

All subjects lived in the most homogeneous and stable district of a west coast city. The district we selected was composed, with a few exceptions, of lower middle-class and blue-collar workers of Caucasian descent. From school records, high school seniors ($N = 52$) who were the youngest members of their families were identified, thereby also locating parents ($N = 54$) who were about to enter the "empty nest" phase. For both groups, names were drawn at random; with one exception, this procedure generated high school and parent subjects who were unrelated. Using public vital statistics, newlyweds ($N = 50$) of less than a year were located, with at least one of each pair living or having lived in this district; for all this was their first marriage, and we interviewed a sample of individuals not couples. The oldest people ($N = 60$) who planned to retire within 2 or 3 years, were located through records of firms or agencies in the area, or suggested by people in the other three groups.

The Five Initial Contacts
The first interviews began in 1968 and usually required a total of 6 to 8 hours to complete. Each of the four remaining interviews was designed to fit within a single 3-hour session. The second interview was conducted between April 1970 and November 1971. The third interview was conducted between February and November 1974, while the fourth was completed between February and August 1977. The fifth set of interviews was completed between April and August 1980. During these multiple contacts, we lost some respondents, and by the time of the last contact our sample was reduced to 168 persons – 78% of the original sample. Not unexpectedly, some respondents had died, 18 in all, primarily but not only the older ones.

Sample Characteristics
The sample was generally representative of traditional blue-collar workers. For the most part upwardly mobile, their ways of living resembled those of the middle and lower-middle classes. They lived in their own small homes in a neighborhood distinguished by the homogeneity of its architecture. Very few held leadership roles in their district or in the city; the primary concern for most lay with the family, both nuclear and extended. Aside from those who were high school seniors at the first interview, a majority had some technical or general education beyond high school – few had completed college. Not surprisingly, the newlyweds were better educated than the middle-aged, who in turn had more schooling than the preretirees. Also reflecting national trends, the older the respondents were more likely to have many siblings, while they themselves have an average of two to three children. Most acknowledged some religious affiliation, with more women than men attending services; many parents who did not participate themselves sent their children to Sunday school or synagogue. More than three-fourths of the women had jobs, frequently on a part-time basis.

The Measures

Activities Checklist

One of the principal interests in the following analyses was the stability in activities that are associated directly or indirectly to social relations. Central to the examination was a 33-item checklist of leisure activities reported by respondents. Each item was scored from 0 ("no participation") to 3 ("frequent participation") by subjects. An initial factor analysis (Fiske & Chiriboga, 1990) indicated the presence of five scales:

1. *Contemplative Activities.* This scale included five items: walking, praying, daydreaming, reminiscing, and writing (alpha = .58).
2. *Housework.* This scale included three items: shopping, cooking, and chores (alpha = .56).
3. *Social Activities.* The scale most directly related to social relations included nine items: cultural activities, travel, picnics, visiting, being visited, parties, eating out, talking, and going to the movies (alpha = .70).
4. *Self-Developmental Activities.* This scale included both solitary and social activities; it included five items: crafts, solitary activities, playing a musical instrument, helping others, and self-improvement activities (alpha = .48).
5. *Sports.* This scale included six items: participant sports, exercise, spectator sports, playing cards, dancing, and lower levels of reading (alpha = .56).

In addition to the five factor-derived scales, an activity scope score was created by summing scores for all 33 items.

Other measures reported in this chapter include family role scope (a count of how many of seven family roles, such as spouse or sibling or child, were occupied by the subject) and total role scope (a count of how many of 13 roles, including friend, neighbor, churchgoer, student, etc. were enacted by the participant). Subjects also were asked Likert-scaled single-item questions concerning how satisfied they were with their general level of activity and how well their marriage compared to those of others.

Life Stressors

Two measures of stressors were included, dealing with life events and hassles. The measure of life events was the 139-item Life Events

Questionnaire (Fiske & Chiriboga, 1990), which respondents completed at the third, fourth, and fifth contacts. In addition to checking off each event that occurred over the past year, respondents also noted whether it was a negative or positive experience. Data included here represent summary totals for negative and positive events from the third and fifth interview contacts. Also included for the same time periods was a summary score from an 11-item hassles inventory (Fiske & Chiriboga, 1990).

Personal and Health Characteristics

Measures from four instruments explored a variety of personal characteristics:

1. *Psychological Symptoms.* A 42-item checklist of symptoms had been developed for the study by three geriatric psychiatrists: Drs. Leonard Micon, Alexander Simon, and Robert Butler (Fiske & Chiriboga, 1990). Drawing heavily on the Cornell Medical Index, this checklist generated a summary score that was used in this chapter.
2. *Bradburn Scales.* Included here are the Bradburn (1969) Affect Balance Scale and a general question ("In general, how happy are you these days? Very happy, somewhat happy, or not too happy").
3. *Self-Reported Health.* Two questions with structured response asked (a) how often the subjects had visited the doctor during the past 12 months, and (b) how healthy they thought they were, compared to others their age.
4. *Adjective Rating List.* A 70-item instrument derived from the Block (1961) Q-Sort method was employed, but was changed to a three-point rating system. Two global scores, positive and negative self-concept, were generated by a principal components analysis (Fiske & Chiriboga, 1990). Seven domains of the self were also identified on the basis of factor analysis. In addition, respondents were asked to circle any characteristic of themselves that they disliked; the result was a self-criticism index.

Comparative Stability in Social Activities

The first step in evaluating stability was to compute correlations between baseline characteristics of all subjects and their status on the same characteristics approximately five years later. For several measures, the stability correlations had to be calculated for two periods later into the study. For example, scores for the life events and hassles measures were compared between the fifth- and tenth-year contacts.

As shown in Table 8.1, the 5-year correlations for the activities measures were in the low moderate range. For the entire sample, the correlations ranged from .41 to .58. While all correlations were significant, it is noteworthy that the activities pertaining specifically to social relations manifest the lowest correlation over time. When the correlations for the four stages are considered individually, it becomes apparent that the younger two groups – especially the newlyweds – manifest lower levels of stability in social activities than did the two older groups. Indeed, the correlations for the two older groups are consistently higher in magnitude than those of the two younger groups. Gender differences, in contrast, are not obvious. The one area of possible differences lies in the areas of housework, where women manifest a relatively a weak correlation ($p = .05$) over time, while the correlation for men was significant at the .001 level.

The stability correlations found for activity measures are higher than some other domains of consideration, and lower than others. For example, the two measures with the greatest 5-year stability were a summary score of positive self-attributes (all sample $r = .63$) and self-reported hassles (all sample $r = .64$). Marital satisfaction and satisfaction with one's activities, both being indicated by single-item measures, were roughly equivalent to the activity measures in reliability. On the lower end of stability were the two measures of morale, the Bradburn Affect Balance Scale (Bradburn, 1969), and the Overall Happiness Score; the measures of positive and negative life events; and number of visits to the doctor. Over all, then, it would appear that measures tapping into the domain of social relations are likely to be relatively stable but would not be expected to manifest the kind of stability that has been found for measures of self-concept and personality (e.g, McCrae et al., 2000).

Generally what these initial correlations demonstrate is that activities, whether specific to social relationships or related to other domains of life, are moderately stable over time. In the case of activities specific to social relationships, as well as for nearly all measures, the results suggest that those in the middle and later years manifest greater stability. What is intriguing about these findings is that the levels of

Table 8.1. Correlations from Baseline Contact to 5-year Follow-up: Transitions Study.

		The Four Stages of the Study				Gender	
Variables	All Rs (N = 186)	High School (N = 46)	Newlywed (N = 46)	Empty Nest (N = 43)	Retirement (N = 51)	Men (N = 91)	Women (N = 95)
1. Activity Checklist							
Contemplative	.46***	-.03	.35*	.45**	.73***	.42***	.51***
Housework	.53***	.46***	.36**	.60***	.69***	.43***	.24*
Social	.41***	.43**	.01	.57***	.52***	.31**	.50***
Self-development	.49***	.34*	.36**	.56***	.55***	.46**	.48***
Sports-oriented	.58***	.36**	.53***	.67***	.58***	.63***	.53***
Scope of Activities	.50***	.38**	.16	.47***	.62***	.47***	.51***
2. Other Relational							
Activity satisfaction	.39***	.31*	.41**	.47**	.28	.59***	.23*
Marital satisfaction	.48***	.40	.37*	.52**	.68***	.50***	.45***
3. Self-Concept							
Negative Self-image	.56***	.33*	.46**	.71***	.61***	.57***	.55***
Positive Self-image	.63***	.51***	.65***	.70***	.68***	.60***	.64***
Self-criticism	.39***	.49***	.17	.53***	.46***	.51***	.30**
4. Emotional							
Affect Balance	.35***	.25	.30*	.45**	.34**	.45***	.28**
Overall Happiness	.21**	.04	.11	.35*	.24	.26*	.16
Psych Symptoms	.46***	.25	.54***	.59***	.45***	.38***	.52***
5. Physical Health							
Perceived Health	.39***	.17	.45**	.52***	.41**	.36***	.41***
Number Dr's Visits	-.04	.13	-.16	.01	-.13	-.10	.18
6. Stressors							
Hassles	.64***	.74***	.41**	.57***	.25	.63***	.63***
Negative Events	.33***	.42**	.32*	.24	.02	.25*	.39***
Positive Events	.38***	.53***	-.13	.33*	-.06	.46***	.31**
7. Other							
Reported Income	.39***	-.17	.41**	.69*	.72***	.39***	.36*
Religiousity	.46***	.22	.38**	.78***	.51***	.53***	.39***

* p = .05   ** p = .01   *** p = .001

Stability and Change

Table 8.2. Correlations between Self-Concept Factors and Indicators of Three Socially Related Activities (as Assessed at Baseline and at the 5-Year Follow-up) and Total Scope of Activities at Baseline.

	\multicolumn{6}{c	}{Indicators of Social Relations}	
	Social		Self-Development		Contemplative		Activity
Factors	Base	5 years	Base	5 years	Base	5 years	Scope
Amiable	.19**	.25***	−.10	.08	.06	.02	.21**
Assertive	.15*	.11	.11	.10	.07	.01	.22***
Controlling	−.11	.00	−.23***	−.22**	−.17*	−.13	−.19**
Dysphoric	−.03	−.09	−.08	−.06	.21**	.17*	.04
Insecure	.06	−.06	.04	.09	.20**	.16*	.13
Polished	−.01	.11	−.16*	−.04	.06	−.17*	.09
Hostile	.02	−.10	.27***	−.10	.15*	.08	.20**

* p = .05   ** p = .01   *** p = .001

stability most likely represent relatively conservative estimates, since all subjects had been specifically selected for study because they were facing major normative transitions that take a number of years to completely unfold.

Relationship of Self-Concept to Social Activities

An aspect of social relations that bears examination lies in their association with the self-image of the individual. As George Herbert Mead commented many years ago, one's self-image is formed at least in part by social exchanges. To consider the relationship between social activities and self-concept in more detail, Table 8.2 shows how five self-concept factors correlated with the social activities. All of the correlations are relatively weak, but at the same time there are patterns that do establish linkages between these two domains of study.

For example, persons who considered themselves higher in attributes reflecting amiability also were more likely to report social activities at both points in time, and also were higher in the overall scope of their activities. Assertive people were higher at baseline in the level of social, as well as overall level of, activities. People who saw themselves as more controlling were likely to be lower in self-development activities at both points in time, and also to be lower in the overall score of their activities. Persons whose self-characterizations reflected a dysphoric quality were more likely to be involved in contemplative, solitary activities; the same was true for those whose self-concepts reflected a sense of insecurity. Those who saw themselves as socially polished were lower in self-development activities (but only at baseline) and were less involved in solitary or contemplative activities 5 years later. Finally, persons with more hostile self-images were higher in activities reflecting self-development and contemplation, but this was true only at baseline. These people were also more active overall in the scope of their activities.

Overall, the results presented in Table 8.2 suggest that social activities and social relationships are associated with individuals' self-assessment of personal attributes. As will be shown later, the self factors that were included in the table demonstrated moderate levels of stability over an 11-year sweep of time. Given that self-concept is a relatively stable domain of the self, these findings are important in establishing that the kinds of social activities that form an important component of social relationships are related to the inner world of the self.

Forces of Change

To examine some of the forces that affect stability in social activities, the next step was to assess 5-year stability in the context of being higher or lower on negative life events. Life events were chosen because they have been shown to affect the stability over time of self-concept indicators (i.e., Chiriboga et al., 1991; Fiske & Chiriboga, 1990). As shown in Table 8.3, both contemplative and social activities were less stable under conditions of high stress, while housework and self-development activities demonstrated higher levels of stability. These findings suggest that social relationships are indeed disrupted. Activities related to sports, in contrast, seemed relatively impervious to the effects of stress exposure.

To put the effects of stress exposure on social activities in perspective, the next step was to consider the effect of stress upon self-concept measures. As shown in Table 8.4, the attributes of self-image that were categorized as reflecting amiability were the most affected by high levels of exposure to stress. The amount of variance (i.e., r^2) explained by the correlation dropped from about 43% to about 5.8%. Amiability, indeed, was the only self-attribute that was clearly affected by stress

Table 8.3. Intracorrelations for Social Activities Variables at Baseline and 5-Year Follow-up, under Conditions of Low and High Stress (Measured by Negative Life Event Score).

	Stress Level	
	Low	High
Contemplative	.51***	.38***
Housework	.47***	.63***
Social	.53***	.20
Self Development	.41***	.58***
Sports	.55***	.56***
Overall Activity Scope	.50***	.44***

* p = .05
** p = .01
*** p = .001

Table 8.4. Intracorrelations for Self-Concept Measures at Baseline and 5-Year Follow-up, under Conditions of Low and High Stress (Measured by Negative Life Event Score).

	Stress Level	
	Low	High
Amiable	.66***	.24*
Assertive	.62***	.56***
Controlling	.49***	.59***
Dysphoric	.41***	.36***
Insecure	.62***	.69***
Polished	.53***	.55***
Hostile	.49***	.46***

* p = .05
** p = .01
*** p = .001

exposure. The stability of the remaining six attributes varied in only minor ways under conditions of greater and lesser stress. Thus, the self-attribute that was most associated with social activities (see Table 8.2) was also the attribute most affected by stress conditions. This helps to explain why the social activities measure demonstrated the lowest stability of all activities.

Stability in Self-Concept Attributes Related to Social Relationships

Here we will consider the stability in seven self-concept factor scores over a period of approximately 11 years. All seven factors represent characteristics, such as amiability and assertiveness, that were shown in Table 8.2 to have a bearing on social relationships. As shown in Table 8.5, the overall correlations over an 11-year period suggest a low to moderate level of stability that approximates the 5-year correlations previously reported for social activities.

In these 11-year intracorrelations, the two older groups once again manifest generally higher levels of stability than the two younger groups. One implication of this finding is that to the extent self-concept attributes affect stability in social relations, middle-aged and older persons should exhibit greater stability than the two younger groups. Referring back to Table 8.1, which covered stability in social relations over a 5-year period of time, some evidence was found for this hypothesis.

SOME CONCLUDING THOUGHTS

In the literature review that began this chapter, the stability of social, leisure, and personal relationships was found to have implications not only for the general topic of social relations but also for research on stress, psychological well-being, and physical health. Because of these implications, there is a growing number of bridging studies, such as that of Coleman and Iso-Ahola (1993), which specifically examine social activities both as a field of study and as important elements in paradigms of stress and health.

The literature presented in this chapter also illustrates how complex and context-dependent the topic of relational stability is. Persons with larger social networks, for example, may exhibit greater relational instability but suffer less from this instability. Those in the oldest stages of life often experience disruptions in their social relationships at a time when they need stability the most. Persons from nonmainstream cultural backgrounds may have important social relationships that fall outside the family and are therefore ignored in much research. Men with relatively small networks may need to actively work at increas-

Table 8.5. Eleven-Year Correlations between Adjective Checklist Factors.

		Stage of the Life Course				Gender	
Factors	All Respondents (N = 154)	High School (N = 40)	Newlywed (N = 40)	Empty Nest (N = 36)	Retirement (N = 38)	Men (N = 71)	Women (N = 83)
Amiable	.35***	-.06	.40**	.47**	.58***	.36**	.30**
Assertive	.53***	.41**	.32*	.63***	.76***	.50***	.51***
Controlling	.41***	.29	.35*	.39*	.54***	.42***	.36***
Dysphoric	.31***	.14	.48**	.38*	.17	.38***	.23*
Insecure	.61***	.34*	.51***	.80***	.80***	.65***	.51***
Polished	.52***	.48**	.44**	.69***	.50**	.41***	.61***
Hostile	.54***	.29	.56***	.55***	.62***	.50***	.61***

* = .05
** = .01
*** = .001

ing the number and quality of their social relationships during times of crisis: For these men, stability in social relationships may create greater vulnerabilities than instability during times of stress.

To begin to examine some of the complexities in stability, a series of analyses were presented. The analyses drew upon a longitudinal study of men and women who originally ranged in age from 16 to their 60s. The sample was relatively unique in being composed of "working class" individuals, whose lives and social context might well have influenced what we found with respect to stability in social activities. These analyses, however, were not designed to be definitive presentations, but rather to demonstrate some of the ways in which relationship stability might be addressed in future research. The linkage between social activities and self-concept, for example, suggests that characteristics of the social context such as stability occur as part of a complex interplay between individuals' inner and outer worlds. Similarly, the impact of negative stressors on the more interpersonally oriented aspects of self-concept suggest that questions of stability must take into consideration the demands being placed on individuals. Clearly the study of stability requires comprehensive and multidisciplinary attention.

Questions of stability in interpersonal relationships are of more than academic interest. For those of us who are interested in very pragmatic issues such as the ability of individuals to provide not only temporary support but sometimes sustained levels of caregiving, stability in relationships becomes a potentially vital target of investigation. In particular, with the rapid growth in the elderly population of the United States, the associated increasing prevalence of chronic disease, the trend toward smaller families, and the high rate of divorce, it is not surprising that many social scientists are concerned about future sources of support for the elderly. In this context of manifest need, the stability of informal support systems will continue to have tremendous significance. In addition, new paradigms of successful aging (e.g., Carver, 1998; Rowe & Kahn, 1998) are incorporating social support and social relationships as critical elements. The emphasis is therefore shifting from one with a focus on problems and dysfunction to one that manifests an appreciation for the positive contributions that social relationships make.

Whatever the focus, a point made repeatedly in this entire volume is that issues of relational stability are complex and multidetermined, and of unexplored but great import. Research is just beginning to identify how this domain of relationships should and can be studied. The identification of appropriate methodologies is of obvious concern. One readily identifiable problem is that studying a dynamic process – which is really what the study of stability in relationships is all about – is extremely difficult if not impossible with standard cross-sectional, panel, and longitudinal methodologies.

Perhaps more important, those studying the stability of relationships are only beginning to identify the critical parameters of study. In this chapter, I have attempted to demonstrate that a life course perspective can provide a useful overview of when and how stability may become important to individuals. I also have documented the salience of stability for understanding how people fare when under conditions of chronic and acute stress. The bottom line, regardless of the perspective adopted, is that there is strong evidence that stability in social relationships plays a vital role in a well-functioning support system.

REFERENCES

Antonucci, T., & Akiyama, H. (1995). Convoys of social relations: Family and friendships within a life span context. In R. Blieszner & V. H. Bedford (Eds.), *Handbook of aging and the family* (pp. 355–371). Westport, CT: Greenwood Press.

Baumeister, R. F., & Leary, M. R. (1995). The need to belong: Desire for interpersonal attachment as a fundamental human motivation. *Psychological Bulletin, 17*, 497–529.

Berkman, L. F., Leo-Summers, L., & Harwitz, R. I. (1992). Emotional support and survival after myocardial infarction. *Annals of Internal Medicine, 117*, 1003–1009.

Block, J. (1961). *The Q-sort method in personality assessment and psychiatric research.* Springfield, IL: Thomas.

Bowlby, J. (1980). *Attachment and loss. Vol. III. Loss: Sadness and depression.* New York: Basic Books.

Bradburn, N. (1969). *The structure of psychological well-being.* Chicago: Aldine.

Brickman, P., & Campbell, D. T. (1971). Hedonic relativism and planning the good society. In M. H. Appley (Ed.), *Adaptation-level theory.* New York: Academic Press.

Bush, D. M. (2000). The evolution of happiness. *American Psychologist, 55*, 15–23.

Carnelley, K. B., Wortman, C. B., & Kessler, R. C. (1999). The impact of widowhood on depression: Findings from a prospective survey. *Psychological Medicine, 29*, 1111–1123.

Carstensen, L., Gross, J., & Fung, H. (1997). The social context of emotional experience. *Annual Review of Gerontology and Geriatrics, 17*, 325–352.

Carver, C. S. (1998). Resilience and thriving: Issues, models and linkages. *Journal of Social Issues, 54*, 245–266.

Chiriboga, D. A. (1994). Of career paths and expectations: Comments on Pearlin and Aneshensel's "Caregiving: The unexpected career." *Social Justice Research, 7,* 391–400.
Chiriboga, D. A., & Pierce, R. C. (1993). Changing contexts of activity. In J. Kelly (Ed.), *Leisure activities in later life* (pp. 42–59). Newbury Park, CA: Sage.
Chiriboga, D. A., Catron, L. S., & Associates. (1991). *Divorce: Crisis, challenge or relief?* San Francisco, CA: Jossey-Bass.
Cohen, S., Doyle, W. J., Skoner, D. P., Rabin, B. S., & Gwaltney, J. M. (1997). Social ties and susceptibility to the common cold. *Journal of the American Medical Association, 277,* 1940–1944.
Coleman, D., & Iso-Ahola, S. E. (1993). Leisure and health: The role of social support and self-determination. *Journal of Leisure Research, 25,* 111–128.
Cumming, E., & Henry, W. E. (1961). *Growing old: The process of disengagement.* New York: Basic Books.
Diener, E. (2000). Subjective well-being: The science of happiness and a proposal for a National Index. *American Psychologist, 55,* 34–43.
Dyck, D. G., Short, R., & Vitaliano, P. P. (1999). Predictors of burden and infectious illness in schizophrenia caregivers. *Psychosomatic Medicine, 61,* 411–419.
Fiske, M., & Chiriboga, D. A. (1990). *Change and continuity in adult life.* San Francisco, CA: Jossey-Bass.
Havighurst, R. J. (1957). The social competence of middle-aged people. *Genetic Psychology Monograph, 56,* 297–375.
Hogan, D. P., & Spencer, L. J. (1993). Kin structure and assistance in aging societies. In G. L. Maddox & M. P. Lawton (Eds.), *Annual review of gerontology and geriatrics* (pp. 169–186). New York: Springer.
Holahan, C. J., Moos, R. H., Holahan, C. K., & Cronkite, R. C. (1999). Resource loss, resource gain, and depressive symptoms: A 10-year model. *Journal of Personality and Social Psychology, 77,* 620–629.
House, J. S., Umberson, D., & Landis, K. R. (1988). Structure and processes of social support. *Annual Review of Sociology, 14,* 293–318.
Jackson, J. S., & Antonucci, T. C. (1992). Social support processes in the health and effective functioning of the elderly. In M. L. Wykle & E. Kahana (Eds.), *Stress and health among the elderly* (pp. 72–95). New York: Springer.
Kiecolt-Glaser, J. K. (1999). Stress, personal relationships, and immune function: Health implications. *Brain, Behavior and Immunity, 13,* 61–72.
Klein Ikkink, K., & van Tilburg, T. (1999). Broken ties: Reciprocity and other factors affecting the termination of older adults' relationships. *Social Networks, 21,* 131–146.
Lemon, B. W., Bengtson, V. L., & Peterson, J. A. (1972). An exploration of the activity theory of aging: Activity types and life satisfaction among in-movers to a retirement community. *Journal of Gerontology, 27,* 511–523.
Lin, N. (1999). Social networks and status attainment. *Annual Review of Sociology, 25,* 467–487.
Lowenthal, M. F., & Haven, C. (1968). Interaction and adaptation: Intimacy as a critical variable. *American Sociological Review, 33,* 20–30.
Martire, L. M., Schulz, R., Mittelmark, M. B., & Newsom, J. T. (1999). Stability and change in older adults' social contact and social support: The

Cardiovascular Health Study. *Journals of Gerontology: Social Sciences, 54B,* S302–S311.
McCrae R. R., et al. (2000). Nature over nurture: Temperament, personality, and life span development. *Journal of Personality and Social Psychology, 78,* 173–186.
McRae, M. B., Thompson, D. A., & Cooper, S. (1999). Black churches as therapeutic groups. *Journal of Multicultural Counseling and Development, 27,* 207–220.
Montgomery, R. J. V. (1999). The family role in the context of long-term care. *Journal of Aging and Health, 11,* 383–416.
Myers, D. G. (2000). The funds, friends and faith of happy people. *American Psychologist, 55,* 56–67.
Neugarten, B. L. (1968). The awareness of middle age. In B. L. Neugarten (Ed.), *Middle age and aging* (pp. 93–98). Chicago: University of Chicago Press.
Oxman, T. E., & Berkman, L. F. (1990). Assessment of social relationships in elderly patients. *International Journal of Psychiatry in Medicine, 20,* 65–84.
Pearlin, L. I. (1999). The stress process revisited: Reflections on concepts and their interrelationships. In C. S. Aneshensel & J. C. Phelan (Eds.), *Handbook of sociology of mental health* (pp. 395–415). New York: Kluwer Academic.
Peek, M. K., & Lin, N. (1999). Age differences in the effects of network composition on psychological distress. *Social Science and Medicine, 49,* 621–636.
Reis, H. T., Sheldon, K. M., Gable, S. L., Roscoe, J., & Ryan, R. M. (in press). Daily well-being: The role of autonomy, competence, and relatedness. *Personality and Social Psychology Bulletin.*
Rosenberg, M. (1979). *Conceiving the self.* New York: Basic Books.
Rowe, J. W., & Kahn, R. L. (1998). *Successful aging.* New York: Pantheon Books.
Sarason, I. G., Sarason, B. R., Shearin, E. N., & Pierce, G. R. (1987). A brief measure of social support: Practical and theoretical implications. *Journal of Social and Personal Relationships, 4,* 497–510.
Sarason, B. R., Sarason, I. G., Irwin, G., & Gurung, R. A. R. (1997). Close personal relationships and health outcomes: A key to the role of social support. In S. Duck et al. (Eds.), *Handbook of personal relationships: Theory, research and interventions,* 2nd ed. (pp. 547–573). Chichester, England: Wiley.
Seeman, T. E. (1996). Social ties and health: The benefits of social integration. *Annals of Epidemiology, 6,* 422–451.
Seeman, T. E., Kaplan, G. A., Knudsen, L., Cohen, R., & Guralnik, J. (1987). Social network ties and mortality among the elderly in the Alameda County Study. *American Journal of Epidemiology, 126,* 714–723.
Thoits, P. A. (1999). Self, identity, stress, and mental health. In C. S. Aneshensel & J. C. Phelan (Eds.), *Handbook of sociology of mental health* (pp. 345–368). New York: Kluwer Academic.
Tooby, J., & Cosmides, L. (1996). Friendships and the banker's paradox: Other pathways to the evolution of adaptations for altruism. *Proceedings of the British Academy, 88,* 119–143.
Unger, J. B., McAvay, G., Bruce, M. L., Berkman, L., & Seeman, T. (1999). Variation in the impact of social network characteristics on physical func-

tioning of elderly persons: MacArthur studies of successful aging. *Journal of Gerontology: Social Sciences, 54B,* S245–S251.

Wenger, G. C., & Jerrome, D. (1999). Change and stability in confidant relationships: Findings from the Bangor Longitudinal Study of Aging. *Journal of Aging Studies, 13,* 269–294.

Williams, R. B., & Chesney, M. A. (1993). Psychosocial factors and prognosis in established coronary artery disease: The need for research on interventions. *Journal of the American Medical Association, 270,* 1860–1861.

Zimmer, Z., Hickey, T., & Searle, M. S. (1995). Activity participation and well-being among older people with arthritis. *The Gerontologist, 35,* 463–471.

CHAPTER NINE

What Microanalysis of Behavior in Social Situations Can Reveal about Relationships across the Life Span

Rebecca M. Warner

OVERVIEW

During face-to-face social interaction, partners engage in a moment-to-moment exchange of behaviors. Each person's smiles, vocalizations, gestures, emotions, and physiological states may vary in predictable ways over time, based on characteristic individual activity rhythms or social scripts. Behaviors may also change in response to changes in partner behaviors (Jones & Gerard, 1967). Global impressions of the quality of a social interaction such as judgments about responsiveness or rapport may be at least partly based on activity patterns and coordination (Bernieri, Reznick, & Rosenthal, 1988; Cappella, 1997). Furthermore, long-term "health" of relationships may depend upon how the partners communicate responsiveness and involvement through their behavioral engagement in everyday social interactions.

MICROANALYSIS OF SOCIAL BEHAVIOR

The Conceptual Terrain

The term *microanalysis* will be used here to refer to any study of social interaction that involves collection of detailed information about the behavior, affect, or physiology of social interaction participants over time. For example, a microanalytic study might involve coding on/off talk and silence patterns four times a second during a 10-minute

---

Address correspondence to Rebecca M. Warner, Department of Psychology, Conant Hall, 10 Library Way, University of New Hampshire, Durham, NH 03824. E-mail address: rmw@hopper.unh.edu.

conversation between two friends. Most microanalytic studies have sampled behaviors at rates ranging from several times a second up to once a minute. Microanalytic data are sometimes summarized in simple ways, for example, by computing the proportion of time spent in each behavioral state, or the overall mean level of physiological arousal or affective involvement. Some of the studies reviewed here used simple descriptive information derived from microanalytic observations, for instance, the ratio of number of positive to number of negative actions in a marital conversation, as a way of describing the social interaction. Other studies used more complicated analyses (including log linear or time series analysis or related methods) to describe predictable patterns in activity over time, or to describe the degree of coordination between the behavior of the social interaction partners. Although these more complex patterns are often of interest, many microanalytic studies involve simple summary statistics (e.g., mean heart rate during an argument).

Definitions of various types of behavioral coordination have been a source of controversy and confusion. Researchers have lacked a consistent vocabulary to describe social behavior patterns in social interaction, and particularly the various ways partner behaviors are coordinated or interdependent. Terms such as *synchrony* are defined differently across studies, and researchers who use similar data analysis methods sometimes apply different verbal labels to their results. Burgoon, Stern, and Dillman (1995) have suggested standard definitions for different types of behavioral coordination, such as matching, mirroring, convergence, interactional synchrony, reciprocity, complementarity, divergence, and compensation. They noted that different underlying processes may produce an appearance of coordination. For example, partner behaviors might be related coincidentally, or through entrainment of biological or behavioral rhythms. On the other hand, coordination might arise because person B deliberately modifies his or her behavior in order to match or respond to person A's behavior (and this adaptation may be unilateral or mutual). This proposed terminology links each term (such as *convergence*) to a specific type of coordination that can be detected through careful analysis of the time series behavioral data.

There may be behavioral patterns or rhythms that indicate "better" or "healthier" social functioning. Most researchers assume that complete absence of any coordination between partner behaviors in social interaction means that something is wrong – there is a lack of involvement, engagement, responsiveness, or rapport. The social significance of highly interrelated behaviors is less clear; extremely high interdependence might indicate psychopathology or rigidity (as described in early work by Gottman, 1979). A few recent studies have yielded curvilinear or context-dependent relations between evaluations of social interaction and various indexes of "predictability of behavior" or partner coordination, such that moderately predictable or coordinated behaviors were evaluated most positively or were predictive of more positive later relationship outcomes. Jaffe, Beebe, Feldstein, Crown, and Jasnow (in press) found that mother–infant dyads with moderately coordinated behaviors had the most positive later attachment status; Warner, Malloy, Schneider, Knoth, and Wilder (1987) found that participants rated moderately rhythmic or predictable conversations most favorably.

Berger and Bradac (1982) suggested that less predictable behavior patterns may be preferred in long-term relationships such as marriage, because unpredictability can provide novelty in a routine that may have become rather boring. In interactions between strangers, however, predictable patterning may be preferred because it reduces the anxiety and uncertainty that many people feel in interactions with strangers. Preference for degree of predictability and coordination might also differ across cultures and individuals (cf. Cappella, 1988). It seems plausible that people need a certain level of contingency and predictability in their lives in order to feel that they have some degree of control (cf. Seligman, 1975). Our face-to-face interactions could potentially be a reassuring form of predictability.

Much of the stress of modern life may be due to the constant stream of novel, high-intensity, unpredictably sequenced information that people are exposed to when they watch television or live in crowded urban environments. Altman, Vinsel, and Brown (1981) theorized that people need to seek privacy after periods of intense social involvement. Perhaps there are several things that we need to balance in our lives: not just high and low intensity of stimulus input, but also high and low levels of predictability of input. Although individuals may differ in their basic preferences for amount or predictability of stimulation (for instance, extraverts may prefer higher levels of activity and sensory stimulation than introverts), these preferences also may be modulated by experiences.

Some types of pathology may be related to disruptions of normal or optimal patterns of predictability/rhythm/coordination. Depression may sometimes be due, at least in part, to dissociations among behavioral, physiological, and social rhythms (Healy & Williams, 1988). The lower incidence of Sudden Infant Death Syndrome (SIDS) in countries where mothers sleep with their infants may be due to the way the mothers' behavioral and physiological rhythms entrain and modulate the infants' rhythms to maintain normal respiration (McKenna, Mosko, Dungy, & McAninch, 1990). Hofer (1984) proposed that grief and bereavement (in humans and in nonhuman animals) may be understood partly as a loss of social synchronizers that are important for normal biological functioning. A similar argument for the importance of behavior coordination and synchrony in healthy infant development was advanced by Field (1985). Theories that suggest rhythm and coordination are essential for good social system functioning were briefly reviewed in Warner (1988, 1991, 1996). It now seems that relationships between the degree of predictable patterning and coordination, and the "health" of a social system, may be quite complex. Moderately predictable and moderately coordinated behavior may be optimal in many social systems.

If we can identify normal versus pathological patterns in behavior and physiology, this may lead to interventions that can help to address potential relationship or developmental problems at an early stage of life. Many questions have yet to be addressed. To what extent is "coordination with a partner" a teachable or learnable skill? If it turns out that people who have difficulty in coordinating their behaviors or emotions with other people are at high risk for poor relationship outcomes, can we teach them to do better? Another related question has to do with "genuineness" versus intentionality of coordination. Some types of behavioral coordination can be done intentionally; a person may mimic the gestures, choices, and opinions of a partner as an ingratiation tactic. It is possible that this type of coordination leads to a feeling of rapport when it occurs naturally, but that it is not evaluated positively when it is perceived as a deliberate influence tactic (Manusov, 1992).

The role of everyday and routine behaviors in determining relationship outcomes and relationship quality may have been understudied and underemphasized (relative to the importance of major life events and crises). It may be that the most important factor in having a long term, happy, stable relationship is being able to have good-quality everyday conversations (Barnes & Duck, 1994) and being able to share and coordinate many different kinds of activities (as represented in the "Relationship Closeness Inventory," Berscheid, Snyder, & Omoto, 1989). The impact of major life events on relationship outcomes may be mediated by the way the life events influence everyday behaviors; for example, it may be less important to adolescents whether their parents are divorced than how this changes the day-to-day quality of the social interactions among the members of the family. If we can identify the problems that occur at this "micro" level, perhaps interventions can be designed that can mitigate the damaging effects of major life effects such as divorce by trying to minimize their impact on the day-to-day relationship patterns.

An ability to share or coordinate behavioral, physiological and/or emotional responses with a partner may be essential in order to be fully involved in a relationship, and may be the basis for empathy, rapport, "emotional contagion," and other aspects of sharing in relationships (Hatfield, Cacioppo, & Rapson, 1992; Levenson & Ruef, 1992). A methodology has also been developed to assess a more "cognitive" sort of empathy, the ability to guess thoughts of a partner while reviewing a videotape of an interaction (Ickes, 1983). Microanalysis of self-reported thoughts that occur during a social interaction (as in Vangelisti, Corbin, Lucchetti, & Sprague, 1999) can add another dimension to future studies of social interaction, which have primarily examined publicly observable behaviors.

Because many of the behaviors examined in microanalytic studies are nonverbal, microanalysis provides a useful way of comparing social interactions across different cultures, different species, or humans before versus after the development of language (Jaffe, Stern, & Peery, 1973). So far, it appears that the similarities in rhythmic patterning across cultures and across age levels in humans are more striking than the differences, although some culture- and age-related differences have been reported (Feldstein & Crown, 1990; Welkowitz, Bond, & Feldstein, 1984). Lomax (1977, 1982) has suggested that cross-cultural differences in temporal patterning of speech, like cross-cultural differences in style of folk song and dance, may be correlated with other characteristics of cultural organization. An anthropology or social psychology of time experience has been emerging, examining the different ways that time is perceived and allocated in different cultures, and the way that negotiations over timing are conducted in different cultural settings (e.g., Bryer, 1979; Hall, 1989; Hiebert, 1976; Levine, 1990, 1997). Some cultures may value the predictable, the cyclic, and the routine in ways that are more conducive to the maintenance of long-term relationships. Other cultures may place such a high value on novelty and stimulation that long-term relationships may be devalued as boring. The loss of family routines such as regular shared mealtimes and holiday celebrations may contribute to the deterioration of families; questions such as this deserve systematic study.

As human interactions with computers become a larger portion of many people's lives, and as some people become involved in communications and even relationships that are computer mediated, issues of "timing" specific to interactions with computers arise (Hesse, Werner, & Altman, 1988). In a human–computer interaction, such as video games or programming, the computer's responses tend to be nearly instantaneous and sometimes highly predictable. A child whose life does not provide much stability or predictability might enjoy computer or video games simply because they provide instant gratification, and a highly predictable result, that gives the child a sense of control and competence. A computer game is an unusual type of social interaction partner – available on demand; immediately responsive; fairly predictable; often a source of rewards; and it can be put on hold when the game player is not interested. It adapts to the tempo set by the human user. Unfortunately, if game players or programmers begin to expect this kind of response from human social interaction partners, they are likely to be disappointed or frustrated. Coordination between human social interaction partners generally requires both partners to make some adaptations in the amount and timing of their behaviors. It is conceivable that some attitudes and skills that are adaptive in working with computers are quite nonadaptive in face-to-face relationships with humans.

Controversies

One of the most popular variables in microanalytic research has been partner influence (which can take such specific forms as matching, mirroring, reciprocity, complementarity, adaptation, and so forth; Burgoon et al., 1995). There is controversy about the most appropriate way to describe coordination, contingency, or dependence between a pair of time series, and there is considerable difference in the choice of statistics across studies. Many researchers have advocated a "causal modeling approach" to the assessment of partner influence, arguing, in effect, that you cannot isolate the partner influence unless you statistically control for or partial out the predictability within each behavior stream

Relationships across the Life Span 213

(e.g., Allison & Liker, 1982; Gottman, 1981). In a related vein, Cappella (1996) has argued that partner influence may involve several different types of adaptation between persons in combination (e.g., there may be both a shared trend in behavior and closely related moment-to-moment changes in behavior), and that the time-series analysis should separate these components. Other researchers have not taken a causal modeling approach in assessing partner influence. Instead, they have used simple descriptive statistics to summarize overall amount of rhythmicity or coordination (Warner, 1992b). Application of the terminology proposed by Burgoon and her colleagues would help to clarify the situation; both types of analysis may be useful, but it needs to be made clear that different statistical indices capture different aspects of coordination. I have argued elsewhere (Warner, 1992a) that both causal modeling and purely descriptive statistical analyses are useful, provided that the differences between these approaches and the limitations of each approach are understood.

MAJOR METHODOLOGICAL CHOICES AND CAVEATS

Sampling Choices

Types of Participants or Dyads
Most microanalytic studies have examined parent–infant, peer, or marital dyads. The following studies are representative examples (this is not an exhaustive list). Because the studies have varied in terms of methodology, data analysis, and results, little can be said to summarize results across studies, but where possible, some tentative generalizations about the findings will be given.

Parent–infant and particularly mother–infant dyads have been studied by Bakeman and Brown (1977); Cohn and Campbell (1992); Cohn, Campbell, Matias, and Hopkins (1990); Feldman, Greenbaum, Yirmiya, and Mayes (1996); Field, Healy, Goldstein, and Guthertz (1990); Isabella (1989, 1991); Lester, Hoffman, and Brazelton (1985); Leyendecker, Lamb, Fracasso, Sholmerich, and Larson (1997); Lutkenau, Grossman, and Grossman (1985); Martin (1981); Tronick and Cohn (1989); and Zlochower and Cohn (1996). Numerous quantitative indexes of pattern and coordination of physiology and behavior in mother–infant dyads have been found to be meaningfully related to clinical diagnostic categories (premature versus full-term birth; depressed versus nondepressed mother) and to relationship outcomes (such as later attachment status). Statistics that describe maternal responsiveness to infant behavior have been found to differ for the mothers of male versus female infants, and for depressed versus nondepressed mothers. Most researchers in this area have argued that at least some degree of contingency between infant and caregiver behavior is desirable in order for the infant to develop well; a complete lack of contingency, or intrusive and insensitive patterns of caregiver response, may result in insecure, anxious, or avoidant attachment.

A few studies have examined social interactions of children; examples include Field et al. (1992); Goldstein, Field, and Healy (1989); Gottman and Parker (1986); Welkowitz et al. (1984); Wade, Ellis, and Bohrer (1973); and Welkowitz, Cariffe, and Feldstein (1976). Some of these, such as Welkowitz et al. (1976) suggest that the ability to coordinate certain behaviors with social partners may increase with maturity; however, a great deal of coordination has been seen even between the behavior of newborns and their caregivers (cf. Jaffe et al., 1973).

Some studies have examined social interactions between adult friends (e.g., Crown, 1991; Ickes, 1983), or in getting-acquainted conversations (e.g., Faraone & Hurtig, 1985; Warner, Malloy, Schneider, Knoth, & Wilder, 1987). Dating, engaged, or cohabiting couples also have been studied, as in Hayes and Cobb (1979); and Talmadge and Dabbs (1990). A variety of outcomes have been reported, and it seems possible that all these can be subsumed under a general model which suggests that moderately rhythmic and coordinated interactions may be preferred (Crown, 1991; Warner, 1996). In addition, factors such as length of relationship may influence the preference for predictability, with a general tendency for strangers to prefer more predictability in their interactions with each other, and for intimate partners to enjoy less predictability.

Numerous researchers have examined marital interactions, including Bradbury and Fincham (1991); Carrere and Gottman (1999a,b); Cook et al. (1995); Feeney, Noller, and Ward (1997); Fitzpatrick (1988); Gottman (1979, 1994, 1998); Gottman and Krokoff (1989); Gottman and Levenson (1992, 1999a); Levenson and Gottman (1985); and Markman and Notarius (1987). Changes in marital satisfaction, and even divorce, can be predicted from microanalysis of small samples of social interaction behavior (sessions as brief as 5 to 15 minutes) within married couples (Gottman, Coan, Carrere, & Swanson, 1998). High levels of physiological arousal, particularly for husbands; high frequencies of behaviors indicating contempt or withdrawal; and low ratios of positive to negative actions seem to be particularly diagnostic of future marital difficulties, according to Gottman and his colleagues. Additional studies suggest that children's future social interaction outcomes may be influenced by the kinds of day-to-day social interactions experienced within the family (Katz & Gottman, 1995).

A handful of studies have examined other types of social situations. McGrath and his colleagues have applied microanalytic methods to small group interactions (e.g., Futoran, Kelly, & McGrath, 1989). A few studies also have been done applying various types of microanalytic methods to psychotherapy sessions (Badalamenti & Lang, 1991; Tracey, 1987). Even computer-mediated communications can be assessed microanalytically in an attempt to see continuities and differences between these and face-to-face interactions (Hesse et al., 1988). At this point, given the small numbers of studies in these areas, it seems premature to generalize or draw conclusions.

Tasks, Situations, Social Contexts

It is difficult to observe naturally occurring social interaction in non-laboratory settings (due to instrumentation requirements, issues of invasion of privacy, and problems in screening out background noise and interruptions). Most studies therefore have taken place in lab settings and dyads have been prompted to interact "on demand." What instructions or tasks would produce the most natural and representative behavior, under such admittedly artificial conditions? For mother–infant dyads, feeding or play situations have been most typical. Sometimes the researcher provides toys or games to structure the interaction. With young adults, it may be easier to obtain a "standardized" social interaction that is comparable across dyads by looking at getting acquainted conversations between strangers; Kellermann, Broetzmann, Lim, and Kitao (1989) found that there is a remarkably consistent "getting acquainted" script. (Conversations in the lab between adult friends who are asked to converse or engage in a cooperative task sometimes seem remarkably awkward.) Married couples are often asked to "Have your usual argument about..." some shared concern, such as money, or to engage in cooperative tasks. Ideally, the task or situation should provide a representative slice of behavior. Ambady and Rosenthal (1992) have shown that for research on expressive behaviors, remarkably brief observation sessions (on the order of 5 minutes) may be sufficient. Ongoing research is beginning to provide more information about which tasks produce the most diagnostically useful information about various types of relationships.

Behavioral, Physiological, Cognitive, Mood Measures

The choice of behaviors or other responses to measure may be driven by theory, as in research on married couples, where the coding systems used to describe behavior are at least to some extent theoretically derived; or it may be influenced by cost and convenience factors. For many variables (such as degree of positive versus negative affect), the judgments of human observers are required. However, some aspects of behavior can be obtained from automated systems (such as the presence or absence of talk within each 1/4-second time interval by the Automatic Vocal Transaction Analysis, or AVTA, system, Jaffe & Feldstein, 1970). The use of automated systems is attractive because of the relatively low cost. However, even for automated systems, reliability and validity should be assessed, and not merely assumed. Useful reviews of issues in observational research and behavior coding systems are found in Bakeman and Gottman (1987), Markman and Notarius (1987), and Sackett (1978).

Various microanalytic studies, cited in previous sections, have employed a wide range of measures: mood or affective states; physiological states such as heart rate; self-reported cognitions that occur during social interactions; observer-coded types of behaviors (positive, negative); amount and types of body movement; on/off patterns of vocalization; and gaze direction (toward/away from the partner). Some researchers (e.g., Cappella, 1996) have employed multiple measures, used correlational methods to assess the degree to which these various behaviors are interrelated over time, and devised composite measures that combine several types of behavioral information.

Level of Measurement: Categorical or Quantitative

Some researchers have found it convenient to use categorical codes for behavior states; categorical time series data can most easily be analyzed using lagged conditional probabilities (as in Markov chain analysis, cf. Jaffe & Feldstein); or by using log linear analysis to model serial dependence (Gottman & Roy, 1990). It is possible to create "continuous" data from binary time series. When talk is coded as present or absent once per second, the data can be aggregated into time blocks to create a quantitative variable such as proportion of time spent talking in each 10-second time window. Other data (such as mood ratings on multiple point scales) naturally come in a continuous form. Continuous time-series data can be analyzed using time-series regression methods or spectral analysis (see Gottman, 1981; Warner, 1998). In spite of the superficial differences between these various analyses, there is an underlying mathematical equivalence in the aspects of pattern in data that these allow us to assess. Serial dependence and interdependence between time series can be assessed using any of the analytic methods named here, although the details of reporting and interpretation will differ according to the type of analysis.

Sampling Frequency (in Relation to Cycles, Reaction Time, Response Latency) and Session Length
The decisions about how often to sample behavior, and how long to make the overall observation session, are quite crucial. Hayes, Meltzer, and Wolf (1970) have pointed out that, like different levels of magnification in a microscope, different sampling frequencies can bring different kinds of structure in behavior into view. For example, speech is organized at multiple temporal levels. When speech samples are taken at a rate of thousands of cycles per second, one can examine fundamental frequency (or pitch), and the phonemic structure of speech sounds. On the order of four samples per second, one can look for on/off patterns of vocalization versus silence, or speech "turns." On the order of 5 seconds per sampling interval, one can look for cycles in amount of talk over the course of a conversation. On the order of 10 minutes per sample, one can look at variations in the amount of conversational speech that occur throughout the course of the day (Hayes and Cobb, 1979).

A researcher needs to know what kind of structure is expected in the time-series data in order to choose the most appropriate sampling frequency. If there may be cycles in the data, then the absolute minimum requirement for sampling frequency is two samples per cycle, but it would be better to have a larger number of observations in order to specify the shape of the cycle waveform. Another issue in choice of sampling frequency is typical response latency. If a mother's response typically occurs within 1 second, then her behavior should be observed at least once per second (or more often, if you want your estimates of individual response latencies to be precise). When using variables that have been employed in past studies, it may be advisable to use the same sampling frequency that has been found satisfactory in past research. In general, when in doubt about the optimum sampling frequency, it is better to sample observations at the highest frequency that is practical. For most studies, observing four times per second, or perhaps one time per second, should be adequate. Observations can always be aggregated into larger time blocks later if that proves to be convenient.

In general, the longer the observation session is, the better (within the limits of practicality). In most time-series analyses the degrees of freedom depend upon the number of observations in the time series. For this reason, if for no other, the number of observations in the time series should be reasonably large (preferably $N > 50$). Of course, there are often practical reasons for keeping sessions brief, such as the difficulty of keeping a very young infant alert and involved in an activity. For research that concerns expressive face-to-face behavior such as talking or nonverbal behavior, Ambady and Rosenthal's (1992) review, and recent work by Gottman and his colleagues, suggest that microanalysis of behavior samples as brief as 5 minutes may be sufficient.

If there are cycles in behavior, the session should be long enough to contain more than one complete cycle, and ideally it should contain at least five to ten repetitions of a cycle. For instance, when Larsen and Kasimatis (1991) assessed 7-day cycles in mood, they collected mood observations on 84 days (12 weeks). It is more convenient for data analysis if the data record contains an integer number of repetitions of the cycle of interest (Warner, 1998).

Other Design Choices

Many early microanalytic studies simply assessed behavior for a dyad at one age level or relationship stage. To address questions about stability or change in dyadic interaction patterns across the life span, and to assess whether microanalytic features of behavior can predict important later relationship outcomes, it is necessary to do longitudinal studies. Such studies might involve assessment of microanalytic features of social interaction, and also assessment of relationship status and perceived communication quality, at two or more age levels or stages in the development of a relationship. While cross-sectional studies may shed some light on possible developmental changes in the structure of social interaction, these have well-known limitations that seriously restrict the kinds of inferences that can be drawn. Ideally, we will want to have multiple time-point longitudinal studies, in which both microanalysis of social interaction and other assessments of relationship quality are done on the same set of dyads at many points in time across the life span. These data would provide information about stability and change in the microanalytic structure of social interaction (both for individuals and for dyads). It would also help us to assess the ways in which day-to-day behaviors in social interaction predict, and perhaps even determine, long-term relationship outcomes.

Research results cited in previous sections indicate that microanalysis of relatively brief caregiver–infant and marital interaction sessions can provide enough information to predict later relationship outcomes. Moderately coordinated behavior in mother–infant dyads predicts secure attachment, while extremely high or low levels of coordination, or inappropriate responses by caregivers, seem to predict attachment problems. The sheer amount of physiological arousal and of negative affect in brief marital interactions, but also the strength of the tendency to reciprocate negative affect, predicts poor marital outcomes. Most of the studies involving interactions between peers (friendship or stranger pairs) have not included the follow-ups necessary to assess whether brief interaction in these types of dyads are diagnostic of later relationship development. One study that did assess later relationship outcomes was done by Van Lear (1991); he reported that cycling between high and low levels of self-disclosure in a series of conversations predicted relationship dissolution.

Research Questions for Future Microanalytic Life Span Studies

When a life span perspective is taken, many questions naturally arise. Microanalytic assessments of coordination in social interaction may be done at one or multiple points in time. Other information about relationship quality or relationship outcomes also may be obtained at one or multiple points in time. One set of questions concerns the development over the life span of the behaviors that are examined within the microanalytic paradigm: Does behavioral synchrony between mother and infant develop gradually during infancy, with the infant slowly becoming more responsive to mother's behaviors? Does this coordination change as the infant becomes a toddler, a child, an adolescent? Is there carry over in an individual's life in the temporal organization of behavior, such that an adolescent's ability to coordinate behavior and emotion with a friend develops out of the coordination experienced in early infancy? So far, not many researchers have collected repeated microanalytic data. A few instances of this include Welkowitz et al.

(1976), who found that congruence of switching pause duration tended to increase with age in children; and Gottman and Levenson (1999b), who found stability in the expression of negative and positive affect in marital interactions across four years. It seems likely that both stability and change will be found in future studies of behavioral coordination and social interaction process across the life span.

A second set of questions has to do with prediction. To what extent can the information from a microanalytic assessment of social interaction predict future relationship satisfaction and relationship outcomes? Do infants who experience poorly coordinated interactions with a parent have developmental difficulties and/or difficulties in later life relationships? Do married couples who exhibit too high a ratio of negative to positive behaviors, or too strong a tendency to reciprocate negative behaviors, have a higher risk of divorce? Studies cited in earlier sections have yielded intriguing results for both parent–infant and marital dyads, suggesting that for infants, their future cognitive development and attachment status may be predictable from the patterning of mother–infant interaction; and that married couples' future satisfaction and risk of divorce may be predictable from small samples of their face-to-face behaviors, affect, and physiological reactions during social interactions.

A third set of questions that has not been addressed involves possible interventions. If pathological patterns in face-to-face social interaction can be detected early in a relationship, a question that naturally arises is whether these can be modified, and whether changing these patterns leads to better relationship outcomes. However, current research is still at the stage of assessing the diagnostic usefulness of behavior patterns; development of interventions will require a better understanding of relationship process.

DIRECTIONS FOR THE FUTURE

What can microanalysis tell us about relationships as they develop and change over the life span? We can use microanalysis to assess what (quantitative) behavior patterns give rise to our "qualitative" impressions (of responsiveness, for example). This may enhance our theoretical understanding of relationship processes and help to answer many of the questions raised in preceding sections of this chapter. Relationships may come to be understood (on one level) as complex systems that involve temporal coordination of behavior, physiology, emotion, and cognition among participants. This perspective may complement other perspectives on relationships, including more qualitative and content-oriented descriptions; it will not replace other perspectives on relationships.

Microanalysis may be used to obtain "diagnostic" information from relatively brief social interactions that may predict later relationship or individual outcomes. This could be quite useful in clinical psychology and counseling, as one means of identifying individuals or dyads whose everyday social interactions may be contributing to the development of longer-term problems.

Microanalysis may be used to identify aspects of "social interaction process," that is, specific behaviors or temporal behavior patterns that may be accessible to clinical interventions. If sensitive responding can be taught, perhaps individuals who do not seem to have this skill naturally might be helped to develop it.

All of this may ultimately lead, as Gottman (1982) once suggested, to the development of a "temporal language" for understanding relationship processes. At this point, many intriguing questions are unanswered, but microanalysis provides new ways of looking at the development of relationships over time.

REFERENCES

Allison, P. D., & Liker, J. K. (1982). Analyzing sequential categorical data: A comment on Gottman. *Psychological Bulletin, 91*, 393–403.

Altman, I., Vinsel, A., & Brown, B. G. (1981). Dialectic conceptions in social psychology: An application to social penetration and privacy regulation. In L. Berkowitz (Ed.), *Advances in experimental social psychology* (Vol. 14, pp. 107–260). New York: Academic Press.

Ambady, N., & Rosenthal, R. (1992). Thin slices of expressive behavior as predictors of interpersonal consequences: A meta-analysis. *Psychological Bulletin, 111*, 256–274.

Badalamenti, A. F., & Lang, R. F. (1991). An empirical investigation of human dyadic systems in the time and frequency domains. *Behavioral Science, 36*, 100–114.

Bakeman, R., & Brown, J. V. (1977). Behavioral dialogues: An approach to the assessment of mother–infant interaction. *Child Development, 48*, 195–203.

Bakeman, R., & Gottman, J. M. (1987). *Observing interaction: An introduction to sequential analysis.* Cambridge: Cambridge University Press.

Barnes, M. K., & Duck, S. (1994). Everyday communicative contexts for social support. In B. Burleson, T. Albrecht, & I. G. Sarason (Eds.), *Communication of social support: Messages, relationships and community* (pp. 175–194). Thousand Oaks, CA: Sage.

Berger, C. R., & Bradac, J. J. (1982). *Language and social knowledge: Uncertainty in interpersonal relations.* London: Edward Arnold.

Bernieri, F. J., Resnick, J. S., & Rosenthal, R. (1988). Synchrony, pseudosynchrony, and dissynchrony: Measuring the entrainment process in mother–infant interactions. *Journal of Personality and Social Psychology, 54,* 243–253.

Berscheid, E., Snyder, M., & Omoto, A. M. (1989). The relationship closeness inventory: Assessing the closeness of interpersonal relationships. *Journal of Personality and Social Psychology, 57,* 792–807.

Bradbury, T. N., & Fincham, F. D. (1991). The analysis of sequence in social interaction. In D. G. Gilbert & J. J. Connolly (Eds.), *Personality, social skills, and development: An individual differences approach.* (pp. 257–287). New York: Plenum Press.

Bryer, K. B. (1979). The Amish way of death: A study of family support systems. *American Psychologist, 34,* 255–261.

Burgoon, J. K., Stern, L. A., & Dillman, L. (1995). *Interpersonal adaptation.* Cambridge: Cambridge University Press.

Campbell, S. B., Cohn, J. F., & Meyers, T. (1995). Depression in first-time mothers: Mother–infant interaction and depression chronicity. *Developmental Psychology, 31,* 349–357.

Cappella, J. N. (1988). Interaction patterns and social and personal relationships. In S. Duck (Ed.), *Handbook of social and personal relationships* (pp. 103–117). New York: Wiley.

(1996). Dynamic coordination of vocal and kinesic behavior in dyadic interaction: Methods, problems, and interpersonal outcomes. In J. Watt & C. A. Van Lear (Eds.), *Dynamic patterns in communication processes* (pp. 353–386). Thousand Oaks, CA: Sage.

(1997). Behavioral and judged coordination in adult informal social interactions: Vocal and kinesic indicators. *Journal of Personality and Social Psychology, 72,* 119–131.

Carrere, S., & Gottman, J. M. (1999a). Predicting the future of marriages. In E. M. Hetherington (Ed.), *Coping with divorce, single parenting, and remarriage: A risk and resiliency perspective* (pp. 3–22). Mahwah, NJ: Erlbaum.

(1999b). Predicting divorce among newlyweds from the first three minutes of a marital conflict discussion. *Family Process, 38,* 293–301.

Cohn, J. F., & Campbell, S. B. (1992). Influence of maternal depression on infant affect regulation. In D. Cicchetti & S. L. Toth (Eds.), *Developmental perspectives on depression: Rochester symposium on developmental psychopathology* (pp. 103–130) Rochester, NY: University of Rochester Press.

Cohn, J. F., Campbell, S. B., Matias, R., & Hopkins, J. (1990). Face-to-face interactions of postpartum depressed and nondepressed mother–infant pairs at 2 months. *Developmental Psychology, 26,* 15–23.

Cook, J., Tyson, R., White, J., Rushe, R., Gottman, J., & Murray, J. (1995). Mathematics of marital conflict: Qualitatitive dynamic mathematical modeling of marital interaction. *Journal of Family Psychology, 9,* 110–130.

Crown, C. L. (1991). Coordinated interpersonal timing of vision and voice as a function of interpersonal attraction. *Journal of Language and Social Psychology, 10,* 29–46.

Faraone, S. V., & Hurtig, R. R. (1985). An examination of social skills, verbal productivity, and Gottman's model of interaction using observational methods and sequential analysis. *Behavioral Assessment, 7,* 349–366.

Feeney, J. A., Noller, P. A., & Ward, C. (1997). Marital satisfaction and spousal interaction. In R. Sternberg & M. Hojjat (Eds.), *Satisfaction in close relationships* (pp. 160–189). New York: Guilford Press.

Feldman, R., Greenbaum, C. W., Yirmiya, N., & Mayes, L. C. (1996). Relations between cyclicity and regulation in mother–infant interaction at 3 and 9 months and cognition at 2 years. *Journal of Applied Developmental Psychology, 17,* 347–365.

Feldstein, S., & Crown, C. (1990). Oriental and Canadian conversational interactions: Chronographic structure and interpersonal perception. *Journal of Asian Pacific Communication, 1,* 247–265.

Field, T. (1985). Attachment as psychobiological attunement: Being on the same wavelength. In M. Reite & T. Field (Eds.), *Psychobiology of attachment* (pp. 415–454). San Diego, CA: Academic Press.

Field, T., Greenwald, P., Morrow, C., Healy, B., Foster, T., Guthertz, M., & Frost, P. (1992). Behavior state matching during interactions of preadolescent friends versus acquaintances. *Developmental Psychology, 28,* 242–250.

Field, T., Healy, B., Goldstein, S., & Guthertz, M. (1990). Behavior-state matching and synchrony in mother–infant interactions of nondepressed versus depressed dyads. *Developmental Psychology, 26,* 7–14.

Fitzpatrick, M. A. (1988). *Between husbands and wives: Communication in marriage.* Newbury Park, CA: Sage.

Futoran, G. C., Kelly, J. R., & McGrath, J. E. (1989). TEMPO: A time-based system for analysis of group interaction process. *Basic and Applied Social Psychology, 10,* 211–232.

Goldstein, S., Field, T., & Healy, B. (1989). Concordance of play behavior and physiology in preschool friends. *Journal of Applied Developmental Psychology, 10,* 337–351.

Gottman, J. M. (1979). *Marital interaction: Experimental investigations.* New York: Academic Press.

(1981). *Time-series analysis: A comprehensive introduction for social sciences.* Cambridge: Cambridge University Press.

(1982). Temporal form: Toward a new language for describing relationships. *Journal of Marriage and the Family, 44,* 943–962.

(1994). *What predicts divorce? The relationship between marital processes and marital outcomes.* Mahwah, NJ: Erlbaum.

(1998). Psychology and the study of marital process. *Annual Review of Psychology, 49,* 169–197.

Gottman, J. M., Coan, J., Carrere, S., & Swanson, C. (1998). Predicting marital happiness and stability from newlywed interactions. *Journal of Marriage and the Family, 60,* 5–22.

Gottman, J. M., & Krokoff, L. J. (1989). Marital interaction and satisfaction: A longitudinal view. *Journal of Consulting and Clinical Psychology, 57,* 47–52.

Gottman, J. M., & Levenson, R. W. (1992). Marital processes predictive of later dissolution: Behavior, physiology and health. *Journal of Personality and Social Psychology, 63,* 221–233.

(1999a). What predicts change in marital interaction over time? A study of alternative medicine. *Family Process, 38,* 143–158.

(1999b). How stable is marital interaction over time? *Family Process, 38,* 159–165.

Gottman, J. M., & Parker, J. G. (1986). *Conversations of friends: Speculations on affective development.* Cambridge: Cambridge University Press.

Gottman, J. M., & Roy, V. (1990). *Sequential analysis: A guide for researchers.* Cambridge: Cambridge University Press.

Hall, E. T. (1989). *Dance of life: Other dimensions of time.* New York: Anchor Books.

Hatfield, E., Cacioppo, J. T., & Rapson, R. L. (1992). Primitive emotional contagion. In M. S. Clark (Ed.), *Emotion and social behavior* (Vol. 14, pp. 151–77). Newbury Park, CA: Sage.

Hayes, D. P., & Cobb, L. (1979). Ultradian biorhythms in social interaction. In A. W. Siegman & S. Feldstein (Eds.), *Of speech and time: Temporal speech rhythms in interpersonal contexts* (pp. 57–70). Hilldsale, NJ: Erlbaum.

Hayes, D. P., Meltzer, L., & Wolf, G. (1970). Substantive conclusions are dependent upon techniques of measurement. *Behavioral Science, 15,* 265–268.

Healy, D., & Williams, J. M. G. (1988). Dysrhythmia, dysphoria and depression: The interaction of learned helplessness and circadian dysrhythmia in the pathogenesis of depression. *Psychological Bulletin, 103,* 163–178.

Hesse, B., Werner, C., & Altman, I. (1988). Temporal aspects of computer-mediated communication. *Computers in Human Behavior, 4,* 147–165.

Hiebert, P. J. (1976). Traffic patterns in Seattle and Hyderabad: Immediate and mediate transactions. *Journal of Anthropological Research, 32,* 326–336.

Hofer, M. A. (1984). Relationships as regulators: A psychobiologic perspective on bereavement. *Psychosomatic Medicine, 46,* 183–197.

Ickes, W. (1983). A basic paradigm for the study of unstructured dyadic interaction. In H. T. Reis (Ed.), *Naturalistic approaches to studying social interaction: New directions for methodology of social and behavioral science* (no. 15, pp. 5–21). San Francisco, CA: Jossey-Bass.

Isabella, R. A. (1989). Origins of infant–mother attachment: An examination of interactional synchrony in the infant's first year. *Developmental Psychology, 25,* 12–21.

(1991). Interactional synchrony and the origins of infant–mother attachment: A replication study. *Child Development, 62,* 373–384.

Jaffe, J., & Feldstein, S. (1970). *Rhythms of dialogue.* New York: Academic Press.

Jaffe, J., Beebe, B., Feldstein, S., Crown, C., & Jasnow, M. (in press). Rhythms of dialogue in infancy: Coordinated timing and social development. *Society for Research in Child Psychology Monographs.*

Jaffe, J., Stern, D. N., & Peery, J. C. (1973). "Conversational" coupling of gaze behavior in prelinguistic human development. *Journal of Psycholinguistic Research, 2,* 321–329.

Jones, E. E., & Gerard, H. B. (1967). *Foundations of social psychology.* New York: Wiley.

Katz, L. F., & Gottman, J. M. (1995). Marital interaction and child outcomes: A longitudinal study of mediating and moderating processes. In D. Cicchetti & S. L. Toth (Eds.), *Emotion, cognition and representation. Rochester symposium on developmental psychopathology* (pp. 301–342). Rochester, NY: University of Rochester Press.

Kellermann, K., Broetzmann, S., Lim, T. S., & Kitao, K. (1989). The conversation MOP: Scenes in the stream of discourse. *Discourse Processes, 12,* 27–61.

Larsen, R. J., & Kasimatis, M. (1990). Individual differences in entrainment of mood to the weekly calendar. *Journal of Personality and Social Psychology, 58,* 164–171.

Lester, B. M., Hoffman, J., & Brazelton, T. B. (1985). The rhythmic structure of mother–infant interaction in term and preterm infants. *Child Development, 56,* 15–27.

Levenson, R. W., & Gottman, J. M. (1985). Physiological and affective predictors of change in relationship satisfaction. *Journal of Personality and Social Psychology, 49,* 85–94.

Levenson, R. W., & Ruef, A. M. (1992). Empathy: A physiological substrate. *Journal of Personality and Social Psychology, 63,* 234–246.

Levine, R. V. (1990). The pace of life. *American Scientist, 78,* 450–459.

——— (1997). *A geography of time.* New York: Basic Books.

Leyendecker, B., Lamb, M. E., Fracasso, M. P., Sholmerich, A., & Larson, C. (1997). Playful interaction and the antecedents of attachment: A longitudinal study of Central American and Euro-American mothers and infants. *Merrill-Palmer Quarterly, 43,* 24–47.

Lomax, A. (1977). A stylistic analysis of speaking. *Language in Society, 6,* 15–36.

——— (1982). Cross cultural variation of rhythmic style. In M. Davis (Ed.), *Interaction rhythms: Periodicity in communicative behavior* (pp. 149–174). New York: Human Sciences Press.

Luetkenhaus, P., Grossmann, K. E., & Grossmann, K. (1985). Infant–mother attachment at twelve months and style of interaction with a stranger at the age of three years. *Child Development, 56,* 1538–1542.

Manusov, V. (1992). Mimicry or synchrony: The effects of intentionality attributions for nonverbal mirroring behavior. *Communication Quarterly, 40,* 69–83.

Markman, H. J., & Notarius, C. I. (1987). Coding marital and family interaction: Current status. In T. Jacob (Ed.), *Family interaction and psychopathology: Theories, methods and findings* (pp. 329–390). New York: Plenum Press.

Martin, J. A. (1981). A longitudinal study of the consequences of early mother–infant interaction: A microanalytic approach. *Monographs of the Society for Research in Child Development, 46,* 1–59.

McKenna, J. J., Mosko, S., Dungy, C., & McAninch, J. (1990). Sleep and arousal patterns of co-sleeping human mother/infant pairs: A preliminary physiological study with implications for the study of Sudden Infant Death Syndrome (SIDS). *American Journal of Physical Anthropology, 83*, 332–346.

Sackett, G. P. (Ed.) (1978). *Observing behavior, Vol. II: Data collection and analysis methods.* Baltimore: University Park Press.

Seligman, M. (1975). *Helplessness.* San Francisco, CA: Freeman.

Talmadge, L. D., & Dabbs, J. M., Jr. (1990). Intimacy, conversation patterns, and concomitant cognitive/emotional processes in couples. *Journal of Social and Clinical Psychology, 9*, 473–488.

Tracey, T. J. (1987). Stage difference in the dependencies of topic initiation and topic following behavior. *Journal of Counseling Psychology, 34*, 123–131.

Tronick, E. Z., & Cohn, J. F. (1989). Infant–mother face-to-face interaction: Age and gender differences in coordination and the occurrence of miscoordination. *Child Development, 60*, 85–92.

Vangelisti, A. L., Corbin, S. D., Lucchetti, A. E., & Sprague, R. L. (1999). Couples' concurrent cognitions: The influence of relational satisfaction on the thoughts couples have as they converse. *Human Communication Research, 25*, 370–398.

Van Lear, C. A. (1991). Testing a cyclical model of communicative openness in relationship development: Two longitudinal studies. *Communication Monographs, 58*, 337–361.

Wade, M. G., Ellis, M. J., & Bohrer, R. E. (1973). Biorhythms in the activity of children during free play. *Journal of the Experimental Analysis of Behavior, 20*, 155–162.

Warner, R. M. (1988). Rhythm in social interaction. In J. E. McGrath (Ed.), *The social psychology of time: New perspectives* (pp. 63–88). Beverly Hills, CA: Sage.

(1991). Incorporating time. In B. Montgomery & S. Duck (Eds.), *Studying interpersonal interaction* (pp. 82–102). New York: Guilford Press.

(1992a). Sequential analysis of social interaction: Assessing internal versus social determinants of behavior. *Journal of Personality and Social Psychology, 63*, 51–60.

(1992b). Speaker, partner and observer evaluations of affect during social interaction as a function of interaction tempo. *Journal of Language and Social Psychology, 11*, 1–14.

(1996). Coordinated cycles in behavior and physiology during face-to-face social interaction. In J. Watt & A. Van Lear (Eds.), *Cycles and dynamic patterns in communication processes* (pp. 327–352). Newbury Park, CA: Sage.

(1998). *Spectral analysis of time-series data.* New York: Guilford Press.

Warner, R. M., Malloy, D., Schneider, K., Knoth, R., & Wilder, B. (1987). Rhythmic organization of social interaction and observer ratings of affect and involvement. *Journal of Nonverbal Behavior, 11*, 57–74.

Welkowitz, J., Bond, R., & Feldstein, S. (1984). Conversational time patterns of Japanese-American adults and children in same and mixed-gender dyads. *Journal of Language and Social Psychology, 3*, 127–138.

Welkowitz, J., Cariffe, G., Feldstein, S. (1976). Conversational congruence as a criterion of socialization in children. *Child Development, 47*, 269–272.

Zlochower, A. J., & Cohn, J. F. (1996). Vocal timing in face-to-face interaction of clinically depressed and nondepressed others and their 4 month old infants. *Infant Behavior and Development, 19*, 371–374.

CHAPTER TEN

Developing a Multifaceted View of Change in Relationships

Ronald D. Rogge and Thomas N. Bradbury

The last 30 years have witnessed an explosion of research on marriage and marital dysfunction. Building on seminal cross-sectional studies contrasting happy couples with distressed couples (for reviews see Bradbury & Fincham, 1987, 1989), one central question has begun to guide the course of marital research: How do marriages change? In contrast to the earlier cross-sectional literature, a large proportion of current marital research seeks to explain how couples can begin their marriages with high levels of satisfaction and then, with surprising regularity, grow to become unhappy in a relatively short period of time. Examining the factors associated with shifts in marital satisfaction is a pragmatic and direct approach to address the problem of marital discord and divorce, and this line of research holds great promise. However, in this chapter we adopt the view that looking at deterioration of marital satisfaction over time is only one facet of understanding change. We believe that relationships can undergo shifts in their basic nature without necessarily demonstrating corresponding changes in satisfaction and that relationships can even experience improvements in satisfaction over time. Focusing too exclusively on deterioration of satisfaction over time precludes the study of these processes. In an effort to expand the focus in this domain, we review previous research within a framework that views change in relationships as a multifaceted process. This will allow us to clarify the strengths and

---

Development of this chapter was supported by the John Templeton Foundation, the National Science Foundation, and the National Institutes of Health. Address correspondence to Ronald Rogge or Thomas Bradbury, UCLA Department of Psychology, Box 951563, Los Angeles, CA, 90095-1563. E-mail addresses: ronrogge@ucla.edu and bradbury@psych.ucla.edu.

limitations of previous work and to highlight a number of new directions for research.

A key distinction that must be established in conceptualizing marital change separates natural change from induced change. This corresponds with the distinction between basic and applied research, or the choice between observing the natural course of relationships over time and striving to change the course of those relationships with an intervention.* Observing natural change can provide a deeper understanding of the processes that generate variability in marital outcomes. However, most basic research on marriage also comes with the limitation that it will be correlational in nature. With the increasing use of longitudinal designs and multivariate statistical techniques like structural equation modeling and hierarchical linear modeling to test competing models, this basic research can begin to provide compelling evidence of causal relationships despite the correlational nature of these designs. But the fact remains that basic studies of "natural" change in marriage will by definition never be experimental in nature. In contrast, analysis of change induced in intervention studies (or other experiments) has the power to put causal mechanisms and theories to a true experimental test. However, inducing change introduces a threat to the external validity of the study because the mechanisms that *can* experimentally induce change in relationships need not be the same mechanisms responsible for shifts in naturally occurring relationships. Of course, this threat is of little concern when the goal is the enhancement of marital outcomes, but it is a major concern when the goal is to capture accurately the means by which marriages develop and change. In this chapter we focus primarily on natural change in marriage, and on developing a framework to view the processes of natural change from a multifaceted perspective. We will say less about change resulting from intervention, although it is this applied goal that motivates much of our work (see Bradbury, in press).

---

* It could be argued that the dimension of natural vs. induced change intersects with the dimension of direction of change (improvement and deterioration). Specifically, natural change involves improvement and deterioration (as well as other changes that may not affect satisfaction), whereas induced change is focused on improvement and preventing deterioration. We would assert that despite their differing foci, studies of natural and induced change will contain all forms of change (improvement, deterioration, and qualitative change) and consequently the dimension of direction of change remains orthogonal to the dimension of natural vs. induced change.

A FRAMEWORK OF CHANGE

Marital relationships offer a tremendous challenge to researchers, because they represent complex and diverse phenomena, marked by as much heterogeneity as homogeneity. Thus, when developing models of marriage and attempting to characterize change within marriage, researchers benefit from a flexible perspective, so that change is viewed from a variety of angles – much as a reporter strives to maintain objectivity and clarity by considering a complex story from many vantage points. Consequently, to fully understand *how* change occurs in relationships we argue that researchers must ask questions within at least three separate domains: (a) *who* changes? (b) *what* changes? (c) *when* does the change occur? We recognize that in developing a framework for conceptualizing change in marital research we will be highlighting areas for future inquiry rather than presenting a comprehensive view of the current understanding of *how couples change*. We feel that this descriptive approach mirrors more closely the stage of understanding that the field of marital research has achieved to this point and is consistent with the view that "we must first do a great deal of describing before we can do even a little explaining" (Moscovici, 1989, p. 424).

Traditionally, asking how couples change has led to the investigation of longitudinal predictors of declines in marital satisfaction in two-wave studies. This methodology has enabled researchers to build a basic understanding of how marriages work, to develop theories on marriage, and to establish a foundation for further research and intervention. Because understanding the factors associated with declines in marital quality is central to building effective models of marriage, the bulk of marital research has focused on examining change with this methodology. Although conceptualizing how couples change in two-wave designs provides a reasonable first step toward understanding change in relationships, it cannot tell the entire story. We propose that broadening the operationalization of change in marital research by including three lines of questioning will enrich and deepen our understanding of how marriages develop, evolve, and deteriorate. First, asking who changes adds to our understanding by embracing the multidetermined nature of marital outcomes, introducing individual variables that can place couples at elevated risk for marital dysfunction and moderate processes of change in their relationships. Second, asking what changes (and what does not change) within marriages leads researchers to challenge and expand the range of process and outcome variables that they examine. This line of questioning also can serve to emphasize the importance of relationship history and relationship expectations in the process of change. Finally, asking when change occurs promotes a developmental view of marriage, and it challenges researchers to move beyond static theories of marriage that fail to distinguish newlyweds from established couples and toward theories that incorporate major developmental transitions such as parenthood. The remainder of this chapter addresses each domain of questioning separately.

BACKGROUND

The last 30 years of research have yielded more than 115 published articles presenting longitudinal findings on marriage from over 68 distinct samples (for reviews see Bradbury & Karney, 1993; Karney & Bradbury, 1995). The large majority of these studies collected data from couples at two time points, separated by as little as 3 months to as many as 45 years, and examined the correlates associated with declines in marital satisfaction between the two time points in an attempt to understand how couples' satisfaction can change over time. Most studies focus on one or two primary predictor variables as the putative source of marital change. As a result, this literature tends to address questions about whether a particular variable predicts change rather than theoretically complex questions about the degree to which change is well accounted for.

Karney and Bradbury (1995) estimate that over 200 variables have been examined in this literature, leaving the field with an overabundance of potential process variables, little integration of them, and a corresponding paucity of conceptual replications. However, partly because of the impact on marital research of social learning theory, which maintains that patterns of coercive interactions would erode relationship satisfaction and stability (e.g., Jacobson & Margolin, 1979), variables reflecting marital communication stand apart as the largest exception to this trend. Communication has received considerable attention in the last 20 years, of course, and consequently it has been assessed in many of the longitudinal studies of marriage. The research literature on communication behavior generally supports a longitudinal association between hostile and attacking behaviors and subsequent marital discord. However, the findings of a handful of studies demonstrate conflicting results, linking negative behaviors to subsequent increases in marital satisfaction instability (see Fincham & Beach, 1999, for a review).

The findings linking observed communication behavior to changes in marital satisfaction present a complex picture in which the exact nature of the behavior and possibly the stage of marriage in which that behavior is expressed qualify the impact of that behavior over time. It would seem that negative behaviors like anger and hostile escalation are deleterious primarily when expressed in newlywed marriages (e.g., Julien, Markman, & Lindahl, 1989; Noller, Feeney, Bonnell, & Callan, 1994; Rogge & Bradbury, 1999a). However, similar negative behaviors might be beneficial when expressed by established couples that have been married an average of 5 or more years (e.g., Heavey, Lane, & Christensen, 1993). This finding could be explained by positing that moderate levels of anger expressed by established couples might actually represent a sustained level of commitment to their marriages. Thus, the developmental stage of marriage may moderate the effects of negative behavior on marital satisfaction.

Alternatively, the seemingly inconsistent findings regarding the longitudinal effects of negative behavior also could be the result of a larger problem facing marital researchers: capturing the full range of behavior expressed in couples' interactions. Part of the appeal of collecting behavioral data is the rich and diverse information it provides over self-report methods. In an attempt to capture that tremendous diversity, coding systems have expanded over the last 30 years, with increasing numbers of codes introduced to capture more of the behavioral variance. Unfortunately, with sample sizes for longitudinal studies typically in the range of 50–250 couples, there is an upper limit to the number of codes a coding system can support before the codes become so rare and infrequent that they lose reliability. In addition, most samples do not have the power to analyze the behavioral data at the level of the individual codes without violating the assumptions of the multivariate statistics and seriously inflating the alpha level of the analyses. To compensate for this lack of power, the field not only has developed a diverse array of coding systems to classify couples' negative and positive communication behaviors, but has also developed a wide range of methods for collapsing these data down to a small number of composite codes to be used in the final analyses. Few studies have offered a direct examination of how the codes between these different coding systems overlap or how the different methods of creating composite codes affect the interpretation of the results. Heyman, Weiss, and Eddy (1995) compared the behavioral variance captured by two different forms of the Marital Interaction Coding System (MICS-III vs. MICS-IV) in a sample of 994 couples. The authors demonstrated that changes in the hierarchy for creating composite codes were associated with significant shifts in the cross-sectional associations of those codes.

In further support of this argument, two sets of analyses in the same sample of newlyweds suggested that negative behavior was beneficial (Karney & Bradbury, 1997) or detrimental (Rogge & Bradbury, 1999a) to marital quality over the first 4 years of marriage, depending on the behavioral coding system employed. These findings would suggest that the seemingly conflicting findings for "negative behavior" may be due to different definitions of that term based on the coding system used and the composite variables created. Given these possible explanations, the findings suggest that although some negative communication behaviors like expressed anger and negative engagement may be beneficial over time, other negative behaviors like contempt and invalidation consistently predict declines in marital satisfaction and stability over time, supporting the self-report findings for negative communication. In light of these conflicting effects of negative behavior, it is not surprising that the overall effect size for negative communication on marital satisfaction is relatively small ($r = .14$, Karney & Bradbury, 1995), accounting for a fraction of the overall variance in satisfaction. Although the size of this effect might be limited by the heterogeneity in the operationalizations of "negative behavior," this finding suggests that researchers must look beyond communication to explain how couples change and grow dissatisfied (see Bradbury, Rogge, & Lawrence, 2001, for further discussion). This finding might also highlight the limits of direct behavioral observation in understanding martial deterioration, suggesting the use of a broader range of methodologies for analyzing the process of change.

In an early attempt to look at additional factors that might influence marital outcomes, Kelly and Conley (1987) followed 247 couples through 45 years of marriage. They examined personality variables, socioenvironmental (family of origin) variables, attitudes toward marriage, and sexual history variables as potential precursors of marital discord and divorce. Their results suggested that the personality variables of husband neuroticism, wife neuroticism, and husband impulse control accounted for approximately half of the variance in marital outcomes. Building on this work, Karney and Bradbury (1997) used HLM analyses to examine the eight wave trajectories of marital satisfaction over the first 4 years of marriage in a sample of 172 newlywed couples, including as predictors both behavioral measures of communication and personality variables like neuroticism. Their analyses revealed that neuroticism was associated with the intercept of these trajectories, but not the slope of the trajectories, and communication behavior was associated with the slope of the trajectories. This would suggest differing roles for communication and neuroticism, in which the level of neuroticism determines how satisfied a couple begins their relationship whereas the quality of their communication determines how their satisfaction will shift over time. Similarly, Belsky and Hsieh (1998) found that enduring personality traits (neuroticism, extraversion, and agreeableness) were associated with initial levels of relationship functioning whereas dyadic behavior during parenting was associated with changes in marital satisfaction over time. Expanding the scope of the discussion beyond the construct of neuroticism, variables ranging from depression (e.g., Fincham, Beach, Harold, & Osborne, 1997) to handling of finances (e.g., Schaninger & Buss, 1986) to demographic variables such as age and parental divorce (e.g., Kurdek, 1993) have been linked to changes in marital satisfaction and stability (see Bradbury, Fincham, & Beach, 2000, for a review).

Although not without methodological limitations, these studies have helped to define how marital satisfaction can change over time. As a group, they provide a useful foundation for future research, calling attention to a set of potential process variables to be explored and highlighting the complexity of the problem.

WHO CHANGES?

The multidetermined nature of marital dysfunction presents a significant theoretical challenge to researchers, as any comprehensive theory on marriage would need to account for the majority of the causal paths without becoming so diverse as to lose all specificity. In other words, it may be difficult to develop a theory to account for a phenomenon like divorce to the extent that each couple experiences the path to that end point very differently. One method of approaching this problem involves asking *who* changes? This approach embraces the multidetermined nature of marital discord and seeks to classify couples into groups representing the most common paths to different marital outcomes instead of trying to force all couples to fit into a common path.

The first step in the process of understanding who changes is to identify the stable risk factors (assessed at the beginning of marriage) that are associated with adverse martial outcomes. A number of studies have used compatibility inventories such as PREPARE/ENRICH and FOCCUS to predict[†] marital outcomes (Fowers & Olson, 1986; Larsen & Olson 1989; Williams & Jurich, 1995). Although the retrospective sampling techniques employed in these studies limit the interpretation of the findings, the authors demonstrated that couple agreement on domains including personality match, conflict resolution, family/friends, children, and sexuality discriminated the couples that remained highly satisfied 3–5 years later from the couples that became distressed or divorced (see Rogge & Bradbury, 1999b, for a review). In addition, numerous studies have demonstrated the importance of stable individual variables in marital functioning. As mentioned above, personality variables like neuroticism have been linked to initial levels of marital functioning (Belsky & Hsieh, 1998; Karney & Bradbury, 1997) and to marital discord (Kelly & Conley, 1987). Individual psychopathology (in particular, depression) has also been linked to marital functioning (e.g., Fincham et al., 1997; Gotlib & Whiffen, 1989; Kurdek, 1998) and to higher rates of marriage in young women (Gotlib, Lewinsohn, & Seeley, 1998). Furthermore, a wide range of demographic factors has been linked to marital functioning. For example, in a sample of 222 newlywed couples, Kurdek (1993) demonstrated that demographic variables (i.e., level of income, level of education, divorce history, and length of courtship) predicted marital dissolution in the first 5 years of marriage. Similarly, Emery, Waldron, Kitzmann, and Aaron (1999) demonstrated that individual characteristics (mothers' adolescent delinquency) and demographic factors (age at marriage, age at childbirth, poverty status, and ethnicity) predicted divorce and nonmarital childbirth in a national sample of 1,204 families.

Taken together, these studies provide a wide array of risk factors that can be used to identify the couples that are at greatest risk for subsequent marital discord. For example, couples planning marriage could

---

[†] Since the discriminant functions used to "predict" outcomes were applied to the same data set from which they were derived, this does not represent prediction in the strictest sense but serves as an estimate of the level of prediction that could be obtained if these discriminant functions were applied to a new data set.

be assessed in these different domains with a brief questionnaire to determine the number of domains in which they are at elevated risk for marital discord, thereby gaining a rough estimate of their individual level of risk. Multivariate techniques like disciminant analysis offer a more systematic approach to assessing risk by integrating a group of risk factors into a single set of linear algorithms that optimally discriminate longitudinal outcomes (see Rogge & Bradbury, 1999a). The results of these studies offer a method for identifying at-risk couples and enable secondary interventions to be targeted to the couples that need them the most. However, identifying key risk factors of adverse marital outcomes is only the first step in understanding who changes. With larger longitudinal samples, it should be possible to develop a classification system to divide couples into groups representing the different pathways of change common to most marriages. For example, relationships marked by severe levels of aggression may undergo processes common to one another but divergent from the experiences of nonaggressive couples (e.g., Lawrence & Bradbury, 2000). Similarly, couples that experience an extramarital affair or some other major violation of trust probably share similarities with one another that they would not share with the majority of married couples. Thus, asking the question "Who changes?" and grouping couples into meaningful categories based on the dynamics of their individual relationships will allow researchers to dissect the multidetermined pathways that lead to discord and divorce.

A handful of studies have attempted to develop taxonomies based on cross-sectional data from large numbers of couples. For example, Fowers and Olson (1992) used cluster analysis in a sample of 5,030 couples that completed the PREPARE marital inventory prior to getting married. Their analyses suggested a four-cluster solution primarily stratified by the couples' overall levels of satisfaction with their relationships. In a separate sample of 8,385 established couples that completed the ENRICH inventory, Lavee and Olson (1993) developed a seven-cluster solution that essentially replicated the four clusters from Fowers and Olson and identified three new clusters representing distinct forms of marital discord. Cluster analysis also has been used in samples of distressed couples seeking marital therapy for the sole purpose of identifying categories of marital discord (e.g., Bayer & Day, 1995; Fals-Stewart, Birchler, Schafer, & Lucente, 1994). Despite the apparent lack of overlap in the clustering variables used between the studies, the analyses in these different samples generated solutions with surprisingly similar characteristics. The cluster analyses typically generated solutions with at least four clusters in which one cluster represented severe levels of distress, one cluster represented avoidant couples, one cluster represented couples with only mild levels of distress, and one cluster represented satisfied couples. Thus, the cross-sectional findings with newlywed, established, and distressed couples provide valuable insights into the question of who changes and suggest a number of distinct paths to distress. However, the cross-sectional nature of these studies prevents a direct examination of those longitudinal pathways, presenting an enticing opportunity for future research.

Belsky and Hsieh (1998) explored these longitudinal pathways more directly by performing cluster analysis on multiwave assessments of marital functioning (satisfaction and level of conflict) taken over the 50 months following the birth of a first child. Husband and wife data generated comparable three-cluster solutions containing a "stays good" group, a "good-gets-worse" group, and a "stays-bad" or "bad-gets-worse" group. As mentioned above, personality variables (i.e., neuroticism, extraversion, and agreeableness) discriminated the groups that start out with low levels of functioning from the remaining groups. In contrast, unsupportive dyadic parenting behavior (undermining the parenting efforts of a partner) helped to identify the couples whose satisfaction deteriorated from the couples that remained satisfied. Thus, by merging cluster analysis with multiwave assessment, the authors expanded the operationalization of change in relationships to include the multidetermined nature of marital outcomes, and they were able to examine the correlates of different longitudinal trajectories of marital functioning. We believe that efforts in this direction represent a crucial step in the process of understanding and accurately describing marital change.

Finally, the question of who changes challenges researchers to search for variables that moderate the relationship between behavior and satisfaction. For example, a number of studies have examined the impact of environmental variables such as negative life events on marriage. In a cross-sectional study of 82 established couples, Whiffen and Gotlib (1989) demonstrated that increased life events and poor coping strategies were associated with husbands' marital distress. In similar cross-sectional studies, life events (Lavee, McCubbin, & Olson, 1987) and their perceived stress (Zelkowitz & Milet, 1997) were shown to be associated with marital distress. Building on this cross-sectional work, Cohan and Bradbury (1997) examined the longitudinal effects of life events on marital functioning in a sample of 57 newlywed couples. The authors demonstrated an interaction between life events and observed communication behavior (expressed anger) on changes in marital satisfaction over 18 months, suggesting that increased numbers of life events exacerbated the relationship between negative behavior and subsequent declines in satisfaction. The authors found additional moderating effects of life events on the relationship between negative behaviors and shifts in depressive symptoms over 18 months. Thus, stressful life events serve a potentiating role in marriage, creating the context in which maladaptive approaches to communication are most clearly associated with declines in marital quality.

Along these lines, the construct of social support also has emerged as a potential moderator variable.[‡] A number of studies have used measures of social support to demonstrate that providing greater levels of social support for partners is associated with higher levels of marital satisfaction (e.g., Acitelli & Antonucci, 1994; Cutrona, 1996; Julien & Markman, 1991). In addition, couples have identified a lack of social support from partners as a key complaint leading to marital distress (Baxter, 1986), and higher levels of marital distress have been linked to seeking support outside the marital relationship (Julien & Markman, 1991) and interference caused by outside support (Julien, Markman, Léveillé, Chartrand, & Bégin 1994). In a sample of 60 newlywed couples, Pasch and Bradbury (1998) extended this work by examining the effects of social support behavior in a longitudinal manner. The authors demonstrated that couples' observed social support behavior was predictive of marital satisfaction 2 years later above and beyond the predictive contribution of conflict behavior, suggesting that the quality of support couples provide each other represents a domain of essential skills for relationships that are distinct from general communication skills. Furthermore, the authors showed that social support behavior moderated the relationship between negative conflict behavior and subsequent marital satisfaction such that couples with poor

---

[‡] The construct of social support is presented in the current section as an example of an individual factor that moderates the link between communication and marital satisfaction. However, social support can also be viewed as a dyadic process variable, which would place it in the category of *what changes*. In this sense, the construct of social support spans both dimensions of change and its placement within the taxonomy is dependent upon the context in which it is being considered.

conflict management skills and poor support skills displayed greater than expected levels of distress 2 years later.

Characterizing moderating variables within models of marriage not only serves to increase the accuracy of those models, but more importantly those moderating variables can serve as potential points of intervention to help prevent marital discord and dissolution. For example, the moderating effect of social support behavior would suggest that couples with poor social support skills are at a higher risk for marital discord and that it could be possible to reduce that risk by teaching them better methods of providing each other support. Thus, moderating variables have the potential to both refine theory and inform clinical practice.

WHAT CHANGES?

Considering the question of *what* changes in marriages shifts attention to the outcome and process variables currently employed in marital research. Most studies of marriage have limited their outcome variables to two dimensions: marital satisfaction and marital stability. This focus has served the field reasonably well in its initial attempts to understand antecedents of marital discord and divorce, but the narrow scope also has obscured other lines of inquiry. For example, the construct of commitment has received relatively little attention in empirical studies despite its tremendous utility when working with couples. Commitment has been shown to account for unique variance in marital satisfaction and for gains in wives' satisfaction following marital therapy, and it mediates the relationship between interdependency and prorelationship behaviors (Beach & Broderick, 1983; Broderick & O'Leary, 1986; Wieselquist, Rusbult, Foster, & Agnew, 1999). Despite this work, few studies of marriage include measures of commitment as potential outcome variables or as mediators of marital outcomes. In addition, although there is a growing literature on the impact of divorce on children and families (see Amato & Keith, 1991, for a review), marital researchers have been slow to include family and child outcomes in their designs. Furthermore, the marital field has begun to include environmental variables such as physical health and work stress into their models as external challenges to the relationship but has not begun to consider general health, work productivity, or even general psychological well-being as potential outcome variables beyond marital satisfaction. The expansion of outcome variables could help to contextualize models of marriage, grounding them more firmly in the real world and providing additional avenues for intervention and a more encompassing perspective on program evaluation.

Asking the question of what changes in relationships also suggests a deeper analysis of potential process variables involved in marital change. As mentioned above, dozens of studies have examined potential mediators of change by measuring them at one time point and then demonstrating their association with changes in marital satisfaction or stability over time. The construct of communication has received widespread attention within this paradigm, demonstrating the predictive validity of self-report and behavioral measures of communication in identifying couples at risk for discord or divorce (e.g., Gottman, 1994; Hill & Peplau, 1998; Lindahl, Clements & Markman, 1998). Despite the relatively low levels of marital discord and divorce in these samples (due to selective attrition and sampling biases), these studies tend to suggest that hostile and negative communication is associated with subsequent declines in marital satisfaction. In a sample of 56 newlywed marriages from the Los Angeles metro area, Rogge and Bradbury (1999a) further clarified the nature of the predictive validity of communication in newlywed marriage. The authors found that initial measures of communication (either self-reported or observationally coded) were predictive of marital discord, whereas initial measures of aggression were predictive of marital dissolution in the first 4 years of marriage. In a subsequent study of 95 couples from Munich, Germany, Rogge, Bradbury, Hahlweg, Engl, and Thurmaier (2000) corroborated these findings, demonstrating that communication was predictive of subsequent marital satisfaction, whereas aggression and psychological distress were predictive of subsequent separation or divorce.

In addition to establishing the predictive validity of communication behavior, the two-wave longitudinal studies of marriage have uncovered a wide array of possible process variables, including social support behavior (e.g., Pasch & Bradbury, 1998), sexual functioning (e.g., Williams & Jurich, 1995), aggression (e.g., O'Leary, Barling, Arias, & Rosenbaum, 1989), attributions for partners' behavior (e.g., Fincham & Bradbury, 1987), expectations (e.g., Craddock, 1980), finance management (e.g., Schaninger & Buss, 1986), psychopathology (e.g., depression; Beach & O'Leary, 1993), and personality traits (e.g., neuroticism; Kelly & Conley, 1987). However, to understand fully the processes underlying changes in marital satisfaction or dissolution, it will be necessary to track potential mediators over time, measuring their fluctuations in direct comparison to changes in marital quality. For example, although there is a large body of literature supporting the predictive validity of communication behavior in marriage, few studies have examined the stability of this behavior over time. In a sample of 33 premarital couples, Noller et al. (1994) examined the stability of conflict behavior in early marriage. The authors demonstrated that with the exception of an increased use of reason and support and a decreased use of manipulation at 1 year of marriage, couples' use of conflict strategies during discussions of problems remained consistent over the first 2 years of marriage. Similarly, Storaasli and Markman (1990) examined the stability of relationship problems in a sample of 84 premarital couples. Contrasting premarital reports of problems with reports taken in early marriage and then again in early parenthood, the authors found that the problems of friends, religion, and jealousy tended to decrease over time, whereas the problems of sex, communication, and recreation tended to increase over time. These studies provide an important step toward understanding what changes in relationships by tracking the changes in potential process variables over time. However, without simultaneously modeling changes in marital quality or stability in these analyses, the linkages between these variables and relationship functioning over time remain unclear.

To address this issue, Karney and Bradbury (2000) used growth curve modeling to examine the covariance between the trajectories of marital satisfaction and maladaptive attributions in the first 4 years of marriage. They found that attributions did in fact change over time, that satisfaction and attributions covaried over time (as satisfaction decreased, maladaptive attributions increased), and that these variables seemed to be causally linked in a bidirectional manner. The authors further demonstrated that neuroticism moderated the trajectories of attributions over time such that spouses with high levels of neuroticism tended to make more stable (negative) attributions over time. Similarly, in a study of 198 newlywed couples, Kurdek (1998) used growth curve modeling to examine associations between the trajectories of marital satisfaction and depression over time, demonstrating that as marital satisfaction decreased over time, depressive symptoms increased. These studies represent an important new step in the longitudinal analysis of marriage as they allow researchers to directly examine the roles of potential process variables over time, revealing the inner nature of marital change as it occurs.

To gain a clear understanding of what changes in relationships, it will also be essential to disentangle the colinearity of the variables being studied. With an array of over 200 potential mediating and moderating variables that have been examined longitudinally, diligent researchers find themselves overwhelmed when trying to design studies that include a comprehensive sampling of these different variables. Reduction analyses (e.g., canonical correlation analysis or principal components analysis) in longitudinal samples would allow experimenters to uncover the primary constructs underlying the current diversity of measures. Separate analyses examining cross-sectional variance, predictive variance, and unique trends of change over time in couples' longitudinal data could help to clarify the major sources of variance involved in marital change, refining current models of marriage and identifying the measures that most directly assess those constructs.

Finally, the question of what changes in marriage raises an interesting line of inquiry regarding the couples' own perceptions of the change in their marriages. A number of studies have examined the predictive validity of the stories that couples tell about their own relationship histories. Orbuch, Veroff, and Holmberg (1993) examined couples' behavior during the narrating of their relationship history and the themes present in those relationship histories in a sample of 264 newlywed couples. The authors found that lower levels of conflict between spouses during the narration were associated with higher levels of marital satisfaction 2 years later after controlling for demographics and initial marital satisfaction. In addition, the presence of "nonromantic positive" themes (e.g., relationship developing out of a friendship) and the absence of "overcoming obstacles" themes (e.g., parents disapproved of marriage) were predictive of higher levels of marital satisfaction 2 years later, once again controlling for initial satisfaction and demographics. In a separate paper from this project, Veroff, Sutherland, Chadiha, and Ortega (1993) demonstrated that the degree to which couples described shared affect regarding the relationship (e.g., "We didn't like fighting" or "We were very much in love") predicted subsequent marital satisfaction. The authors interpreted these expressions of couple affect as indicative of a communal orientation to the relationship, indicating a high level of dedication to the marriage. Buehlman, Gottman, and Katz (1992) explored the predictive validity of couples' behavior during an oral history interview in a sample of 52 established couples. The authors found that increased expressions of fondness and "we-ness" during the interview and decreased expressions of disappointment and negativity were associated with lower levels of marital discord and divorce 3 years later. These studies would suggest that, independent of the accuracy of their narrations, the manner in which couples speak about their relationships and the content they choose to include in those histories are predictive of their subsequent marital satisfaction.

WHEN DO COUPLES CHANGE?

The question of *when* couples change promotes a developmental perspective on relationships and on models of marital functioning. Although models of marriage like the vulnerability-stress-adaptation model proposed by Karney and Bradbury (1995) are beginning to incorporate developmental components such as external events and adaptive processes, most current models of marriage do not take into account the stage of marriage; newlywed couples and established couples are not always distinguished. It is fair to assume that some basic marital processes might be independent of the developmental stage of the marriages. However, the findings of Storaasli and Markman (1990) would suggest that as couples transition into marriage and then into the roles of parents, the nature of the problems they face changes across those transitions. The literature on communication behavior suggests also that negative behavior that is disruptive in the early years of marriage might be beneficial in established marriages that have survived the initial high-risk period for divorce. Thus, the developmental stage of marriage can moderate the effects of variables like behavior, suggesting the need for models of marriage that are developmentally sensitive.

The transition to parenthood underscores this point. With the birth of a child, a marital relationship is confronted suddenly with an array of new factors and issues that did not exist prior to the baby's arrival. In addition to the stress that young parents must contend with, couples with a new baby must redefine themselves and their relationship to incorporate their new roles as parents. Consequently, this transition has been shown to be associated with increased conflict and decreased marital satisfaction (Belsky & Rovine, 1990; Belsky, Spanier, & Rovine, 1983; Cowan et al., 1985; Crohan, 1996; Ruble, Fleming, Hackel, & Stangor, 1988), particularly if the pregnancy was unplanned or the parents are struggling with depressive symptoms (Cox, Paley,

Burchinal, & Payne, 1999). This shift in marital satisfaction has been linked with declines in leisure activities, decreases in positive interchanges, and disappointment from unmet role expectations as division of household labor becomes more traditional, leaving wives with the bulk of the household and childrearing duties (Belsky & Pensky, 1988; Cowan & Cowan, 1988; Kluwer, Heesink, & Van De Vliert, 1997). Furthermore, Belsky, Lang, and Huston (1986) demonstrated that the negative effect of traditionalizing roles on marital satisfaction is potentiated by wives' perceptions of themselves, such that the negative effects are enhanced for wives that view themselves as less feminine (gender typical). Interestingly, when couples making the transition to parenthood are compared with matched samples of couples without children, the results indicate no differences between the groups, suggesting that the declines in satisfaction demonstrated in prior work may simply represent a normative erosion of marital quality independent of parenthood (McHale & Huston, 1985; White & Booth, 1985). Despite this important qualification, a large body of work suggests that the transition to parenthood presents a number of distinct challenges to couples that can cause conflict and marital dissatisfaction if they are not navigated successfully. Thus, the question of when couples change can encourage researchers to adopt a developmental view of marriage that accommodates major life transitions such as parenthood.

Another developmental issue in the study of marital change concerns trends of divorce in the United States. The first 4 years of marriage have been shown to be a high-risk period for marital instability, with about 40% of all divorces occuring within this short span of time (National Center for Health Statistics, 1990). Growth curve modeling of marital satisfaction trajectories over this period indicate significant linear (and sometimes quadratic) trends in the data, suggesting rapid declines in marital satisfaction immediately following marriage (Kurdek, 1998). Furthermore, Karney and Bradbury (1997) demonstrated that rapid declines in satisfaction following marriage were strongly associated with divorce in the first 4 years of marriage. These findings suggest that for many couples the transition to marriage is very difficult and is associated with a rapid erosion of the relationship ending in an early divorce. The existence of this "failure to thrive" in early marriage has a number of implications. First, this supports the idea that divorce is a multidetermined outcome with many possible paths. In other words, couples who become distressed and divorce in the first few years of marriage most likely differ in important ways from couples whose relationships slowly decline over 10 to 15 years, ultimately ending in divorce (e.g., Huston, Caughlin, Houts, Shebilski, & Smith, 1999). Thus, the longitudinal trajectory leading to divorce could serve as an important moderator of the correlates associated with the process of marital deterioration. Second, the findings highlighting a large proportion of early divorces suggest the presence of a potentially powerful selection effect in samples of established couples. When researchers use samples of established marriages (e.g., couples that have been married for 6 years on average) to understand the processes leading to marital dissolution, that sampling strategy necessarily excludes a large proportion of the couples of interest, as established samples will no longer contain those couples who divorced in the first four years of marriage. Introducing a developmental perspective helps to clarify this discrepancy and qualifies the interpretation of findings from newlywed or established samples. Third, the presence of a rapidly unstable group of marriages suggests the importance of examining the courtship phase of relationships in order to track the process of change from its beginnings. Although the study of dating relationships introduces an entire array of logistical problems (e.g., adequate sampling, attrition due to breakup before marriage), the study of dating or engaged samples enables researchers to examine carefully the event of getting married as any other major life transition, tracking the course of marital functioning and satisfaction across that transition in order to better understand the impact that marriage has on relationships.

Finally, one of the main challenges in building developmental models of marriage involves identifying discrete stages of marriage. We, like others, often recruit samples of newlywed couples, thereby using couples' wedding dates to homogenize the developmental stage of the samples. Although the transition into legal marriage is no doubt a major transition, this method makes two main assumptions about the process of marital change. First, it tends to assume that all couples who have been married one month share more similarities with one another than they do with all other couples. This assumption fails to recognize that variables like age at marriage, length of courtship, and level of income can be important predictors of marital outcomes. These findings suggest that to fully homogenize the developmental stage of a sample, either newlywed couples should be matched on these demographic factors as well or the effects of these demographic factors should be statistically controlled in all analyses. Second, the use of newlywed samples to synchronize the developmental stages assumes further that the passage of time in relationships effects change in a manner similar to child development – essentially asserting that marital change is a time-based process. Christensen (1998) argues that an event-based approach might be more appropriate and suggests that a couple that has just had its first child after 3 years of marriage would have more in common with other couples that are first-time parents (regardless of length of marriage) than they would with childless couples that have also been married for 3 years. This perspective emphasizes shared experiences rather than the passage of time as the main source of variance in marital change and suggests event-based developmental models focusing on major life transitions as well as event-based sampling of couples to test those models.

CROSS-DOMAIN QUESTIONS

Although the three primary domains of questioning have been addressed separately thus far, they are by no means isolated from each other and in fact their regions of overlap encourage additional conceptualizations of change. For example, asking the higher-order question of *what changes when* in relationships leads researchers to examine both outcome variables and process variables from a developmental perspective, recognizing that different processes might become more salient at different stages of marriage. Studies that make use of multiwave assessments and growth curve analysis to model satisfaction and process variables simultaneously exemplify this direction of inquiry (e.g., Karney & Bradbury, 2000; Kurdek, 1998). This methodology enables a developmental analysis of the process of change as it occurs, allows researchers a number of methods for assessing the directionality of causation within the longitudinal associations between variables (see Karney & Bradbury, 2000), and illuminates the unique contributions of the factors involved by controlling for the effects of all variables simultaneously. Thus, combining the questions of *what changes* and *when does that happen* challenges researchers to analyze the dynamics of change with greater precision and accuracy over time.

Another domain of overlap asks the question, *who changes when* in relationships; this introduces a developmental perspective on the analysis of the multidetermined nature of marital outcomes. For example, although much of the work on developing experimental taxonomies of marriage has used cross-sectional designs, Belsky and Hsieh (1998) performed cluster analyses on multiwave assessments of marital functioning. With this methodology, the authors were able to identify common trajectories of marriage and examine their associations with predictor and process variables, thereby establishing distinct profiles of change. Once again, merging the questions of *who changes* and *when does that happen* demands a greater flexibility in how change is operationally defined. The combination of multiwave assessment and cluster analysis provides an operationalization of change in relationships that encorporates both the developmental and multi-determined natures of that process.

Finally, merging the questions of *who changes* and *what changes* challenges researchers to consider the intersection of process variables and contextual factors like stressful events or enduring vulnerabilities. As mentioned above, contextual variables can serve as moderators of the relationships between marital processes and outcomes. For example, the inability to provide social support to a partner can exacerbate the effects of poor communication, leading to greater declines in marital satisfaction (Pasch & Bradbury, 1998). Thus, the search for individual factors that serve to moderate basic marital processes represents a merging of these two domains and helps to refine models of marriage so that they approximate more closely the actual experiences of couples.

CONCLUSIONS AND IMPLICATIONS

The taxonomy of change developed in this chapter provides a framework for organizing previous research, clarifying what has been established in an understanding of change in marriage and illuminating areas for additional study. The majority of previous work has examined *how couples change* by demonstrating the predictive validity of different variables in two-wave designs. Although this provides a foundation of research rich with potential process variables to be explored further, operationalizing the study of marital change in this manner restricts the range of hypotheses that can be explored.

First, expanding the conceptualization of change to include the domain of *who changes* allows researchers to begin testing the multi-determined nature of marital outcomes with the possibility of developing a taxonomy to identify the major paths that marriages can take. Asking who changes further challenges researchers to begin looking for more intricate relationships among process variables, identifying the moderating variables that enable general models to be tailored to predict individual cases more precisely. Second, expanding the perspective on change to include *what changes* calls into question the limited range of process variables used in marital research. Asking what changes also calls for a longitudinal analysis of process variables, using multiwave studies to track their variance over time concomitantly with changes in marital satisfaction. Finally, expanding the taxonomy of change to include the domain of *when change occurs* promotes a developmental view of marriage, incorporating major life transitions as event-dependent stages.

This multifaceted perspective on change suggests a number of implications for future research. First, this framework helps to highlight the power of multiwave assessment in marital research. Only by sampling couples at multiple points over time is it possible to track change as it is occurring; this in turn allows a deeper analysis of the mechanisms involved in that change. Second, this framework argues for a broader range of outcome variables. Although the study of marital satisfaction and stability has produced a wealth of data, expanding the repertoire of outcome variables to include factors such as dimensions of commitment, individual mental and physical health, child adjustment, and work productivity would increase the scope of marital research, thereby placing models of marital functioning into the larger context of global functioning. Third, this multifaceted perspective suggests the need for conceptual replications across studies and more direct attempts to identify and reduce the colinearity among variables. With over 200 potential process variables already identified in the longitudinal literature thus far, colinearity is a matter of fact rather than of conjecture, and yet it has received little systematic attention in the field. The framework presented in this chapter helps to inform the process of construct validation by emphasizing distinct domains of validity to be assessed in the search for unique variance. Fourth, the framework also reveals the need for increased study of contextual moderators of marital processes. To describe marital change effectively, we believe that a model of marital functioning must recognize that relationship processes do not occur in a vacuum, and that contextual factors can have a dramatic impact on the salience of different processes for individual couples. Finally, the framework presented highlights the power of multivariate techniques like cluster analysis and growth curve modeling. These techniques take full advantage of multiwave longitudinal data and afford more sophisticated analyses of change in marriage.

The field of marital research has built a preliminary but useful foundation of knowledge using primarily two-wave longitudinal designs that examine the correlates of change in satisfaction over time. As a result, the field has reached a point where that conceptualization of change is providing diminishing returns. The multifaceted framework of change developed in this chapter illuminates a new set of options for examining change in relationships and emphasizes a number of promising methodologies to facilitate that process.

REFERENCES

Acitelli, L. K., & Antonucci, T. C. (1994). Gender differences in the link between marital support and satisfaction in older couples. *Journal of Personality and Social Psychology, 76*, 688–698.

Amato, P. R., & Keith, B. (1991). Parental divorce and the well-being of children: A meta-analysis. *Psychological Bulletin, 110*, 26–46.

Baxter, L. A. (1986). Gender differences in the heterosexual relationship rules embedded in break-up accounts. *Journal of Social and Personal Relationships, 3*, 289–306.

Bayer, J. P., & Day, H. D. (1995). An empirical typology based on differentiation. *Contemporary Family Therapy, 17*, 265–271.

Beach, S. R., & Broderick, J. E. (1983). Commitment: A variable in women's response to marital therapy. *American Journal of Family Therapy, 11*, 16–24.

Beach, S. R., & O'Leary, K. D. (1993). Dysphoria and marital discord: Are dysphoric individuals at risk for marital maladjustment? *Journal of Marital and Family Therapy, 19*, 355–368.

Belsky, J., & Hsieh, K. H. (1998). Patterns of marital change during the early childhood years: Parent personality, coparenting, and division-of-labor correlates. *Journal of Family Psychology, 12*, 511–528.

Belsky, J., & Pensky, E. (1988). Marital change across the transition to parenthood. *Marriage and Family Review, 12*, 133–156.

Belsky, J., & Rovine, M. (1990). Patterns of marital change across the transition to parenthood: Pregnancy to three years postpartum. *Journal of Marriage and the Family, 52*, 5–19.

Belsky, J., Lang, M., & Huston, T. L. (1986). Sex typing and division of labor as determinants of marital change across the transition to parenthood. *Journal of Personality and Social Psychology, 50*, 517–522.

Belsky, J., Spanier, G. B., & Rovine, M. (1983). Stability and change in marriage across the transition to parenthood. *Journal of Marriage and the Family, 45*, 567–577.

Bradbury, T. N. (in press). Research on relationships as a prelude to action. *Journal of Social and Personal Relationships*.

Bradbury, T. N., & Fincham, F. D. (1987). Affect and cognition in close relationships: Towards an integrative model. *Cognition and Emotion, 1*, 59–87.

(1989). Behavior and satisfaction in marriage: Prospective mediating processes. In C. Hendrick et al. (Eds.), *Close relationships* (pp. 119–143). Newbury Park, CA: Sage.

Bradbury, T. N., & Karney, B. R. (1993). Longitudinal study of marital interaction and dysfunction: Review and analysis. *Clinical Psychology Review, 13*, 15–27.

Bradbury, T. N., Fincham, F. D., & Beach, S. (2000). Research on the nature and determinants of marital satisfaction: A decade in review. *Journal of Marriage and the Family, 62*, 964–980.

Bradbury, T. N., Rogge, R. D., & Lawrence, E. (2001). Reconsidering the role of conflict in marriage. In A. Booth, N. Crouter, & M. Clements (Eds.), *Couples in conflict* (pp. 59–81) Hillsdale, NJ: Erlbaum.

Broderick, J. E., & O'Leary, K. D. (1986). Contributions of affect, attitudes, and behavior to marital satisfaction. *Journal of Consulting and Clinical Psychology, 54*, 514–517.

Buehlman, K. T., Gottman, J. M., & Katz, L. F. (1992). How a couple views their past predicts their future: Predicting divorce from an oral history interview. *Journal of Family Psychology, 5*, 295–318.

Christensen, A. (1998). On intervention and relationship events: A marital therapist looks at longitudinal research on marriage. In T. N. Bradbury (Ed.), *The developmental course of marital dysfunction* (pp. 377–392). Cambridge: Cambridge University Press.

Cohan, C. L., & Bradbury, T. N. (1997). Negative life events, marital interaction, and the longitudinal course of newlywed marriage. *Journal of Personality and Social Psychology, 73*, 114–128.

Cowan, C. P., & Cowan, P. A. (1988). Who does what when partners become parents: Implications for men, women, and marriage. *Marriage and Family Review, 12*, 105–132.

Cowan, C. P., Cowan, P. A., Heming, G., Garrett, E., Coysh, W. S., Curtis-Boles, H., & Boles, A. J. (1985). Transitions to parenthood: His, hers, and theirs. *Journal of Family Issues, 6*, 451–481.

Cox, M. J., Paley, B., Burchinal, M., & Payne, C. C. (1999). Marital perceptions and interactions across the transition to parenthood. *Journal of Marriage and the Family, 61*, 611–625.

Craddock, A. E. (1980). Marital problem-solving as a function of couples' marital power expectations and marital value systems. *Journal of Marriage and the Family, 42*, 185–196.

Crohan, S. E. (1996). Marital quality and conflict across the transition to parenthood in African American and white couples. *Journal of Marriage and the Family, 58*, 933–944.

Cutrona, C. E. (1996). Social support as a determinant of marital quality: The interplay of negative and supportive behaviors. In G. R. Pierce & B. R. Sarason (Eds.), *Handbook of social support and the family* (pp. 173–194). New York: Plenum.

Emery, R. E., Waldron, M., Kitzmann, K. M., & Aaron, J. (1999). Delinquent behavior, future divorce or nonmarital childbearing, and externalizing behavior among offspring: A 14-year prospective study. *Journal of Family Psychology, 13*, 568–579.

Fals-Stewart, W., Birchler, G. R., Schafer, J., & Lucente, S. (1994). The personality of marital distress: An empirical typology. *Journal of Personality Assessment, 62,* 223–241.
Fincham, F. D., & Beach, S. R. (1999). Conflict in marriage: Implications for working with couples. *Annual Review of Psychology, 50,* 47–77.
Fincham, F. D., & Bradbury, T. N. (1987). The impact of attributions in marriage: A longitudinal analysis. *Journal of Personality and Social Psychology, 53,* 510–517.
Fincham, F. D., Beach, S. R., Harold, G. T., & Osborne, L. N. (1997). Marital satisfaction and depression: Different causal relationships for men and women? *Psychological Science, 8,* 351–357.
Fowers, B. J., & Olson, D. H. (1986). Predicting marital success with PREPARE: A predictive validity study. *Journal of Marital and Family Therapy, 12,* 403–413.
(1992). Four types of premarital couples: An empirical typology based on PREPARE. *Journal of Family Psychology, 6,* 10–21.
Gotlib, I. H., & Whiffen, V. E. (1989). Depression and marital functioning: An examination of specificity and gender differences. *Journal of Abnormal Psychology, 98,* 23–30.
Gotlib, I. H., Lewinsohn, P. M., & Seeley, J. R. (1998). Consequences of depression during adolescence: Marital status and marital functioning in early adulthood. *Journal of Abnormal Psychology, 4,* 686–690.
Gottman, J. M. (1994). *What predicts divorce? The relationship between marital processes and marital outcomes.* Hillsdale, NJ: Erlbaum.
Heavey, C. L., Layne, C., & Christensen, A. (1993). Gender and conflict structure in marital interaction: A replication and extension. *Journal of Consulting and Clinical Psychology, 61,* 16–27.
Heyman, R. E., Weiss, R. L., & Eddy, J. (1995). Marital Interaction Coding System: Revision and empirical evaluation. *Behavior Research and Therapy, 33,* 737–746.
Hill, C. T., & Peplau, L. A. (1998). Premarital predictors of relationship outcomes: A 15-year follow-up of the Boston Couples Study. In T. N. Bradbury (Ed.), *The developmental course of marital dysfunction* (pp. 237–278). Cambridge: Cambridge University Press.
Huston, T. L., Caughlin, J. P., Houts, R. M., Shebilski, L. J., & Smith, S. E. (2001). The connubial crucible: Newlywed years as predictors of marital delight, distress, and divorce. *Journal of Personality and Social Psychology, 80,* 237–252.
Jacobson, N. S., & Margolin, G. (1979). *Marital therapy: Strategies based on social learning and behavior exchange principles.* New York: Brunner/Mazel.
Julien, D., & Markman, H. J. (1991). Social support and social networks as determinants of individual and marital outcomes. *Journal of Social and Personal Relationships, 8,* 549–568.
Julien, D., Markman, H. J., Léveillé, S., Chartrand, E., & Bégin, J. (1994). Networks' support and interference with regard to marriage: Disclosures of marital problems to confidants. *Journal of Family Psychology, 8,* 16–31.
Julien, D., Markman, H. J., & Lindahl, K. M. (1989). A comparison of a global and a microanalytic coding system: Implications for future trends in studying interactions. *Behavioral Assessment, 11,* 81–100.

Karney, B. R., & Bradbury, T. N. (1995). The longitudinal course of marital quality and stability: A review of theory, method, and research. *Psychological Bulletin, 118,* 3–34.

— (1997). Neuroticism, marital interaction, and the trajectory of marital satisfaction. *Journal of Personality and Social Psychology, 72,* 1075–1092.

— (2000). Attributions in marriage: State or trait? A growth curve analysis. *Journal of Personality and Social Psychology, 78,* 295–309.

Kelly, E. L., & Conley, J. J. (1987). Personality and compatibility: A prospective analysis of marital stability and marital satisfaction. *Journal of Personality and Social Psychology, 52,* 27–40.

Kluwer, E. S., Heesink, J. A. M., & Van De Vliert, E. (1997). The marital dynamics of conflict over the division of labor. *Journal of Marriage and the Family, 59,* 635–653.

Kurdek, L. A. (1993). Predicting marital dissolution: A five-year prospective longitudinal study of newlywed couples. *Journal of Personality and Social Psychology, 64,* 221–242.

— (1998). The nature of predictors of the trajectory of change in marital quality over the first 4 years of marriage for first-married husbands and wives. *Journal of Family Psychology, 4,* 494–510.

Larsen, A. S., & Olson, D. H. (1989). Predicting marital satisfaction using PREPARE: A replication study. *Journal of Marital and Family Therapy, 15,* 311–322.

Lavee, Y., & Olson, D. H. (1993). Seven types of marriage: Empirical typology based on ENRICH. *Journal of Marital and Family Therapy, 19,* 325–340.

Lavee, Y., McCubbin, H. I., & Olson, D. H. (1987). The effect of stressful life events and transitions on family functioning and well-being. *Journal of Marriage and the Family, 49,* 857–873.

Lawrence, E., & Bradbury, T. N. (2000). Physical aggression and marital dysfunction: A longitudinal analysis. Manuscript submitted for publication.

Lindahl, K., Clements, M., & Markman, H. (1998). The development of marriage: A nine-year perspective. In T. N. Bradbury (Ed.), *The developmental course of marital dysfunction* (pp. 205–236). Cambridge: Cambridge University Press.

McHale, S. M., & Huston, T. L. (1985). The effect of the transition to parenthood on the marriage relationship. *Journal of Family Issues, 6,* 409–433.

Moscovici, S. (1989). Preconditions for explanation in social psychology. *European Journal of Social Psychology, 19,* 407–430.

National Center for Health Statistics (1990). Advance Report of Final Marriage Statistics, *Monthly Vital Statistics Report, 38,* Supplement.

Noller, P., Feeney, J. A., Bonnell, P., & Callan, V. (1994). A longitudinal study of conflict in early marriage. *Journal of Social and Personal Relationships, 11,* 233–252.

O'Leary, K. D., Barling, J., Arias, I., & Rosenbaum, A. (1989). Prevalence and stability of physical aggression between spouses: A longitudinal analysis. *Journal of Consulting and Clinical Psychology, 57,* 263–268.

Orbuch, T. L., Veroff, J., & Holmberg, D. (1993). Becoming a married couple: The emergence of meaning in the first years of marriage. *Journal of Marriage and the Family, 55*, 815–826.

Pasch, L. A., & Bradbury, T. N. (1998). Social support, conflict, and the development of marital dysfunction. *Journal of Consulting and Clinical Psychology, 66*, 219–230.

Rogge, R. D., & Bradbury, T. N. (1999a). Till violence does us part: The differing roles of communication and aggression in predicting adverse marital outcomes. *Journal of Consulting and Clinical Psychology, 67*, 340–351.

(1999b). Recent advances in the prediction of marital outcomes. In R. Berger & M. T. Hannah (Eds.), *Preventive approaches in couples therapy* (pp. 331–360). Philadelphia: Brunner/Mazel.

Rogge, R. D., Bradbury, T. N., Hahlweg, K., Engl, J., & Thurmaier, F. (2000). *Prediction of marital satisfaction and dissolution of 5 years: Refining the two-factor hypothesis.* Manuscript submitted for publication.

Ruble, D. N., Fleming, A. S., Hackel, L. S., & Stangor, C. (1988). Changes in the marital relationship during the transition to first-time motherhood: Effects of violated expectations concerning division of household labor. *Journal of Personality and Social Psychology, 55*, 78–87.

Schaninger, C. M., & Buss, W. C. (1986). A longitudinal comparison of consumption and finance handling between happily married and divorced couples. *Journal of Marriage and the Family, 48*, 129–136.

Storaasli, R. D., & Markman, H. J. (1990). Relationship problems in the early stages of marriage: A longitudinal investigation. *Journal of Family Psychology, 4*, 30–99.

Veroff, J., Sutherland, L., Chadiha, L. A., & Ortega, R. M. (1993). Predicting marital quality with narrative assessments of marital experience. *Journal of Marriage and the Family, 55*, 326–337.

Whiffen, V. E., & Gotlib, I. H. (1989). Stress and coping in maritally distressed and nondistressed couples. *Journal of Social and Personal Relationships, 6*, 327–344.

White, L., & Booth, A. (1985). The transition to parenthood and marital quality. *Journal of Family Issues, 6*, 435–449.

Wieselquist, J., Rusbult, C. E., Foster, C. A., & Agnew, C. R. (1999). Commitment, prorelationship behavior, and trust in close relationships. *Journal of Personality and Social Psychology, 77*, 942–966.

Williams, L., & Jurich, J. (1995). Predicting marital success after five years: Assessing the predictive validity of FOCCUS. *Journal of Marital and Family Therapy, 21*, 141–153.

Zelkowitz, P., & Milet, T. H. (1997). Stress and support as related to postpartum paternal mental health and perceptions of the infant. *Infant Mental Health Journal, 18*, 424–435.

PART THREE

CONTEXTS: SOCIAL ENVIRONMENTS FOR STABILITY AND CHANGE

To fully understand personal relationships, one must attend to the context in which those relationships exist. Context, as we use this term, includes both proximal factors – i.e., the larger social network in which the dyadic relationship is embedded – and distal factors – i.e., cultural-historical factors that influence the dyad. The impact of the former, although commonly noted, is seldom investigated. It is readily apparent, however, that dyadic relationships rarely, if ever, exist in a social vacuum; instead, they are linked to wider social networks by virtue of the partners' participation in multiple dyadic relationships. As for the latter, only recently have relationship researchers begun to consider the moderating role that cultural-historical contexts may play. Some of this impact is based on technological innovation. For example, advances in medicine and social hygiene throughout the twentieth century (e.g., birth control, standards of gynecological care that allow women to enjoy sexual intercourse without pain) have radically altered the nature of sexuality in relationships. Similarly, developments in communication technology, beginning with the telephone and extending more recently to the Internet, afford opportunities to maintain and even initiate relationships without or with limited face-to-face contact.

Sprecher, Felmlee, Orbuch, and Willetts begin this section by making a strong case for the importance of social networks and their influence on personal (dyadic) relationships. After reviewing prior work, these authors offer a detailed, far-reaching analysis of how and why network processes may influence stability and change in premarital, marital, and other committed relationships. Because networks themselves may reflect social forces, Sprecher and her colleagues further argue that a number of macrolevel social processes may affect networks and the relationships that comprise them. Finally, in discussing questions that might be addressed by future studies, the authors show that any theoretical explanation of stability and change in relationships is incomplete without acknowledgment of the potent effects of social networks.

Wheeler and Christensen focus their attention on a particular context for change: the therapeutic intervention, and specifically Integrative Behavioral Couple Therapy (IBCT). Therapeutic settings, they propose, are ripe for examining processes associated with stability and change in romantic relationships, because couples usually enter therapy with the explicit goal of change – for example, to rid themselves of stable, ongoing problems. Wheeler and Christensen argue that IBCT is a particularly effective method to help couples attain this goal. They do so in part by contrasting IBCT with Traditional Behavioral Couple Therapy (TBCT), and also by describing several techniques used in IBCT that promote relationship change. By explaining how and why IBCT offers couples a context for change, Wheeler and Christensen illuminate mechanisms and circumstances that may facilitate relational change in nontherapeutic contexts.

Next, Hatfield and Rapson discuss historical and cultural influences on conceptualizations of romantic love. They offer compelling arguments concerning historical and cultural forces that may affect individuals' perceptions and enactments of passionate love and sexual desire. The vivid examples they provide suggest room for both stability and change in people's understanding of love and sexual desire over time and across cultural boundaries. Hatfield and Rapson also provide a fascinating forecast of future trends in gender equality, the pursuit of happiness, and the ability of individuals to enhance their lives. Their analysis reminds us that many aspects of romantic relationships may be more malleable than is typically assumed.

In the final chapter of this volume, Cappella and Pelachaud take readers "back to the future" in describing a context for relationships that is likely to be realized soon: virtual interactions. They argue that current technological trends will create computers that are socially and emotionally responsive. Because previous research indicates that people prefer to interact with computers and computer agents that are humanlike, Cappella and Pelachaud propose that virtual interactions should be modeled on human interactions. This importantly involves responsiveness, which the authors define, and whose significance they outline in describing several rules for "realistic," responsive interactions between human and nonhuman agents. Cappella and Pelachaud's analysis vividly demonstrates people's sensitivity to the microelements of social interaction and social relationships.

CHAPTER ELEVEN

Social Networks and Change in Personal Relationships

Susan Sprecher, Diane Felmlee, Terri L. Orbuch, and Marion C. Willetts

Intimate relationships begin, develop, are maintained, change, and dissolve within a larger environment. Although personal characteristics of the pair members and properties that emerge from their interaction (e.g., love) affect the temporal course and outcome of a relationship, the larger environment also is important, and, in fact, can influence the properties that emerge in the pair's interaction. The environment includes both physical forces (e.g., proximity, physical setting) and social networks. The focus of this chapter is on social networks of family and friends and their influences on *change and stability* in intimate relationships.

Social scientists interested in relationship development, satisfaction, commitment, stability, and other relationship phenomena have generally neglected social environmental explanations, as noted many years ago (e.g., Ridley & Avery, 1979) and also more recently (Berscheid, 1999; Berscheid & Reis, 1998). However, theoretical and empirical contributions on the influence of social networks on intimate relationships have been growing. In the first section of this chapter, we provide a synthesis of previous theoretical statements linking social networks with personal relationships and highlight what we believe to be the network processes and attributes most likely to influence relationships. Next we discuss how these network processes and attributes are related to the formation, development, and stability versus dissolution of premarital relationships. The third section provides a review of the influence of

Address correspondence to Susan Sprecher at the Department of Sociology and Anthropology, Illinois State University, Normal, IL 61790-4660. E-mail address: sprecher@ilstu.edu. Other affiliations are the University of California at Davis (D. F.), Oakland University (MI) (T. L. O.), and Illinois State University (M. C. W.).

social networks on marriage and other committed relationships. Then we broaden our focus by speculating on how macrolevel social processes affect changes in social networks and the intimate relationships embedded in them. We end the chapter with suggestions for issues that need further investigation on how the social environment influences change and stability in personal relationships.

THEORETICAL SYNTHESIS

There have been several theoretical statements on how social networks may influence intimate relationships (e.g., Klein & Milardo, 1993; Marsiglio & Scanzoni, 1995; Milardo, 1986; Parks, 1997; Parks & Eggert, 1991; Ridley & Avery, 1979; Surra, 1988; and Surra & Milardo, 1991). From this past work, we highlight the network processes and attributes that we believe are most relevant to understanding the effects of social networks on change in intimate relationships. Our theoretical synthesis is summarized in Fig. 11.1 and discussed below.

Change in the Dyad

We represent relationship change with Levinger's (1974; Levinger & Snoek, 1972) model of pair relatedness. At Level 0, *zero contact*, P (Partner) and O (Other) are not aware of each other. The first stage (Level 1) of a potential relationship is *awareness*. P becomes aware of O; O may become aware of P at the same time or at a later time. At Level 2, *surface contact*, P and O have initial contact, which is usually superficial. If positive impressions are formed, the relationship may progress to Level 3, a continuum representing degrees of mutuality, which include mutual disclosure, discovery, and investment (Levinger, 1974). Social networks can influence whether and how P and O move through the stages of awareness and surface contact and on through levels of mutuality, as well as whether the relationship dissolves at some point along this continuum.

Processes by Which Networks Influence the Pair

In Fig. 11.1 we list three major ways in which social networks have an impact on close dyads. The first is *opportunity*. Social networks are useful in providing individuals with the opportunity to meet potential partners through introductions and by helping to locate and select possible partners. In addition, an individual's social network itself can be

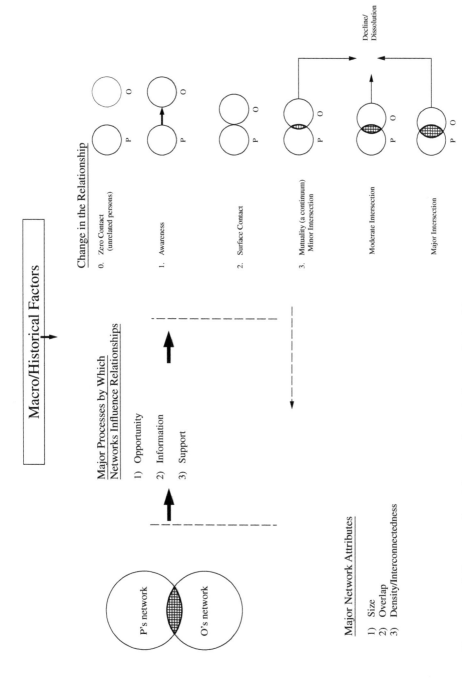

Figure 11.1. Influences of social networks on intimate relationships.

a source of coupling opportunities, such as when individuals become romantically involved with a friend or acquaintance. In some cultures, significant others, especially parents, determine an individual's mate through the practice of arranged marriages.

Information is a second way in which social networks influence dyads. Social networks provide various types of information to couples, such as suggestions for activities that may aid in enhancing a couple's relationship. They also can provide normative advice regarding appropriate and inappropriate behavior that may decrease the likelihood of partner conflict and increase social acceptance of a couple in their wider environment. Network members, too, may be an important source of information about one partner to the other, which can help reduce uncertainty about a partner (e.g., Berger, 1979; Parks & Adelman, 1983).

Finally, social networks are a potential source of *support* for couples. One type of support is relationship directed. For example, family and friends may express their approval of a relationship and over time treat the two individuals as a couple. A second type is general personal support (i.e., assistance). For example, network members can act as sounding boards and emotional outlets for individuals facing relationship dilemmas and can provide a safety net for couples in times of stress. In addition, the assistance can be practical or financial.

The role of social networks in a couple's life is not always as supportive as is often assumed, however. Significant others may block opportunities to meet a potential partner, provide information to dyads that is uninformative, incorrect, or even misleading, and express opposition to, or withhold support from the pair. Furthermore, even positive opportunities, information, and support offered by the network can have negative effects for a couple, or for one or both partners, as when the network encourages a dysfunctional couple to stay together.

Network Attributes

Numerous aspects of social networks have been examined in empirical work. In this chapter, we emphasize three: size, overlap, and density, which are referred to frequently in the literature on changes in dyadic relationships. *Size* refers to the number of distinct individuals included in a network. However, the size may depend on the type of network. A distinction has been made between the psychological network, those whom an individual perceives as significant, and the interactive

Social Networks

network, those with whom one interacts regularly (e.g., Surra & Milardo, 1991). *Overlap* refers to the extent to which partners share the same social network members. Partners are likely to have some of the same friends and over time to develop friends that are "couple specific." Upon marriage, a pair begins to share an array of mutual relatives (e.g., in-laws). *Density* (sometimes called *interconnectedness*) refers to the proportion of network ties to all potential network ties, or, more generally, the degree to which P's network members have connections with each other separate from their ties to P.

The Direction of Influence

In Fig. 11.1, solid arrows show that network attributes and processes influence change in the pair. This direction of influence is the major focus of the chapter. However, dashed arrows lead from the dyad to the network attributes and processes, and indicate that change in the dyad also can contribute to change in the networks. For example, we discuss how size and overlap of networks change as couples become more involved. In addition, dyad members may influence the network to obtain the opportunities, information, and support they seek.

NETWORKS AND THE FORMATION, DEVELOPMENT, AND DISSOLUTION OF PREMARITAL RELATIONSHIPS

The influence of social networks on intimate relationships may be greatest in the formation stages. Social networks can affect a person's readiness to begin a relationship, the likelihood that P (Person) becomes aware of a particular O (Other), whether and how P and O have surface contact (i.e., meet for the first time), how deeply the relationship develops once a mutual relationship begins, and whether the relationship ends before reaching a higher stage of commitment (e.g., marriage). All of these issues will be discussed in this section. In addition, we discuss how social networks change as the premarital relationship progresses through relationship stages or dissolves.

Networks and the "Readiness" to Form Partnerships

Even before P has a chance to become aware of O, a potential partner, social networks influence P's interest in forming a relationship. North America and most other Western societies emphasize the romantic pair. As agents of the larger society, networks of friends and family often exert pressure on adolescents and young adults to enter romantic relationships (Ryder, Kafka, & Olson, 1971). For example, parents and friends may ask about possible partners or arrange opportunities for P to meet available and desirable others.

Social networks also provide normative information about the pairing process. For example, adolescent (particularly female) networks emphasize norms that stress the importance of romantic relationships, particularly those that are exclusive, monogamous, and opposite sex (e.g., Simon, Eder, & Evans, 1992). Social networks also provide information about who would make an appropriate partner (Kerckhoff, 1974). Evidence suggests that similarity in social characteristics is emphasized, although pairing with someone with more desirable attributes also is encouraged, especially for females (e.g., Prather, 1990).

In some cases, social networks may discourage rather than encourage the pairing process. For example, parents are not always ready for their teenage children to begin dating or to have a serious involvement (Leslie, Johnson, & Huston, 1986). Some friendship networks also may discourage committed pair involvement. At the other end of the life span, a widowed aging parent may be discouraged by his or her adult children from finding a new partner (Atchley, 1994). Similarly, children of divorced families may be reluctant to see their parents form new partnerships (Montgomery, Anderson, Hetherington, & Clingempeel, 1992).

Networks and the Likelihood That "P" Becomes Aware of and Interacts with "O"

Networks can influence, either directly or indirectly, the likelihood that P and O move to awareness and surface contact. First, social networks can influence the work, school, and social settings in which P and O occupy time. Parents choose neighborhoods in which to live and send their children to particular schools; people attend parties, events, and informal gatherings because they are invited by friends or relatives; people obtain particular jobs because they learn about them from network members. Hence, social networks indirectly influence the likelihood that P and O will meet due to their influence on P's and O's placement in social settings.

Furthermore, P and O may have a greater chance of meeting if their networks overlap (i.e., they have friends in common). Parks and Eggert (1991) provided evidence that P often meets a member of O's network before meeting O. Approximately 66% of the college and high school students in their sample reported that they had met at least one of their dating partner's (or friend's) network members prior to meeting their partner (friend). Network overlap is likely to increase the chances that P and O meet through the processes listed in Fig. 11.1. Having friends in common is probably associated with the likelihood that P and O will be in the same social situation at the same time (i.e., have the *opportunity* to meet). In addition, a mutual friend may provide *information* to one or both about the other prior to a meeting, as well as offer *support* for the P–O initial interaction.

The influence of networks on the likelihood that P meets a particular O is sometimes more direct. A network member who knows both P and O may introduce them. Many studies have found that a large proportion (1/3 to over 1/2) of the relationships of college students and adults begin through an introduction by a third party (e.g., Knox & Wilson, 1981; Laumann, Gagnon, Michael, & Michaels, 1994; Parks & Eggert, 1991; Simenauer & Carroll, 1982). However, there is no research on whether a third-party introduction, in comparison to a self-introduction, increases the likelihood that P and O move beyond surface contact to form a relationship. This is because P–O interactions that do not result in relationship involvement, as a baseline comparison, are not easy to observe or recall. We can speculate, however, about the possible benefits of an introduction. First, an introduction by a third party may be the only way that a person who is shy will move from awareness to surface contact with O. Second, P may believe that his or her friend is vouching for the fact that O is available and potentially compatible with P. Third, P may be forecasting, based on the introduction, that it will be easy to integrate O into his or her social network, a benefit noted by Laumann, et al. (1994). It also may be that the introduction itself is less important than other behaviors that follow, such as the network member providing P with additional information about O that helps to reduce uncertainty about him or her (e.g., Berger, 1979) and helping to arrange for further interactions.

Networks and the Development of Mutuality in a Specific Relationship

Social networks also influence whether the relationship moves to a close partnership and some degree of mutuality. Friends and family can do this in a number of ways. If they want the relationship to develop, friends and family can help arrange for *opportunities* for the two to interact, provide positive *information* about O to P, and express *support* for the relationship. If they do not want the relationship to develop, they may ignore it or possibly try to sabotage it.

In a study of college students, Leslie et al. (1986) identified the specific types of behaviors engaged in by parents directed toward the P–O relationship. The most common approving behaviors included asking about the partner, being pleasant to the partner, letting the two have time alone together, and inviting the two as a couple to do things. Disapproving behaviors included talking about others P could date, encouraging P to wait until he or she is older to get involved with someone, and not talking to the partner. Leslie et al. also found that most of the young adults attempted to influence their parents' impressions of their partner, most frequently by talking about the good points of the partner and relationship. Sometimes, however, young adults conceal information about their relationship from network members, particularly parents, most often because they anticipate a negative reaction (Baxter & Widenmann, 1993).

Do parental and friend reactions to a dyad affect how the dyad members feel about each other? Most of the evidence on this topic suggests that positive reactions from others for the romantic dyad are associated with the greater likelihood that the relationship grows to greater intersections of mutuality and experiences of love and commitment. More specifically, perceived network support for the relationship has been found to be associated with emotional attachment, an expectation that the relationship will continue, satisfaction, commitment, and love (Eggert & Parks, 1987; Parks, Stan, & Eggert, 1983; Sprecher, 1988; Sprecher & Felmlee, 1992). In addition, longitudinal data have indicated that perceived social support at one time is related to an increase in commitment or other feelings of attachment over time (Lewis, 1973; Sprecher & Felmlee, 1992). One notable exception to the evidence for the positive effect of network support, however, is the "Romeo and Juliet" effect found by Driscoll, Davis, and Lipetz (1972). They found that parental interference (and not parental support) was correlated positively with romantic love for the dating couples. Increases in parental interference over several months also were associated with increases in romantic love.

Driscoll (personal communication, 1993), writing several years later about the failure of the Romeo and Juliet effect to be replicated after his initial investigation, offered an elaboration to the original paper:

The Romeo and Juliet effect occurs only within a *window* of opportunity. Parental interference prior to the window, before the connection is sufficiently strong, will cause the couple to break up. And continuing interference, after the window has passed, will lead to a deteriorating relationship and failing love. Only within a small window will parental interference intensify love.... Shakespeare understood the window of opportunity, as Romeo and Juliet played out their saga in a brief three days and were dead and done with it. What if she had awakened in time, and they continued in exile and tried to make a life together cut off from everything they loved? I imagine it could have gotten very old very quickly. (Richard Driscoll, personal correspondence to Keith Davis, March 31, 1993)

In general, further research is needed on the parameters of the Romeo and Juliet effect, including how it is affected by life stage (adolescence vs. young adulthood) and the relationship between the adolescents or young adults and their parents.

Networks and the Stability vs. Dissolution of the Relationship
As noted above, if Romeo and Juliet had lived, their relationship was likely to have ended had it continued to receive opposition from the Capulets and the Montagues. One reason that support from others for the relationship is important for relationship stability, according to a symbolic interactionist perspective, is that these positive reactions help in developing a pair's sense of identity as a couple (Lewis, 1973, 1975). In addition, according to cognitive balance theory (e.g., Heider, 1958), positive social support from network members is related to dyadic stability; networks that are mutually supportive and contain participants who like each other are apt to consist of subgroups that are balanced and unstressful.

Research shows that support rather than opposition from the social network increases relationship longevity. The perception of network support was one of the strongest predictors of relationship stability in two longitudinal studies (Parks & Adelman, 1983; Parks et al., 1983). Support from a partner's social network also was found to decrease the likelihood of a subsequent premarital breakup over several months, even when controlling for individual and dyadic factors (Felmlee, Sprecher, & Bassin, 1990). Approval from the female partner's family and friends was a significant predictor, too, of the stability of romantic relationships (Sprecher & Felmlee, 1992) and reduced the likelihood of dissolution over several years (Sprecher & Felmlee, in press). Finally, increases in approval from one's own friends, and increases in approval from a partner's family and friends, were associated with decreases in breakup rates over a 3- to 5-month period (Felmlee, 1999).

Although the overwhelming evidence indicates that positive network support is associated with relationship stability, there may be a brief "window of opportunity," as noted above by Driscoll, in which couple stability is enhanced by interference or lack of support from social networks. However, to the extent that there is a Romeo and Juliet effect on romantic breakups, it appears to be quite limited and may appear only from certain network sectors, that is, parents, and in particular situations, that is, when opposition is slight, or when opposition from parents occurs at the same time that friends are supportive and close (e.g., Felmlee, 1999; Parks et al., 1983).

The approval or disapproval network members have for a particular P–O relationship is also reflected in the *opportunities* and *information* they present to P or O. For example, the social network can act in ways that constrain the opportunities for P and O to meet potential partners. As a couple becomes more involved, the network members may interact more with the pair as a unit and less with each member independently (e.g., Johnson & Leslie, 1982). In this situation, interdependence with the network is likely to grow (Milardo, 1982). Increases in network interaction and overlap probably decrease the opportunity for meeting alternatives to the current relationship and thus lower the probability of breakup. Individuals are apt to be hesitant to end a current liaison if they have a limited chance of coming into contact with an attractive alternative partner (e.g., Felmlee et al., 1990; Rusbult, 1983). Network members, in expressing their support for a relationship, also may relay positive information about one partner to the other, which can reduce uncertainty (e.g., Berger, 1979). Parks and Adelman (1983) found that individuals who communicated more frequently with a partner's social network experienced less uncertainty and were less likely to break up over a 3-month period.

Of course, it is also feasible that network members can intentionally (or unintentionally) increase opportunities for P and O to meet attractive others and provide negative information about one partner to the other, which may have the consequences of increasing the likelihood that the relationship terminates. Network members also can increase the likelihood of a breakup simply by being good alternative sources of companionship and intimacy. Networks can be characterized by their *substitutability*, that is, the degree to which individuals in a network engage in similar exchange patterns with a person (Marsiglio & Scanzoni, 1995). In cultures where marital relationships are formed for intimacy and companionship needs, if someone's basic needs for intimacy and companionship are readily met by significant others (i.e., high substitutability), then his or her chances of a breakup may be increased. Some support for this prediction has been documented empirically. Felmlee (1999) found that the closer participants felt to their best friends, the greater was the chance that their dating relationship would break up over a period of 3 to 5 months, even while controlling for other factors. Presumably a very close friend represents an alternative source of companionship and a situation of high substitutability (see, also, Drigotas & Rusbult, 1992).

Changes in Social Networks as a Function of Changes in the Premarital Relationship

Not only do friends and family influence the formation, development, and stability vs. dissolution of romantic relationships, but as premarital relationships advance (or deteriorate) in mutuality and courtship stages, their networks change in response. For example, as P and O become closer, they tend to withdraw from their networks to focus on each other, which has been called *dyadic withdrawal* (Huston & Burgess, 1979; Johnson & Leslie, 1982; Slater, 1963). Cross-sectional research demonstrates that network size (e.g., number of friends and relatives considered important) and amount of interaction with the network (especially with friends) decrease as the couple advances in courtship stages, from casually dating through marriage (e.g., Johnson & Leslie, 1982; Milardo, Johnson, & Huston, 1983). Furthermore, romantic partners have been found to engage in fewer leisure activities with network members as they move to marriage (Huston, Surra, Fitzgerald, & Cate, 1981). Couple withdrawal has been explained, in part, by increased time investment in a partner, which often means less time available for others. In addition, the withdrawal may occur as part of the couple's attempt to see themselves as a unit separate from others (Krain, 1977; Lewis, 1973).

However, couple withdrawal does not seem to be spread equally across all network sectors. For example, Johnson and Leslie (1982) did not find an overall decline in the number of kin their participants listed as important, although they found that the variance in number of kin increased at engagement and marriage, indicating that some couples increased their involvement with kin whereas others decreased it. Furthermore, through reports of daily social interactions collected at two points in time (separated by 3 months), Milardo et al. (1983) found that withdrawal occurred primarily for acquaintances and intermediate friends and less for best friends and relatives. In addition, Parks et al. (1983) found that individuals who were more romantically involved (as compared to those who were less involved) had more contact and communication with their partner's friends and family. Research also suggests that romantic partners experience an increase in overlap in networks as their relationship progresses (Kim & Stiff, 1991; Milardo, 1982; Milardo et al., 1983). Hence, some scholars (e.g., Parks et al., 1983) have stated that *dyadic realignment* may better describe what occurs to couples as they progress in involvement. As part of their growing mutuality, couples form mutual friends, continue to interact with close relatives and friends (often together), but withdraw from less important friends.

The amount of support offered from the network for the romantic pair is also likely to change as the public status of the relationship changes. For example, traditionally, an important function of the engagement period was for the couples to obtain acceptance and support for their relationship from friends and especially from family. Very little research, however, has examined changes in network support over courtship stages. In a cross-sectional study, Johnson and Milardo (1984) found that university students who were dating exclusively, as compared to students who were either dating casually or married, reported a greater proportion of network members who tried to interfere with their relationship. They speculated that network interference may be highest at the dating exclusively stage because this is a time when couples withdraw from their friends and relatives, creating anxiety in the larger network (Slater, 1963). In a five-year longitudinal study of premarital couples, Sprecher and Felmlee (2000) found that perceived network approval tended to increase over time for the couples whose relationship remained intact. Furthermore, in the subsample of couples who became engaged during the study, both men and women perceived more support from the male's friends after engagement than before.

Reactions from the social network for the relationship also are likely to change if the relationship begins to dissolve. In his descriptive model of the breakup process, Duck (1982) states that an important phase of the breakup is to seek social network support for the termination. Hence, even if a particular P–O relationship was approved of while it was intact, both P and O are likely to receive support from their networks for its termination. With longitudinal data collected from couples, Sprecher and Felmlee (2000) reported on the perceived network reactions the couples received prior to the breakup and the social reactions the couples received after the breakup (for the breakup). Even though the couples had initially reported high network support for the relationship, the couples who broke up during the study reported, after the breakup, that their network supported the dissolution. However, the more support participants, especially men, had received *for the relationship* (prior to the breakup), the less approval they reported *for the breakup*. The men and women also reported significant decreases in affection for partner's network from before to after the breakup, which would be consistent with balance theory (e.g., Newcomb, 1961).

SOCIAL NETWORKS AND MARRIAGE

There appears to be a disjunction in the literature between the work on networks during the early stages of relationships and the work on marriage and divorce. First, less research has been conducted on the link between social networks and relationship processes in marital or other long-term relationships. Perhaps there is an implicit assumption that social networks (or the external environment) are less significant once relationships enter a more "committed" or maintenance stage. We argue, however, along with others (e.g., Bott, 1957; Bryant & Conger, 1999; Milardo & Allan, 1996), that networks continue to influence relationship processes even after the relationship enters major intersections of mutuality.

Next, similar to the wider literature on marriage and divorce, the research on networks and marriage is plagued by methodological and design issues, such as attrition of married couples, the mobility of families, and the difficulty in conducting prospective studies of divorce or obtaining representative samples of divorced spouses. Thus, longitudinal research on networks and marriage or divorce is limited. Furthermore, those longitudinal studies that do examine marriage and divorce seem to be more driven by the goal of understanding what factors keep marriage together and happy rather than on whether network processes within marriage (or after divorce) change over time.

The Bott Hypotheses

The general proposition that the social environment is linked to the internal dynamics of marriage was first examined by Bott (1957/1971). Bott conducted a qualitative study of 20 urban, working-class English families and concluded that husbands and wives who had close-knit networks (now referred to as network density) were more likely than husbands and wives who had less close-knit networks to engage in role-segregated activities and to generally follow traditional male–female distinctions. Although Bott examined only one network attribute, connectedness or density, this "hypothesis" has been the focus of many subsequent studies.

Bott's thinking intrigued social scientists largely because she linked two distinct social systems – the external social network and the internal marriage arrangement. Bott also gave social psychological interpretations to the connection – mainly that close-knit networks (dense networks) are more binding of couples to norms. Although it was never clear why the norms had to lead to gender role differentiation, traditional gender role differentiation, and sex-segregated activities may have been existing norms for English marriages at the time.

Another implicit hypothesis in Bott's work, as suggested by Milardo and Allan (1996), is that husbands and wives who have close-knit networks are more likely to engage in role-segregated activities because of their constant mutual exchange of support and aid with their network members. Bott's data suggest that spouses in close-knit networks, because of their investment in their networks, have less time and fewer resources to assist and support one another. Furthermore, the association may be bi-directional – spouses in close-knit networks are more likely to rely on network members, rather than their spouses, for support and assistance (household labor, child care, and leisure time), and thus segregated roles emerge.

Over the years, subsequent research aimed at testing Bott's original hypotheses has provided inconsistent findings (Aldous & Straus, 1966; Gordon & Downing, 1978; Rogler & Procidano, 1986; Udry & Hall, 1965). Milardo and Allan (1996) reviewed 14 empirical tests of the Bott hypotheses and concluded that five were generally supportive and two provided mixed results. The other studies provided either no association between network density and role segregation or only a modest relationship. In defense of the underlying connection between social structure and marital processes, Milardo and Allan (1996) argued that we should not reject the hypotheses completely.

Social Networks and Marital Processes

When a couple marries, a major, yet difficult task is to blend the partners' networks. The blending of networks, and the resulting increased network overlap, can have positive effects on the quality of the relationship. Kin and friend network members who are involved with both P and O are likely to validate their relationship, give them positive feedback, and strengthen their dyadic identity as a couple, processes that are likely to increase the satisfaction experienced in the relationship. Furthermore, if spouses are involved with overlapping networks (rather than separate networks), they may be influenced by the same norms and values, leading to homogeneity within the marital dyad and greater marital harmony (e.g., Ackerman, 1963). Research indicates that marital satisfaction is associated with greater network overlap between spouses (e.g., Julien & Markman, 1991; Stein, Bush, Ross, & Ward, 1992), especially if the joint network has a balanced inclusion of each partner's kin (Julien, Chartrand, & Bégin, 1999; Stein et al., 1992). Marital satisfaction also is linked to receiving positive support from the network for the marriage (Bryant & Conger, 1999).

Furthermore, the more integrated a couple is with their social networks, the more likely they are to receive general support from their network members, which increases the likelihood of a successful and happy marriage. Integrated couples (those who are close to their networks) can count on others for support, child care, and help in putting perspective on marital problems.

For example, Veroff, Douvan, and Hatchett (1995) found that, in the early years of marriage, the greater the number of relatives reported to be potentially supportive in time of need, the greater were husbands' and wives' marital happiness.

Increasing network overlap and involvement, however, also may have negative consequences for the marital relationship. Couples may become so enmeshed or so supported within their family and friend networks that they feel an enormous burden to conform to network demands. Some of these demands may come in the form of disapproval of the relationship, which can decrease marital satisfaction (e.g., Veroff et al., 1995). In addition, the partners may have little opportunity for independent thought and time.

The degree and nature of the effects of social networks on marital dynamics seem to depend on characteristics of the spouse, couple, and networks. For example, findings suggest that husbands' connections with kin (i.e., degree of interaction and closeness), rather than wives' connections, are more important to the marital well-being and stability of a marriage (Cotton, Antill, & Cunningham, 1993; Cotton, 1995; Milardo & Allan, 1996). Furthermore, this link between husbands' social networks and the well-being of the marriage appears to be stronger among black husbands than white husbands (Orbuch, Veroff, & Hunter, 1999; Timmer, Veroff, & Hatchett, 1996).

Social networks also have different implications for the marriage depending on whether kin ties or friendships are included in the social network of wives or husbands. Cotton (1995) found that if wives interact with and feel close to dense friend networks, husbands report lower marital satisfaction. Burger and Milardo (1995) reported similar results; husbands experienced lower love and greater ambivalence and conflict when their wives had high frequencies of social interaction with close friends. The implications of the effects of friends versus kin network members on marital processes is further confounded by whether the couple has children. Wives, particularly those with children, report fewer friendships and more leisure time spent with kin, as compared to husbands (e.g., Huston & Vangelisti, 1995; McHale & Huston, 1985). This reliance on different social network members, depending on the gender of the spouse and life-course stage of the couple, may have consequences for the well-being and stability of marriages.

The degree to which couples engage in or withdraw from their larger social networks may further vary as a function of the couples' life stage. Socioemotional selectivity theory (e.g., Carstensen, 1992, 1999) suggests that as couples grow older, they actively select their socioemotional partners and narrow their interactions, in such a way as to maximize positive emotional experiences. As couples mature, they become aware that time is limited and they focus less on trivial relationships and more on those that are emotionally meaningful. This may mean that older individuals in marriages or partnerships concentrate on enhancing and maintaining positive affective experiences within their interpersonal and network relationships.

Research also suggests that interaction with and support from families are more relevant for the well-being and stability of African American families and marriages than they are to white families and marriages (Orbuch et al., 1999; Stack, 1974; Taylor, Chatters, & Jackson, 1993). Stack (1974) found that neighborhood support was particularly important to the well-being of black women raising their children. Orbuch et al. (1999) commented that the support African Americans derive from their families may be especially critical for them to withstand the disruptive forces on marriages that occur in a racist society. Families can provide the interactive reassurance that helps one or the other spouse, perhaps husbands in particular, feel more comfortable about their threatened position in such a society. Alternatively, the cultural context of marriage and what is important for the success and well-being of marriage could differ for different ethnic groups; African American culture historically may have placed a greater focus on social networks and their importance to individuals.

Social Networks and Divorce

Theories of divorce or commitment argue that social networks can serve as a barrier force keeping couples in their marriage (e.g., Johnson, 1991; Levinger, 1979). In support of these theories, cross-sectional research indicates that couples who remain married report more network support (and less opposition) before and during marriage than those who divorce (e.g., Thornes & Collard, 1979). In addition, Bryant and Conger (1999) found that greater perceived network support for the marriage was associated with the decreased intention of divorcing or separating. Furthermore, retrospective studies, in which divorced individuals are asked why their relationship ended, indicate that many report that interference from networks (in-laws, in particular) had at least some role in the breakup (e.g., Burns, 1984; Cleek & Pearson, 1985; Kitson & Sussman, 1982). Unfortunately, there is very little prospective research that has examined how social network properties measured early in marriage predict longevity vs. dissolution. However, Veroff et al. (1995) found that closeness to family predicted marital stability over time, although only for black couples (see, also, Timmer & Veroff, in press).

Individuals experiencing a divorce often turn to their networks for support. Milardo (1987) reported that friends may be more supportive of divorced individuals than kin (Bell, 1981; Spanier & Thompson, 1984), and that the amount of friendship support is directly related to the stress of the divorced individual. However, the link between friendship support and postdivorce stress may be moderated by gender. Women may be more likely to maintain separate friendships during marriage and thus report more support from these friends following divorce. Alternatively, women may be socialized to be more relationship oriented, and thus be more likely to receive and give support from others, regardless of the state of their primary, intimate relationship.

Social networks affect the divorce decision and process, but social networks also are likely to change in the aftermath of a divorce, although this is an issue that has been examined primarily through retrospective research. Findings suggest that both network size and density decrease when individuals become separated or divorce (Bohannan, 1970; Milardo, 1987; Spanier & Thompson, 1984; Weiss, 1975). Of course, network overlap also decreases as each person withdraws from his or her partner's kin and friends (Rands, 1988). Not only are general network attributes likely to be affected by divorce, but, more poignantly, individual network members are affected. The divorce literature indicates that divorce or separation has consequences for the well-being of individual spouses, children, and the social network members connected to the couple (Johnson, 1982; Orbuch, 1992; Spanier & Thompson, 1984; Weiss, 1975).

INFLUENCES OF SOCIAL NETWORKS ON INTIMATE RELATIONSHIPS: A HISTORICAL PERSPECTIVE

Not only have relationship scientists tended to ignore the social environmental context of relationships, as noted in the introduction, but they also have ignored how larger macroforces influence long-term changes in intimate relationships. Levinger (1994) and Marsiglio and Scanzoni (1995) have provided excellent discussions of how intimate relationships can be affected by such social forces as industrialization and economic change, women's involvement in the labor force, and other demographic trends. In this section, we discuss how such macroforces can affect intimate relationships through their effects on changes in social network attributes and processes. As sociologists, we believe it is important to consider how the impact of social network processes depends on the historical and societal context.

One result of the increase in women's labor force participation is an increase in the *opportunities* women (and men) have to meet potential partners through their networks. Furthermore, men and women increasingly interact with each other in social networks away from their respective partner's supervision. Therefore, the number of attractive alternatives has increased in the social networks of both men and women, making dissolution of an existing relationship more likely (e.g., Berscheid & Campbell, 1981).

Another historical event has been the increased *social acceptance* of divorce (Allan, 1998), which includes the transition to no-fault divorce. The increased social acceptance of divorce has led to less social pressure (from network members) to keep the marriage together, which reduces a barrier to dissolution (e.g., Allan, 1998; Attridge & Berscheid,

1994; Berscheid & Campbell, 1981; Levinger, 1994). The increased acceptance of divorce, though, also means that social networks sometimes have to assist multiple times in finding a new partner for P. It also means that network members who were previously committed become available again as possible partners.

A demographic trend that has affected social networks and the relationships embedded in them is the increase in average age at first marriage (U.S. Bureau of the Census, 1989a). This is associated with other demographic trends including the delay of parenthood and a lower fertility rate (U.S. Bureau of the Census, 1989b). The resulting impact on intimate dyads (as was the case with female labor force participation) includes the increased availability of attractive alternatives in the network and the reduction in social barriers to divorce resulting from the decrease of children and kin in one's network.

Another historical trend influencing social networks and intimate dyads is the increasing presence of technology. Certainly, the development of the automobile provided single individuals with greater opportunities to interact, as young people increasingly engaged in leisure activities with friends outside of the home, rather than with kin (Scanzoni, 1995). Furthermore, the development of the automobile was critical for the practice of dating to emerge and in the reduction of the influence of kin network members, who historically chaperoned visits during courtship. The development of the telephone and the increasing ease of long distance travel, made possible in large part by airplanes, also have changed the structural attributes of networks and the process by which networks influence intimate dyads. For example, individuals are better able to maintain ties with their network members who reside at some distance. As a result, there is likely to be a greater discrepancy between P's psychological and interactive networks (Surra & Milardo, 1991). In addition, network members are now more geographically dispersed, which means that network members may not be able to coordinate their efforts in influencing the P–O relationship.

Furthermore, the development of the Internet has provided an explosion of opportunities with regard to meeting potential social network members and partners. Internet chat rooms allow individuals to form networks with those they have never met face-to-face. The potential for heterogamous social networks is great, as the Internet could theoretically bring together people from various backgrounds in terms of religion, age, race, social class, and propinquity (Wellman et al., 1996). Furthermore, the Internet provides opportunities for individuals to meet potential partners with little influence from social networks. The result is that the function provided by networks to assist in the development and maintenance of intimate relationships is weakened. Intimate couples may experience greater difficulty in maintaining their relationships without this social support. For example, such couples may receive less positive information about O from network members, or may be less likely to be discouraged from considering alternatives, since network members do not personally know O. This lack of support may be particularly problematic in terms of relationship stability if the couple is heterogamous as a function of meeting through the Internet (as heterogamous couples experience higher dissolution rates; Heaton, Albrecht, & Martin, 1985).

Despite the potential impact of the Internet on social networks and intimate relationships, existing research indicates that friendships formed on the Internet are generally weak, suggesting that the influence of Internet social network members in terms of the formation, maintenance, and dissolution of intimate relationships is minor, at least at this point in time (Kraut, Mukhopadhyay, Szczypula, Kiesler, & Scherlis, 1998a; Kraut, Patterson, Lundmark, Kiesler, Mukhopadhyay, & Scherlis, 1998b). Furthermore, increased use of the Internet is associated with decreases in family communication and the size of one's interactive network, as well as increases in loneliness and depression. This research suggests that the Internet, and relationships formed through it, may detract from the quality of preexisting relationships without compensating for this loss. Furthermore, while acquaintances formed on-line may provide useful information through chat rooms, listserves, etc., on various subjects, it is rare that information about potential partners is provided (Kraut et al., 1998b). In short, Internet relationships appear to be poor substitutes for relationships initially formed through other means, and indeed seem to detract from these other relationships while contributing to lower levels of psychological well-being.

FUTURE RESEARCH DIRECTIONS AND CONCLUSIONS

We have summarized the various ways in which social networks influence change in relationships, beginning with early stages of relationship development. In general, more research is needed linking the social environment to the internal dynamics of the relationship. For example, we need more research on the importance of network influence (e.g., introductions) in relationship initiation, the window in which a Romeo and Juliet effect might operate, the role of networks in the dissolution of relationships, and the degree to which networks influence role behaviors and satisfaction in marriage and the mechanisms by which this occurs. In addition, we need to consider how the effects of social networks may depend on the historical period and the cultural milieu.

The focus of our conceptual model and review of the literature was on the influence of networks on *change in the intimate dyad*. Although we discussed briefly how networks can change as a result of changes in the dyad (e.g., couple withdrawal vs. couple realignment), most prior research has treated the social network as static. We encourage more research that examines simultaneous or sequential changes in both networks and dyads over time. For example, we know very little about how social networks change with certain relationship transitions (moving in together, parenthood, divorce, empty nest) and the subsequent effects of these changes on the intimate pair. To assess these mutual influences, network attributes need to be measured at multiple times and from the perspectives of both dyad members and network members.

A related omission in the literature is the degree to which and the way that pair members attempt to manipulate their social environment. The assumption of most past theory and research is that network influence originates in the network. However, pair members may be instrumental in manipulating their networks to obtain the type of opportunity, information, or support they desire for their relationship. This has been referred to as endogenous network effects, distinct from the exogenous effects which originate within the network (Berscheid & Lopes, 1997). We encourage more research on the outcomes of endogenous vs. exogenous network processes. As one example, an introduction of P and O by a third party may be initiated by either P or O (an endogenous force) or by the third party (an exogenous force). The likelihood that the P–O pairing becomes an actual relationship may depend on who initiated the introduction, an issue yet to be studied.

Furthermore, if research focused to a greater degree on obtaining data from the network members themselves, it also should be possible to examine the *intent* of network members for the P–O relationship. More specifically, opportunities, information, and support (or lack thereof) coming from social networks for the P–O relationship may be either intentional and deliberate or simply happenstance. An example of the former would be a person going out of her or his way to match two friends. An example of the latter would be a person simply being polite and introducing one friend to another friend because they both happen to be in the same social setting. The outcome of network processes may depend on the degree to which the network processes are intentional and planned (rather than happenstance).

A social network is usually thought of as a collection of individuals composed of family members, other kin, friends, and acquaintances. However, the network also can be viewed as consisting of a collection of other P–O pairs, likely to influence and be influenced by a particular P–O relationship. For example, in young adulthood, a particular P–O pair may begin sexual activity, enter cohabitation, or even marry as other couples in their networks take similar leaps. Later in the life cycle, several couples in a network may divorce at nearly the same time, as they are influenced by each others' decisions. Friendship pairs from the network are also likely to influence romantic dyads. We encourage more research on the effects of *networks of couples and friendship pairs* on the romantic dyad, and vice versa.

An increased understanding of the effects of social networks on intimate relationships has practical implications. Therapists who treat troubled couples and lonely individuals seeking intimacy often focus on improving communication skills or changing attitudes and cognitions. We argue that it also is important that therapists equip themselves with knowledge about how couples and individuals may arrange their social environment to receive the opportunities, information, and support they need from their networks to promote positive, healthy interactions and relationships. A first step in this direction is to help people become more aware of how their relationships and potential relationships are affected by the social environment. Research indicates that when people are asked why they experience attraction, love, or satisfaction in a relationship, they are unlikely to refer to the influence of parents and friends (e.g., Aron, Dutton, Aron, & Iverson, 1989; Berscheid, 1999; Sprecher, 1998). Yet the research, as reviewed in this chapter, suggests that the social environment can be very important in the development, maintenance, and dissolution of intimate relationships.

REFERENCES

Ackerman, C. (1963). Affiliations: Structural determination of differential divorce rates. *American Sociological Review, 69,* 13–20.

Aldous, J., & Straus, M. A. (1966). Social networks and conjugal roles: A test of Bott's hypothesis. *Social Forces, 44,* 576–580.
Allan, G. (1998). Friendship, sociology and social structure. *Journal of Social and Personal Relationships, 15,* 685–702.
Aron, A., Dutton, D. G., Aron, E. N., & Iverson, A. (1989). Experiences of falling in love. *Journal of Social and Personal Relationships, 6,* 243–257.
Atchley, R. C. (1994). *Social forces and aging: An introduction to social gerontology,* 7th ed. Belmont, CA: Wadsworth.
Attridge, M., & Berscheid, E. (1994). Entitlement in romantic relationships in the United States: A social-exchange perspective. In M. J. Lerner & G. Mikula (Eds.), *Entitlement and the affectional bond: Justice in close relationships* (pp. 117–147). New York: Plenum.
Baxter, L. A., & Widenmann, S. (1993). Revealing and not revealing the status of romantic relationships to social networks. *Journal of Social and Personal Relationships, 10,* 321–337.
Bell, R. R. (1981). Friendships of women and of men. *Psychology of Women Quarterly, 5,* 402–417.
Berger, C. R. (1979). Beyond initial interaction: Uncertainty, understanding, and the development of interpersonal relationships. In H. Giles & R. St. Clair (Eds.), *Language and social psychology* (pp. 122–144). Oxford: Basil Blackwood.
Berscheid, E. (1999). The greening of relationship science. *American Psychologist, 54,* 260–266.
Berscheid, E., & Campbell, B. (1981). The changing longevity of heterosexual close relationships: A commentary and forecast. In M. J. Lerner & S. C. Lerner (Eds.), *The justice motive in social behavior* (pp. 209–234). New York: Plenum.
Berscheid, E., & Lopes, J. (1997). A temporal model of relationship satisfaction and stability. In R. J. Sternberg & J. Hojjat (Eds.), *Satisfaction in close relationships* (pp. 129–159). New York: Guilford Press.
Berscheid, E., & Reis, H. T. (1998). Attraction and close relationships. In D. T. Gilbert, S. T. Fiske, & G. Lindzey (Eds.), *The handbook of social psychology* (Vol. 2, 4th ed.) (pp. 193–281). New York: McGraw-Hill.
Bohannan, P. (1970). The six stations of divorce. In P. Bohannan (Ed.), *Divorce and after* (pp. 33–62). New York: Anchor Books.
Bott, E. (1957/1971). *Family and social networks.* London: Tavistock.
Bryant, C. M., & Conger, R. D. (1999). Marital success and domains of social support in long-term relationships: Does the influence of network members ever end? *Journal of Marriage and the Family, 61,* 437–450.
Burger, E., & Milardo, R. M. (1995). Marital interdependence and social networks. *Journal of Social and Personal Relationships, 12,* 403–415.
Burns, A. (1984). Perceived causes of marriage breakdown and conditions of life. *Journal of Marriage and the Family, 46,* 551–562.
Carstensen, L. L. (1992). Social and emotional patterns in adulthood: Support for socioemotional selectivity theory. *Psychology and Aging, 7,* 331–338.
  (1999). Taking time seriously: A theory of socioemotional selectivity. *American Psychologist, 54,* 165–181.

Cleek, M., & Pearson, T. A. (1985). Perceived causes of divorce: An analysis of interrelationships. *Journal of Marriage and the Family, 47,* 179–191.

Cotton, S. (1995). *Support networks and marital satisfaction.* Unpublished manuscript, Macquarie University, Sidney, Australia.

Cotton, S., Antill, J., & Cunningham, J. (1993). Network structure, network support, and the marital satisfaction of husbands and wives. *Australian Journal of Psychology, 45,* 176–181.

Drigotas, S. M., & Rusbult, C. E. (1992). Should I stay or should I go? A dependence model of breakups. *Journal of Personality and Social Psychology, 62,* 62–87.

Driscoll, R., Davis, K. E., & Lipetz, M. E. (1972). Parental interference and romantic love: The Romeo and Juliet effect. *Journal of Personality and Social Psychology, 24,* 1–10.

Duck, S. W. (1982). A topography of relationship disengagement and dissolution. In S. W. Duck (Ed.), *Personal Relationships 4: Dissolving Personal Relationships.* New York: Academic Press.

Eggert, L. L., & Parks, M. R. (1987). Communication network involvement in adolescents' friendships and romantic relationships. In M. L. McLaughlin (Ed.), *Communication yearbook* (Vol. 10, pp. 283–322). Newbury Park, CA: Sage.

Felmlee, D. H. (1999). *No couple is an island: Social networks and the stability of romantic dyads.* Paper presented at the American Sociological Association, Chicago.

Felmlee, D., Sprecher, S., & Bassin, E. (1990). The dissolution of intimate relationships: A hazard model. *Social Psychology Quarterly, 53,* 13–30.

Gordon, M., & Downing, H. (1978). A multivariate test of the Bott hypothesis in an urban Irish setting. *Journal of Marriage and the Family, 40,* 585–593.

Heaton, T. B., Albrecht, S. L., & Martin, T. K. (1985). The timing of divorce. *Journal of Marriage and the Family, 47,* 631–639.

Heider, F. (1958). *The psychology of interpersonal relations.* New York: Wiley.

Huston, T. L., & Burgess, R. L. (1979). The analysis of social exchange in developing relationships. In R. L. Burgess & T. L. Huston (Eds.), *Social exchange in developing relationships* (pp. 3–28). New York: Academic Press.

Huston, T. L., & Vangelisti, A. L. (1995). How parenthood affects marriage. In M. A. Fitzpatrick (Ed.), *Explaining family interactions* (pp. 147–176). Thousand Oaks, CA: Sage.

Huston, T. L., Surra, C., Fitzgerald, N., & Cate, R. (1981). From courtship to marriage: Mate selection as an interpersonal process. In S. Duck & R. Gilmour (Eds.), *Personal relationships* (Vol. 2, pp. 53–88). London: Academic Press.

Johnson, M. P. (1991). Commitment in personal relationships. In W. H. Jones & D. W. Perlman (Eds.), *Advances in personal relationships* (Vol. 3, pp. 117–143). London: Jessica Kinglsey.

Johnson, M. P., & Leslie, L. (1982). Couple involvement and network structure: A test of the dyadic withdrawal hypothesis. *Social Psychology Quarterly, 45,* 34–43.

Johnson, M. P., & Milardo, R. M. (1984). Network interference in pair relationships: A social psychological recasting of Slater's theory of social regression. *Journal of Marriage and the Family, 46,* 893–899.

Julien, D., Chartrand, E., & Bégin, J. (1999). Social networks, structural interdependence, and conjugal adjustment in heterosexual, gay, and lesbian couples. *Journal of Marriage and the Family, 61,* 516–530.

Julien, D., & Markman, H. (1991). Social support and social networks as determinants of individual and marital outcomes. *Journal of Social and Personal Relationships, 8,* 549–568.

Kerckhoff, A. C. (1974). The social context of interpersonal attraction. In T. L. Huston (Ed.), *Foundations of interpersonal attraction* (pp. 61–78). New York: Academic Press.

Kim, H. J., & Stiff, J. B. (1991). Social networks and the development of close relationships. *Human Communication Research, 18,* 70–91.

Kitson, G., & Sussman, M. (1982). Marital complaints, demographic characteristics and symptoms of mental distress in divorce. *Journal of Marriage and the Family, 44,* 87–101.

Klein, R., & Milardo, R. M. (1993). Third-party influence on the management of personal relationships. In S. Duck (Ed.), *Social context and relationships* (pp. 55–77). Newbury Park, CA: Sage.

Knox, D., & Wilson, K. (1981). Dating behaviors of university students. *Family Relations, 30,* 255–258.

Krain, M. (1977). A definition of dyadic boundaries and an empirical study of boundary establishment in courtship. *International Journal of the Family, 7,* 107–123.

Kraut, R., Mukhopadhyay, T., Szczypula, J., Kiesler, S., & Scherlis, W. (1998a). Communication and information: Alternative uses of the Internet in households. In *Proceedings for the Association for Computing Machinery, Special Interest Group on Computer–Human Interaction* (pp. 368–375). New York: Addison-Wesley and the Association for Computing Machinery.

Kraut, R., Patterson, M., Lundmark, V., Kiesler, S., Mukhopadhyay, T., & Scherlis, W. (1998b). Internet paradox: A social technology that reduces social involvement and psychological well-being? *American Psychologist, 53,* 1017–1031.

Laumann, E. O., Gagnon, J. H., Michael, R. T., & Michaels, S. (1994). *The social organization of sexuality: Sexual practices in the United States.* Chicago: University of Chicago Press.

Leslie, L. A., Johnson, M. P., & Huston, T. L. (1986). Parental reactions to dating relationships: Do they make a difference? *Journal of Marriage and the Family, 48,* 57–66.

Levinger, G. (1974). A three-level approach to attraction: Toward an understanding of pair relatedness. In T. L. Huston (Ed.), *Foundations of interpersonal attraction* (pp. 99–120). New York: Academic Press.

(1979). A social exchange view on the dissolution of pair relationships. In R. L. Burgess & T. L. Huston (Eds.), *Social exchange in developing relationships* (pp. 169–193). New York: Academic Press.

(1994). Figure versus ground: Micro- and macroperspectives on the social psychology of personal relationships. In R. Erber & R. Gilmour (Eds.),

Theoretical frameworks for personal relationships (pp. 1–28). Hillsdale, NJ: Erlbaum.

Levinger, G., & Snoek, J. D. (1972). *Attraction in relationships*. Morristown, NJ: General Learning Press.

Lewis, R. A. (1973). Social reactions and the formation of dyads: An interactionist approach to mate selection. *Sociometry, 36*, 409–418.

——— (1975). Social influences on marital choice. In S. E. Dragastin & G. H. Elder, Jr. (Eds.), *Adolescence in the life cycle* (pp. 211–225). New York: Hemisphere.

Marsiglio, W., & Scanzoni, J. (1995). *Families and friendships*. New York: HarperCollins.

McHale, S. M., & Huston, T. (1985). A longitudinal study of the transition to parenthood and its effect on the marriage relationship. *Journal of Family Issues, 6*, 409–433.

Milardo, R. M. (1982). Friendship networks in developing relationships: Converging and diverging social environments. *Social Psychology Quarterly, 45*, 162–172.

——— (1986). Personal choice and social constraint in close relationships: Applications of network analysis. In V. J. Derlega & B. A. Winstead (Eds.), *Friendship and social interaction* (pp. 145–166). New York: Springer-Verlag.

——— (1987). Changes in social networks of women and men following divorce: A review. *Journal of Family Issues, 8*, 78–96.

Milardo, R. M., & Allan, G. (1996). Social networks and marital relationships. In S. Duck, K. Dindia, W. Ickes, R. Milardo, R. Mills, & B. Saranson (Eds.), *Handbook of personal relationships* (pp. 505–522). London: Wiley.

Milardo, R. M., Johnson, M. P., & Huston, T. L. (1983). Developing close relationships: Changing patterns of interactions between pair members and social networks. *Journal of Personality and Social Psychology, 44*, 964–976.

Montgomery, J. J., Anderson, E. R., Hetherington, E. M., & Clingempeel, W. G. (1992). Patterns of courtship for remarriage: Implications for child adjustment and parent–child relationship. *Journal of Marriage and the Family, 54*, 686–698.

Newcomb, T. M. (1961). *The acquaintance process*. New York: Holt, Rinehart & Winston.

Orbuch, T. L. (Ed.) (1992). *Close relationship loss: Theoretical approaches*. New York: Springer.

Orbuch, T. L., Veroff, J., & Hunter, A. G. (1999). Black couples, white couples: The early years of marriage. In E. M. Hetherington (Ed.), *Coping with divorce, single-parenting, and remarriage* (pp. 23–46). Hillsdale, NJ: Erlbaum.

Parks, M. R. (1997). Communication networks and relationship life cycles. In S. Duck (Ed.), *Handbook of personal relationships* (pp. 351–372). New York: Wiley.

Parks, M. R., & Adelman, M. B. (1983). Communication networks and the development of romantic relationships: An expansion of uncertainty reduction theory. *Human Communication Research, 10*, 55–79.

Parks, M. R., & Eggert, L. L. (1991). The role of social context in the dynamics of personal relationships. In W. Jones & D. Perlman (Eds.), *Advances in personal relationships* (Vol. 2, pp. 1–34). London: Jessica Kinglsey.

Parks, M. R., Stan, C. M., & Eggert, L. L. (1983). Romantic involvement and social network involvement. *Social Psychology Quarterly, 46,* 116–131.

Prather, J. E. (1990). "It's just as easy to marry a rich man as a poor one!": Students' accounts of parental messages about marital partners. *Mid-American Review of Sociology, 14,* 151–162.

Rands, M. (1988). Changes in social networks following marital separation and divorce. In R. M. Milardo (Ed.), *Families and social networks* (pp. 127–146). Newbury Park, CA: Sage.

Ridley, C. A., & Avery, A. W. (1979). Social network influence in the dyadic relationship. In R. L. Burgess and T. L. Huston (Eds.), *Social exchange in developing relationships* (pp. 223–246). New York: Academic Press.

Rogler, L., & Procidano, M. (1986). The effects of social networks on marital roles. *Journal of Marriage and the Family, 48,* 693–702.

Rusbult, C. E. (1983). A longitudinal test of the investment model: The development and deterioration of satisfaction and commitment in heterosexual involvements. *Journal of Personality and Social Psychology, 45,* 101–117.

Ryder, R. G., Kafka, J. S., & Olson, D. H. (1971). Separating and joining influences in courtship and early marriage. *American Journal of Orthopsychiatry, 4,* 450–464.

Scanzoni, J. (1995). *Contemporary families: Reinventing responsibility.* New York: McGraw-Hill.

Simenauer, J., & Carroll, D. (1982). *Singles: The new Americans.* New York: Simon & Schuster.

Simon, R. W., Eder, D., & Evans, C. (1992). The development of feeling norms underlying romantic love among adolescent females. *Social Psychology Quarterly, 55,* 29–46.

Slater, P. E. (1963). On social regression. *American Sociological Review, 28,* 339–358.

Spanier, G. B., & Thompson, L. (Eds.) (1984). *Parting: The aftermath of separation and divorce.* Beverly Hills, CA: Sage.

Sprecher, S. (1988). Investment model, equity, and social support determinants of relationship commitment. *Social Psychology Quarterly, 51,* 318–328.

(1998). Insiders' perspectives on reasons for attraction to a close other. *Social Psychology Quarterly, 61,* 287–300.

Sprecher, S., & Felmlee, D. (1992). The influence of parents and friends on the quality and stability of romantic relationships: A three-wave longitudinal investigation. *Journal of Marriage and the Family, 54,* 888–900.

(2000). Romantic partners' perceptions of social network attributes with the passage of time and relationship transitions. *Personal Relationships, 7,* 325–340.

Stack, C. B. (1974). *All our kin: Strategies for surviving in a black community.* New York: Harper & Row.

Stein, C. H., Bush, E. G., Ross, R. R., & Ward, M. (1992). Mine, yours and ours: A configural analysis of the networks of married couples in relation to marital satisfaction and individual well-being. *Journal of Social and Personal Relationships, 9,* 365–383.

Surra, C. A. (1988). The influence of the interactive network on developing relationships. In R. M. Milardo (Ed.), *Families and social networks* (pp. 48–81). Newbury Park, CA: Sage.

Surra, C., & Milardo, R. (1991). The social psychological context of developing relationships: Psychological and interactive networks. In D. Perlman & W. Jones, *Advances in personal relationships* (Vol. 3, pp. 1–36). London: Jessica Kingsley.

Taylor, R. J., Chatters, L. M., & Jackson, J. S. (1993). A profile of familial relations among three-generation black families. *Family Relations, 42*, 332–341.

Thornes, B., & Collard, J. (1979). *Who divorces?* London: Routledge & Kegan Paul.

Timmer, S. G., & Veroff, J. (in press). Discontinuity of divorce: Family ties and the marital happiness of newlywed couples from intact and nonintact families. *Journal of Marriage and the Family*.

Timmer, S. G., Veroff, J., & Hatchett, S. (1996). Family ties and marital happiness: The different marital experiences of black and white newlywed couples. *Journal of Social and Personal Relationships, 13*, 335–359.

Udry, J. R., & Hall, M. (1965). Marital role segregation and social networks in middle-class, middle-aged couples. *Journal of Marriage and the Family, 27*, 392–395.

U.S. Bureau of the Census. (1989a). Marital status and living arrangements: March 1988. Current Population Reports, Series P-20, No. 437. Washington, DC: U.S. Government Printing Office.

(1989b). Fertility of American women: June 1988. Current Population Reports, Series P-20, No. 436. Washington, DC: U.S. Government Printing Office.

Veroff, J., Douvan, E., & Hatchett, S. J. (1995). *Marital instability: A social and behavioral study of the early years*. Westport, CT: Praeger.

Weiss, R. S. (1975). *Marital separation*. New York: Basic Books.

Wellman, B., Salaff, J., Dimitrova, D., Garton, L., Gulia, M., & Haythornthwaite, C. (1996). Computer networks as social networks: Collaborative work, telework, and virtual community. *Annual Review of Sociology, 22*, 213–238.

CHAPTER TWELVE

Creating a Context for Change
Integrative Couple Therapy

Jennifer Wheeler and Andrew Christensen

Although there is little that is more private than the details of a couple's intimate relationship, a couple that has become distressed may decide to "expose" their relationship problems to a helping professional such as a couple therapist. In this way, couple therapists have a unique opportunity to observe the behaviors of couples in distress, and to create an environment for couples that will help facilitate relationship change. Throughout the last few decades, observations and interventions of couple therapists have been studied extensively to better understand factors that contribute to and detract from couples' satisfaction and their capacity for changing problematic behavior. Such research has provided valuable information, not only about the development and maintenance of couple distress, but also about therapeutic approaches that influence behavior change and improve relationship satisfaction.

"CHANGE" AND COUPLE THERAPY

Distressed couples seeking therapy have experienced profound changes in their relationship. They started out happy and hopeful, but over time became increasingly dissatisfied in their relationship (see review of longitudinal research on marriage, Karney & Bradbury, 1997). Compared to their nondistressed counterparts, they are more negative and withdrawn in their behaviors toward one another, have more negative and blaming interpretations of each other's behavior, and have

---

Preparation of this chapter was supported in part by Grants MH56165-03 and MH56233-02 and from the National Institute of Mental Health. The authors wish to dedicate this work in memory of Neil S. Jacobson. Address correspondence to Andrew Christensen, Department of Psychology, 405 Hilgard Avenue, University of California, Los Angeles, CA 90095-1563. E-mail address: christensen@psych.vcla.edu.

less positive and more negative emotion toward one another (e.g., Weiss & Heyman, 1997). From therapy, they seek profound changes in their relationship to bring back the satisfaction they once enjoyed. Perhaps partners attribute the deterioration in their relationship to changes that the other has made since the beginning of the relationship. Or perhaps one or both partners were aware of problems from the beginning of the relationship but stayed in the relationship hoping that the other would change with time. Given the implicit or explicit demand for change in a distressed relationship, the couple therapist is thus presented with the challenge of facilitating positive changes that will increase the couple's happiness. How each couple therapist approaches this challenge may vary widely.

For two decades, the "gold standard" for the treatment of couple distress has been behavioral couple therapy (see Christensen & Heavey, 1999; Baucom, Shoham, Kim, Daiuto, & Stickle, 1998; and Jacobson & Addis, 1993, for reviews of couple therapies). First applied to couple distress by Stuart (1969) and Weiss, Hops, and Patterson (1973), traditional behavioral couple therapy (TBCT) uses basic behavioral principles of reinforcement, modeling, and behavioral rehearsal to facilitate collaboration and compromise between partners, and ultimately to create positive behavioral changes in the relationship. For example, one TBCT technique is "Behavior Exchange," which is intended to help couples identify the pleasing things (i.e., reinforcing behaviors) that each partner can do for the other, and to increase the frequency of those behaviors in their daily lives. Other TBCT techniques include "Communication and Problem Solving Training," which teaches couples how to discuss problems and negotiate change without resorting to destructive tactics such as coercion and polarization. (See Jacobson & Margolin, 1979, for a more complete discussion of TBCT strategies.) Thus, the focus of TBCT is teaching couples new skills that will ideally change their problematic or unsatisfying relationship behaviors.

In early studies, change-oriented behavioral techniques demonstrated significant empirical success in the treatment of couple distress (for reviews see Christensen & Heavey, 1999; Baucom et al., 1998; and Jacobson & Addis, 1993). Despite the apparent success of change-oriented techniques, outcome research also revealed some limitations in the efficacy and generalizability of traditional behavioral techniques. Many couples demonstrate no benefit from these techniques (Jacobson, Schmaling, & Holtzworth-Munroe, 1987), and many couples who benefit initially experience a relapse within a couple of years (Jacobson et al., 1984; Jacobson et al., 1987). Overall, outcome research suggests that traditional behavioral techniques are effective and demonstrate long-term benefit for only about one-half of the distressed couples who present for therapy. Furthermore, comparative treatment studies have failed to demonstrate any increment in efficacy by various enhancements to traditional behavioral techniques (e.g., Baucom & Epstein, 1990; Baucom, Epstein, & Rankin, 1995; Baucom et al., 1998; Floyd, Markman, Kelly, Blumberg, & Stanley, 1995).

Research on the treatment response of distressed couples has identified several factors that appear to affect the success of traditional change-oriented techniques. Compared to couples who respond positively to traditional behavioral techniques, couples who are regarded as "treatment failures" are generally older, more emotionally disengaged, more polarized on basic issues, and more severely distressed than couples who are regarded as "treatment successes" (Baucom & Hoffman, 1986; Hahlweg, Schindler, Revenstorf, & Brengelmann, 1984; Jacobson, Follette, & Pagel, 1986; see Jacobson & Christensen, 1996, for a review). Each of the factors above has an obvious deleterious effect on a couple's ability to collaborate, compromise, and facilitate positive behavioral change. For example, older couples have had more time than younger couples to become "stuck" in their destructive behavioral patterns. Couples who are more polarized on fundamental issues may never be able to reach a mutually satisfying compromise. And couples who are extremely disengaged from one another may be completely unable to collaborate. Each of these factors is likely to be associated with long-standing, deeply entrenched behavioral patterns. Thus, it should come as no surprise that the change-oriented techniques of traditional behavioral couple therapy are ineffective for these couples.

"STABILITY" AND COUPLE THERAPY

The factors associated with "difficult to treat" couples seem to represent deeply entrenched behavioral patterns; in fact, many of the problems that are identified as a source of a couple's distress may be the result of partners' long-standing differences and incompatibilities. In the early stages of a relationship, differences in partners' backgrounds, personalities, goals, and interests may be appealing. Those that are not may be downplayed or ignored – or perhaps both partners expect the other to eventually compromise or change to "their way" of doing things. Over time, these incompatibilities are inevitably exposed.

Differences that were once regarded as novel, interesting, or challenging may ultimately be perceived as impediments to one's own goals and interests, and these incompatibilities may acquire undue or exaggerated significance. How partners respond to these differences and incompatibilities may further exacerbate their problem (and may become even more problematic than the incompatibilities themselves), leading to an increasingly destructive conflict.

Traditional behavioral techniques might approach such incompatibilities by trying to change one partner or the other, despite the fact that outcome data suggest that this approach will be least helpful for the couples in greatest need (i.e., more fundamentally disengaged and polarized couples). Therefore, an additional approach is needed to help those couples who do not benefit from traditional change techniques alone, one that emphasizes the stable nature of couples' differences and incompatibilities and how these contribute to and maintain partners' distress.

Based on these data as well as their own clinical experience with TBCT, Christensen and Jacobson developed a treatment, which they called Integrative Behavioral Couple Therapy (IBCT; Christensen, Jacobson, & Babcock, 1995; Jacobson & Christensen, 1996), designed to address the problems associated with TBCT. We first describe the conceptual framework of IBCT and how it is similar to and different from TBCT. Then we describe the more specific strategies of IBCT.

CONCEPTUAL FRAMEWORK FOR TRADITIONAL AND INTEGRATIVE BEHAVIORAL COUPLE THERAPY

Both TBCT and IBCT are behavioral approaches and are thus, in essence, contextual approaches. Each creates change in behavior by changing the context in which that behavior occurs. Couple therapists become part of the context of the couple's life and through their behavior, they alter the actions, thoughts, and feelings of the couple. However, TBCT and IBCT approach this task in fundamentally different ways.

The central difference between TBCT and IBCT can be found in Skinner's (1966) distinction between rule-governed behavior and contingency-shaped behavior. Although both may look very similar, they are elicited by different stimuli and reinforced by different stimuli. And they feel different. In rule-governed behavior, the eliciting stimulus is a "rule"; one gets reinforcement for following the rule or punishment for violating it. If Fred and Diane have come to an agreement to kiss each other before going to sleep at night, their behavior is under the guidance of this rule: Violations of the rule might receive sanctions from the other; compliance with the rule may create some comfort or satisfaction. If, however, Diane kisses Fred because she notices how attractive he is or because she feels gratitude for his assistance or because she feels proud of his accomplishment, her kiss is elicited, not by a rule, but by particular contingencies in the current environment. Also, the reinforcement comes not from compliance with the rule (or sanctions for violations of the rule) but from the experience itself and its aftermath (Fred's kiss back and his obvious pleasure in her attention serve to reinforce the kiss).

In their efforts to bring about therapeutic change, TBCT places a greater reliance on rule-governed behavior, while IBCT places a greater reliance on contingency-shaped behavior. TBCT therapists promote certain rules and use reason to justify them. For example, in an effort to promote greater reinforcement between partners, therapists may suggest that members of a couple "focus on what you can do for your partner, not on what your partner can do for you." After helping couples generate lists of positive actions that would be pleasing for the other, IBCT therapists may instruct couples to "engage in items from the list." TBCT therapists may teach couples rules of good communication, such as "talk about your feelings in reaction to your partner's specific behavior rather than criticizing your partner." In addition to providing "rules," TBCT therapists may help couples develop their own relationship rules. In problem solving, for example, the couple generates a plan (or rule) for solving a particular problem. For instance, to combat their emotional distance from each other, a couple may agree to the rule that they go out on a date once a week. During treatment, the therapist provides reinforcement for couples following the rules. The therapist assumes that the rules will generate positive behavior that will eventually provide its own reinforcement and thus maintain the rules, even after treatment has ended.

IBCT is much more skeptical of the efficacy of rule-governed strategies, particularly for couples who are experiencing strong negative emotions toward each other. Couples may be unable to follow rules such as being positive with one another. They may sabotage rules of communication so that they, for example, use the rules as another way to criticize their partner ("You didn't communicate the way we were told"). They may not follow through with agreements, such as their plan to have a date night. Even if they do follow through with a plan, it may be experienced negatively. On their date night, they may spend the evening arguing. Therefore, the focus in IBCT is much more on contingency-shaped behavior than on rule-governed behavior.

Rather than provide rules and advice for couples, IBCT therapists try to change the context of their interaction by calling attention to aspects of each partner's behavior and experience that may elicit different reactions from them both. For example, if a husband makes a strong statement of his demands for his wife, an IBCT therapist would not try to teach him a different way of talking to his wife. Instead the IBCT therapist might say something such as "I wonder if you are uncertain, maybe even anxious, that your wife won't listen to what is important to you, so you come on really strong to try to ensure that she will hear you." This statement could direct the couple's attention away from the strong, negative flavor of the husband's statement and toward his anxiety that may have stimulated it. If the intervention is successful in redirecting the couple's attention, it may interrupt the wife's usual response to her husband, namely, shutting down. As another example, let's assume the husband makes a strong, demanding statement to his wife and she turns away, looks hopeless, and is unresponsive. The therapist might say, "I just saw something happen now, where you (husband), made a strong statement of your (husband's) needs and you (wife) shut down. I wonder if that happens frequently in your relationship." This intervention directs the couple's attention away from each other and onto their interaction pattern. They may begin to talk about the problem in a different way, as a sequence that occurs between the two of them rather than as the negative actions of the other ("She never listens to me," "He always attacks me").

In addition to calling attention to previously ignored aspects of their interaction, IBCT therapists may themselves provide potent behavioral cues to each partner that elicit and shape different responses from each. The most common dysfunctional communication that occurs when couples discuss problems is probably some version of blame on the one hand and defense, withdrawal, and counterattack on the other. To create a nonblaming, nondefensive but engaged interaction, IBCT therapists take a validating stance toward each partner, not only for the goals that each partner has, but even for the often dysfunctional way each goes about achieving those goals. IBCT therapists would endorse the husband's desire to have his wife understand his needs and would understand the frustration that leads him to come on so strong to her as a way of trying to get heard. But IBCT therapists would also validate the wife's need to protect herself from his critical and demanding messages by shutting down. Finally, IBCT therapists would comment on the ironic dilemma that their interaction creates: Despite his best efforts, he still doesn't get heard; despite her best efforts at protection, she still gets attacked. IBCT therapists engage in these validating actions to shift the context away from that of attack and defend to a context of understanding and empathy that may elicit feelings of concern for each other, in spite of the conflict.

In their efforts to change the context, IBCT therapists may directly elicit new behavior. During a moment when the couple is beginning to go through its pattern of demand and shut down, the therapist may ask the wife to describe what is going on with her emotionally or ask the husband to describe what it feels like for him. If the husband and wife discuss previously unrevealed aspects of their experience during the moment of that experience, then the adversarial context of their interaction gets shifted. If the wife talks about her fear or how her husband's comments remind her of how her dad used to talk to her, the husband may begin to experience her not as someone who is deliberately holding out on him, but as someone who is intimidated by him. If the husband can talk about how helpless he feels in getting someone to care about him, his wife may experience him not as an intimidating presence, but as someone who needs her.

IBCT therapists may also guide behavior in ways that elicit new reactions. The therapist may ask the husband and wife to replay the sequence of husband demanding and wife shutting down. Because the stimulus for this enactment comes from the therapist rather than from the usual cues that guide this sequence, the couple will be unable to completely re-create the sequence. They may be unable to create the usual emotions or usual intensity; they may even laugh at their difficulty in re-creating a sequence that they normally enact daily. Even if they are able to re-create the sequence somewhat, the emotions are liable to be attenuated and conversation about the sequence facilitated. Thus, the therapist has changed the context around this particular problematic sequence. The couple is able to experience it differently from the way they normally experience it.

Because this pattern of "demand and shut down" is painful for the couple, they may want to change it dramatically, to exorcise it from their relationship. The wife may never want to face his demands again; he may never want to face her withdrawal again. However, the pattern of interaction may be long-standing, with a rich causal history and strong current determinants. He often "plays tough" when he senses his needs may not be met – and that often works for him. She often shuts down as a way of dealing with noxious events – and that works for her. In fact, maybe there was even some appeal in these differences: She liked his assertiveness (when not directed at her); he liked the fact that she was not challenging of him. With such a powerful causal background, it is unlikely that any therapist can delete this problematic pattern from any future interaction. A more realistic goal is that as a result of these IBCT interventions, conducted over a period of time, the couple may come to "accept" this interaction and the role each plays in it. When the pattern occurs, it may not create as much pain as it did before. Husband and wife may be able to interrupt the pattern more frequently or recover from it more quickly. Although they may not be able to conquer this problem, they may be able to manage it. In addition, the husband, having a new experience and richer knowledge of his wife, may on his own, without any rules or advice from the therapist, try to come across more gently to her in the future. Similarly, she may decide to stay in the interaction more frequently.

Because of its emphasis on contingency-shaped behavior, IBCT is much less structured and much more experiential than TBCT. Therapists don't know the contingencies that will shape new behavior in each partner. Although IBCT therapists have the clear goal of shifting couples away from the adversarial or alienated contexts which they have generated, IBCT therapists do not know what particular comments or techniques will make headway toward that goal. A comment that might be very effective for one couple may fall flat with the next. Because each partner and each couple has different histories and different causal forces operating on them, therapists must first assess each couple to determine their major problematic patterns and the likely determinants of each. From this assessment, which culminates in a formulation of the couple's problems, IBCT therapists can engage in a series of specific strategies to alter the context of these problems. Because of the enormous variability in couples, there will always be some trial and error in this work. However, the formulation of the couple and the strategies for altering the context in which problems occur, serve as guidelines for IBCT treatment. We describe these guidelines below.

INTEGRATIVE BEHAVIORAL COUPLE THERAPY

IBCT, which has sometimes been labeled "acceptance therapy," promotes the acceptance of each other as a means of generating positive relationship change. Rather than trying to eliminate a couple's longstanding conflicts and incompatibilities, IBCT helps couples develop a new understanding of apparently irreconcilable differences. IBCT uses these differences to promote each partner's sense of intimacy, empathy, and compassion for the other. With its focus on acceptance, IBCT creates an environment for couples to understand each other's behavior before deciding if and how they might change it. It is the job of the IBCT therapist to identify and reframe a couple's incompatibilities in a way that minimizes their destructive nature while maximizing the couple's level of intimacy and relationship satisfaction. In this way, the IBCT therapist helps couples change the destructive patterns of interaction that have led to their current relationship distress.

In couple therapy, "change" typically refers to modifying each partner's *public* behavior that is offensive to the other, such as his or her activity (e.g., sloppy housework), inactivity (e.g., lack of affection), or verbal behavior (e.g., criticism). But with IBCT, the expectation of change also includes each partner's *private* behavior, such as his or her emotional response to and understanding of the other partner's offensive behavior. When a couple's problem feels "irreconcilable," the IBCT therapist must help each partner find a new approach to their "same old" conflict. Specifically, the IBCT therapist first helps each partner change his or her *response* to the other's "offending" behavior, rather than trying to first change that offending behavior. The IBCT therapist helps partners develop a new understanding of each other's behavior so that their original "complaints" are transformed into less destructive responses. In addition, this change in a partner's *reaction – his or her acceptance of the other –* often has a salutary impact on the frequency or intensity of each partner's "offending" behavior. Sometimes this "acceptance work" is followed by direct efforts to change "offending behavior."

For example, consider a husband (Lou) and wife (Betty) who frequently argue about money. Lou, who is very concerned about the family's finances, insists that Betty consult with him before she spends any of their money. Betty, who resents having to ask Lou's permission to make family purchases, regularly spends money without consulting Lou. Every time the topic of money arises, both Lou and Betty become deeply entrenched in their respective sides of the argument, and neither partner is willing to yield to the other. Lou continues to insist that Betty must consult with him, and Betty refuses to comply with Lou's demand that he be consulted.

For the IBCT therapist, the goal is not to make Betty comply with Lou's request, nor is it to make Lou "give in" to Betty's refusal. Rather, the goal would be to help Lou and Betty find a new way of responding to each other and to their conflict. Perhaps the IBCT therapist would help Lou appreciate that, because Betty viewed her own mother as financially "controlled" by her father, it is very important to Betty that she be able to make independent financial decisions. At the same time, the IBCT therapist might help Betty develop empathy for Lou's deepest fear that he will fail to adequately provide for his family and thus cause their financial ruin. By helping Lou and Betty understand and accept the reasons for each other's behavior, the IBCT therapist provides them with a new way of approaching their old conflict. Ideally, this new a perspective will help facilitate a long-term change in their relationship.

It is important to note that in the context of IBCT, *acceptance* should not be confused with *resignation*. While resignation involves one partner grudgingly giving in to the other – perhaps unwillingly tolerating what is seen as an unyielding status quo – acceptance involves one partner letting go of the struggle to change the other. Instead of encouraging one partner to give in to the other, acceptance work focuses on transforming a couple's differences into a vehicle for promoting closeness and intimacy. A goal of IBCT is to end the ongoing struggle that has been historically generated by these differences. Ideally, partners let go of the struggle not grudgingly, but rather as a result of having a new appreciation for their partner's experience. By understanding their distress in terms of their differences, and by learning to accept each other's differences, it is hoped that the distress generated by the struggle to change each other will be reduced.

Formulation

The organizing principle of IBCT is the *formulation*. The formulation refers to the way the therapist conceives of and describes the couple's problem in terms of their long-standing and stable differences, incompatibilities, and the associated discord. One of the most basic goals of IBCT is for the couple to adopt the formulation as part of their relationship history. The couple can use the formulation both during and after therapy, as a context for understanding their relationship and their conflicts. The formulation gives couples a language to describe and discuss their problems, and it allows couples to put distance between themselves and their problems.

The formulation comprises three basic components: a *theme*, a *polarization process*, and a *mutual trap*. The *theme* is the description of the couple's primary conflict, usually described using a phrase that captures the nature of the couple's differences. The theme is a shorthand way of describing the function of each partner's behavior during his or her typical conflicts. For example, a theme common to many distressed couples is that of "Closeness–Distance," where one partner is seeking greater intimacy while the other partner is trying to maintain his or her optimal level of distance. Lou and Betty's theme might have been called "Autonomy–Control."

The *polarization process* refers to the destructive interaction process that ensues when a distressed couple enters into a theme-related conflict. A natural response for a couple confronted with their differences is for each partner to try to change the other. When this happens, their differences may be exacerbated and the two partners become polarized in their conflicting positions. After they have become polarized, further attempts to change each other merely increase the conflict and perpetuate their polarized stances. For example: Lou and Betty became polarized when Lou insisted that Betty consult with him but Betty insisted upon making decisions independently. Lou's attempts to "control" Betty's spending only furthered Betty's desire for autonomy, while Betty's attempts at gaining autonomy only fueled Lou's desire to have more control.

The *mutual trap* describes the outcome of the polarization process and is called a "trap" because it typically leaves the couple feeling "stuck" or "trapped" in their conflict. Partners in a mutual trap are reluctant to give up their efforts to change each other, since this would mean resigning themselves to an unsatisfying relationship. As a result they become more entrenched in their respective positions over time. In the example of Lou and Betty, Lou's fears about failing to protect the family prevent him from giving more control to Betty. To "give in" to Betty would exacerbate his fear of failure, so Lou is trapped in his position. Meanwhile, Betty's fear of being "controlled" by Lou prevents her from complying with Lou's request. To "give in" to Lou would make her feel controlled, so she is trapped in her position. As a result of their respective fears, both partners appear to have no way out of this conflict.

The experience of partners who are so polarized and "trapped" is one of helplessness and futility. This experience may rarely (if ever) be discussed openly between them, or it is discussed with such an overlay of blame and accusation that each partner may be unaware that the other partner also feels trapped. Making each partner aware of the other's sense of entrapment is an important part of acceptance work, and encouraging each partner to experience the other's sense of "stuckness" is the first step toward promoting empathy and intimacy between partners.

It is important to remember that the formulation is a dynamic concept that may require alteration and modification (or "reformulation") throughout treatment. In addition, any given session may include smaller "reformulations" of particular relationship incidents as part of the couple's acceptance work. In other words, the overall formulation is only the beginning of the couple's new way of perceiving and approaching their relationship.

Assessment

The primary goal of the assessment phase is for the therapist to develop a formulation based on the couple's *problem areas*, their *current circumstances*, *their individual histories*, and their relationship's *developmental history*. The assessment will help the therapist to determine whether to intervene first with change techniques or techniques to promote acceptance.

First, the IBCT therapist assesses the couple's *presenting problem*(s). The therapist should evaluate how distressed the couple is, how committed each partner is to the relationship, what are their divisive issues and why, what are the couple's strengths, and what is the extent of the couple's collaborative set (Jacobson & Margolin, 1979). The "collaborative set" refers to the couple's joint perspective that they share responsibility for the problems in their relationship, and that they will both have to change in order for the relationship to change. The strength of this set determines whether change-oriented or acceptance-oriented interventions are indicated. The stronger the couple's collaborative set, the more successful change-oriented interventions will likely be.

The therapist should also spend time during the assessment to learn more about each partner as an individual, specifically to understand how each partner's *current circumstances and his or her developmental history* might contribute significantly to the couple's formulation. *Current circumstances* refer to changes or dynamic factors in a partner's life (e.g., parenting, losing a job) that directly or indirectly impact his or her relationship. For example, a wife whose job is extremely socially oriented and demanding may want to spend her evenings retreating into aloneness. Or a husband whose work puts him in the role of barking orders to his crew may quite naturally fall into such a "commanding" role with his family.

Developmental history should include the features of each partner's history that may have influenced the current relationship problems. These experiences might include each partner's significant childhood events, previous relationship experiences, or how each partner perceived his or her own parent's marriage. In the example of Lou and Betty, Betty's developmental history was very important to their formulation. Betty felt her father controlled her mother, and she did not want to replicate such a dynamic in her own marriage to Lou. Lou's fear of financial failure can be traced in part to a risky business adventure, early in his career, that forced him to apply for bankruptcy. Although a couple's current circumstances and developmental history are not necessarily going to be a part of their formulation, the therapist should consider each area and its potential relevance to the couple's distress.

The therapist also asks couples about the *history of their relationship*. The goal here is for the therapist to gain a good understanding of the couple's attachment to one another, and to use this information in developing the couple's formulation. For example, in the case of Lou and Betty the therapist might discover that part of Lou's attraction to Betty was that Betty was so independent and self-assured, and that part of Betty's attraction to Lou was the fact that he seemed so stable, secure, and organized. Each of these characteristics – Betty's independence and Lou's stability – is related to the very same qualities that are now the source of Lou and Betty's frequent conflicts about money. This ambivalence toward characteristics in the other can be part of a formulation that moves the couple to greater acceptance.

Building Emotional Acceptance

Treatment generally begins with a focus on promoting acceptance. The exception would be when a couple is able to collaborate with one another ("the collaborative set") and both members want to make specific changes in their relationship. In that case, change-oriented strategies may be indicated.

In doing acceptance work, the actual content of the therapy sessions is determined by the couple. Discussions of recent emotionally salient incidents are the best means of exploring the couple's theme, polarization process, and mutual traps, and are useful for implementing the acceptance-building strategies of *empathic joining around the problem, unified detachment from the problem,* and *tolerance building.*

Empathic joining refers to the process by which couples cease to blame one another for their emotional suffering, and instead develop empathy for each other's experience. The first step toward empathic joining is the therapist's general reformulation, which is presented in the feedback session. In subsequent sessions, the therapist adapts and applies this formulation to the daily incidents that upset each partner and which illustrate the couple's theme. The therapist reformulates partners' behaviors, even their offensive behaviors, as efforts to cope with their thematic differences. Although these actions may exacerbate the very differences they were intended to solve, they are understandable actions to take in the face of the obstacles that each perceives.

In making the reformulation of each partner's behavior, it is important that the IBCT therapist emphasize the pain that each partner is experiencing. One strategy for building empathy between partners is through the use of "soft disclosures." Often partners express their emotional pain by using "hard disclosures" of feelings such as anger or disgust. Although hard disclosures are easier to make because they do not reveal vulnerability, they are more difficult for the other partner to hear because they imply blame. It is the combination of "pain and blame" that results in discord. But if the therapist can encourage partners to express their pain *without* expressing blame, the result will hopefully be increased acceptance from the other partner. In the case of Lou and Betty, the IBCT therapist might encourage Lou's soft disclosures by suggesting "soft" feelings such as his fear of failing to provide for his family and the shame associated with that failure. Although soft disclosures are more difficult to make because they reveal vulnerability, they are easier for the other partner to hear and to empathize with. It may be easier for Betty to hear Lou's disclosures of shame and fear than it is for her to hear him criticize her for not consulting with him before spending money. Although Betty is different from Lou in that she doesn't share his fears of financial failure, she might certainly be able to empathize with the emotions of fear and shame. Thus, empathic joining is promoted by reformulating a couple's discord as a result of common differences and their understandable reactions to those differences, and through the use of soft disclosures to express painful emotions.

Unified detachment refers to an IBCT technique that allows partners to describe and discuss a problem without placing blame – or responsibility to change – on either partner. In this way, the partners engage in *unified detachment* from their problematic interactions. The therapist engages the couple in a dialogue about the sequence of a particular conflict, including what factors trigger their reactions, how specific events are connected to one another, and how the couple can diffuse or override the conflict. The approach is that of an intellectual analysis of the problem, in which partners see the problem in an emotionally detached manner as an "it" rather than as a "you" or "me." By detaching themselves from the problem, couples have an opportunity to discuss their conflict without becoming emotionally "charged" by it. In this way, they can try to understand the conflict from a more neutral, objective stance. They may even at times be able to see the humor in their conflicts. When possible, the therapist should give the couple's theme, polarization process, or mutual traps a name, and should use this name, or metaphors of their struggle, to further define the problem as an "it." In the case of Lou and Betty, the therapist might refer to their conflict as the "check-check" – since Lou wants Betty to check with him before she writes a check.

Building acceptance may be most challenging when one partner experiences intense emotional pain as a result of the other partner's behavior. In these circumstances, the IBCT therapist must help a partner build tolerance for the other partner's "offending" behavior. By *building tolerance*, partners will ideally experience a reduction in the pain caused by the behavior. In order to build tolerance, however, partners must cease efforts to prevent, avoid, or escape the partner's behavior. Instead, partners must expose themselves to the behavior without the associated struggle, which will hopefully reduce their sensitivity and pain from the "offending" behavior.

One strategy for building tolerance is through positive reemphasis, or focusing on the *positive aspects of a partner's negative behavior*. For example, what one partner sees as the other partner's "uptightness" might be the "stability" that first attracted her (as in the case of Lou and Betty). Alternatively, what one partner sees as the other's "flakiness" or "irresponsibility" might be the "free-spiritedness" or "rebelliousness" that had so attracted him in the beginning of their relationship. The IBCT therapist must help couples notice the positive aspects of what they have come to see as purely negative behavior. And often this behavior is in some way related to a quality they once found attractive about the other.

Another strategy for building tolerance for each other's differences is by focusing on the *ways in which these differences complement each other*, and presenting these differences as part of what makes the relationship "work." One partner's stability might balance the other's free-spiritedness. The therapist might describe for the couple the ways in which they would be "worse off" if those differences did not exist. The differences can become a positive aspect of the couple's relationship, something they can be proud of rather than something that is seen as a destructive threat.

A third technique for building tolerance to a partner's behavior is by *preparing couples for inevitable slip-ups and lapses* in behavior. This is especially important when couples first begin to detect changes in their partner's behavior, and they begin to feel positive about the progress they are making in therapy. It is during this time that the therapist should congratulate the couple for their hard work and progress, and then warn them that "backsliding" is still a likely occurrence. The couple should be asked to suggest some circumstances in which a slip-up is likely to occur and to consider possible responses to the slip-up in advance. The therapist may ask the couple to rehearse their responses to a slip-up in the session. In the case of Betty and Lou, they might prepare for the next time Lou gets upset with Betty for spending money without consulting him. Working out how they will face such lapses will help partners build their tolerance for them.

A related strategy for building tolerance is instructing couples *to fake negative behavior* while they are at home. Each partner is instructed to engage in a designated "bad behavior" between sessions – with the stipulation that the couple is to engage in this behavior only on occasions when they are not feeling like doing so. The instructions are given in front of both partners, so that both know that a bad behavior in their future might actually be a faked bad behavior. For example, Betty would be instructed to pretend she has made a major purchase without talking about it first with Lou. Lou would also be instructed to pretend to get upset with Betty for spending money on something, which would not ordinarily upset him (e.g., on groceries). This "public" announcement of the impending "bad" behavior introduces an ambiguity into the future negative behaviors that might affect the partner's response to them. More important, however, is that faking behavior gives both partners an opportunity to observe the effects of their negative behavior on their partner. Specifically, because they are performing the bad behavior during a time when they do not feel like it, they can make these observations when they are in a calm emotional state that allows them to be more sympathetic. The faker is also instructed to let the other partner know about the faked behavior soon after it is performed – this will prevent the situation from escalating, and will give the couple an opportunity to "debrief" following their "experiment."

One unavoidable source of pain for many partners is when they feel that the other partner is failing to meet their needs in some important way. However, it is rarely the case that one partner will be able to fulfill all of the needs of the other. An important aspect of acceptance building is for partners to increase their own self-reliance, or *self-care*, in getting their needs met. Partners should be encouraged to find alternative ways to care for themselves when their partner is not able to do so. Partners may need to learn to seek support from friends and family in times of stress, or to find new ways to define and solve a problem on their own. As self-reliance increases, reliance on partners to meet all of their emotional needs will decrease. Ideally, this will result in partners' decreased sensitivity to the others' failure to meet their needs, thereby reducing conflict.

Using Both Acceptance and Change Techniques

For some couples, direct change interventions, such as those used in TBCT, may be indicated. Whether an IBCT therapist begins by implementing "acceptance" techniques or "change" techniques will depend primarily on the couple's collaborative set and on their specific treatment needs. In general, however, change techniques will be most effective if implemented later in therapy, after much acceptance work has been done.

Stability, Change, and Outcome

The previous sections have described the conceptual background of IBCT as well as its strategies for promoting emotional acceptance between partners and for promoting behavioral change. The fate of IBCT rests, however, not on the strength of its conceptual framework or the appeal of its treatment strategies, but on whether it brings about larger and more enduring improvements in relationship satisfaction and stability than other treatment approaches such as TBCT.

Short-Term vs. Long-Term Benefit
A recently published small clinical trial provides some evidence for the short-term success of IBCT (Jacobson, Christensen, Prince, Cordova, & Eldridge, 2000). A sample of 21 maritally distressed couples were randomly assigned to a maximum of 25 sessions of TBCT or IBCT. Pre- to posttreatment measures of relationship satisfaction revealed that 80% of couples who had received IBCT showed statistically reliable improvements in relationship satisfaction, compared to 64% of couples who had received TBCT. Seventy percent of IBCT couples but only 55% of TBCT couples not only made reliable improvements in relationship satisfaction but reached levels of satisfaction characteristic of nondistressed couples. A second study (Cordova, Jacobson, & Christensen, 1998), conducted on a sample of 6 IBCT and 6 TBCT couples from the first study, all of whom had each of their therapy sessions videotaped, examined mechanisms that could possibly account for the changes in outcome. Spouses' behavior during randomly selected videotapes from early, middle, and late therapy sessions were coded for soft emotions, hard emotions, detachment from the problems, or engaging in the problem during therapy. Couples who received IBCT increased their use of detachment over the course of therapy and were significantly more likely to use detachment both in the middle and at the end of therapy than were couples in the TBCT group. IBCT couples also used substantially more soft emotions than TBCT couples. Although no group or time differences were found between IBCT and TBCT couples in their use of hard emotions, IBCT couples significantly reduced their use of hard emotions from beginning to end of therapy. The development of nonblaming discussions of mutual problems, such as occurs in "unified detachment," was strongly correlated with decreases in marital distress and seemed to be crucial elements in therapy. A moderate correlation between the use of soft emotions and decrease in marital distress was also found.

In addition to these two studies conducted by the founders of IBCT and their associates, two small, independent, but currently unpublished studies have examined IBCT. One found that IBCT administered in groups was superior to a no-treatment control; the other found that IBCT for married, depressed women performed as well as cognitive behavior therapy (Christensen & Heavey, 1999). Thus, there is promising evidence that IBCT is an efficacious treatment for marital discord, at least in the short run.

However, the real test of a therapy is not whether it provides amelioration in the short term, but whether those positive changes are enduring. To provide a more definitive test of the relative impact of TBCT and IBCT, a large clinical trial, designed by Neil S. Jacobson and Andrew Christensen, is currently underway in which approximately 130 couples are being randomly assigned to TBCT or IBCT. Each couple receives up to 25 sessions of therapy, which typically occurs over 6 to 9 months of treatment. Comprehensive assessments are conducted prior to treatment, midway through treatment, at the end of treatment, and every 6 months following treatment for 2 years. Data from this study will address the long-term impact of each treatment.

Future Directions: Individual and Child Outcome

In addition to the traditional measures of couple therapy outcome (i.e., relationship quality and satisfaction), the current two-year longitudinal study is evaluating "non-traditional" measures of couple therapy outcome. Such measures include assessments of each partner's physical and emotional health, and assessments of children who have been living in the couple's home. By broadening the definition of "positive outcome" following couple therapy, we hope to account for couples whose lives are somehow improved *despite* the status of their relationship. This definition challenges previous approaches to couple therapy outcome by asking questions such as *Can divorce be a 'positive' outcome?* and *Is it always best to stay married for the children's sake?* This broader perspective forces us to consider other types of "positive outcome" following couple therapy, and to assess both individual and child outcomes in addition to assessing relationship satisfaction (see Christensen & Heavey, 1999).

CONCLUSION

It is our hope that IBCT will provide couples with an environment to create long-term, positive relationship change. Whether applied alone, or in conjunction with traditional techniques, the acceptance-based approach of IBCT gives even the most "stuck" couples a new approach to their long-standing conflicts and a new perspective on their otherwise irreconcilable differences. The pilot data on IBCT look good; however, it is only the more extensive clinical trial, now under way, that will provide definitive evidence on the effects of IBCT.

REFERENCES

Baucom, D. H., & Epstein, N. (1990). *Cognitive behavioral marital therapy*. New York: Brunner/Mazel.

Baucom, D. H., Epstein, N., & Rankin, L. A. (1995). Cognitive aspects of cognitive behavioral marital therapy. In N. S. Jacobson & A. S. Gurman (Eds.), *Clinical handbook of couple therapy* (pp. 65–90). New York: Guilford Press.

Baucom, D. H., & Hoffman, J. A. (1986). The effectiveness of marital therapy: Current status and application to the clinical setting. In N. S. Jacobson & A. S. Gurman (Eds.), *Clinical handbook of marital therapy* (pp. 597–620). New York: Guilford Press.

Baucom, D. H., Shoham, V. M., Kim, T., Daiuto, A. D., & Stickle, T. R. (1998). Empirically supported couple and family interventions for marital distress and adult mental health problems. *Journal of Consulting and Clinical Psychology, 66*, 53–88.

Christensen, A., & Heavey, C. L. (1999). Interventions for couples. *Annual Review of Psychology* (Vol. 50, pp. 165–190). Palo Alto, CA: Annual Reviews.

Christensen, A., & Jacobson, N. S. (2000). *Reconcilable differences*. New York: Guilford Press.

Christensen, A., Jacobson, N. S., & Babcock, J. C. (1995). Integrative Behavioral Couple Therapy. In N. S. Jacobson & A. S. Gurman (Eds.), *Clinical handbook of couple therapy* (pp. 31–64). New York: Guilford Press.

Cordova, J. V., Jacobson, N. S., & Christensen, A. (1998). Acceptance versus change interventions in behavioral couple therapy: Impact on couples' in-session communication. *Journal of Marriage and Family Counseling, 24*, 437–455.

Floyd, F. J., Markman, H. J., Kelly, S., Blumberg, S. L., & Stanley, S. M. (1995). Preventive intervention and relationship enhancement. In N. S. Jacobson & A. S. Gurman (Eds.), *Clinical handbook of couple therapy* (pp. 212–230). New York: Guilford Press.

Hahlweg, K., Schindler, L., Revenstorf, D., & Brengelmann, J. C. (1984). The Munich marital therapy study. In K. Hahlweg & N. S. Jacobson (Eds.), *Marital interaction: Analysis and modification* (pp. 3–26). New York: Guilford Press.

Jacobson, N. S. (1977). Problem solving and contingency contracting in the treatment of marital discord. *Journal of Consulting and Clinical Psychology, 45*, 92–100.

——— (1978). Specific and nonspecific factors in the effectiveness of a behavioral approach to the treatment of marital discord. *Journal of Consulting and Clinical Psychology, 46*, 442–452.

Jacobson, N. S., & Addis, M. E. (1993). Research on couple therapy: What do we know? Where are we going? *Journal of Consulting and Clinical Psychology, 61*, 85–93.

Jacobson, N. S., & Christensen, A. (1996). *Acceptance and change in couple therapy: A therapist's guide for transforming relationships*. New York: W. W. Norton.

Jacobson, N. S., & Margolin, G. (1979). *Marital therapy: Strategies based on social learning and behavior exchange principles*. New York: Brunner/Mazel.

Jacobson, N. S., Christensen, A., Prince, S. E., Cordova, J., & Eldridge, K. (2000). Integrative Behavioral Couple Therapy: An acceptance-based, promising new treatment for couple discord. *Journal of Consulting and Clinical Psychology, 68*, 351–355.

Jacobson, N. S., Follette, W. C., & Pagel, M. (1986). Predicting who will benefit from behavioral marital therapy. *Journal of Consulting and Clinical Psychology, 54*, 518–522.

Jacobson, N. S., Follette, W. C., Revenstorf, D., Baucom, D. H., Hahlweg, K., & Margolin, G. (1984). Variability in outcome and clinical significance of behavior marital therapy: A reanalysis of outcome data. *Journal of Consulting and Clinical Psychology, 52*, 497–564.

Jacobson, N. S., Schmaling, K. B., & Holtzworth-Munroe, A. (1987). Component analysis of behavioral marital therapy: Two-year follow-up and prediction of relapse. *Journal of Marital and Family Therapy, 13*, 187–195.

Karney, B. R., & Bradbury, T. N. (1997) Neuroticism, marital interaction, and the trajectory of marital satisfaction. *Journal of Personality and Social Psychology, 72*, 1075–1092.

Skinner, B. F. (1966). Contingencies of reinforcement in the design of a culture. *Behavioral-Science, 11*, 159–166.

Stuart, R. B. (1969). Operant interpersonal treatment for marital discord. *Journal of Consulting and Clinical Psychology, 33*, 675–682.

Weiss, R. L., & Heyman, R. E. (1997). A clinical-research overview of couples interactions. In W. K. Halford & H. J. Markman (Eds.), *Clinical handbook of marriage and couples interventions* (pp. 13–41). New York: Wiley.

Weiss, R. L., Hops, H., & Patterson, G. R. (1973). A framework for conceptualizing marital conflict, technology for altering it, some data for evaluating it. In L. A. Hamerlynck, L. C. Handy, & E. J. Mash (Eds.), *Behavior change: Methodology, concepts, and practice*. (pp. 309–342). Champaign, IL: Research Press.

CHAPTER THIRTEEN

Passionate Love and Sexual Desire
Cultural and Historical Perspectives

Elaine Hatfield and Richard L. Rapson

Today, the scholarly world is in a state of creative ferment. Western views are yielding to more global perspectives, academic isolation to multidisciplinary cooperation; important intellectual territories are being staked out, new questions posed, and new methodologies utilized in the quest for new kinds of answers.

Few multidisciplinary marriages offer more promise than that between history and psychology. Until recently, history was, in the main, the study of the public arena and of power – of kings, presidents, generals, and war; now it has become the study of Everyone. Once historians were interested in history from the "top down." Today, a generation of psychological historians is committed to exploring the activities of humankind from the "bottom up." Their pioneering research has cast a dazzling light into the dark corners of history. These scholars have much to say about such "private" and "psychological" concerns as marriage, love, sexuality, and intimacy; family life, women's issues, child rearing, and emotions.

Their observations and conclusions are fascinating in and of themselves; in addition, by opening up windows to the past, they also furnish social scientists with a wider perspective on the past, present, and future. Psychology, like the other social sciences, once focused almost exclusively on one area, the West, and on one dimension of time, the present. But now new and exciting possibilities present themselves. Historians help us gain an understanding of culture's impact on

---

Address correspondence to Elaine Hatfield, Department of Psychology, 2430 Campus Road, University of Hawaii, Honolulu, HI 96822. E-mail address: elainehi@aol.com. Or write to Richard Rapson, Department of History, University of Hawaii, Honolulu, HI 96822-2383. E-mail address: rapson@aol.com.

people's attitudes, emotions, and behavior. In this era – when it has become faddish to attribute *all* gender and human differences to our evolutionary heritage and biology – cultural and historical insights provide a much needed balance. History reminds us that people's greatest strength may be the diversity and flexibility that has allowed us to survive and prosper in an amazing array of ecological niches; to explore this planet and beyond. A knowledge of history also provides a perspective that allows us make informed guesses about the future of ourselves, our families, and the planet. So valuable is this research that we wish all social scientists could know more about it. (To help to advance this goal, we'll cheerfully send our bibliography of this psychological/historical research, conducted over the past 20 years, to anyone who writes us asking for it.)

DEFINITIONS OF PASSIONATE LOVE AND SEXUAL DESIRE

Passionate love (sometimes called "obsessive love," "infatuation," "lovesickness," or "being-in-love") is a powerful emotional state. It has been defined as:

A state of intense longing for union with another. Passionate love is a complex functional whole including appraisals or appreciations, subjective feelings, expressions, patterned physiological processes, action tendencies, and instrumental behaviors. Reciprocated love (union with the other) is associated with fulfillment and ecstasy. Unrequited love (separation) with emptiness, anxiety, or despair (Hatfield & Rapson, 1993, p. 5).

The Passionate Love Scale was designed to assess the cognitive, physiological, and behavioral indicents of such love (Hatfield & Sprecher, 1986).

Social psychologists tend to use the terms *passionate love* and *sexual desire* almost interchangeably. This is not surprising. Passionate love has been defined as "a longing for union," while sexual desire has been defined as "a longing for *sexual* union" (Hatfield & Rapson, 1995, p. 3). As Susan and Clyde Hendrick (1987) noted:

It is apparent to us that trying to separate love from sexuality is like trying to separate fraternal twins: they are certainly not identical, but, nevertheless, they are strongly bonded. (p. 282)

In a recent study, Pamela Regan and Ellen Berscheid (Regan & Berscheid, 1995) found that most young people assume that although platonic love exists, one cannot be "in love" with someone unless he or she is sexually attracted to the beloved.

Overview

Today, anthropologists and evolutionary psychologists generally take it for granted that passionate love and sexual desire are cultural universals. Cross-cultural researchers and historians point out, however, that culture may have a profound impact on people's perceptions and feelings and on their ideas as to what is appropriate and permissible in the expression of romantic and passionate feelings. Let us review what these scholars have learned about the nature of passionate love and sexual desire.

ANTHROPOLOGICAL AND EVOLUTIONARY PERSPECTIVES

Recently, anthropologists have found compelling evidence in support of the contention that passionate love is a cultural universal. William Jankowiak and Edward Fischer (1992), for example, argued that romantic love is a pan-human characteristic. They searched for evidence of romantic love in a sampling of hunting and gathering societies included in the Standard Cross-Cultural Sample. They relied on five indicators to ascertain whether or not romantic love was present in a given tribal society: (a) accounts depicting personal anguish and longing; (b) the existence of love songs or folklore about such love; (c) elopement due to mutual affection; (d) native accounts affirming the existence of passionate love; and (e) the ethnographer's affirmation that romantic love was present. They found clear evidence of passionate love in 147 of the 166 tribal cultures. In only one society was there no compelling evidence of romantic love.

HISTORICAL PERSPECTIVES

The earliest Western literature abounds in tales of lovers caught up in a sea of passion and violence: Odysseus and Penelope, Orpheus and Eurydice, Daphnis and Chloë, Dido and Aeneas, Abelard and Eloise, Dante and Beatrice, Romeo and Juliet. In those stories, love was not expected to end well. Romeo and Juliet, Ophelia and Hamlet, Abelard and Eloise did not fall in love and live happily ever after. Romeo swallowed poison. Juliet stabbed herself. Ophelia went mad and drowned herself. Hamlet was felled by a poisoned sword point. Peter Abelard (a real person) was castrated and his beloved Eloise retired to a nunnery.

Passionate Love and Sexual Desire

For more than 4,000 years, China's art and literature have been filled with stories of passionate love and sexual yearning. In the Song Dynasty (A.D. 960–1279), the *Jade Goddess* recounted the story of a passionate young couple who defied their parents' wishes and eloped, only to fall into desperate straits (Ruan, 1991). In Japan, love suicides have been an institution since the end of the 17th century (Mace & Mace, 1980).

It is clear, however, that throughout the world, people's attitudes toward passionate love and sexual desire have changed markedly over time.

In the Medieval Western world, a number of social factors conspired to make sexual activity unappealing – if not terrifying. The early Catholic Church urged Christians to be celibate. Reay Tannahill (1980) observed:

> It was Augustine who epitomized a general feeling among the Church Fathers that the act of intercourse was fundamentally disgusting. Arnobius called it filthy and degrading, Methodius unseemly, Jerome unclean, Tertullian shameful, Ambrose a defilement. In fact there was an unstated consensus that God ought to have invented a better way of dealing with the problem of procreation. (p. 141)

The only conceivable excuse married couples had for engaging in nonpassionate, tepid, duty-bound sexual activity was the desire to produce children. So, for married couples, sex was grudgingly permitted. But, as Tannahill (1980) points out:

> Though not very often. Some rigid theologians recommended abstention on Thursdays, in memory of Christ's arrest; Fridays, in memory of his death; Saturdays, in honor of the Virgin Mary; Sundays, in honor of the Resurrection; and Mondays, in commemoration of the departed. Tuesdays and Wednesdays were largely accounted for by the ban on intercourse during fasts and festivals – the forty days before Easter, Pentecost, and Christmas; the seven, five, or three days before Communion; and so on. (p. 146)

Secular authorities contributed to the fear-mongering clamor. Until the 18th century, physicians generally assumed that masturbation was unhealthy. Even well into the Enlightenment, Swiss physician Samuel Tissot (1766/1985) claimed that masturbation drained away men and women's strength and left them vulnerable to almost every ailment known to humankind, including pimples, blisters, constipation, tuberculosis, blindness, insomnia, headaches, genital cancer, insanity, feeblemindedness, weakness, jaundice, nose pain, intestinal disorders, confusion, insanity, and a host of other grotesque maladies. Daniel Defoe (1727), too, warned about the pitfalls of sexual excess: "Whence come Palsies and Epilepsies, Falling-Sickness, trembling of the Joints, pale dejected Aspects, Leanness, and at last Rottenness, and other filthy and loathsome Distempers, but from the criminal Excesses of their younger times?" (p. 91).

Until 1500 and continuing well into 1800, men wielded all the power. As with the Chinese during Mao's Cultural Revolution, sexual intercourse generally lasted only a few minutes. Most couples had never even heard of foreplay. Men simply climbed on top, thrust for a few minutes, and ejaculated. Women rarely enjoyed sex or experienced orgasm. Women's pleasure in sex was also tempered by their fear of getting pregnant and perhaps dying in childbirth.

In the Early Modern period, the double standard reigned. Men's extramarital affairs were ignored; women's were not. Women were regarded as the sexual property of men. Their value was diminished if they were "loaned" out to anyone other than their legal owner. In 1700, De la Rivière Manley, observed of a "fallen" woman:

"If she had been a man, she had been without Fault: But the Charter of that Sex being much more confin'd than ours, what is not a Crime in Men is scandalous and unpardonable in Woman" (Cited in Needham, 1951, p. 272).

As late as 1825, Sir John Nicholls declared that "forgiveness on the part of a wife . . . is meritorious, while a similar forgiveness on the part of a husband would be degrading and dishonorable" (cited in Thomas, 1959, p. 202).

Perhaps temptation was less rife in the early days of the Early Modern era. Lawrence Stone (1977) pointed out that in this period, young men and women were unlikely to encounter anyone who was very sexually appealing in their daily lives. People's hair was caked with lice. They had bad breath and rotting teeth. They rarely bathed and their skin crawled with eczema, scabs, running sores, oozing ulcers, and other disfiguring skin diseases.

Men and women who engaged in sexual relations were likely to catch any number of venereal diseases. (James Boswell, the 18th-century biographer, contracted gonorrhea at least 17 times.) Women suffered from gynecological problems – vaginal infections, ulcers, tumors, and bleeding – which made sexual intercourse uncomfortable, painful, or impossible (Shorter, 1995).

Nor did people generally have much excess energy to "squander" on sex. Robert Darnton (1984) described French peasant life in the 16th and 17th centuries this way:

Men labored from dawn to dusk, scratching the soil on scattered strips of land with plows like those of the Romans and hacking at their grain with primitive syckles.... Women married late – at age twenty-five to twenty-seven – and gave birth to five or six children, of whom only two or three survived to adulthood. Great masses of people lived in a state of chronic malnutrition, subsisting mainly on porridge made of bread and water with some occasional, home-grown vegetables thrown in. They ate meat only a few times a year, on feast days ... [and] often failed to get the two pounds of bread (2,000 calories) a day that they needed to keep up their health. (p. 24) ...
Whole families crowded into one or two beds and surrounded themselves with livestock in order to keep warm. So children became participant observers of their parents' sexual activities. No one thought of them as innocent creatures or of childhood itself as a distinct phase of life....
The peasants of early modern France inhabited a world of stepmothers and orphans, of inexorable, unending toil, and of brutal emotions, both raw and repressed. The human condition has changed so much since then that we can hardly imagine the way it appeared to people whose lives really were nasty, brutish, and short. (p. 29)

In the 300 years from 1500 to 1800, England and America showed stunning change in *mentalité*. People began to question patriarchal and repressive attitudes and to adopt more individualistic, egalitarian, and permissive attitudes toward passionate love and sexuality.

By the 1800s, most people had adopted a more individualistic orientation. They possessed a stronger sense of personal autonomy and a stronger desire for personal freedom, the pursuit of happiness, and privacy; they became less concerned with kin and community. Couples were now bound together by affection, sexual attraction, and habit rather than by ties of political, familial, or economic interest. They were more sexually liberated and less guilt ridden; they began to countenance birth control to limit pregnancy.

In the early 1900s – fueled by rapidly changing notions as to the value of individualism, personal freedom, and personal happiness and by advances in birth control – the sexual revolution began to pick up speed. In the 1960s, the women's movement sparked an explosion of change. There is no question that today, in the 21st century, a startling change has occurred in the way men and women in the West view sensuality and sexuality. There is, of course, no guarantee that this evolution in sexual freedom will continue forever. (The AIDS epidemic has already slowed the pace of change.) America may be poised on the threshold of another pendulum swing. But the best bet is that there will never be a return to the kind of sexual "repression" or "restraint" (the term you use depends upon your value system) that existed prior to 1500. The West is likely to continue to view sexual desire and expression positively. The debate over how much affective individualism and how much communitarianism, how much sexual freedom and how much sexual restraint are ideal, is taking place over a narrower range and around a more tolerant base. (Readers interested in other histories of Western sexuality should see Bullough, 1990; D'Emilio & Freedman, 1988; or Tannahill, 1980.)

One particularly intriguing and important phenomenon: It took the West over 500 years (from the Renaissance into the present) to accept "modern" ideas concerning love, sex, and intimacy. In many non-Western cultures, however, these same historical changes seem to be occurring in a mere 50 years or less. These changes come about as TV, MTV, movies, the Internet, DVDs, and expanded travel weave their webs. It is as if some historical deity has pushed the fast-forward button on global change.

Recently, of course, there has begun to be a worldwide backlash. Non-Western ethnic groups have begun to celebrate their own cultures, traditions, and religions, and to resist wholesale Western cultural expansionism. Throughout the world, people have begun to speculate about the possibilities of taking the best that the West has to offer, integrating it with cultural traditions that are uniquely their own, and rejecting the rest (Kağitçibasi, 1990). Some feel it is best to turn back the clock and reject Westernization entirely, as was attempted by Ayatollah Khomeini in Iran and Mao during China's disastrous Cultural Revolution. The dialectic between Westernization and resistance to it defines much of international life today, and different societies are seeking different balances. It remains to be seen whether a nation can accept science, technology, rock and roll, and capitalism and keep out gender equality, democracy, avaricious materialism, and individualism. (In this chapter, space is necessarily limited. For readers interested in the history of sex in China and other non-Western nations, see Hatfield & Rapson, 1995; Kon, 1993; and/or Ruan, 1991.)

Currently, the historical perspective suggests several questions for researchers interested in personal relationships: What aspects of love, sex, and intimacy are universal? Which are social constructions? Is the world becoming one and homogeneous, or are traditional cultural practices more tenacious and impervious to this sort of deep transformation than some have supposed?

CROSS-CULTURAL PERSPECTIVES

Cross-cultural researchers point out that culture has a profound impact on how susceptible people are to falling in love, with whom they fall in love, and how passionate affairs work out.

The world's cultures differ profoundly in the extent to which they emphasize individualism or collectivism (although some cross-cultural researchers would focus on related concepts: independence or interdependence, modernism or traditionalism, urbanism or ruralism, affluence or poverty). Individualistic cultures such as the United States, Britain, Australia, Canada, and the countries of northern and western Europe tend to focus on personal goals. Collectivist cultures such as China, many African and Latin American nations, Greece, southern Italy, and the Pacific Islands, in contrast, press their members to subordinate personal interests to those of the group (Markus & Kitayama, 1991; Triandis, McCusker, & Hui, 1990).

At one time theorists argued that passionate love was a uniquely Western phenomenon. Harry Triandis and his colleagues (1990), for example, pointed out that in individualistic cultures, young people are allowed to "do their own thing." In collectivist cultures, the group comes first. Godwin Chu (1986; Chu & Ju, 1993) argued that although in America, romantic love and compatibility are of paramount importance, in China such things matter little. Traditionally, parents and go-betweens arranged young peoples' marriages. Parents' primary concern is not love and compatibility but *men tang hu tui*. Do the families possess the same social status? Are they compatible? Francis Hsu (1985) and L. Takeo Doi (1963, 1973) contended that passionate love was a Western phenomenon, almost unknown in China and Japan, and so incompatible with Asian values and customs that it was unlikely ever to gain a foothold among young Asians.

Recent scientific evidence suggests that the cross-cultural theorists were wrong.

The Cross-Cultural Data

Susceptibility to Passionate Love

It has been claimed that Americans are preoccupied with love and passion (Murstein, 1974). Early researchers (Goode, 1959; Rosenblatt, 1967) assumed that romantic love was prevalent only in modern, industrialized nations. The emerging evidence, however, suggests

Table 13.1. Intensity of Passionate Love in Various Ethnic Groups.

Ethnic Group	Average PLS Score Men	Women
Euro Americans (Mainland USA)	97.50	110.25
Euro Americans (Hawaii)	100.50	105.00
Filipino Americans	106.50	102.90
Japanese Americans	99.00	103.95

that men and women in a variety of cultures are every bit as romantic as Americans. Susan Sprecher and her colleagues (1994) interviewed 1,667 men and women in the United States, Russia, and Japan. Passion was found to be far more common worldwide than the researchers expected. Sprecher and her colleagues found that the percentage of those "currently in love" was surprisingly high in all three societies. They had expected American men and women to be most vulnerable to love, the Japanese the least. In fact, 59% of American college students, 67% of Russians, and 53% of Japanese students said they were in love at the time of the interview. In all three cultures, men were slightly less likely than were women to be in love at the present time. Surveys of Mexican American, Chinese American, and Euro-American students have found that in a variety of cross-national groups, young men and women show high rates of reporting being in love at the present time (Aron & Rodriguez, 1992; Doherty, Hatfield, Thompson, & Choo, 1994).

Intensity of Passionate Love

What impact does culture have on how passionately men and women love one another? In one study, Elaine Hatfield and Richard Rapson (1987) asked men and women of European, Filipino, and Japanese ancestry to complete the Passionate Love Scale. To their surprise, once again they found that men and women from the various ethnic groups – individualist or collectivist – seemed to love with equal passion (see Table 13.1). In a survey of European Americans, Chinese Americans, Filipino Americans, Japanese Americans, and Pacific Islanders, William Doherty and his colleagues (1994) secured similar results.

In summary, the preceding studies suggest that any stunning differences that may have once existed between Westernized, modern, urban, industrial societies and Eastern, modern, urban, industrial societies are fast disappearing. Today, those interested in cross-cultural variations may be forced to search for them in the most underdeveloped, developing, and collectivist of societies – such as in Africa or Latin America, in China, or in the Arab countries (Egypt, Kuwait, Lebanon, Libya, Saudi-Arabia, Iraq, or the United Arab Emirates). It may well be, of course, that even there the winds of Westernization, individualism, and social change are blowing.

DIRECTIONS FOR FUTURE RESEARCH

Thus far, we have focused on what cross-cultural, historical, and social psychological researchers have learned about the nature of love and sexual desire. What about the future? What directions might we expect theorists and researchers from these and other disciplines to take?

Historical Differences in the *Meaning* of Passionate Love and Sexual Desire

During the Middle Ages, Western Crusaders, troubadours, and courtiers spun tales of the joys and searing torments of pure love. Andreas Capellanus (1174/1941), in *The Art of Courtly Love*, set down the cruel rules of chivalry. To be worthy of love, a woman must put herself beyond it; she must be noble, chaste, and so utterly virtuous as to be forever unattainable. In his turn, the true lover must eagerly embrace not his beloved, but the Grail-like quest for love. He must be willing to perform any deed, suffer any torment, to attest to the purity of his doomed love (Gay, 1986; Murstein, 1974; Tannahill, 1980).

In the 7th and 8th centuries, Arab storytellers told a more complex tale of romantic, erotic, love. One source of the tales were the professional storytellers, who flourished in the cities of the Near East. Reay Tannahill (1980) observed:

> The repertoire of these men, especially the Persians among them, was astonishingly varied. They drew on the *Bible* and the *Vedas*, recounted the exploits of Greek heroes, Roman warriors, and Egyptian queens, told of angels and djinns, winged horses and magic carpets, of treasure houses on earth and dancing girls in paradise. Their word pictures had a wild, exotic glamour that took possession of the Arab imagination. (p. 235)

Often, their stories were tales of the purest of love. Pure love was a spiritual, romantic, and eternal kind of love. The beloved was usually a dimly glimpsed woman, chaste, and forever unattainable. (Generally, the beloved was a devout Muslim wife, imprisoned in a *harām*.) This sort of love promised only yearning and exquisite torture.

Seductive slave singers, on the other hand, offered another vision of romance – love-desire. This was a happier, rougher, sexier, and transient kind of love. Here, the woman who caught the lover's eye (for the moment) was generally a slave singer – cultured, exquisite, deceitful, and very sexy. Love-desire was not expected to last forever. Men buzzed from flower to flower, enjoying whichever slave-singer or adolescent boy happened to catch their attention at the moment (Tannahill, 1980).

Although the Western Crusaders, troubadours, and courtiers and the Arab storytellers and slave singers tended to separate falling in love and making love, tenderness and lust, throughout history, for many people, the two were tightly connected.

In the last decade, social psychologists have become increasingly interested in laypersons' "naïve" perceptions of a variety of emotions, including love. Social psychologists such as Beverley Fehr (1993, 1994; Fehr & Russell, 1991) and Julie Fitness and Garth Fletcher (1993) have used a "prototype analysis" to explore people's mental representations of passionate love and sexual desire (see also Shaver, Schwartz, Kirson, & O'Connor, 1987).

Researchers find that there are cultural/historical differences in the way men and women view and have viewed passionate love. In one study, Shelley Wu and Philip Shaver (1992; Shaver, Wu, & Schwartz, 1991) interviewed young people in America, Italy, and the People's Republic of China about their emotional experiences. Passionate love is by definition a bittersweet experience. Whether the emphasis is on the sweet or the bitter, however, seems to depend on one's culture. American and Italian subjects tended to equate passionate love with happiness. Chinese students, however, had a darker view. In Chinese, there are few "happy-love" ideographs. Love tends to be associated with sadness, pain, and heartache. Chinese men and women generally associated passionate love with such ideographs as infatuation, unrequited love, nostalgia, and sorrow-love.

We suspect that in the next few years social psychologists (utilizing such techniques) will devote increasing attention to the way that passionate love and sexual desire are defined and the meanings they have had at various times and places. If theorists do set out on such explorations, historians, cross-cultural psychologists, and social psychologists offer some speculations on which they might choose to build.

Social psychologists interested in the social construction of emotions have pointed out that people may possess various mental representations of passionate love and may differ markedly in the ways in which such love is perceived, interpreted, labeled, and expressed (see Fehr, 1993, 1994; Fehr & Russell, 1991; Fitness & Fletcher, 1993; Hatfield & Rapson, 1993, 1995).

What about sexual desire? Theorists have also speculated as to the various social constructions and meanings that sexual desire and sexual activity have had throughout time. This work is probably less well known by personal relationship researchers than is the research on cultural differences in the meaning of "love," so we will discuss it in some detail.

Historians such as John D'Emilio and Estelle B. Freedman (1988) point out that throughout history, people have assumed that it is appropriate to engage in sexual activity for a variety of very different reasons. They observe:

Sexuality has been associated with a range of human activities and values: the procreation of children, the attainment of physical pleasure (eroticism), recreation or sport, personal intimacy, spiritual transcendence, or power over others. (p. xv)

Others, too, have observed that in different historical eras, the words "love," "sex," and "intimacy," have carried profoundly different meanings (see also Bullough, 1990; Degler, 1980; D'Emilio & Freedman, 1988; Gay, 1984, 1986; Gillis, 1985; Hatfield & Rapson, 1995; Mintz & Kellogg, 1988; Phillips, 1988; Stone, 1977, 1990).

To determine the meanings that sexuality has in a given historical era, historians ask a number of questions: In what kinds of sources do references to "sexuality" appear – sacred or secular, personal or public? What is the language of sexuality – are the dominant metaphors religious, medical, romantic, or commercial?

They find that in different historical eras, men and women have assumed that people should and do choose to engage in sexual activity for a variety of very different reasons. For the thousand years in Europe after the fall of Rome, the Church sanctioned only *procreation* as a legitimate justification for "sinful" activity, although the exercise of *power* (mostly, though not exclusively of men over women) constituted a large part of the reality of sexual behavior.

In the modern era, among the new meanings – sometimes culturally sanctioned, sometimes not – which D'Emilio and Freedman and other historians have ascribed to sex are passionate love, spiritual transcendence, procreation, kindness (a "mercy fuck"), eroticism (the attainment of physical pleasure, recreational sex, "sport fucking"), self-esteem, mental and physical health (see China's recent emphasis on sex education), the formation of alliances, appeasement (the Bonobo), curiosity, excitement seeking and thrills, self-aggrandizement, a desire to save the world, duty, power over others, submission to others (the other side of power), political revolt, revenge, to make a point, money, and health and long life (Yin and Yang)!

Sex researchers and sociologists, too, have explored the various meanings of sex. They document that men and women from various groups cite many of the preceding reasons in explaining why they choose to engage in sexual activity (see, for example, the landmark research of DeLamater & MacCorquodale, 1979; and Nelson, 1979).

We speculate that in the next decade, social psychologists will discover a great deal more as to the meanings that have been ascribed to passionate love and sexual desire in various cultures and at different times.

GAZING INTO THE FUTURE

Yale historian Robin Winks once said that writing history is "like nailing jelly to the wall." Setting out to describe sweeping historical trends and *then* attempting to predict future trends in love, sex, and intimacy is even more difficult. But despite the fact that history does not always move in a linear direction, let us make – with good cheer and a large, necessary dose of humility – a tentative effort.

First, recent evidence suggests that men and women in the West and in most modern societies are moving slowly and bumpily in the direction of social equality and freedom for all in the arenas of passionate love and sexual desire (although tolerance can be slowed by events such as the AIDS epidemic, backlash against permissiveness, and religious revivals). The global village created by worldwide communication, computers and satellites, information exchange, travel, and trade makes it hard to imagine that non-Western cultures can long hold off the advancing currents of individualism or that they can forever restrain the spirit of sexual equality and experimentation. Of course, that revolution is far from being consummated – and healthy, honorable disagreement about the revolution remains ongoing.

We would predict that people throughout the world will come increasingly to accept a transforming trio of powerful ideas. First is a belief in the equality of women and members of minority groups. Second is a belief that the pursuit of happiness and the avoidance of pain are desirable goals in life. Third is a belief that it is possible to improve life and that action is preferable to the passive acceptance of age-old traditions. Let us end this chapter by briefly considering this trio of revolutionary ideas.

From Male Supremacy to Gender Equality

The women's movement may be the most momentous social upheaval taking place in our lifetimes. Though its sources lie in Euro-America, it is rapidly spreading around the world.

Of course, the world is still far from achieving gender equality. As we enter the 21st century, male supremacy continues to be the rule worldwide – even in the West. When Western and developing-world women joined together to speak for the first time at United Nations human rights conferences in Geneva in 1993 and Cairo in 1994, they itemized the staggering array of human rights violations that are routinely inflicted upon women throughout the world. Girls are ritually mutilated in the Sudan and Somalia. In Burma and Thailand very young girls are coerced into prostitution. In Saudi Arabia and Kuwait, household maids are often beaten and raped. The list of abuses includes female infanticide, genital mutilation, the sale of brides, dowry murders, *suttee* (in India, widows are still sometimes required to immolate themselves on their husbands' funeral pyres), and discriminatory laws against women's civic, social, and legal equality.

Yet, there are signs around the world that existing assumptions of the worthlessness of women (and the absolute rights of men to have their way over them) may not be immutable doctrines. The recent Geneva and Cairo conferences are two examples. Dramatic transformations in the role of women are infiltrating into some sanctuaries of the most deeply entrenched male-dominated cultures.

If these changes occur, they will continue to have an impact on the issues with which many of us are concerned. In the arena of love and sex, we would expect men and women to move toward gender equality in their sexual preferences, feelings, and experiences. We might expect to see the continued erosion of the sexual double standard. We might see greater acceptance of heterosexuality, bisexuality, and homosexuality. We might see broader cultural definitions of the institution of family combined with more creative social measures to support families while women work outside the home, with or without mates.

The Pursuit of Happiness and the Avoidance of Pain

The subversive notion that lies behind all modernization is the simple idea that in life people are entitled to pursue happiness and avoid pain. Traditionally, many religions – including Christianity and most varieties of Hinduism and Buddhism, laboring to stem the tide of individualism and self-interest – asked people to accept what was given, to repress individual desire, indeed to regard such desire as sin. Authoritarians, political and religious, have worked with great success to sell these propositions to their constituencies; they have been concerned with maintaining order and keeping down the unwashed masses.

Although the validation of the pursuit of happiness only regained currency in the 18th century Enlightenment (after a very long absence), there is now evidence that the notion of pleasure and Thomas Jefferson's "pursuit of happiness" as a *desideratum* is gaining increasing acceptance worldwide. If this trend continues, we might expect societies around the world to begin to accept a more positive view of passionate love and sexual desire (no longer seeing them as evil).

We might also expect to see an increase in premarital sexual activity and sexual permissiveness, a growing acceptance of birth control, and a belief that individuals should be permitted to marry for love (rather than submitting to arranged marriages), and perhaps, even more important, permitted to terminate unhappy marriages by divorce. Some historians (such as Lawrence Stone, 1990) regard the movement from nonseparating to separating societies as among the most significant of all historical developments.

A Belief That Things Can Change for the Better

Modernism has wrought its most far-reaching change with its onslaught on fatalism. The possibility of progress outweighs hopelessness and resignation in most places in the world.

Each year, Richard L. Rapson teaches a graduate seminar in which students spend the semester attempting to imagine what life will be like in the 21st century. They consider the changes in the world that have occurred since 1500 and, given contemporary innovations, attempt to predict what is likely to happen if such trends continue. The futurists at the University of Hawaii, fully cognizant of the perils of such an enterprise, have come up with the following predictions:

In the *economic/practical* realm: both spouses working outside the home; a continuation of the movement toward gender and economic equality; more consensual unions; more long-distance relationships; and more cyberspace relationships.

In the *technological* realm: improvement in birth control and abortion technology; more test-tube babies, clones, babies without fathers; a cure for AIDS and for male and female impotence, both of which may eventuate (for better or worse) in greater sexual permissiveness; increased availability of pornography; and technological sex.

In the *cultural* realm: increasing acceptance of interracial relationships; of homosexuality; and of more varied definitions of what society will mean by "family." (The last would suggest that there will be many more childless marriages and, on the other side of the coin, better childcare services – each, along with consensual and homosexual unions, eroding the traditional dominance of the nuclear family.) Men and women will be more experienced about sexual relationships. The norm will not be stability but change.

All of our readers surely possess their own theoretical frameworks in the arenas of love, sex, and intimacy. Whether or not you agree with our playful speculations, the attempt to look ahead into some sort of future has several advantages: (a) it provides an exciting test of existing psychological and historical theories and it introduces the element of time into our research; (b) it encourages interdisciplinary work and the intersections of disciplines offers some of the most productive intellectual activity that is taking place these days. (The combining of cross-cultural, historical, and psychological insights is likely to yield new knowledge); (c) when one looks at the broader picture, it helps to put theorizing based primarily upon contemporary findings into a broader perspective.

By all this, we mean to suggest there is an explosion of new questions to ask and new ways to find answers. We may be at the threshhold of an expansive and quite remarkable moment in intellectual inquiry.

REFERENCES

Aron, A., & Rodriguez, G. (1992). Scenarios of falling in love among Mexican-, Chinese-, and Anglo-Americans. Paper presented at the Sixth Conference of the International Society for the Study of Personal Relationships, Orono, ME.

Bullough, V. L. (1990). History and the understanding of human sexuality. *Annual Review of Sex Research, 1,* 75–92.
Capellanus, A. (1174/1941). *The art of courtly love* (J. J. Parry, Trans.). New York: W.W. Norton.
Chu, G. C. (1985). The changing concept of self in contemporary China. In A. J. Marsella, G. DeVos, & F. L. K. Hus (Eds.), *Culture and self: Asian and Western perspectives* (pp. 252–277). London: Tavistock.
Chu, G. C., & Ju, Y. (1993). *The great wall in ruins.* New York: State University of New York Press.
Darnton, R. (1984). *The great cat massacre.* New York: Basic Books.
Defoe, D. (1727). *Conjugal lewdness: Or, matrimonial whoredom.* London: T. Warner.
Degler, C. N. (1980). *At odds: Women and the family in America from the Revolution to the present.* New York: Oxford University Press.
DeLamater, J., & MacCorquodale, P. (1979). *Premarital sexuality: Attitudes, relationships, behavior.* Madison: University of Wisconsin Press.
D'Emilio, J., & Freedman, E. (1988). *Intimate matters: A history of sexuality in America.* New York: Harper & Row.
Doherty, R. W., Hatfield, E., Thompson, K., & Choo, P. (1994). Cultural and ethnic influences on love and attachment. *Personal Relationships, 1,* 391–398.
Doi, L. T. (1963). Some thoughts on helplessness and the desire to be loved. *Psychiatry, 26,* 266–272.
——— (1973). *The anatomy of dependence* (J. Bester, Trans.). Tokyo: Kodansha International.
Fehr, B. (1993). How do I love thee? Let me consult my prototype. In S. Duck (Ed.), *Individuals in relationships: Understanding relationship processes series* (Vol. 1, pp. 87–120). Newbury Park, CA: Sage.
——— (1994). Prototype-based assessment of laypeople's views of love. *Personal Relationships, 1,* 309–331.
Fehr, B., & Russell, J. (1991). The concept of love viewed from a prototype perspective. *Journal of Personality and Social Psychology, 60,* 425–438.
Fitness, J., & Fletcher, G. J. O. (1993). Love, hate, anger, and jealousy in close relationships: A prototype and cognitive appraisal analysis. *Journal of Personality and Social Psychology, 65,* 942–958.
Gay, P. (1984). *The bourgeois experience: Victoria to Freud. Education of the senses.* (Vol. 1). New York: Oxford University Press.
——— (1986). *The bourgeois experience: Victoria to Freud. The tender passion.* (Vol. 2). New York: Oxford University Press.
Gillis, J. R. (1985). *For better, for worse: British marriages, 1600 to the present.* New York: Oxford University Press.
Goode, W. J. (1959). The theoretical importance of love. *American Sociological Review, 24,* 38–47.
Hatfield, E., & Rapson, R. L. (1987). Gender differences in love and intimacy: The fantasy vs. the reality. In W. Ricketts & H. L. Gochros (Eds.), *Intimate relationships: Some social work perspectives on love* (pp. 15–26). New York: Hayworth Press.
——— (1993) *Love, sex, and intimacy: Their psychology, biology, and history.* New York: HarperCollins.

(1995). *Love and sex: Cross-cultural perspectives*. Boston: Allyn and Bacon.
Hatfield, E., & Sprecher, S. (1986). Measuring passionate love in intimate relations. *Journal of Adolescence, 9,* 383–410.
Hendrick, S. S., & Hendrick, C. (1987). Love and sexual attitudes, self-disclosure, and sensation-seeking. *Journal of Social and Personal Relationships, 4,* 281–297.
Hsu, F. L. K. (1985). The self in cross-cultural perspective. In A. J. Marsella, G. DeVos, & F. L. K. Hsu (Eds.), *Culture and self: Asian and Western perspectives* (pp. 24–55). London: Tavistock.
Jankowiak, W. R., & Fischer, E. F. (1992). A cross-cultural perspective on romantic love. *Ethology, 31,* 149–155.
Kağitçibaşi, C. (1990). In J. J. Berman (Ed.), Family and socialization in cross cultural perspective: A model of change. *Nebraska Symposium on Motivation: 1989: Cross-Cultural Perspectives, 37,* 136–200. Lincoln: University of Nebraska Press.
Kon, I. (1993). Sexuality and culture. In I. Kon & J. Riordan (Eds.), *Sex and Russian society* (pp. 15–43). Bloomington: Indiana University Press.
Mace, D., & Mace, V. (1980). *Marriage: East and West.* New York: Dolphin Books.
Markus, H. R., & Kitayama, S. (1991). Culture and self: Implications for cognition, emotion, and motivation. *Psychological Review, 98,* 224–253.
Mintz, S., & Kellogg, S. (1988). *Domestic revolutions: A social history of American family life.* New York: Free Press.
Murstein, B. I. (1974). *Love, sex, and marriage through the ages.* New York: Springer.
Needham, G. B. (1951). Mrs. Manley: An eighteenth-century wife of Bath. *Huntington Library Quarterly, 14,* 259–284.
Nelson, P. A. (1979). *Personality, sexual functions, and sexual behavior: An experiment in methodology.* Unpublished doctoral dissertation. Gainsville: University of Florida.
Phillips, R. (1988). *Putting asunder: A history of divorce in Western society* (pp. 630–640). Cambridge: Cambridge University Press.
Rapson, R. L. (1988). *American yearnings: Love, money, and endless possibility.* Lanham, MD: University Press of America.
Regan, P. C., & Berscheid, E. (1995). Gender differences in beliefs about the causes of male and female sexual desire. *Personal Relationships, 2,* 345–358.
Rosenblatt, P. C. (1967). Marital residence and the function of romantic love. *Ethnology, 6,* 471–480.
Ruan, F. F. (1991). *Sex in China: Studies in sexology in Chinese culture.* New York: Plenum.
Shaver, P., Schwartz, J., Kirson, D., & O'Connor, C. (1987). Emotion knowledge: Further exploration on a prototype approach. *Journal of Personality and Social Psychology, 52,* 1061–1086.
Shaver, P. R., Wu, S., & Schwartz, J. C. (1991). Cross-cultural similarities and differences in emotion and its representation: A prototype approach. In M. S. Clark (Ed.), *Review of personality and social psychology,* Vol. 13 (pp. 175–212). Beverly Hills, CA: Sage.

Shorter, E. (1995). *Women's bodies: A social history of women's encounters with health, ill-health, and medicine.* New York: Transaction.
Sprecher, S., Aron, A., Hatfield, E., Cortese, A., Potapova, E., & Levitskaya, A. (1994). Love: American style, Russian style, and Japanese style. *Personal Relationships, 1,* 349–369.
Stone, L. (1977). *The family, sex, and marriage: In England 1500–1800.* New York: Harper & Row.
    (1990). *Road to divorce: England 1530–1987.* New York: Oxford University Press.
Tannahill, R. (1980). *Sex in history.* New York: Stein & Day.
Thomas, K. (1959). The double standard. *Journal of the History of Ideas, 20,* 202.
Tissot, S. A. D. (1766/1985). *Onanism.* New York: Garland.
Triandis, H. C., McCusker, C., & Hui, C. H. (1990). Multimethod probes of individualism and collectivism. *Journal of Personality and Social Psychology, 59,* 1006–1020.
Wu, S., & Shaver, P. R. (1992). Conceptions of love in the United States and the People's Republic of China. Paper presented at the Sixth Conference of the International Society for the Study of Personal Relationships, Orono, ME.

CHAPTER FOURTEEN

Rules for Responsive Robots
Using Human Interactions to Build Virtual Interactions

Joseph N. Cappella and Catherine Pelachaud

Computers seem to be everywhere and to be able to do almost anything. Automobiles have global positioning systems to give advice about travel routes and destinations. Virtual classrooms supplement and sometimes replace face-to-face classroom experiences with web-based systems (such as Blackboard) that allow postings, virtual discussion sections with virtual whiteboards, as well as continuous access to course documents, outlines, and the like. Various forms of "bots" search for information about intestinal diseases, plan airline reservations to Tucson, and inform us of the release of new movies that might fit our cinematic preferences. Instead of talking to the agent at AAA, the professor, the librarian, the travel agent, or the cinemaphile two doors down, we are interacting with electronic social agents. Some entrepreneurs are even trying to create toys that are sufficiently responsive to engender emotional attachments between the toy and its owner.

These trends are seen by some as the leading edge of a broader phenomenon – not just interactive computer agents but emotionally responsive computers and emotionally responsive virtual agents. Nicholas Negroponte (1996) answers the obvious question: "Absurd? Not really. Without the ability to recognize a person's emotional state, computers will remain at the most trivial levels of endeavor.... What you remember most about an influential teacher is her compassion and enthusiasm, not the rigors of grammar or science" (p. 184). The editors

Address correspondence to Joseph N. Cappella, Annenberg School for Communication, University of Pennsylvania, 3620 Walnut St., Philadelphia, PA 19104-6220. Fax: (215) 898-2024; Tel: (215) 898-7059. E-mail address: jcappella@asc.upenn.edu. Or write to Catherine Pelachaud, Università di Roma "La Sapienza," Dipartimento di Informatica e Sistemistica, Via Buonarroti, 12, 00185 Roma Italy. E-mail address: cath@dis.uniroma1.it.

of *PC Magazine* do not consider emotionally responsive computers science fiction. "[I]n the not so distant future, your computer may know exactly how you feel" (*PC Magazine*, 1999, p. 9). Researchers at Microsoft are developing lifelike avatars to represent their owners and who could participate in a virtual meeting while the owner remains at the office available only remotely (Miller, 1999, p. 113).

Computer gurus are not the only people predicting the "emotionalization" of the human–computer interface. Scholars, such as Rosiland Picard (1997), have given serious attention to the possibility and value of programming computers and computer agents to be responsive emotionally. Part of her interest in this possibility is based on how people typically respond to computers.

Reeves and Nass (1996) have built a strong case for the "media equation," namely that people treat computers and new media like real people. Their claim is that people are primarily social beings ready to default to social judgments and evaluations even when they are dealing with inanimate entities such as computers. For example, in one of their studies people were led to believe that they were evaluating a teaching program run by one computer. When asked by the computer that had taught them how effective the teaching program was, participants offered more positive assessments than when the same evaluation of the teaching computer was asked by a different computer.

The authors argue that this result is explained by a norm of social politeness. Just as a person might direct less criticism to their own (human) teacher but direct harsher criticism toward the teacher when asked by a third party, so they did with the computer stations. The social rule of politeness was adopted as the default even when acting in a nonsocial context. In a different study, computers employing a dominant verbal style of interaction were preferred by users who possessed a dominant personality while those with submissive personalities preferred computers with a submissive style. This pattern parallels the social preferences that people have for other humans. Across a wide variety of studies, Reeves and Nass have shown that people are first and foremost social in their interactions, even when those interactions are with inanimate media rather than flesh and blood *Homo sapiens*.

Picard (1997) reasons that if people are social even in nonsocial interactions, then human users should prefer to interact with computers and their representative systems that are more rather than less human. To be social and to be human is in part to be emotionally responsive.

Picard's treatment of emotionally responsive computers involves reviewing literature on human emotional expression and recognition as well as recent thinking on emotional intelligence (Gardner, 1983, 1993; Goleman, 1995). She reports recent advances in automatic recognition of emotion and in work on the animation of facial displays of emotion.

The automated recognition and expression of emotion present immense problems for programmers. However, even if these problems are solved, a large gap will remain. Affective interaction in human–computer interchanges cannot be reduced to sequences of recognition and expression. The fundamental feature of human interaction is contingent responsiveness, which is not reducible to a mere sequence of recognition and expression by two agents. This chapter is about what it means to act in a way that is contingently responsive.

Our argument is essentially that modeling social interaction as it is experienced by humans requires certain mechanisms or rules without which simulated interactions are little more than the juxtaposition of two monologues.

We present our position by (a) defining responsiveness; (b) discussing computer simulation tools; (c) presenting empirical models of two-person interactions; (d) describing the importance of responsive and unresponsive interactions to people; and (e) concluding with general rules for realistic virtual interaction between human and nonhuman agents.

VIRTUAL INTERACTIONS AND HUMAN RELATIONSHIPS

Before taking up these issues, it is fair to ask what this chapter has to do with human relationships. The development of computer simulations of human interactions is well underway. Service industries that provide simple transactions such as banking exchanges, fast food services, and so on are anxious to replace their service personnel with autonomous agents who will be the friendly, responsive representatives of the company that their more expensive, late, and sometimes surly and uncivil human counterparts are not. However, the models for such simulations – if they are to be accepted as viable replacements for humans – must have human social abilities.

Much of what is known about human social interaction is ignored by computer modelers. Instead, they often import their own assumptions into their models. Attend even one computer conference on "real characters" and you will find fascinating models, elegantly presented, but with little empirical foundation. Understanding the human and empirical basis for social interaction is crucial for artificial intelligence (AI) specialists. The science of relationships – especially human interaction in relationships – needs to be imported into the science of modeling interactions.

But does modeling virtual relationships have anything to do with understanding human relationships? The answer is an unequivocal "Yes!" in at least two senses. First, to provide useful information to computer simulators requires very precise claims and a very solid empirical base. This is a challenge to researchers who study human relationships. Our work will have little influence unless it is precise and empirically well founded.

In *Zen and the Art of Motorcycle Maintenance*, Robert Pirsig explores the differences between classical and romantic conceptions of knowing. Complex devices, such as motorcycles, can be appreciated for the beauty of their superficial structure and function or for their underlying causal operation. The latter, classical view, leads Pirsig's hero on an intellectual journey exploring what it can mean to know the underlying, unobserved structure and function of physical and social systems. He concludes that deep knowledge is knowledge that allows one to build a replica of the system being scrutinized. So it is with models of human interaction – deep understanding comes when research and theory allow the simulation of the behaviors being modeled. The data we present on responsiveness in human interaction are pertinent to both the principles that will guide the simulations of virtual human interaction and to the parameters needed to tune the simulations.

Second, and this may sound truly strange, interactions between virtual agents or between virtual agents and human agents are a new form of relationship. Although this claim may sound like science fiction, it represents a future not far removed. What form such mediated interactions take and what implications they might have for the human agents behind them are a matter for speculation. However, their reality will depend on their programming, which in turn will depend in part on the assumptions imported to the model. Successful virtual interactions between agents require realistic assumptions about the nature of human interactions. The study of virtual interactions, then, may provide insights into human relationships in the same way that studying the successes and failures of any model of any system can provide insight into the function and design of the focal system. We may find ourselves studying virtual interactions to learn about human interactions.

DEFINING RESPONSIVE HUMAN INTERACTIONS

The defining feature of human social interaction is responsiveness. What does it mean to be responsive? Responsiveness is not simply the generation or recognition of social signals. Nor is it just receiving and sending such signals. Neither can responsive interaction be reduced to the interweaving of two monologues, as if responsive interaction could be created from the behavior of two separate individuals juxtaposed. Responsive interactions are the regularized patterns of messages from one person that influence the messages sent in turn by the other over and above what they would otherwise be (Cappella, 1994). On this view, my rude remark to you during cocktails is not an interaction. Rather it is just a rude remark. But when my rude remark is followed by your sarcastic reply and, then, my biting insult, we have been responsive to one another, if not very polite.

Davis has defined responsive social interaction in terms of two kinds of contingency (Davis & Perkowitz, 1979). The first refers to the probability of a person's response to the actions of a partner in an interaction. The second concerns the proportion of responses related to the content of the previous message. Davis and colleagues have been able to show that both of these measures of responsiveness are related to attraction to responsive others and to feelings of acquaintance. Responsiveness has been applied to physical pleasure and to verbal reinforcements as well (Davis & Martin, 1978; Davis & Holtgraves, 1984).

Our definition of responsiveness is a conceptual relative of Davis's but more narrowly focused. Consider a conversation between two persons, A and B. Let the behavioral repertoire of person A be denoted by the set $X = (X_1, X_2, \ldots, X_N)$, where the values X are the N discrete behaviors that can be enacted by person A at discrete intervals of time. No real loss of generality is entailed by assuming that the behaviors are discrete rather than continuous or measured on a clock base rather than event time. Let the behavioral repertoire of person B be denoted by the set (Y) identical to the set X for A. Responsiveness is defined by two features of the contingent probability between the set of behaviors (X) and the set (Y):

$$P[X_i(t+1) \mid Y_i(t)] > 0, \qquad (1)$$

$$P[X_i(t+1) \mid Y_j(t)] > \text{ or } < P[X_j(t+1)] \qquad (2)$$

for at least some combination of the behaviors *I* and *J*. In words, equations 1 and 2 mean that B's behavior (the *j*th one, in fact) must influence the probability of A's behavior (the *i*th behavior) at some significant level and, more importantly, that the size of the probability must be greater than the probability that A will emit the behavior in the absence of B's prior behavior [2]. These two features ensure that A's response level in the presence of B's behavior is above A's normal baseline behavior. A similar pair of equations can be written for A's influence on B. Together they constitute the necessary and sufficient conditions for mutual responsiveness.

Much of the research in modeling human interaction has been given over to coordinating components of a single person's expression. For example, generating a hostile remark requires coordination among semantic, vocal, gestural, and visual systems. Even simple matters such as head movements when improperly timed with bursts of speech can produce an odd appearance. The problems of modeling a realistic expression require attention to a range of physical systems and detailed knowledge about their interplay. The same is true for recognition systems. These individually based processes present enormous technical and theoretical problems that must be solved before realistic interactions can be built. But solving these individual problems will not solve the problem of realistic social interaction by themselves. Realistic interaction requires modeling agents who are mutually responsive.

Our central claim in this chapter is that building virtual humans capable of engaging in social interaction requires building responsive humans. What a "responsive virtual human" might be requires understanding what a "responsive human" is. To investigate this question we will proceed as follows:

1. Review literature on modeling human interaction as practiced in artificial intelligence.
2. Present data on human responsiveness showing that
   a. pairs of people in interaction *cannot* be constructed from the predispositions of individuals.
   b. being responsive depends on reacting contingently and appropriately to the behavior of others.

Rules for Responsive Robots

  c. being responsive requires sensitivity to the context of contingent responses.
  d. being responsive is the sine qua non of human interaction, but the degree and magnitude of responsiveness is highly variable.
 3. People are sensitive to responsiveness in others (although they deny it) and they are specifically sensitive to how emotionally responsive and polite people are to one another.

SIMULATION TOOLS: MODELING VIRTUAL INTERACTION IN ARTIFICIAL INTELLIGENCE

In this section, our goal is to sketch a few of the tools employed in simulations of virtual interactions. By "agent" we mean a robot or human. The techniques of artificial intelligence and the methods of cognitive science provide the tools to build virtual humans with interactive capacity. However, the data, the rules, and the theory upon which modeling occurs must come from the study of human interaction.

Simulating the Behavior of Agents

Structure
Different levels of information are needed to describe and manipulate an agent. One level describes the structure of an agent. For example, an agent can be a set of joints and limbs. These settings are simple for a single-legged robot, but much more complex for a human agent.

Procedure
The next level corresponds to procedures acting directly on the jointed figures. These procedures are used to build complex motions (Zhao & Badler, 1994). For example, to animate Marilyn Monroe and Humphrey Bogart, Magnenat-Thalmann and Thalmann (1987) used abstractions of muscle actions. They worked on specific regions, almost all of which corresponded to a single muscle.

Function
Walking (Ko, 1994), grasping an object (Rijpkema & Girard, 1991), keeping one's balance (Phillips & Badler, 1991) or expressing a facial emotion (Lee, Terzopoulos, & Waters, 1995) are very difficult to simulate if one has to work at the level of joint movements or of their

equations of motion. Instead, such behaviors can be built up as functions from the lower levels of description. For example, facial animation is simulated by integrating the representation of the various layers of the facial tissue with dynamic simulation of the muscle movement (Lee et al., 1995). The skin is constructed from a lattice whose points are connected by springs. To carry out an animation, the user selects which muscles to contract.

Manipulation Techniques

Different methods have been proposed to manipulate virtual agents: key-frame, script language, "performance animation," and task specification.

The Key-Frame Technique
Key-frame requires a complete description of each frame of activity. The user places each object in the virtual world and has total control of its location and position. The main disadvantage of this method is that the total specification of the model requires immense amounts of data.

Script Language
Script language offers the possibility of performing complex animations (Kalra, Mangili, Magnenat-Thalmann, & Thalmann, 1991; Moravetz, 1989). Detailed lists of actions – in parallel or sequentially – and their location and duration are specified. Examples of scripts include smile while saying "hello," or start the action "walk" at time t, start action "wave hand" at time $t + 1$, end action "wave hand" at time $t + 2$. Script language provides a simple mechanism for scheduling actions and their sequences.

Performance Animation
"Performance animation" consists of recording the movement of an actor or an object through the use of sensors (DeGraf, 1990; Patterson, Litwinowicz, & Greene, 1991; Litwinowicz, 1994; Guenter, Grimm, Malvar, & Wood, 1998). For example, sensors are placed on various points on the person being tracked. The movements of the points over time are used as input for a three-dimensional synthetic model. The synthetic model moves by imitation.

This technique is mainly used in advertising and entertainment. Its main advantage is to produce complex animations quickly and cheaply.

Rules for Responsive Robots

However, each new animation requires new data. The synthetic agent has no knowledge simply reproducing the motions recorded.

Task Specification

The task specification approach allows the user to give task-level instructions to an agent: "Go to the wooden door and open it." The program decomposes tasks into subgoals (walk to the door, avoid any obstacle, find the type of door, grab the handle, open the door depending on its type (slide it or turn the knob and push the door)). Each subgoal must be programmed using lower level functions: e.g., walking or grasping (Brooks, 1991; Zeltzer, 1991; Webber et al., 1995). The agent needs to evaluate and understand a situation (Chopra-Khullar & Badler, 1999) and must make decisions based on world knowledge and current goals.

Simulating Conversation between Agents

Communication in face-to-face interactions is expressed through a variety of channels, including the body, the voice, the face, and the eyes. When talking, humans move their hands (beats, batons, deitics) and heads (nods on accented items, gaze at the listener during back channel) among other things. They accentuate words and raise their eyebrows to punctuate a question mark or express affect. Speakers use facial expression, gaze, and gesture not only to reinforce their talk but also to convey their emotion and to evaluate their partner's reaction. Moreover, these nonverbal signals are synchronized with the dialogue and with the agent's activity (gaze follows hand movement while performing a task). To have a believable animation, a synthetic agent must deploy each of these behaviors in a way that is appropriate and well timed.

Face-to-Face Conversation between Synthetic Agents

The goal of many simulations (Cassell et al., 1994) is to simulate interaction in which one agent helps the other to achieve a goal. Each agent is implemented as semiautonomous, keeping its own representation of the state of the world and the conversation. The agent's behavior is determined by these representations. The appropriate intonation, gesture, gaze, and facial expressions are computed based on the semantic content and the dialogue generated by a discourse planner.

In this model the two agents do not sense each other's behaviors. This is a significant limitation because responsive interactions require dynamic adjustments to each agent's behaviors. Without sensing the partner's behavior, no adjustment by the agent to ongoing actions by the partner is possible. Instead the complexities of this version are found in the coordination within an agent's behavioral systems rather than between agents.

Face-to-Face Conversation between a Synthetic Agent and a User

Takeuchi and Nagao (1993; Nagao & Takeuchi, 1994) move a step closer to realistic responsive interactions. They employ a categorization of facial expressions that depends on communicative meaning. Chovil (1991) postulates that facial expressions are not only a signal of the emotional state of the sender but also a social communication whose conveyed meanings have to be interpreted in the context in which the expressions are emitted. She found that facial displays occurring during speech are linked to current semantic content.

Based on these insights, Takeuchi and Nagao consider 26 facial displays stored in a library. When a response is computed in the speech dialogue module, a corresponding facial display is generated simultaneously. A signal is sent to the animation module, which deforms the facial model to show the requested facial displays. In this model, the facial actions of agent B depend on the semantic content presented by agent A. Although simplistic, there is a rudimentary form of responsiveness with agent A's actions dependent on those of B.

More recent conceptual advances include the development of the embodied agent – that is, one encompassing conversational skills and able to exhibit nonverbal communicative behaviors (Andre, Rist, van Mulken, Klesen, & Baldes, 2000; Badler et al., 2000; Cassell, Bickmore, Campbell, Vilhjalmsson, & Yan, 2000; Rickel & Johnson, 2000; Lester, Towns, Callaway, Voerman, & FitzGerald, 2000; Poggi & Pelachaud, 2000; Poggi, Pelachaud, & de Rosis, 2000). The goal of this work is to develop an agent capable of understanding the user's verbal and nonverbal behaviors, as well as being able to generate human-like communicative behaviors.

Ymir (Thórisson, 1997) is an architecture to simulate face-to-face conversation between the agent, Gandalf, and a user. The system takes as sensory input hand gesture, eye direction, intonation, and body position of the user. Gandalf's behavior is computed automatically in real time. He can exhibit context-sensitive facial expressions, eye movement, and pointing gestures as well as generate turn-taking signals. Nevertheless, Gandalf has limited capacity to analyze discourse at a semantic level and therefore to generate semantically driven nonverbal signals.

Rea, the real estate agent, is capable of multimodal conversation: She can understand and answer in real time (Cassell et al., 1999). She moves her arms to indicate and to take turns. She uses gaze, head movements, and facial expressions for functions such as turn taking, emphasis, and greetings as well as back channels to give feedback to the user speaking to her. Poggi and Pelachaud (2000) developed a system of an animated face that can produce the appropriate facial expression according to the performative of the communicative act being performed, while taking into account information on the specific interlocutor and the specific physical-social situation at hand.

Conclusions and Future Directions

We have reported different techniques to simulate complex animations and behaviors during conversation. They offer tools to analyze, manipulate, and integrate systems so that models of communication between agents can be realistic. But to take full advantage of these techniques in simulating human interaction requires clear ideas about how humans interact in general and in the specific context of cooperative exchanges.

Current simulations of social interaction have a variety of shortcomings. The interface between the synthetic agent interacting with a human requires a better sensing and recognition system. Current systems limit the role of humans to simple spoken utterances with some head and hand motions, as well as a few facial expressions. Moreover, while dialoguing with a synthetic agent, most of the time no interruption by the user is allowed (however, see Cassell et al., 1999). Also the set of utterances used by the system is small.

We believe that successful models require not only production and recognition systems, not only coordination among gestural, vocal, and semantic subsystems, but also models that incorporate responsive agents. Responsiveness implies the ability to adjust to the dynamically changing behavior of the partner in ways that mimic at least approximately the alterations that humans would make to one another in similar, usually cooperative contexts.

EMPIRICAL MODELS OF HUMAN SOCIAL INTERACTION

A comprehensive model of human social interaction would include both semantic and emotional components. In the data presented here only emotional components will be considered. Human emotion is carried in a variety of ways in social interaction, but the nonverbal channel, including face, voice, and body, is the primary vehicle of emotional communication (Cappella, 1991). Social attachment and affective reaction are conveyed and understood in the patterns of emotional signaling through the voice (Scherer, 1986) and face (Ekman, 1971) as well as body position (Hatfield, Cacioppo, & Rapson, 1994) and less observable physiological indicators (Ekman, Levenson, & Friesen, 1983).

In this section our attention will be focused on the ways that nonverbal signs of affect are expressed and responded to in ordinary social interaction. By understanding the patterns of exchange and response between humans in cooperative interactions, we hope to be able to infer some specific and general rules for virtual interaction.

Much of the information that researchers have gathered about human interaction is based on static data or, at best, scenarioes in which two exchanges are monitored. The data to be reported here come from interactions that take place over 20- to 30-minute periods. The behaviors enacted in those periods are audio- and video-recorded for later coding.

The archive of interactions we have consists of about 100 interactions. They include same-sex and opposite-sex pairs, dyads with longer histories (greater than six months as friends) and strangers, partners with similar and different attitudes, and expressive and reticent pairs (see Cappella & Palmer, 1990 for more details on the design and procedures for data collection). This group of persons offers maximum variance of behavioral response in part due to their expressive differences. Their interactions were informal and not directed by the researcher in any way. The interactions scrutinized in this chapter come from a set of 19 interactions of 15-minute duration.

A number of behaviors were coded for later analysis. These include vocalic behaviors, eye gaze, smiles and laughter, head nods, back channels, posture, illustrator gestures, and adaptor gestures. Vocal behaviors allow us to obtain information about conversational tempos that are known to be related to arousal and excitation. Overlapping speech patterns can be read as impolite as people are seen to usurp conversational resources. Positive affect is carried in part by facial smiles and laughter. Head nods provide feedback while listening as well as emphasis during

Rules for Responsive Robots

speech. Gaze can be a regulator of interaction, a method of monitoring threat, or a sign of attention and positive regard. Gestures can function as signs of anxiety and spillover of energy and as a means of carrying information that is redundant with or supplementary to speech. Back channels are signals listeners offer speakers that they are being attentive while not necessarily trying to wrest the floor away. Postural states may be signals of involvement or of detachment.

Behaviors are carefully and reliably assessed using trained coders and computerized data acquisition techniques.* Codes are "on and off" values at each 0.1 second yielding long time series for each behavior and each person. The series are synchronous with a common time base. These series give a temporally precise picture of the behaviors enacted by partners during ordinary social interaction. Since some of these behaviors carry information about affect, they provide the basis for describing emotional responsiveness.

Analytic Strategy

The long-term goal of our research is to model the sequential structures of human interaction, specifically the behaviors indicative of emotional reaction. Our approach identifies states of the individual and the interaction. Writing rules that describe changes in these states over time and that correspond to the empirical realities is the essence of the enterprise of modeling. Consider the case of smiling and the rules that might govern its enactment.†

To describe interaction, two types of rules need to be understood. One set concerns *sequence* or when to change a state. For example, do people break mutual gaze by both looking away at the same time or does one look away first? The other concerns *distributional* rules or how long to remain in a state before leaving. For example, how frequent is a gaze of more than 6 seconds? Is this a common or uncommon occurrence? Because these rules are probabilistic, the range of observed probabilities can provide guidance to modelers about what humans find acceptable and unacceptable changes in behavior during interaction.

A second issue concerns the source of probabilities for rules of sequence and distribution. Can we study the behavior of individuals

---

* Reliabilities are reported in Cappella and Palmer (1990) or are available upon request from the first author.
† In this chapter space limitation requires that we focus on only one behavior. We have selected smiles. Interested parties may contact the first author for similar analyses of gaze, gesture, and voice.

Table 14.1. Transition Probability Matrix for Four Behaviors at Individual Level: Composite, Low, and High Values.

Adaptors	Off	On	Total
Off: Average	.5362	.0047	.5410
(Low–High)	(.0980–.9516)	(.0014–.0140)	
On: Average	.0047	.4543	.4590
(Low–High)	(.0013–.0140)	(.0400–.8978)	

Gaze			
Off: Average	.1854	.0136	.1990
(Low–High)	(.0100–.3538)	(.0027–.0224)	
On: Average	.0135	.7873	.8008
(Low–High)	(.0026–.0226)	(.6419–.9630)	

Illustrators			
Off: Average	.9128	.0044	.9172
(Low–High)	(.6207–.9827)	(.0002–.0128)	
On: Average	.0044	.0784	.0828
(Low–High)	(.0002–.0128)	(.0009–.2198)	

Smiles			
Off: Average	.9274	.0034	.9308
(Low–High)	(.8566–.9841)	(.0011–.0077)	
On: Average	.0034	.0658	.0692
(Low–High)	(.0011–.0077)	(.0133–.1451)	

Note: The first entry in each cell is the average probability across 38 people, the second is the lowest, and the third the highest probability.

to see how and when they change, or must we focus on the behavior of pairs of persons within interaction? Are interactions homogeneous regarding distributional and sequential rules, or do the rules change from one section to the next? This is sometimes called *context sensitivity*. Are interactional rules context sensitive or not? We will take up each of these questions in turn.

Rules from the Behavior of Individuals

In Table 14.1, probabilities of individual change in four behaviors are presented. The behavior is assumed to be either "on" or "off." The

Rules for Responsive Robots

matrix is the probability of moving from a prior to a subsequent state. These probabilities are derived from treating each person in the interaction as if he or she did not have a partner. The cell of each matrix contains an average probability and a high and low value. The number of observations is more than 300,000.

Two things are immediately apparent. First, some behaviors are much more frequent than others. Body gestures occur roughly 45% of the time, while smiles and illustrator gestures are "off" the vast majority of the time. Gaze directed at the partner is on at the rate of 80% on average. Second, there is considerable variability across persons. The high and low values can differ by huge amounts, at times spanning the full range of probabilities.

What is not so obvious from these data are their implications for responsiveness. Can individual transition probabilities be used to create sequences for pairs of people in interaction? The answer is "no" on two grounds. The variability in individual response implies that the average values will not provide good fit for any particular dyad. Also when two people are paired in interaction, there is good evidence that they adjust their behaviors to those of the partner, for example, in cooperative interactions smiling together and converging in their interactive tempos (Burgoon, Stern, & Dillman, 1995; Cappella, 1981, 1991). This implies that we cannot predict well A's interaction with C based on A's interaction with B and C's interaction with D (Cappella, 1980).

The first rule of interaction, then, is the *synthesis rule*. The behavior of persons is insufficient for synthesizing the behaviors of dyads. Studying the behaviors of individuals can never produce realistic descriptions of dyads. Put a bit more technically, the probabilities that describe a dyad when derived from the probabilities that describe persons will yield unrealistic models of interaction (virtual or otherwise).[‡]

Predicting Sequential Rules from Dyads

In order to study the sequences of behavior in dyads, we first need to create state definitions for pairs of people in interaction. If these descriptions are to avoid the synthesis problem, then they must be sensitive to the behavior of the partner and not just the behavior of the person. The usual means for doing so is to define states for the pair of persons as follows:

[‡] For a detailed description of the synthesis rule, see Cappella (1980).

Table 14.2. Transition Probability for Dyadic State: Average, High, and Low Values for Smiles and Laughter ($N = 170586$).

	Neither on	A on only	B on only	Both on	Row Total
Neither on	.8830	.0029	.0018	.0001	.8878
	.7341–.9468	.0009–.0073	.0002–.0046	0–.0004	
A on only	.0029	.0544	.0000	.0011	.0583
	.0009–.0072	.0071–.1228	0–.0001	.0003–.0020	
B on only	.0019	.0000	.0253	.0007	.0279
	.0003–.0050	0–.0001	.0027–.0548	.0001–.0014	
Both on	.0000	.0011	.0008	.0241	.0260
	0–.0004	.0004–.0021	.0002–.0022	.0071–.0797	

State Definitions for Any Two-Person, on–off Behavior (Example for Smiles)

A's Behavior	B's Behavior	Dyad's Behavior
Smile is off (= 0)	Smile is off (= 0)	Neither smiling (00)
Smile is on (= 1)	Smile is off (= 0)	A Only smiling (10)
Smile is off (= 0)	Smile is on (= 1)	B Only smiling (01)
Smile is on (= 1)	Smile is on (= 1)	Both smiling (11)

Using these state definitions, we can follow the sequences among the various dyadic states. These are represented by transition matrices, but now the transition matrices describe movements by pairs of people over time rather than individuals changing. A matrix representing 19 different dyads aggregated together is presented in Table 14.2.

What do transition matrices tell us? First, the diagonal elements (upper left to lower right) indicate the probability that the dyad continues in the state that it is already in. The off-diagonal elements tell us about changes from one condition to the next – for example, from only person A smiling to both A and B smiling together. In effect, the diagonal elements give information about stability of a state while the off-diagonals give information about change.

Let us work with the case of smiling and laughter, because this is a crucial variable in some later studies we will be discussing. Smiles and laughter are mostly off for the dyad. When the dyad changes state the paths it does *not* take include

Rules for Responsive Robots

00 → 11 (Neither → Both)
10 → 01 (A only → B only)
01 → 10 (B only → A only)
11 → 00 (Both → Neither)

That is, the cross-diagonals (lower left to upper right) are zero. People do not change from one person smiling alone to the other smiling alone or from both smiling to neither smiling or neither to both smiling. In human terms, they negotiate.

Instead to get from one mutual state to another or to get from one person smiling alone to another smiling alone, the following paths are used:

00 → 01 → 11
    or
  10 → 11

10 → 00 → 01
    or
  11 → 01

01 → 00 → 10
    or
  11 → 10

11 → 01 → 00
    or
  10 → 00

When neither is smiling, an overture by one is required before acceptance by the other is possible. When both are smiling, termination by one is required before termination by both. Most interestingly, smiling by one can only become smiling by the other through moments of mutuality. What does not happen is alternation of smiling alone or a sequence when smiling together follows neither smiling or neither smiling follows smiling together. This kind of dyadic behavior appears to be forbidden in human interaction and, therefore, should be forbidden in virtual interactions as well.[§]

[§] One possible objection to the findings is the limited sample size and narrow time window (sampling at 0.1 seconds). A structurally similar transition matrix based on 40 dyads of various types and a sampling interval of 0.3 seconds shows the counter-diagonal probabilities with the same pattern as in Table 14.2. They are all near zero, confirming the claim that there is mutuality and negotiation in changing smiling states for people in cooperative interaction (data for this matrix can be seen in Cappella, 1993, or are available from the first author by request).

Two conclusions obtain. First, mutuality is a crucial state for how the dyad changes its conditions of smiling. Second, to have mutuality requires a person knowing his or her own state as well as that of the partner. A realistic model of smiling in interaction cannot be built from studying the behavior of individuals or through simple sequences of expression and recognition guided by individual rules.

When other behaviors are examined, such as gaze and gesture, patterns similar to those observed with smiles are found. Adaptor gestures show the greatest variability, with the diagonal probabilities varying from very low to very high. Behaviors that are mostly on (e.g., gaze) and mostly off (e.g., gestures) have smaller ranges of variation.

In general, the dyadic matrices exhibit more empirical constraint than the individual matrices do. The off-diagonal probabilities carry information about changes in the state of the pair of persons. In all cases, the cross-diagonal elements are zero or nearly zero. This constraint implies that when the dyad changes state, it does so along a particular path and avoids other paths completely. The paths people choose are through moments of sharing the same state. This simultaneity is a kind of mutual responsiveness that is not required in principle but is required by the social nature of human beings.

Context Effects

In the study of grammars, one distinguishing feature of types of grammar is whether they are context sensitive or not. Are there features of the surrounding linguistic context that determine the application of one rather than another rule? Context sensitivity may also apply to the study of the grammar of emotional exchange.

An important context in all interactions is the exchange of speaker and hearer roles, also called *turn-taking* (Duncan & Fiske, 1977). Speakers and hearers are different behaviorally in many ways. Speakers are generally under greater cognitive load than listeners are (Cappella, 1980). They look at listeners less and, of course, gesture more (Cappella, 1985). The kinds of head nods used are very different, tending to be more related to packets of stressed speech than the deliberate nods of listeners (Duncan & Fiske, 1977). Too, holding the floor is controlling an important conversational resource that must be shared or, if not, wrestled away from the partner in order to gain access.

The listener-hearer role may be one important context within which other social and emotional exchanges occur. To determine whether

Rules for Responsive Robots

Table 14.3. Defining Speaker–Listener States According to the Rules of Jaffe and Feldstein (1970).

Person A Speaking	Person B Speaking	Floor?	State Description	State Code
No	No	A	Both silent, A floor	00A
Yes	No	A	A Only	10A
Yes	Yes	A	Both talk, A floor	11A
No	No	B	Both silent, B floor	00B
No	Yes	B	B Only	01B
Yes	Yes	B	Both talk, B floor	11B

sequential rules are context sensitive, we first need to define states and sequences of states for two-person speaker–hearer exchanges and, then, embed social-emotional exchange rules into these contexts.

States for turn taking are presented in Table 14.3 and are based on the definitions of Jaffe and Feldstein (1970). The definitions depend on two important features. First is that having the floor is the same as being the only speaker. Second, a person has the floor from the person's first unilateral vocalization to the first unilateral vocalization by the partner. In Table 14.3 there are six rather than four dyadic states of previous representations. This is because "holding the floor" is ambiguous when both are silent or both are talking. The ambiguity is resolved by giving the person who has most recently had the floor responsibility for the floor in subsequent moments of mutual silence or mutual talk.

With six speaker–hearer states, a first-order transition matrix will have 36 (= 6 × 6) cells. But some of these cells have structural zeros because certain sequences are forbidden by definition. For example, the dyad cannot change from both talking and person A holding the floor to both talking and person B holding the floor. In the 6 × 6 transition matrix, there are 12 such constraints (also called *structural zeros*).

To test for context sensitivity, the sequential matrices for emotion and social behavior must be embedded within the speaker–hearer transition matrix producing a rather daunting 24 × 24 matrix with 12 × 16

Table 14.4. Four Speaker–Listener Contexts That May Alter Emotional Interaction Patterns.

Context	Elements of Context	State Changes
Switching speaker & listener roles	Smoothly w/switching pause	10A → 01B
	Smoothly w/o switching pause	00A → 01B
	Interruptive w/o switching pause	11A → 01B
Simultaneous contests for speaker role	Contesting	11A → 11A
	End contesting	11A → 10A
	Begin contesting	10A → 11A
Within-speaker role	Normal continuation with speech	10A → 10A
	without speech	00A → 00A
		00A → 10A
	End hesitation	10A → 00A
	Begin hesitation	11A → 00A
Awkward moments:	Whose turn?	00A → 11A

(= 192) structural zeroes. The general matrix is very complex and is only presented in the Appendix. The complexity suggests that even simple codes for behavior (such as on and off) can quickly produce very involved representations just by requiring dyadic rather than individual representations and context sensitivity rather than context independence.

The complexity of context-sensitive affective exchanges can be reduced by noticing that certain transitions can be grouped conceptually. We divided the subcomponents of this transition matrix into four speaker–listener contexts summarized in Table 14.4. They include the most common types of speaker–hearer exchanges: ordinary speaker exchanges; ordinary continuations of the speaker role; contests for the speaker role won by the original speaker; and awkward moments where it is not clear who will get the floor next.

Context sensitivity asks: Are the sequential rules for smiling, gesturing, and gazing the same or different across the contexts of speaker–hearer interaction? The summary matrix for smiles within the four speaker–listener contexts is presented in Appendix A. First the composite matrix is listed, followed by smile sequences during turn switches, simultaneous turns, within turns, and awkward turns.

The large sample sizes ensure that the smile sequences are reliably different from the composite for the different contexts. The match between the composite and the smile sequences for the "within-turn" context is very close, mostly because 88% of the observations for the composite come from moments in the interaction when a person is continuing to hold the floor. The other three smile sequence matrices differ from the composite by amounts that can be appreciable.

Specifically, the row totals for smiling *are higher* during turn switches and awkward, or simultaneous turns than during within-turn interaction. Although the data are not presented here, there is more mutual gaze during turn switches, simultaneous turns, and awkward turns than during within-turn segments. In effect, smiling and mutual gaze tend to pile up during those moments in interaction when speaker–listener roles are being exchanged, the roles are being contested, or when awkward moments such as an attempted interruption followed by mutual silence. By contrast, when speakers are engaged in serial monologue, mutual smiling is lowered. To put too simple a point on these data: Social and emotional rules of interaction depend on turn-taking context.

Sometimes the differences described in the preceding sections appear to be rather small. However, both participants in and observers of interactions use these differences in responsiveness in the judgments they render about interlocutors.

THE IMPORTANCE OF RESPONSIVE AND UNRESPONSIVE INTERACTIONS

One could respond to our findings so far as "much ado about nothing." Small changes like these could not matter much to ordinary interactants. We undertook a series of studies to test whether the microprocesses of interaction matter.

From the 100 or so dyadic interactions in our archive, eight were selected. Four of these met criteria for highly responsive interactions and four were low in responsiveness. Responsiveness was defined using time series methods with equations similar to equations 1 and 2 presented earlier. From these eight, 2 one-minute segments from each were chosen (see Cappella, 1997 for further details).

Three studies were conducted. The first simply showed the 16 one-minute segments in a fixed order. People evaluated each immediately after seeing the segments. Four questions were asked, each assessing some component of responsiveness. In a second study, facial cues were removed by superimposing a mosaic on the faces. Motion was still visible but specific features were not. In a third study, both facial and vocal cues were eliminated. Vocal cues were completely eliminated in Study 3, while in Study 1 words could not be understood, although vocal tempo and variation could be.

Students in Study 1 denied that they could make reliable judgments of responsiveness. They were incorrect in their denials because judgments were reliable within person, within study, and across studies. People were sensitive to responsive interactions, being able to distinguish responsive from nonresponsive interaction in all three studies. Observers judged partners to be responsive when they smiled in synchrony with one another and when their gaze and gesture were complementary. One way of describing this is that partners were judged synchronous when they were emotionally responsive and polite. Interactants liked one another more when their smiles were mutual ones. Judged responsiveness too accounted for people's attraction to one another.

The implications of these results are, we think, very important for building virtual interactions. If people are going to judge virtual social interactions as real, then simulations must be sensitive to micromomentary responsiveness and unresponsiveness between partners. People are sensitive to responsive partners whether they are participating in the interaction or just observing it. They may not be able to say what it is about an interaction that makes it feel right or wrong, but they do perceive unresponsive partners in less favorable terms.

CONCLUSION AND IMPLICATIONS

Among researchers in the AI community, there has been a sharp upsurge of interest in creating synthetic agents with at least some capacity for interaction with human agents. Many researchers (e.g., Picard, 1997) have argued that computerized tools need to be "emotionalized," in part because people feel comfortable treating computers and other media in social terms and in part because emotion is as important a component of the learning process as rationality is. Making computers, or their virtual agents, more user friendly involves adaptation in both rational and emotional ways.

The task of creating emotionally responsive synthetic agents is enormously complex. Multiple systems must be coordinated within a given synthetic agent just to make the agent's actions appear roughly normative. These subsystems include the semantic, vocal, gestural, facial, visual, and so on. However, to fabricate a synthetic agent with the capacity for interaction with a human or another synthetic agent

Rules for Responsive Robots

requires responsiveness *between* agents. And responsiveness between agents is more than a sequence of interleaved expressions, no matter how realistic those expressions might be. Realistic virtual interactions require agents responsive to one another's behavior just as human interaction, if it is to be human, requires responsiveness between partners.

Many of the tools employed in AI modeling efforts make assumptions that simplify the processing load by avoiding the inclusion of recognition systems or building in preestablished goals and plans. These simplifications are understandable at the earlier stages of modeling. However, simulations that produce realistic virtual interactions will need to include agents with the ability to sense their own state as well as that of the partner and the capacity to dynamically alter their behavior in response to that of the partner and to the surrounding context.

Our data from the human sphere made very clear that interactions cannot be modeled by studying the behavior of individuals disaggregated from their partners. Rather, partners must be studied together. You cannot build models of dyads from the behavior of individuals. The reason is simply that people adjust to their partners' behaviors – that is, they are responsive. There is an aggregation problem in moving from persons to dyads.

People are also sensitive to the context of their actions. For example, smiling (and gazing) were more frequent when partners were switching speaker and listener roles or contesting those roles than when carrying out a lengthy monologue. Virtual agents will need the capacity to know what context their actions are in so that minor modifications in affective cues such as smiles can be made.

The perceived realism of an interaction depends in part on these microadjustments. Humans who participate in or observe interactions that involve less-responsive others sense it and evaluate the interaction less favorably. Although current synthetic agents may behave in ways that are too crude to worry about microadjustments in smiles, gaze, gestures, and head nods, eventually they will need to. The models employed as the tools for simulation will require assumptions that allow for responsive, context-sensitive agents.

The study of interpersonal relations is about to face a new set of entities for its empirical and theoretical scrutiny. These entities will be the robots, virtual and synthetic agents that will interact with one another and with human agents. Whether the tools used in the study of personal and social relationships will be useful in this new domain of relationships is unclear. What is clear is that scholars of interpersonal relations have the opportunity not only to study but to participate in the creation of the objects of study.

REFERENCES

Andre, E., Rist, T., van Mulken, S., Klesen, M., & Baldes, S. (2000). The automated design of believable dialogues for animated presentation teams. In J. Cassell, J. Sullivan, S. Prevost, & E. Churchill (Eds.), *Embodied conversational agents* (pp. 220–255). Cambridge, MA: MIT Press.

Badler, N., Bindiganavale, R., Allbeck, J., Schuler, W., Zhao, L., & Palmer, M. (2000). Parameterized action representation for virtual human agents. In J. Cassell, J. Sullivan, S. Prevost, & E. Churchill (Eds.), *Embodied conversational agents* (pp. 256–286). Cambridge, MA: MIT Press.

Brooks, R. A. (1991). A robot that walks: Emergent behaviors from a carefully evolved network. In N. I. Badler, B. A. Barsky, & D. Zeltzer (Eds.), *Making them move: Mechanics, control, and animation of articulated figures* (pp. 99–108). San Mateo, CA: Morgan-Kaufmann.

Burgoon, J. K., Stern, L. A., & Dillman, L. (1995). *Interpersonal adaptation: Dyadic interaction patterns.* Cambridge: Cambridge University Press.

Cappella, J. N. (1980). Talk and silence sequences in informal social conversations II. *Human Communication Research, 6,* 130–145.

(1981). Mutual influence in expressive behavior: Adult and infant–adult dyadic interaction. *Psychological Bulletin, 89,* 101–132.

(1985). Production principles for turn-taking rules in social interaction: Socially anxious vs. socially secure persons. *Journal of Language and Social Psychology, 4,* 193–212.

(1991). The biological origins of automated patterns of human interaction. *Communication Theory, 1,* 4–35.

(1993). The facial feedback hypothesis in human interaction: Review and speculations. *Journal of Language and Social Psychology, 12,* 13–29.

(1994). The management of conversational interaction in adults and infants. In M. L. Knapp & G. R. Miller (Eds.), *The handbook of interpersonal communication,* 2nd ed. (pp. 380–419). Thousand Oaks, CA: Sage.

(1997). Behavioral and judged coordination in adult informal social interactions: Vocal and kinesic indicators. *Journal of Personality and Social Psychology, 72,* 119–131.

Cappella, J. N., & Palmer, M. T. (1990). Attitude similarity, relational history, and attraction: The mediating effects of kinesic and vocal behaviors. *Communication Monographs, 57,* 161–183.

Cassell, J. B., Bickmore, T., Billinghurst, M., Campbell, J., Chang, K., Vilhjalmsson, L., & Yan, H. (1999). Embodiment in conversational interfaces: Rea. In *CHI '99 conference proceedings,* 520–527, Pittsburgh, PA.

Cassell, J. B., Bickmore, T., Campbell, J., Vilhjalmsson, L., & Yan, H. (2000). Human conversation as a system framework: Designing embodied conversational agents. In J. Cassell, J. Sullivan, S. Prevost, & E. Churchill

(Eds.), *Embodied conversational agents* (pp. 29–63). Cambridge, MA: MIT Press.
Cassell, J., Pelachaud, C., Badler, N., Steedman, M., Achorn, B., Becket, T., Douville, B., Prevost, S., & Stone, M. (1994). Animated conversation: Rule-based generation of facial expression, gesture and spoken intonation for multiple conversational agents. *Computer graphics annual conference Series*, 413–420.
Chopra-Khullar, S., & Badler, N. (1999). Where to look? Automating attending behaviors of virtual human characters. In *Proceedings of autonomous agents '99*, Seattle, WA.
Chovil, N. (1991). Social determinants of facial displays. *Journal of Nonverbal Behavior, 15*, 141–154.
Davis, D., & Holtgraves, T. (1984). Perceptions of unresponsive others: Attributions, attraction, understandability, and memory for utterances. *Journal of Experimental Social Psychology, 20*, 383–408.
Davis, D., & Martin, H. J. (1978). When pleasure begets pleasure: Recipient responsiveness as a determinant of physical pleasuring between heterosexual dating couples and strangers. *Journal of Personality and Social Psychology, 36*, 767–777.
Davis, D., & Perkowitz, W. T. (1979). Consequences of responsiveness in dyadic interaction: Effects of probability of response and proportion of content-related responses on interpersonal attraction. *Journal of Personality and Social Psychology, 37*, 534–550.
DeGraf, B. (1990). "Performance" facial animation. In *State of the art in facial animation* (Vol. 26, 10–14). ACM Siggraph'90.
Duncan, S. D., Jr., & Fiske, D. W. (1977). *Face-to-face interaction: Research., methods, and theory.* Hillsdale, NJ: Erlbaum.
Ekman, P. (1971). Universal and cultural differences in facial expressions of emotion. In J. Cole (Ed.), *Nebraska symposium on motivation* (pp. 207–283). Lincoln: University of Nebraska Press.
Ekman, P., Levenson, R. W., & Friesen, W. V. (1983). Autonomic nervous system activity distinguishes among emotions. *Science, 221*, 1208–1210.
Gardner, H. (1983). *Frames of mind.* New York: Basic Books.
(1993). *Multiple intelligences: The theory in practice.* New York: Basic Books.
Goleman, D. (1995). *Emotional intelligence.* New York: Bantam.
Guenter, B., Grimm, C., Malvar, H., & Wood, D. (1998). Making faces. *Computer graphics proceedings*, Annual Conference Series, *ACM*.
Hatfield, E., Cacioppo, J. T., & Rapson, R. L. (1994). *Emotional contagion,* New York: Cambridge University Press.
Jaffe, J., & Feldstein, S. (1970). *Rhythms of dialogue.* New York: Academic Press.
Kalra, P., Mangili, A., Magnenat-Thalmann, N., & Thalmann, D. (1991). SMILE: A multilayered facial animation system. In T. L. Kunii (Ed.), *Modeling in computer graphics* (pp. 189–198). New York: Springer-Verlag.
Ko, H. (1994). Kinematic and dynamic techniques for analyzing, predicting, and animating human locomotion. Unpublished Ph. D. Dissertation, University of Pennsylvania, Philadelphia.

Lee, Y., Terzopoulos, D., & Waters, K. (1995). *Computer graphics annual conference series*, 1995.

Lester, J., Towns, S., Callaway, C., Voerman, J., & FitzGerald, P. (2000). Deictic and emotive communication in animated pedagogical agents. In J. Cassell, J. Sullivan, S. Prevost, & E. Churchill (Eds.), *Embodied conversational agents* (pp. 123–154). Cambridge, MA: MIT Press.

Litwinowicz, P. C. (1994). Animating images with drawings. *Computer graphics annual conferences series*, 413–420.

Magnenat-Thalmann, N., & Thalmann, D. (1987). The direction of synthetic actors in the film *Rendez-vous à Montréal. IEEE Computer graphics and applications*, December: 9–19.

Miller, M. J. (1999). Computers will be more human. *PC Magazine*, June 22.

Moravetz, C. (1989) A high level approach to animating secondary human movement. Master's thesis, School of Computing Science, Simon Fraser University: Bournaby, BC, Canada.

Nagao, K. N., & Takeuchi, A. (1994). Speech dialogue with facial displays: Multimodel human–computer conversation. In *ACL '94*, 102–109.

Negroponte, N. (1996). Affective computing. *Wired*, April.

Patterson, E. C., Litwinowicz, P. C., & Greene, N. (1991). Facial animation by spatial mapping. In N. Magnenat-Thalmann & D. Thalmann (Eds.), *Computer animation '91* (pp. 45–58). New York: Springer-Verlag.

PC Magazine (1999). Emotional computing. July.

Phillips, C. B., & Badler, N. I. (1991). Interactive behaviors for articulated figures. *Computer Graphics*, 25, 359–362.

Picard, R. (1997). *Affective computing*. Cambridge, MA: MIT Press.

Poggi, I., & Pelachaud, C. (2000). Performative facial expressions in animated faces. In J. Cassell, J. Sullivan, S. Prevost, & E. Churchill (Eds.), *Embodied conversational agents* (pp. 155–188). Cambridge, MA: MIT Press.

Poggi, I., Pelachaud, C., & de Rosis, F. (2000). Eye communication in a conversational 3d synthetic agent. Special Issue on Behavior Planning for Life-Like Characters and Avatars of AI Communications, 2000.

Reeves, B., & Nass, C. (1996). *The media equation*. Cambridge: Cambridge University Press.

Rickel, J., & Johnson, W. L. (2000). Task-oriented collaboration with embodied agents in virtual worlds. In J. Cassell, J. Sullivan, S. Prevost, & E. Churchill (Eds.), *Embodied conversational agents* (pp. 95–122). Cambridge, MA: MIT Press.

Rijpkema, H., & Girard, M. (1991). Computer animation of hands and grasping. *Computer Graphics*, 25, 339–348.

Scherer, K. R. (1986). Vocal affect expression: A review and a model for future research. *Psychological Bulletin*, 99, 143–165.

Takeuchi, A., & Nagao, K. (1993). Communicative facial displays as a new conversational modality. In *ACM/IFIP INTERCHI '93*, Amsterdam.

Thórisson, K. R. (1997). Layered modular action control for communicative humanoids. In *Computer Animation '97*, Geneva: IEEE Computer Society Press.

Webber, B., Badler, N., Di Eugenio, B., Geib, C., Levison, L., & Moore, M. (1995). Instructions, intentions and expectations. *Artificial Intelligence Journal, 73*, 253–269.

Zeltzer, D. (1991). Task-level graphical simulation: Abstraction, representation, and control. In N. I. Badler, B. A. Barsky, & D. Zeltzer (Eds.), *Making them move: Mechanics, control, and animation of articulated figures* (pp. 3–33). San Mateo, CA: Morgan-Kaufmann.

Zhao, J., & Badler, N. I. (1994). Inverse kinematics positioning under nonlinear programming for highly articulated figures. *ACM Transactions on Graphics, 13*, 313–336.

APPENDIX A. VIRTUAL INTERACTION

Two tables follow. Table 14.A.1 is a transition matrix for smiles within context. The contexts are determined by speaker–hearer roles in conversation and transitions between those roles. Embedded within each role and role transition are dyadic sequences for smiling and laughter. Table 14.A.2 is a set of five matrices. The first is the composite matrix for dyadic smile sequences, identical to that presented in earlier tables. The next four are the matrices for the same behavior and same sequences but in the context of switching between speaker and hearer roles, simultaneous speaking, within-turn speaking, and awkward turns.

Table 14.A.1. Transition Matrix Necessary to Detect Context Sensitivity of Behavioral Sequences: Example of Smile.

Floor	Smile	00A 00	00A 10	00A 01	00A 11	10A 00	10A 10	10A 01	10A 11	11A 00	11A 10	11A 01	11A 11	00B 00	00B 10	00B 01	00B 11	01B 00	01B 10	01B 01	01B 11	11B 00	11B 10	11B 01	11B 11
00A	010		wt																						
00A	10		wt																						
00A	01		wt																						
00A	11		wt																						
10A	00													x	x	x						x	x	x	x
10A	10													x	x	x						x	x	x	x
10A	01													x	x	x						x	x	x	x
10A	11													x	x	x						x	x	x	x
11A	00													x	x	x	x					x	x	x	x
11A	10													x	x	x	x					x	x	x	x
11A	01													x	x	x	x					x	x	x	x
11A	11													x	x	x	x					x	x	x	x
00B	00	x	x	x	x					x	x	x	x												
00B	10	x	x	x	x					x	x	x	x												
00B	01	x	x	x	x					x	x	x	x												
00B	11	x	x	x	x					x	x	x	x												
10B	00	x	x	x	x					x	x	x	x												
10B	10	x	x	x	x					x	x	x	x												
10B	01	x	x	x	x					x	x	x	x												
10B	11	x	x	x	x					x	x	x	x												
11B	00	x	x	x	x					x	x	x	x												
11B	10	x	x	x	x					x	x	x	x												
11B	01	x	x	x	x					x	x	x	x												
11B	11	x	x	x	x					x	x	x	x												

Note: A and B refer to agent 1 and to agent 2; floor: 0: pause, 1: talk, floor to agent A or B; smile: 1: smile or laughter, 0: no smile or laughter; wt: within-turn; "x" implies forbidden transition

Table 14.A.2. Transition Matrices for Smiles: Composite and by Context of Occurrence.

Smile

Composite (N = 170586)

	Neither	A Only	B Only	Both	Total
Neither	0.882951	0.002861	0.001799	0.000141	0.887752
A Only	0.002854	0.054371	0.000018	0.001070	0.058304
B Only	0.001883	0.000006	0.025320	0.000691	0.027900
Both	0.000059	0.001079	0.000761	0.024130	0.026029

Turn Switches (N = 4590)

	Neither	A Only	B Only	Both	Total
Neither	0.849455	0.006100	0.002614	0.000218	0.858387
A Only	0.003922	0.067756	0.000000	0.000871	0.072549
B Only	0.002832	0.000000	0.033987	0.001089	0.037908
Both	0.000000	0.001089	0.000871	0.029194	0.031154

Simultaneous Turn (N = 15562)

	Neither	A Only	B Only	Both	Total
Neither	0.839352	0.006297	0.003920	0.000386	0.849955
A Only	0.003084	0.069207	0.000000	0.002121	0.074412
B Only	0.002185	0.000064	0.039070	0.001349	0.042668
Both	0.000000	0.001542	0.001285	0.030138	0.032965

Within Turn (N = 150252)

	Neither	A Only	B Only	Both	Total
Neither	0.888581	0.002396	0.001551	0.000113	0.892641
A Only	0.002802	0.052385	0.000020	0.000965	0.056172
B Only	0.001824	0.000000	0.023614	0.000612	0.026050
Both	0.000067	0.001032	0.000705	0.023334	0.025138

Awkward Turn (N = 182)

	Neither	A Only	B Only	Both	Total
Neither	0.807692	0.010989	0.005495	0.000000	0.824176
A Only	0.000000	0.087912	0.000000	0.000000	0.087912
B Only	0.000000	0.000000	0.043956	0.000000	0.043956
Both	0.000000	0.000000	0.000000	0.043956	0.043956

Author Index

Aaron, J. 235
Achorn, B. 333
Acitelli, L. K. 137, 140, 238
Ackerman, C. 271
Addis, M. E. 21, 286
Adelman, M. B. 260, 265–266
Agnew, C. R. 239
Ahadi, S. 40
Ahrens, K. 72
Ainsworth, M. D. S. 40–41
Akiyama, H. 187, 189
Alansky, J. A. 42
Albersheim, L. 8, 17
Albrecht, S. L. 49, 123, 276
Alden, L. 21
Aldous, J. 139, 270
Allan, G. 269–271, 274
Allbeck, J. 334
Altemeyer, B. 85
Altman, I. 69, 209, 212, 215
Amato, P. R. 59, 63, 66, 116, 239
Ambady, N. 215, 218
Anderson, E. R. 262
Anderson, K. E. 43
Anderson, S. M. 7, 15
Andre, E. 334
Antill, J. 271
Antonucci, T. 187, 189–190, 238
Aquilino, W. S. 139–140
Arbuckle, J. 74

Argyle, M. 115
Arias, I. 135, 240
Aron, A. 19, 278, 314
Aron, E. N. 19, 278
Arriaga, X. B. 156, 158–161, 163–165, 168, 174
Asendorpf, J. B. 2, 46
Ashmore, R. D. 7
Atchley, R. C. 262
Attridge, M. 274
Averill. J. R. 13
Avery, A. W. 257–258
Axelson, L. J. 121
Axinn, W. G. 139

Babcock, J. C. 18, 288
Badalamenti, A. F. 215
Badler, N. 331, 333–334
Bagarozzi, D. 122
Bahr, H. M. 156–157
Bahr, K. S. 156–157
Bakeman, R. 213, 216
Baldes, S. 334
Baldwin, M. W. xiii, 5, 7–8, 15, 17
Ball, F. 143
Baltes, P. B. 52
Banaji, M. R. 11, 23
Bandler, R. 137
Bandura, A. 68
Bank, L. 44–45

Bargh, J. A. 23
Barkley, R. A. 39
Barling, J. 135, 240
Barnes, M. K. 210
Barnett, P. A. 15
Barr, P. K. 108
Bar-Tal, D. 157, 166, 178
Bartholomew, K. 5, 9, 138, 146, 169–170
Bassin, E. 265–266
Bates, J. E. 43
Baucom, D. H. 19–21, 286–287
Baum, A. 15
Baumeister, R. F. 184
Baxter, L. A. 264
Bayer, J. P. 236
Beach, S. R. 232, 234–235, 239–240
Becket, T. 333
Bedrosian, R. 62
Beebe, B. 209
Bégin, J. 238, 271
Behrens, B. C. 20, 59, 64
Beier, E. G. 119
Bell, R. Q. 37
Bell, R. R. 273
Belsky, J. 18, 63, 234–235, 237, 243–244, 246–247
Bem, D. J. 45–46
Bengston, V. 59, 184
Benoit, P. J. 108–109
Benoit, W. J. 108–109
Benson, P. R. 163
Bera, S. 9
Berger, C. R. 209, 260, 263, 266
Berkman, L. F. 183, 185–186, 189
Bernieri, F. J. 207
Berscheid, E. xiii–xiv, 6, 23, 211, 257, 274–275, 277–278, 307
Bickmore, J. 334–235
Billinghurst, M. 335
Bilsker, D. 171
Bindiganavale, R. 334
Birchler, G. R. 236

Black, D. 72
Blakeley-Smith 139
Blehar, M. C. 40–41
Block, J. 194
Blumberg, S. 158, 287
Bodenhausen, G. 145
Bohannan, P. 274
Boles, A. J. 243
Bolger, N. 107–108
Bond, R. 211, 214, 219–220
Bonnell, D. 131, 232, 241
Book, R. 72
Booth, A. 59, 63, 66, 123, 244
Bott, E. 269–270
Bouchard, T. J. Jr. 84–85, 87, 94–95
Bower, G. H. 14
Bowlby, J. 5, 7, 10, 23–24, 52, 63, 138, 188
Bozicas, G. 62
Bradac, J. J. 209
Bradburn, N. 194–195
Bradbury, T. N. 17, 20, 25, 49–50, 58, 65, 68, 105, 129–130, 214, 228–229, 231, 233–236, 238, 240–241, 243–244, 246–247, 285
Bradshaw, D. 5
Braiker, H. 116–117
Brandwein, R. 66
Brazelton, T. B. 213
Brengelmann, J. C. 287
Brennan, K. 146
Bretherton, I. 7
Broderick, J. E. 239
Broetzmann, S. 215
Brooks, R. A. 333
Brooks-Gunn, J. 11
Brown, B. G. 209
Brown, C. 66
Brown, D. 72
Brown, J. D. 9
Brown, J. V. 213
Bruce, M. L. 183, 185, 189
Bryant, C. M. 2, 68, 269, 271, 273

Author Index

Bryer, K. B. 211
Buehlman, K. T. 242
Buhrmester, D. 60
Bullough, V. L. 312, 317
Bulter, R. 194
Burchinal, M. 243–244
Burge, D. 17
Burger, E. 272
Burgess, R. L. 267
Burgoon, J. K. 208, 212–213, 339
Burke, P. 58
Burns, A. 130, 273
Bush, D. M. 184
Bush, E. G. 271
Buss, D. M. 51, 84, 86, 90, 118
Buss, W. C. 234, 240
Buttenweiser, P. 143

Cacioppo, J. T. 211, 336
Callan, V. J. 131, 232, 241
Callaway, C. 334
Campbell, B. 274–275
Campbell, S. B. 213
Campbell, L. 334–335
Cancian, F. M. 173
Cannon, K. L. 120
Capaldi, D. 65
Cappella, J. N. 207, 209, 213, 216, 256, 329, 336, 339, 341–342, 345
Cappellanus, A. 315
Cariffe, G. 214
Carlston, D. E. 9, 11
Carnelley, K. B. 186
Carrere, S. 124, 163, 214
Carroll, D. 263
Carstensen, L. L. 52, 124, 186–187, 272
Carver, C. S. 202
Cascardi, M. 58–59
Caspi, A. 45–46, 84, 86
Cassell, J. 333–335
Cassidy, J. 7, 18, 63
Cate, R. M. 117–118, 142, 267

Catron, L. S. 185, 187–188, 198
Caughlin, J. P. 114, 245
Chadiha, L. A. 242
Chang, K. 335
Chartrand, E. 238, 271
Chatters, L. M. 272
Chen, S. 7
Chesney, M. A. 186
Chiriboga 104, 184–185, 187–188, 190, 193–194, 198
Chodorow, N. 171
Choo, P. 314
Chopra-Khullar, S. 333
Chovil, N. 334
Christensen, A. 18–20, 58, 113, 132, 142–143, 145, 232, 246, 256, 286–288, 302–303
Chu, G. C. 313
Clark, M. S. 167
Clark, S. 65
Cleek, M. 273
Clemens, A. W. 121
Clements, M. 133, 136, 140–141, 144, 163, 240
Clingempeel, W. G. 262
Clore, G. L. 13
Cloven, D. H. 112
Coan, J. 124, 163, 214
Cobb, L. 214, 217
Cohan, C. L. 58, 65, 238
Cohen, R. 185
Cohen, S. 186, 190
Cohn, D. A. 18
Cohn, J. F. 213
Coie, J. D. 36, 43
Cole, S. W. 15
Coleman, D. 200
Collard, J. 273
Collins, N. L. 5, 7, 146
Collins, W. A. xiv
Conger, R. D. 2, 57, 63–69, 269, 271, 273
Conley, J. J. 50, 233, 240

Conry, R. F. 21
Conte, H. 157
Cook, K. 214
Cooper, S. 190
Corbin, S. D. 211
Cordova, J. V. 19, 302
Cortese, A. 314
Cosmides, L. 184
Cotton, S. 271–272
Courtright, J. A. 122
Cowan, C. P. 18, 143, 243–244
Cowan, P. A. 18, 143, 243–244
Cox, L. 156, 158–161, 163–165, 168, 174
Cox, M. J. 243–244
Coysh, W. S. 243
Craddock, A. E. 240
Crick, N. R. 44
Crnic, K. 18
Crocker, J. 10–12
Crohan, S. E. 107, 120, 243
Cross, S. 6
Crowell, J. 8, 17
Crown, C. L. 209, 211, 214
Cumming, E. 183
Cunningham, J. 271
Curtis-Boles, H. 243
Cutrona, C. E. 238

Dabbs, J. M. Jr. 214
Daiuto, A. D. 21, 286–287
Darnton, R. 311
Davila, J. 17
Davis, D. 329
Davis, K. E. 146, 264–265
Day, H. D. 236
Defoe, D. 310
De Fries, J. C. 84
Degler, C. N. 317
DeGraf, B. 332
DeLamater, J. 318
DeLongis, A. 107–108
DelVecchio, W. F. 36

D'Emilio, J. 312, 317–318
de Rosis, F. 334
Deutsch, F. M. 11
DeWolff, M. S. 41
Dickson-Markman, F. 134, 146
Diener, E. 40
Di Eugenio, B. 333
Dill, D. 172–173
Dillman, L. 208, 212–213, 339
Dimitrova, D. 275
Dishion, T. J. 44–45
Dodge, K. A. 36, 43–44
Doherty, R. W. 314
Doi, L. T. 313
Dostal, C. 62, 66, 70
Douvan, E. 57, 137, 140, 271, 273
Douville, B. 333
Downey, G. xiii
Downing, H. 270
Doyle, W. J. 186, 190
Drigotas, S. M. 156, 158–161, 163–165, 168, 174, 267
Driscoll, R. 264–266,
Duck, S. W. 210, 268
Duncan, S. D. Jr. 342
Dungy, C. 210
Dunn, J. 60
Durkheim, E. 183
Dutton, D. G. 278
Dyck, D. G. 189

Easterbrooks, M. A. 17
Eaves, L. J. 84
Eddy, J. 233
Eder, D. 262
Edwards, J. 63
Edwards, R. 112
Egeland, B. 17
Eggert, L. L. 258, 262, 264–268
Ekman, P. 336
Elder, G. H. Jr. 45–46, 57, 64–67
Eldridge, K. 19, 302
Ellis, M. J. 214

Author Index

Ellsworth, P. C. 13
Emery, R. E. 235
Engl, J. 240
Enns, V. 8
Epstein, N. 19, 287
Epstein, S. 23
Erikson, J. 17
Eskew, R. W. 120, 123
Evans, C. 262
Evans, W. 100
Eysenck, H. J. 84

Fals-Stewart, W. 236
Faraone, S. V. 214
Feeney, J. 58, 68, 103–104, 131–132, 134, 137, 139, 141, 144, 146, 150, 169, 214, 232, 241
Fehr, B. 5, 8, 17, 316–317
Fehsenfeld, D. A. 118
Feingold, L. M. 84
Feldman Barrett, L. 2, 6, 24
Feldman, R. 213
Feldman, S. 59, 70
Feldstein, S. 209, 211, 214, 216, 219–220, 343
Felmlee, D. H. 68, 150, 255, 264–268
Feng, D. 59
Ferguson, L. W. 143
Field, D. 134
Field, T. 210, 213–214
Fincham, F. D. 12, 17, 214, 228, 232, 234–235, 240
Fisher, E. F. 308
Fisher, H. 83
Fisher, L. 59, 70
Fiske, D. W. 342
Fiske, M. 184–185, 193–194, 198
Fiske, S. T. 6, 8–13, 24
Fitness, J. 9, 20, 316–317
Fitzgerald, N. 267
FitzGerald, P. 334
Fitzpatrick, M. A. 115, 141, 143

Fleeson, J. xii, xiv
Fleming, A. S. 11, 120, 243
Fletcher, G. J. O. 5, 8, 9, 12, 316–317
Floyd, F. J. 287
Follette, W. C. 286–287
Fong, G. T. 11, 17
Ford, C. 21
Forgas, J. P. 14
Foster, C. A. 239
Foster, T. 214
Fowers, B. J. 235–236
Fox, E. 66
Fracasso, M. P. 213
Frease-McMahan, L. 172–173
Fredrickson, B. 14
Freedman, E. 312, 317–318
Friesen, W. V. 336
Frost, P. 214
Frye, N. 59
Fuhrman, R. W. 20
Fuller, T. L. 17
Fung, H. 187
Furman, W. 60
Futoran, G. C. 215

Gable, S. L. 184
Gaelick, L. 145
Gagnon, J. H. 263
Gardner, H. 327
Garrett, E. 243
Garton, L. 275
Gay, P. 315, 317
Ge, X. 65–67
Gecas, V. 58
Geib, C. 333
Gerard, H. B. 207
Giarusso, R. 59
Gilligan, C. 171
Gillis, J. R. 317
Girard, M. 331
Glenn, N. 69
Goldberg, W. A. 17

Goldscheider, C. 66
Goldscheider, F. 66
Goldsmith, H. H. 42
Goldstein, S. 213–214
Goleman, D. 327
Goode, W. J. 313
Gordon, L. 65
Gordon, M. 270
Gotlib, I. H. 15, 107, 235, 237
Gottman, J. M. 13, 20, 57, 60, 64, 68, 113, 124, 131, 143, 149, 158, 163, 209, 213–218, 220–221, 240, 242
Gowen, L. 59, 70
Greenbaum, C. W. 213
Greenberg, D. F. 38
Greenberg, E. 62
Greenberg, J. R. 24
Greenberg, L. S. 19, 21, 25
Greene, N. 332
Greenwald, A. G. 23
Greenwald, P. 213–214
Griffin, D. 9, 13
Grimm, C. 332
Grinder, J. 137
Gross, J. 187
Grossmann K. 8, 213
Grossmann, K. E. 8, 213
Guenter, B. 332
Guetzkow, H. 115
Gulia, M. 275
Guralnik, J. 185
Gurung, R. A. R. 186
Guthertz, M. 213–214
Gwaltney, J. M. 186, 190

Hackel, L. S. 120, 243
Hahlweg, K. 20–21, 240, 286–287
Halberstadt, J. B. 14, 24
Halford, G. 57
Halford, W. K. 20, 59, 64
Hall, E. T. 211
Hall, M. 270

Hamilton, C. E. 17
Hamilton, D. 13
Hammen, C. 17
Hammersala, J. F. 172–173
Hanson, E. 109
Hanson, L. R. 13
Harold, G. T. 57, 234–235
Harper, L. V. 37
Hartup, W. W. 45
Harwitz, R. I. 186
Hatchett, S. 57, 271–273
Hatfield, E. 211, 256, 307, 312, 314, 317, 336
Haven, C. 189
Havighurst, R. J. 183
Hayes, D. P. 214, 217
Hayes, S. C. 18
Haythornthwaite, C. 275
Hazan, C. 5, 9, 63, 132, 138, 146–147, 170
Healy, B. 213–214
Healy, D. 210
Heath, A. C. 84
Heaton, T. B. 49, 123, 276
Heavey, C. L. 20, 113, 143, 145, 232, 286, 302–303
Heesink, J. A. M. 244
Heider, F. 265
Heiss, J. 172
Heller, C. 138
Heller, K. 132
Heming, G. 243
Henderson, M. 115
Hendrick, C. 307
Hendrick, S. S. 307
Henry, W. E. 183
Herbener, E. S. 84, 86
Hesse, B. 212, 215
Hesse, E. 18
Hetherington, E. M. 262
Heyman, R. E. 163, 233, 286
Hickey, T. 183–184
Hiebert, P. J. 211

Author Index

Higgins, E. T. 16
Hill, C. T. 118, 148–149, 240
Hinde, R. 103
Hinkley, K. 7, 15
Hodges, S. D. 7
Hofer, M. A. 210
Hoff, N. 108, 111–112
Hoffman, J. 213
Hoffman, J. A. 287
Hogan, D. P. 190
Holmberg, D. 242
Holmes, J. G. 5, 9, 13, 15, 19
Holtgraves, T. 329
Holtzworth-Munroe, A. 19, 286–287
Honeycutt, J. M. 112
Hopkins, J. 213
Hornyak, L. M. 163
Horowitz, L.M. 5, 169
House, J. S. 57, 121, 123, 190
Houts, R. M. 58, 68, 135–136, 245
Hsieh, K. H. 234–235, 237, 246
Hsu, F. L. K. 313
Hubbard, M. 8
Huck, S. 72
Hui, C. H. 313
Hunter, A. G. 272
Hurtig, R. R. 214
Huston, T. 58, 68, 119, 121, 129, 134–136, 141–143, 244–245, 262, 264, 267, 272

Ickes, W. 211
Ifert, D. 124
Innes-Ker, A. H. 14, 24
Irwin, G. 186
Isabella, R. A. 63, 213
Iso-Ahola, S. E. 200
Iverson, A. 278

Jack, D. C. 156, 171–173
Jackson, J. S. 190, 272
Jackson, S. 108–109

Jacobs, S. 108–109
Jacobson, N. S. 18–21, 231, 286–288, 296, 302–303
Jaffe, J. 209, 211, 214, 216, 343
James, P. L. 21
Jankowiak, W. R. 308
Janoff-Bulman, R. 11, 13, 22
Jardine, R. 84
Jensen, A. R. 84
Jerrome, D. 187
John, O. P. 5, 13
Johnson, K. L. 103, 110–114, 117–118
Johnson, M. P. 69, 165, 262, 264, 266–268, 273–274
Johnson, S. M. 19, 21, 25
Johnson, W. B. 143
Johnson, W. L. 334
Jones, E. E. 207
Ju, Y. 313
Julien, D. 141, 232, 238, 271
Jurich, J. 235, 240

Kafka, J. S. 262
Kağitçibaşi, C. 312
Kahn, R. L. 202
Kalra, P. 332
Kanouse, D. E. 13
Kaplan, G. A. 185
Kaplan, K. 7, 18, 63
Karlsson, J. 39
Karney, B. R. 17, 20, 25, 49–50, 58, 65, 68, 129–130, 231, 233–235, 241, 243–244, 246, 285
Katz, L. F. 60, 242
Keelan, J. P. R. 8
Keith, B. 59, 239
Keith, V. 52
Kellermann, K. 215
Kelley, H. H. xiv, 113, 116–117, 158, 164, 167
Kellogg, S. 317
Kelly, A. 57

Kelly, C. 142
Kelly, E. L. 50, 233, 240
Kelly, J. R. 215
Kelly, S. 287
Kerckhoff, A. C. 262
Kessler, R. C. 38, 107–108, 186
Kiecolt-Glaser, J. K. 144, 190
Kiefer, D. M. 108
Kiesler, S. 276
Kim, H. J. 268
Kim, T. 286–287
Kimmerly, N. L. 42
Kininmonth, L. 8
Kirchler, E. 134
Kirkpatrick, L. A. 9, 138, 146–147, 170
Kirson, D. 316
Kitao, K. 215
Kitayama, S. 313
Kitson, G. C. 121, 273
Kitzmann, K. M. 235
Klein Ikkink, K. 187–188
Klein, R. 258
Klesen, M. 334
Klohnen, E. C. 9
Kluwer, E. S. 244
Knee, C. R. 23
Knoth, R. 214
Knox, D. 263
Knudsen, L. 185
Ko, H. 331
Kohlhepp, K. A. 120, 123
Koh-Rangarajoo, E. 8
Kojetin, B. A. 84
Kon, I. 312
Kraft-Hanak, S. 144
Krain, R. 267
Kramer, L. 60
Krantz, S. 14
Krause, N. 52
Kraut, R. 276
Kressin, N. R. 51
Krokoff, L. J. 131, 143, 158, 214

Kunce, L. J. 169–170
Kunda, Z. 8–9, 11, 16–17
Kupersmidt, J. B. 36, 43
Kurdek, L. A. 50–51, 108, 110, 129–130, 133, 147, 234–235, 241, 244, 246

Landis, K. 57, 190
Lang, F. R. 52
Lang, M. 244
Lang, R. F. 215
Langhinrichsen-Rohling, J. 62, 66, 70
Larsen, A. S. 235
Larsen, R. J. 218
Larson, C. 213
Laumann, E. O. 263
Laurenceau, J. P. 2
Lavee, Y. 236–237
Lawrence, E. 233, 236
Layne, C. 232
Leary, M. R. 184
Lee, Y. 331–332
Lemon, B. W. 184
Leonard, K. E. 58, 68, 134–135
Leo-Summers, L. 186
Lepper, M. R. 8
Lerner, H. G. 156, 171
Leslie, L. A. 262, 264, 266–267
Lester, B. M. 213
Lester, G. W. 20
Lester, J. 334
Léveillé, S. 238
Levenson, R. W. 13, 124, 143, 149, 163, 211, 214, 220, 336
Levine, R. V. 211
Levinger, G. 165, 167, 258, 273–275
Levison, L. 333
Levitskaya, A. 314
Lewinsohn, P. M. 235
Lewis, R. A. 147, 264–265
Leyendecker, B. 213
Liang, J. 52

Author Index

Lim, T. S. 215
Lin, K. 65
Lin, N. 188–189
Lindahl, K. 133, 136, 140–141, 163, 232, 240
Lindsey, B. 100
Lindsey, S. 24
Linville, P. W. 9, 11
Lipetz, M. E. 264
Lipkus, I. 116, 162
Litwinowicz, P. C. 332
Lloyd, S. A. 109, 117
Lomax, A. 211
Long, E. C. J. 117–118
Longstreth, M. 117
Lopes, J. 277
Lorenz, F. 57, 64–67
Lorenz, K. 91
Lowenthal, M. F. 189
Lucchetti, A. E. 211
Lucente, S. 236
Lucy, L. 72
Lundmark, V. 276
Luetkenhaus, P. 213, 225
Lykken, D. T. 2–3, 51, 84–85, 87, 90, 92, 94–95, 97, 100
Lytton, H. 37, 43

Ma, H. K. 157
MacCorquodale, P. 318
MacDermid, S. M. 121
Mace V. 309
Mace, D. 309
Magnenat-Thalmann, N. 331–332
Magnusson, D. 37
Main, M. 7–8, 18, 23, 63
Malone, J. 135
Malvar, H. 332
Mangili, A. 332
Manusov, V. 210
Marcia, J. 171
Marcussen, K. 57
Margolin, G. 19–20, 231, 286, 296

Markman, H. J. 20–21, 57, 104, 113, 133, 136, 140–141, 144, 146, 156, 158, 160–161, 163–165, 167–168, 174–175, 214, 216, 232, 238, 240–241, 243, 271, 287
Markus, H. R. 7–8, 16, 313
Marsiglio, W. 258, 266, 274
Martin, H. J. 329
Martin, J. A. 213
Martin, N. G. 84
Martin, T. K. 276
Martire, L. M. 189
Masheter, C. 122
Matias, R. 213
Matthews, L. 63–64, 68–69
Mayer, K. U. 52
Mayes, L. C. 213
McAninch, J. 210
McAvay, G. 183, 185
McCrae, R. R. 190, 195
McCubbin, H. I. 237
McCusker, C. 313
McGonagle, K. A. 107
McGrath, J. E. 215
McGue, M. 84–85, 87, 92, 94–95
McGuire, C. V. 11
McGuire, W. J. 11
McHale, S. M. 121, 244, 272
McKenna, J. J. 210
McMillan, D. 8
Mead, G. H. 197
Mead, M. 100
Melby, J. N. 72
Meltzer, L. 217
Mero, R. P. 121, 123
Merrick, S. 8, 17
Metzger, N. J. 69
Michael, R. T. 263
Michaels, S. 263
Micon, L. 194
Miell, D. 5
Mikulincer, M. 146, 170
Milardo, R. M. 258, 261, 266–275

Milet, T. H. 237
Mill, J. S. 99–100
Millar, F. E. 122
Miller, L. C. 11
Miller, M. J. 326
Mills, J. 167
Mintz, S. 317
Mitchell, S. A. 24
Mittlemark, M. B. 189
Moffitt, T. E. 45
Montemayor, R. 109
Montgomery, J. J. 262
Montgomery, R. J. V. 189
Moore, M. 333
Moravetz, C. 332
Morrow, C. 214
Moscovici, S. 230
Mosko, S. 210
Moylan, S. J. 14
Mukhopadhyay, T. 276
Murphy, J. V. 39
Murray, J. 214
Murray, S. L. 5, 9, 13, 15, 19
Murstein, B. I. 84, 313, 315
Muser, K. T. 21
Mutchler, L. 72
Myers, D. G. 183

Nachshon, O. 146, 170
Nagao, K. 334
Napier, A. Y. 20
Nass, C. 326
National Center for Health Statistics 244
Nay, W. 62
Needham, G. B. 310
Negroponte, N. 325
Nelson, G. 19
Nelson, P. A. 318
Neugarten, B. L. 186
Newcomb, T. M. 269
Newman, D. L. 45
Newsom, J. T. 189

Newton, T. L. 144
Niedenthal, P. M. 14, 24
Noller, P. 58, 68, 103–104, 131–132, 134, 137, 139, 141, 144–146, 150, 157, 214, 232, 241
Norton, R. 132
Notarius, C. 113, 158, 163, 214, 216

O'Connor, C. 316
Ogilvie, D. M. 7
O'Leary, D. 58–59
O'Leary, K. D. 135, 141, 143–144, 240
Olson, D. H. 149, 235–237, 262
Omoto, A. M. 211
O'Neil, R. 62
Orbuch, T. L. 121, 123, 139, 242, 255, 272, 274
Ortega, R. M. 242
Osborne, L. N. 234–235
Oxman, T. E. 189
Ozer, D. J. 84, 86

Pagel, M. 287
Paley, B. 243–244
Palmer, M. 334
Palmer, M. T. 336
Pam, A. 157
Paris, M. 19
Parke, R. 58, 62
Parker, G. 63, 70
Parker, J. G. 214
Parks, M. R. 258, 260, 262–268
Pasch, L. A. 238, 240, 247
Patterson, E. C. 332
Patterson, G. R. 37, 44–45, 286
Patterson, M. 276
Payne, C. C. 243–244
Pearlin, L. I. 186
Pearson, J. L. 18
Pearson, T. A. 273
Peek, M. K. 188
Peery, J. C. 211, 214

Author Index

Pelachaud, C. 256, 333–335
Pennebaker, J. W. 18
Pensky, E. 244
Peplau, L. A. 118, 148–149, 240
Perkowitz, W. T. 329
Peterson, J. A. 184
Petty, R. E. 23
Phelps, J. L. 18
Phillips, C. B. 331
Phillips, G. M. 69
Phillips, R. 317
Picard, R. 326, 346
Pierce, G. 131, 149
Pietromonaco, P. R. 2, 6, 24
Pillemer, K. 121, 135
Pirsig, R. 328
Pistole, C. 170
Planalp, S. 5, 7, 11, 13
Plomin, R. 84
Plutchik, R. 157
Poggi, I. 334–335
Pollard, S. 39
Potapova, E. 314
Prather, J. E. 262
Pratto, F. 13
Prentice, D. A. 11
Prevost, S. 333
Prince, S. E. 19, 302
Procidano, M. E. 132, 270

Rabin, B. S. 186, 190
Raffaelli, M. 109
Rands, M. 274
Rankin, L. A. 287
Rapson, R. L. 211, 256, 307, 312, 314, 317, 320, 336
Read, S. J. 5, 7, 11, 146
Reber, E. 11, 17
Reeves, B. 326
Regan, P. C. 307
Reis, H. T. xiii–xiv, 6, 23, 184, 257
Repinski, D. 72
Resick, P. A. 108

Revenstorf, D. 286–287
Reznick, I. 7, 207
Rholes, W. S. 146
Rickel, J. 334
Ridley, C. A. 257–258
Rijpkema, H. 331
Rist, T. 334
Rivers, M. 11, 13
Roberts, B. W. 36
Roberts, L. 58, 68, 134–135
Roberts, M. K. 84
Roberts, N. 150
Rodriguez, G. 314
Rogers, L. E. 122
Rogers, S. J. 72, 116
Rogge, R. D. 105, 233, 235–236, 240
Rogler, L. 270
Rollins, B. C. 120
Roloff, M. E. 103, 110–114, 117–118, 124
Romney, D. M. 43
Rosanowski, J. 9
Roscoe, J. 184
Rosenbaum, A. 135, 240
Rosenberg, M. 186
Rosenblatt, P. C. 313
Rosenthal, R. 207, 215, 218
Ross, J. 72
Ross, L. 8
Ross, M. 8
Ross, R. R. 271
Rothbard, J. C. 8, 17
Rothbart, M. 10–12, 43
Rovine, M. 243
Rowe, J. W. 202
Roy, K. 63, 70
Roy, V. 216
Rozendal, F. 63
Ruan, F. F. 309, 312
Rubin, Z. 118, 171,
Ruble, D. N. 11, 120–121, 243
Ruby, N. L. 108
Rueter, M. 64–65, 67, 72

Rusbult, C. E. 69, 116, 156, 158–161, 163–165, 168, 174, 239, 266–267
Ruscio, J. 51
Rushe, R. 214
Russell, J. 316–317
Ruzzene, M. 145
Ryan, R. M. 184
Ryder, R. G. 262

Safran, J.D. 5, 7
Sagrestano, L. M. 113
Salaff, J. 275
Salovey, P. 5
Sameroff, A. J. 37
Sanders, M. R. 20, 59, 64
Sanitioso, R. 11, 17
Sarason, B. 131, 149, 186
Sarason, I. 131, 149, 186
Satir, V. 137
Sawyer, J. 115
Sayers, S. L. 20
Scanzoni, J. 258, 266, 274–275
Schaeffer, N. C. 110
Schafer, J. 236
Schafer, W. D. 42
Schaninger, C. M. 234, 240
Scharfe, E. 9, 138, 146
Scherer, K. R. 336
Scherlis, W. 276
Schiedel, D. 171
Schilling, E. A. 107–108
Schindler, L. 287
Schmaling, K. B. 286–287
Schneider, K. 214
Schooler, T. Y. 24
Schuler, W. 334
Schulz, R. 189
Schwartz, J. C. 316
Schwarz, N. 13
Scott, C. K. 20
Searle, M. S. 183–184
Seeley, J. R. 235

Seeman, T. E. 183, 185
Segal, N. 87, 94
Seligman, M. 209
Shanahan, M. 65
Shaver, P. R. 5, 8, 17, 63, 132, 138, 146, 169–170, 316
Shebilski, L. J. 245
Sheldon, K. M. 184
Sher, T. G. 20
Shoham, V. 21, 286–287
Sholmerich, A. 213
Short, R. 189
Shorter, E. 310
Sillars, A. L. 123
Silva, P. A. 45
Silvern, L. 144
Silvestri, S. 62
Simenauer, J. 263
Simon, R. 57
Simon, R. W. 262
Simons, R. 64–67
Simpson, J. A. 146, 170
Singer, J. L. 5
Skinner, B. F. 288
Skinner, M. L. 45
Skoner, D. P. 186, 190
Slater, P. E. 267–268
Sloane, D. 163
Slovik, L. F. 116, 162
Smith, C. A. 13
Smith, D. A. 141, 143–144
Smith, E. R. 7–8, 22
Smith, S. E. 245
Snoek, J. D. 258
Snyder, M. 211
Spanier, G. B. 147, 243, 273–274
Speigel, D. K. 108
Spencer, L. J. 190
Spiro III, A. 51
Spitze, G. 121
Sprague, R. L. 211
Sprecher, S. 68, 255, 264–266, 268, 278, 307, 314

Author Index

Srole, L. 183
Sroufe, L. A. xii, xiv, 8, 17, 36
Stack, C. B. 272
Stan, C. M. 264–268
Stangor, C. 8, 11, 120, 243
Stanley, S. M. 104, 156, 158–161, 164–165, 167–168, 174–175, 287
Staudinger, U. M. 52
Stavros, T. 72
Steedman, M. 333
Stein, C. H. 271
Steinmetz, S. K. 116, 120, 123
Stern, D. N. 5, 7, 211, 214
Stern, L. A. 208, 212–213, 339
Sternberg, D. P. 119
Sternberg, R. J. 5
Stevens, J. G. 146
Stickle, T. R. 286–287
Stiff, J. B. 268
Stone, L. 310, 317, 320
Stone, M. 333
Stoolmiller, M. 45
Storaasli, R. D. 241, 243
Strauss, A. 115
Strauss, M. A. 135, 270
Stuart, R. B. 20, 286
Suitor, J. J. 120–121, 135
Sullaway, M. 132
Surra, C. A. 117, 258, 261, 267, 275
Sussman, M. B. 121, 273
Sutherland, L. 242
Swann, W. B. Jr. 8, 9
Swanson, C. 124, 163, 214
Sweet, J. J. 108
Swenson, C. H. 120, 123
Szczypula, J. 276

Takeuchi, A. 334
Tallman, I. 58
Tannahill, R. 309, 312, 315–316
Tannen, D. 144
Taylor, D. 69
Taylor, L. 63, 70

Taylor, R. J. 272
Taylor, S. E. 7–10, 24
Tellegen, A. 84–85, 87, 89–92, 95
Terman, L. M. 143
Terzopoulos, D. 331–332
Thagard, P. 11
Thalmann, D. 331–332
Thibaut, J. W. 158, 164, 167
Thoits, P. A. 186, 189
Thomas, G. 5
Thompson, D. A. 190
Thompson, K. 314
Thompson, L. 273–274
Thompson, R. A. 42
Thórisson, K. R. 334
Thornes, B. 273
Thornton, A. 66, 139
Thurmaier, F. 240
Tice, D. M. 11
Timmer, S. G. 272–273
Tissot, S. A. D. 309
Todorov, T. 157
Tomkins, S. S. 5
Tooby, J. 184
Towns, S. 334
Trapp, R. 108, 111–112
Treboux, D. 8, 17
Triandis, H. C. 313
Tronick, E. Z. 213
Tucker, J. S. 51
Tudor, M. 19
Tyree, A. 135
Tyson, R. 214

Udry, J. R. 270
Umberson, D. 57, 190
Unger, J. B. 183, 185

Vaillant, C. O. 123
Vaillant, G. E. 123
van Aken, M. A. G. 46
van den Boom, D. C. 41–43
Van De Vliert, E. 244

van IJzendoorn, M. H. 41
Van Lange, P. A. M. 156, 158–161, 163–165, 168, 174
Van Lear, C. A. 219
van Mulken, S. 334
van Tilburg, T. 187–188
Vangelisti, A. L. 114, 119, 129, 134–135, 141–143, 211, 272
Vanzetti, N. A. 163
Verette, J. 116, 162
Veroff, J. 57, 137, 140, 242, 271–273
Vilhjalmsson, L. 334–335
Vinsel, A. 209
Vitaliano, P. P. 189
Vivian, D. 141, 143–144
Voerman, J. 334
von Salisch, M. 60
Vuchinich, S. 108–109, 111, 115

Wade, M. G. 214
Walczynski, P. 142
Waldron, M. 235
Wall, S. 40–41
Waller, N. G. 84–85
Walster, E. 83
Walster, G. W. 83
Ward, C. 144, 214
Ward, M. 271
Ward, R. A. 121
Warner, R. M. 104–105, 209–210, 213–214, 217–218
Waters, E. 8, 17, 40–41
Waters, K. 331–332
Webber, B. 333
Webster, P. S. 121, 123
Wegener, D. T. 23
Weinfield, N. S. 17
Weishaus, S. 134
Weiss, R. L. 145, 163, 233, 286
Weiss, R. S. 274
Welkowitz, J. 211, 214, 219–220
Wellman, B. 275

Wells, J. 63
Wenger, G. C. 187
Westman, J. 100
Weston, D. 8
Wheeler 256
Whiffen, V. E. 235, 237
Whitbeck, L. 64, 66–67
White, G. L. 84
White, J. 214
White, L. K. 123, 244
Whitney, G. A. 116, 162
Whitton, S. 104, 174–175
Whyte, K. 149
Wickrama, K. A. S. 57, 64, 68–69
Widenmann, S. 264
Wieselquist, J. 239
Wilder, B. 214
Willetts, M. C. 255
Williams, J. M. G. 210
Williams, K. M. 118
Williams, L. 235, 240
Williams, R. B. 186
Wilpers, S. 46
Wilson, D. P. 143
Wilson, K. 263
Wilson, T. D. 7, 24
Winks, R. 318
Wippman, J. 8
Witcher, B. 156, 158–161, 163–165, 168, 174
Witteman, H. 115
Wolf, G. 217
Wood, D. 332
Wortman, C. B. 186
Wright, W. 87
Wu, S. 316
Wurf, E. 7
Wyer, R. 145
Wyer, R. S. Jr. 20

Yan, H. 334–335
Yirmiya, N. 213

Zagacki, K. S. 112
Zanna, M. 13
Zelkowitz, P. 237
Zeltzer, D. 333
Zhao, L. 331, 334
Zietlow, P. H. 123
Zimmer, Z. 183–184
Zlochower, A. J. 213

Subject Index

activity theory, 183
Adult Attachment Interview, 18, 41
aggression, 37–38, 53
  aggression–counteraggression, 44
  aggressive-rejected children, 44
  childhood aggressiveness, 44–45
  and conflict, 37–38, 135–136
  and marital dissolution, 240
  and peers, 43–44
  physical, 59
  verbal, 112, 136
agreeableness, 48
altruism, 157
attachment, 7, 17, 104, 138–139, 169–171
  adult attachment, 146–147, 169
  anxious, 42, 138, 146
  avoidant, 42
  behavioral observations, 43
  classifications in children, 8–9
  and communication, 131
  and infants, 40
  maternal sensitivity, 41
  parents' security, 41
  and relationships, 7
  secure, 41–42, 138, 146, 149, 170
  and social support, 132, 138
  temperament, 42–43, 52
  theory of, 40–41, 63, 169
attributions, 62–63, 68
  and neuroticism, 241
Automatic Vocal Transaction Analysis, 216
autonomy-control, 295

balance theory, 265
behavioral continuity hypothesis, 65
behavioral coordination (see also communication; responsiveness)
  and adult friendships, 214
  compensation, 208
  complementarity, 208
  convergence, 208
  and depression, 209
  divergence, 208
  and divorce, 214, 220
  and emotions, 211
  genuineness, 210
  human-computer interaction, 212, 215
  intentionality, 210
  and intervention, 210–211
  and marital interactions, 214
  and marital satisfaction, 214, 220
  matching, 208

Subject Index

mirroring, 208
parent–infant interaction, 213–214, 219
partner coordination, 209–210
reciprocity, 208
rhythm, 208–211
and small group interactions, 215
social synchronizers, 210
synchrony, 208, 210, 219
temporal patterning, 211
behavior exchange, 286
behaviorism, 37
Berkeley Guidance Study, 45–46
Berlin Aging Study, 52
Bradburn Affect Balance Scale, 194

closeness-distance, 295
cluster analysis, 236
  multiwave assessments, 246–247
codependency, 156
cognitions (*see also* attributions)
  affect, 24–25, 104
  attitudes, 23
  relationship related, 62
  self-concept, 23
  stereotyping, 23
cognitive balance theory, 265
commitment, 69, 73–74, 76–77, 83, 104
  and couple identity, 167
  and interdependency, 239
  and marital satisfaction, 239
  and marital therapy, 239
communication, 240 (*see also* behavioral coordination; nonverbal accuracy; responsiveness)
  assertiveness, 73
  diary studies, 134
  listener responsiveness, 73
  quality, 134–135, 141–142

quantity, 134–135, 141–142
and relationship satisfaction, 129, 240
standard content paradigm, 137
two-wave longitudinal studies, 240
Communication Patterns Questionnaire, 132, 136
Communication and Problem Solving Training, 286
conflict (*see also* serial arguing)
  change in, 136
  coercive behavior, 64, 73
  contempt, 215
  destructive patterns of, 149
  and distrust, 110
  and economic stress, 67
  and family of origin, 63
  frequency, 135, 142
  gender roles in, 143
  and interdependence, 110
  interpersonal, 48
  and intimacy, 110
  and mother–child relationships, 37–38
  negativity, 64, 136, 140, 143, 148
  patterns of, 130
  and personal distance, 110
  relational power, 108, 110
  sentiment override, 145
  serial arguments, 103, 107–124
  situational cues, 15
  violated expectations, 110
  withdrawal, 131, 136, 215
connectionist models, 22
conscientiousness, 48
contextual cues, 14–17
costs, 159
couple identity, 167
cross-lagged panel design, 37, 52; *see also* Longitudinal research

DEARR model, 60–78
demand-withdraw
  conflict pattern, 20, 114, 143
  and therapy, 291–292
depression, 241
disengagement theory, 183
discriminant analysis, 236
distressed couples, 236–237
  attribution differences, 12–13
  blaming, 285
  and marital therapy, 285
  and negativity, 285
  and social support, 238–239
  and withdrawal, 285
divorce
  and conflict, 121–122
  and demographic factors, 235
  genetics of, 92–96
  influence on children, 62–63
  risk of, 214, 220, 235–236
  trends in, 244–245
dyadic friendship, 45
dynamic-interactional view, 37

economic hardship, 67
emotions
  contagion effect, 211
  empathy, 211
  lability, 41–42
  stability of, 65
ENRICH, 235–236
event-based approach, 246
expectations, 8, 110–111, 244

family of origin, 58–60
  demographic characteristics, 65–67
  and interpersonal skills, 59
  and marital quality, 59
  sibling or parent socialization hypothesis, 64
  siblings, 60
  and warmth, 70–76

Feminist Theory, 171–173, 175, 177
FOCCUS, 235

growth curve modeling, 241; *see also* longitudinal research

hostility, 64, 70, 73–76, 144

individual differences (*see* personality)
influence, 212
  assessing partner influence, 212–213
  causal-modeling approach, 212–213
  and predictability, 212
Integrative Behavioral Couple Therapy
  acceptance, 293–294, 297–298,
  assessment of, 296–297
  benefits of, 302–303
  complaints, 293
  contingency-shaped behavior, 288–292
  demand and shut down, 291–292
  distinguished from Traditional Behavioral Couple Therapy, 288–290
  empathic joining, 298–299
  formulation, 294–296
  mutual trap, 295–296
  polarization process, 295
  private behavior, 293
  public behavior, 293
  resignation, 294
  themes, 295
  unified joining, 299
interdependence theory, 158, 164, 167
internal or external changes, 14
internal working models, 5, 7, 10, 131

Subject Index

interpersonal competence
   hypothesis, 69

longitudinal research (*see also*
   cross-lagged panel design;
   growth curve modeling)
  behavioral data, 232
  benefits of, 130–131, 248
  coding systems, 232
  and communication, 231, 240
  effects of negative behavior, 232
  limitations of two-wave designs, 230
  and marital satisfaction, 230, 232
  sample sizes, 232
  self-report data, 232
  and social networks, 268
love (*see also* passionate love)
  companionate, 83
  romantic, 83–84
  and sacrifice, 157
  and shyness, 48

Marital Communication Inventory, 132–133
Marital Communication Scale, 132
marital instability (*see* divorce)
Marital Interaction Coding System, 233
marital interventions
  behavioral marital therapy, 20, 150; *see also* Traditional Behavioral Couple Therapy
  and change, 285–287
  cognitive-behavioral, 20
  cognitive restructuring, 20
  emotionally focused therapy, 21
  integrative couples therapy, 18–19, 256; *see also* Integrative Behavioral Couple Therapy
  reframing, 18–19, 25
  and stability, 287–288
mate selection, 84–92

microanalysis
  adult friendships, 214
  cross-sectional analysis, 218
  definition of, 207
  diagnostic information, 221
  human–computer interaction, 212, 215
  marital interaction, 214
  multiple time-point longitudinal data, 218
  observational data, 217–218
  parent–infant interaction, 213–214, 219
  small group interaction, 215
  social interaction process, 221
  time-series analysis, 217–218
Minnesota Twin Registry, 84, 92
Monte Carlo simulation studies, 40
mood, 14–15
  attributions of mood, 14
  negative mood, 107
  and relationship representations, 15
motivation, 15
Multidimensional Personality Inventory, 85

negativity (*see also* conflict)
  benefits of, 233
  and conflict, 64, 136, 140, 143, 148
  contempt, 233
  impulse control, 50, 233
  invalidation, 233
  negative behavior, 233
negotiation, 115–116
neuroticism, 49, 53, 65, 233–234
  and marital instability, 50, 65
  and negative attributions, 241
  neuroticism-dissatisfaction correlation, 50
  neuroticism-divorce correlation, 50

New Zealand Dunedin
  Longitudinal Study, 45–46
nonverbal accuracy, 137–138, 140,
  145, 148 (*see also*
  communication)
  negativity bias, 145
  positivity bias, 145

observational learning hypothesis,
  64

parenting
  influence of, 62–63
  mother–infant interaction, 41–42,
    213–214
  parent–infant interaction,
    213–214
  patterns and coordination,
    213–214
  and personality, 41
  and relationship representations,
    18
  styles of, 37
  traditional roles of, 244
parenthood
  transition to, 237, 243–244
passionate love, 256
  anthropological perspectives on,
    308
  cross-cultural perspectives on,
    313–315
  cultural realm, 321
  definitions of, 307
  economic/practical realm, 321
  evolutionary perspectives on,
    308
  and gender, 318–320
  historical perspectives on,
    308–312
  intensity of, 314–315
  meaning of, 315–317
  modernism, 320–321
  susceptibility to, 313–314
  technological realm, 321
peer relationships, 44–49
perpetual problems model, 58
personality (*see also* neuroticism)
  aggressiveness, 43–45
  attachment, 40–43
  Big Five personality
    characteristics, 49
  and change in knowledge
    representations, 17
  conscientiousness, 51
  evocation, 51
  gene-environment interaction, 51
  manipulation, 51–52
  and marital outcomes, 46, 49–51,
    237
  nature vs. nurture, 51, 97
  obstacles to studying, 36–40
  and parenting, 37, 40–43
  and peer relationships, 43–49
  personality-relationship
    interpretation, 50
  relationship effects, 36
  selection, 51
  shyness, 45–49
positive illusions, 9, 19
positive reinforcement, 73
predictability of behavior, 209
  novelty, 209, 212
  and stimulation, 212
PREPARE, 235–236
problem-solving skills, 64
psychoanalysis, 37

Quality Marriage Index, 132

Relationship Closeness Inventory,
  211
relational knowledge (*see*
  relationship representations)
relational maintenance, 117–118

Subject Index

relationship representations
  accessibility, 16
  book keeping system, 10–11
  breadth of change in, 12–13
  characteristics of change in, 10–14
  conversion, 10–11
  direction of change in, 13–14
  and emotions, 13
  and enduring contexts, 17–22
  gender-specific schemas, 171
  internal working models, 5, 10, 17, 131
  interpersonal schemas, 5
  lay relationship theories, 5
  mechanisms of change in, 14–22
  momentum of change in, 11–12
  positive relationship representations, 13
  prototypes, 5
  scripts, 5, 7
  speed of change in, 10–11
  stability in, 8–9, 36
  and temporary contexts, 14–17
relationship schemas (see relationship representations)
responsiveness, 40–41, 329–331 (see also behavioral coordination; communication)

Sacrifice
  accommodation, 162–163
  and commitment, 161, 165, 174, 176–177
  definition of, 158–160
  editing, 162–163
  interdependence, 164, 174
  negative effects of, 168–173
  perceptions of, 174–176
  positive effects of, 160–168
  and satisfaction, 160–161

scripts (see also relationship representations)
  "if-then" contingencies, 7
  "if-then" production rules, 20
self-concept
  esteem, 186
  representations of self, 7–8, 16, 19
  self-knowledge representations, 5
  self-other units, 19
  and social activities, 197–198
self-disclosure, 117–118
self-esteem (see self-concept)
serial arguing (see also conflict)
  affect, 124
  antecedents of, 116–123
  and child rearing, 120–121
  and division of labor, 120
  elements of, 108–115
  escalation, 112, 114
  form of, 113–114
  in courtship, 116–118
  interdependence, 116, 118
  issue expansion, 113–114
  negotiation and, 115–116
  parent–child conflict, 121
  participant role, 114
  patterns of, 111–112
  relational consequences of, 123–124
  situational cues, 112
  transient mood, 112
  verbal aggression, 112
sexual desire (see passionate love)
shyness, 46–48
Silencing the Self Scale, 172
similarity, 84–87
situational cues, 15, 17
social activities
  and self-concept, 197–198
  stability in, 194–197

social learning theory, 231
social networks, 185, 255, 257
   attributes of, 260–261
   in African American families, 272–273
   couple withdrawal in, 267–268
   and courtship, 267–269
   density, 260–261
   and divorce, 273–274
   historical perspective on, 274–276
   influence of, 258–260, 276
   methodological issues, 269
   negative effects of, 260
   overlap, 260–263, 271
   positive effects of, 265–266
   presence of technology, 275
   relationship termination, 268
   role-segregated activities, 270
   Romeo and Juliet effect, 264–265
   and satisfaction, 271
   size of, 260
   and stability, 265
   substitutability, 266
social support, 104, 131–132, 138–139, 147 (see also social networks)
   and age, 185
   caregiving, 189–190
   families, 190
   and gender, 185
   and marital satisfaction, 238–239
   mediating effects of, 190
   minority groups, 190
   moderating effects of, 238
   relationships over time, 186–187
   and self-esteem, 186
   stability and instability, 187–188
   and well-being, 184–186
Social Support Inventory, 132
socioeconomic status, 65–66, 77

socioemotional selectivity theory, 272
stories
   and marital satisfaction, 242
   nonromantic positive themes, 242
   overcoming obstacles, 242
   and scripts, 5
   shared affect in, 242
   we-ness in, 243
Strange Situation, 8, 40–42
stress
   financial resources and, 66–67
   hassles, 193–194
   life stressors, 193–194
   mediators, 182, 190
   negative life events, 237
   outcomes, 182
   stressors, 182
Sudden Infant Death Syndrome, 210
symbolic interactionist perspective, 265

Traditional Behavioral Couple Therapy
   benefits of, 286–287, 302–303
   change-oriented behavioral techniques, 286
   contextual approaches, 288
   difficult to treat couples, 287–288
   failures of, 287
   rule-governed behavior, 288–290
   and stability, 287–288
   successes of, 287

violence, 59 (see also aggression)
virtual interactions, 256, 327–329
   context effects, 342–345
   emotionally responsive computers, 325
   empirical models of, 336–337

Subject Index

manipulation techniques, 332–333
modeling in artificial intelligence, 331–332
politeness, 326
responsiveness, 329–331, 345–346
rules of behavior, 326, 338–342
simulating conversation, 333–335

For EU product safety concerns, contact us at Calle de José Abascal, 56–1°, 28003 Madrid, Spain or eugpsr@cambridge.org.

www.ingramcontent.com/pod-product-compliance
Ingram Content Group UK Ltd.
Pitfield, Milton Keynes, MK11 3LW, UK
UKHW020350060825
461487UK00008B/605